A PRIMER IN Positive Psychology

A PRIMER IN

Positive Psychology

CHRISTOPHER PETERSON

2006

OXFORD
UNIVERSITY PRESS

Oxford University Press, Inc., publishes works that further
Oxford University's objective of excellence
in research, scholarship, and education.

Oxford New York
Auckland Cape Town Dar es Salaam Hong Kong Karachi
Kuala Lumpur Madrid Melbourne Mexico City Nairobi
New Delhi Shanghai Taipei Toronto

With offices in
Argentina Austria Brazil Chile Czech Republic France Greece
Guatemala Hungary Italy Japan Poland Portugal Singapore
South Korea Switzerland Thailand Turkey Ukraine Vietnam

Published by Oxford University Press, Inc.
198 Madison Avenue, New York, New York 10016

www.oup.com

Library of Congress Cataloging-in-Publication Data
Peterson, Christopher, 1950 Feb. 18–
A primer in positive psychology / by Christopher Peterson.
p. cm.
Includes bibliographical references and indexes.
ISBN-13 978-0-19-518833-2

1. Positive psychology. I. Title.
BF204.6.P48 2006
150.19′8—dc22 2005029442

9 8 7 6 5 4

Printed in the United States of America
on acid-free paper

I dedicate this book

with love and gratitude

to my parents,

who taught me

to love learning,

to work hard, and

to get along with others

Preface

Positive psychology as an explicit perspective has existed only since 1998, but enough relevant theory and research now exist concerning what makes life most worth living to fill a book suitable for a semester-long college course. This is that book. Writing occupied me during 2005, and I wrote with an audience of college students in mind. Perhaps they had previously studied psychology, perhaps not. Regardless, all the material here is accessible and—I hope—interesting and informative.

In writing about this new field, I did so from the viewpoint of general psychology. Positive psychology is psychology, and psychology is science. I have tried to do justice to the science of the good life in covering topics ranging from pleasure and happiness to work and love. What do we know, and how do we know it? And what remains unknown?

I also wrote with a more general audience in mind, given growing popular interest in positive psychology. Perhaps even more so than psychology students, for whom critical thinking is explicitly urged by their instructors, the general public needs a fair and balanced presentation of what psychologists know and what they do not. Positive psychology is plenty exciting without the need to run far ahead of what has already been established.

Who am I? My personality will show itself in the pages to come. But more formally, I am a baby boomer who grew up in the Midwest. I went to school at the University of Illinois, then the University of Colorado, and finally the University of Pennsylvania. I have been a psychology professor at the University of Michigan since 1986, where I have taught a variety of courses, including introductory psychology, psychopathology, research methods, and—of course—positive psychology, to more than 20,000 students. I am the former director of our Clinical Psychology Training Program, but my identity is now that of a positive psychologist. I spent most of my professional career concerned with depression, despair, and demoralization. I am now a different kind of psychologist, one concerned with happiness, character, and purpose.

It has been said that physical scientists stand on the shoulders of their predecessors, whereas social scientists step in their faces (Zeaman, 1959). My story is different because as a member of the Positive Psychology Steering Committee, I have been able to stand next to and to work with some remarkable scholars who have shaped positive psychology from the beginning: Mike Csikszentmihalyi, Ed Diener, Kathleen Hall Jamieson, George Vaillant, and—first among equals—Marty Seligman.

The positive psychology research which has so energized me has been generously supported by the Mayerson Foundation, the Templeton Foundation, the Annenberg/Sunnylands Trust Foundation, Atlantic Philanthropies, and the U.S. Department of Education. And much of what I have written here had its beginning in collaborative projects with Nansook Park and Marty Seligman.

Writing this book went smoothly, in no small part because I worked with Oxford University Press, in particular associate publisher Joan Bossert and associate editor Jennifer Rappaport, unwavering supporters of positive psychology and my own writing. Lisa Christie carefully edited what were rough chapters and suggested useful resources for each chapter. Vincent Colapietro, Ed Diener, Steve Maier, Nansook Park, Stephen Post, Lilach Sagiv, and George Vaillant helped me to track down some specific citations. Thanks to all.

Contents

A PRIMER IN Positive Psychology

What Is Positive Psychology?

The chief purpose of education is to teach young people to find pleasure in the right things. —PLATO (~400 BCE)

If it is possible, talk to your parents about the day your were born. Not how or where or when, but what they were thinking and feeling when they first held you. I suspect that what rushed through them was a mix of fears and hopes. The fears included whether you were healthy and safe and whether they would be able to take care of you. The hopes included the wishes that you would grow up to be happy, that you would live a fulfilling life, that you would have skills and talents, that you would learn how to use these in a productive way, that you would someday have your own family and friends, and that you would become a valued member of a social community.

Now think about the very end of your life, whenever that might be. Suppose you have the time to think back over your life in its final moments. What would be your greatest satisfactions? And what would be your greatest regrets? I suspect that your thoughts and feelings would play out along the same lines as those of your parents decades earlier. Was your life a good and fulfilling one? Did you do your best, even when it was difficult? Did you have people in your life who loved you and whom you loved in return? Did you make a difference for the better in your community? I doubt that your regrets would include not eating more Fritos, not working longer shifts, or not watching—for the 10th time—cable television reruns of *Law & Order*. I doubt that you would wish you had taken more shortcuts in life, that you had put your own needs more frequently ahead of other people's needs, or that you had never thought about what life means.

Positive psychology is the scientific study of what goes right in life, from birth to death and at all stops in between. It is a newly christened approach within psychology that takes seriously as a subject matter those things that make life most worth living. Everyone's life has peaks and valleys, and positive psychology does not deny the valleys. Its signature premise is more nuanced but nonetheless important: What is good about life is as genuine as what is bad and therefore deserves equal attention from psychologists. It assumes that life entails more than avoiding or undoing problems and hassles. Positive psychology resides somewhere in that part of the human landscape that is metaphorically north of neutral. It is the study of what we are doing when we are not frittering life away.

In this book, I describe positive psychology and what positive psychologists have learned about the good life and how it can be encouraged. Some of you are reading this book because it has been assigned for a college course. Others of you are reading it simply because you are curious and want to learn more. In either case, I will voice one more suspicion: You will find some food for thought here and an action plan that might make your own life a better one.

Positive Psychology: A Very Short History With a Very Long Past

You may already have studied psychology. If so, perhaps you encountered this terse characterization of the field by Herman Ebbinghaus, one of the field's luminaries: "Psychology has a long past, but only a short history" (Boring, 1950, p. ix). What this means is that psychology has been a formal discipline for little more than 100 years but that its enduring issues were phrased centuries before by philosophers, theologians, and everyday people. How do we know the world? How and why do we think and feel? What is the essence of learning? What does it mean to be a human being?

Let me borrow this characterization and assert that positive psychology has a very long past but only a very short history. The field was named[1] in 1998 as one of the initiatives of my colleague Martin Seligman in his role as president of the American Psychological Association (Seligman, 1998, 1999). One of the triggers

1. If this history is to be accurate, it needs to acknowledge that the phrase *positive psychology* appeared in print long before Seligman popularized it (Strümpfer, 2005). Abraham Maslow, one of the central figures in humanistic psychology a generation ago, used the phrase to describe his emphasis on creativity and self-actualization (Maslow, 1954, p. 353), although he later labeled what he was doing more clumsily as health-and-growth psychology (Maslow, 1962, p. 201). He referred to the rest of psychology—what I dub business-as-usual psychology—as low-ceiling psychology (Maslow, 1954, p. 356). In Russia, there is a similar approach known as *acmeology* (roughly, the science of high points; Rean, 2000), and in South Africa, there is a field known as *psychofortology* (roughly, the psychology of strength; Wissing & van Eeden, 2002). Positive psychology also has some close cousins, which will be mentioned later in the book, including positive organizational studies and positive youth development (chapter 11).

for positive psychology was Seligman's realization that psychology since World War II had focused much of its efforts on human problems and how to remedy them. The yield of this focus on pathology has been considerable. Great strides have been made in understanding, treating, and preventing psychological disorders. Widely accepted classification manuals—the *Diagnostic and Statistical Manual of Mental Disorders* (*DSM*) sponsored by the American Psychiatric Association (1994) and the *International Classification of Diseases* (*ICD*) sponsored by the World Health Organization (1990)—allow disorders to be described and have given rise to a family of reliable assessment strategies. There now exist effective treatments, psychological and pharmacological, for more than a dozen disorders that in the recent past were frighteningly intractable (Barrett & Ollendick, 2004; Evans et al., 2005; Hibbs & Jensen, 1996; Kazdin & Weisz, 2003; Nathan & Gorman, 1998, 2002; Seligman, 1994).

But there has been a cost to this emphasis. Much of scientific psychology has neglected the study of what can go right with people and often has little more to say about the good life than do pop psychologists, inspirational speakers, and armchair gurus. More subtly, the underlying assumptions of psychology have shifted to embrace a disease model of human nature. People are seen as flawed and fragile, casualties of cruel environments or bad genetics, and if not in denial then at best in recovery. This worldview has crept into the common culture of the United States. We have become a nation of self-identified victims, and our heroes and heroines are called survivors and sometimes nothing more.

Positive psychology proposes that it is time to correct this imbalance and to challenge the pervasive assumptions of the disease model (Maddux, 2002). It calls for as much focus on strength as on weakness, as much interest in building the best things in life as in repairing the worst, and as much attention to fulfilling the lives of healthy people as to healing the wounds of the distressed (Seligman, 2002; Seligman & Csikszentmihalyi, 2000). Psychologists interested in promoting human potential need to start with different assumptions and to pose different questions from their peers who assume only a disease model.

The past concern of psychology with human problems is of course understandable. It will not and should not be abandoned. People experience difficulties that demand and deserve scientifically informed solutions. Positive psychologists are merely saying that the psychology of the past 60 years is incomplete. As simple as this proposal sounds, it demands a sea change in perspective.

The most basic assumption that positive psychology urges is that human goodness and excellence are as authentic as disease, disorder, and distress. Positive psychologists are adamant that these topics are not secondary, derivative, illusory, epiphenomenal, or otherwise suspect. The good news is that these generalizations about business-as-usual psychology over the past 60 years are simply that—generalizations. There are many good examples of psychological research, past and present, that can be claimed as positive psychology.

The very long past of positive psychology stretches at least to the Athenian philosophers in the West and to Confucius and Lao-Tsu in the East (Dahlsgaard, Peterson, & Seligman, 2005). In the writings of these great thinkers can be found the same questions posed by contemporary positive psychologists. What is the good life? Is virtue its own reward? What does it mean to be happy? Is it possible to pursue happiness directly, or is fulfillment a by-product of other pursuits? What roles are played by other people and society as a whole?

Somewhat later but still many centuries ago, we encounter the ideas of religious figures and theologians—Jesus, the Buddha, Mohammed, Thomas Aquinas, and many others—who also posed deep questions about the meaning of the good life and its attainment. When we identify common themes across the disparate world views they advanced, we see that they advocated service to other individuals, to humankind as a whole, and to a higher power and purpose, however it is named. Today's positive psychologists also emphasize a life of meaning and emphasize that it can be found in both spiritual and secular pursuits. In so doing, positive psychology places the psychology of religion in a central place it has rarely occupied in the history of the discipline (Emmons & Paloutzian, 2003).

Within psychology, the premises of positive psychology were laid out long before 1998. In the beginning, psychologists were greatly interested in genius and talent as well as in fulfilling the lives of normal people. Setting the immediate stage for positive psychology as it currently exists were humanistic psychology as popularized by Rogers (1951) and Maslow (1970); utopian visions of education like those of Neill (1960); primary prevention programs based on notions of wellness—sometimes dubbed *promotion programs*—as pioneered by Albee (1982) and Cowen (1994); work by Bandura (1989) and others on human agency and efficacy; studies of giftedness (e.g., Winner, 2000); conceptions of intelligence as multiple (e.g., Gardner, 1983; Sternberg, 1985); and studies of the quality of life among medical and psychiatric patients that went beyond an exclusive focus on their symptoms and diseases (e.g., Levitt, Hogan, & Bucosky, 1990).

Today's positive psychologists do not claim to have invented notions of happiness and well-being, to have proposed their first theoretical accounts, or even to have ushered in their scientific study. Rather, the contribution of contemporary positive psychology has been to provide an umbrella term for what have been isolated lines of theory and research and to make the self-conscious argument that what makes life worth living deserves its own field of inquiry within psychology, at least until that day when all of psychology embraces the study of what is good along with the study of what is bad (Peterson & Park, 2003).

FAQs About Positive Psychology

Positive psychology is not without its critics (Cowen & Kilmer, 2002; Lazarus, 2003; Taylor, 2001). Up to a point, those of us who are positive psychologists welcome criticism because it means that people are paying attention and, more important, because we can learn from it. Here are some of the frequently asked questions (FAQs) that I have encountered in the past few years when I speak and write about positive psychology (Seligman & Pawelski, 2003). Some of the questions come from the general public and others from my academic colleagues.

My experience is that everyday people find it exciting and the sort of thing psychology should be doing (Easterbrook, 2001). Despite the pervasiveness of a victim mentality, everyday people seem to know that the elimination or reduction of problems is not all that is involved in improving the human condition. In contrast, the academic community is often skeptical of positive psychology. Contributing to skepticism are widespread assumptions within the social sciences about human nature as flawed and fragile, notions more explicit among social scientists than the general public. From this starting point, the field can only be seen as the study of fluff—perhaps even as a dangerous diversion while the world goes to hell. Social scientists are doubtful about the existence of the good life and certainly about the ability of people to report on it with fidelity. We too are mindful of the dangers of self-report but point out that "social desirability" is hardly a nuisance variable when one studies what is socially desirable (Crowne & Marlowe, 1964).

Is Positive Psychology Just Happiology?

When positive psychology is featured in the popular media, it seems that no one in charge of layout can resist accompanying the story with a graphic of Harvey Bell's clichéd smiley face,[2] beaming at readers in its jaundiced glory (e.g., *U.S. News & World Report*, September 3, 2001; *Newsweek*, September 16, 2002; *USA Weekend*, March 9, 2003; *Time*, September 17, 2005; *Psychology Today*, February 2005). This iconography is terribly misleading because it equates positive psychology with the study of happiness and indeed with a superficial form of happiness.

All other things being equal, smiling is of course pleasant to do and pleasant to observe, but a smile is not an infallible indicator of all that makes life most worth living. When we are highly engaged in fulfilling activities, when we are speaking from our hearts, or when we are doing something heroic, we may or may not be smiling, and we may or may not be experiencing pleasure in the moment. All of these are central concerns to positive psychology, and they fall outside the realm of happiology.

To foreshadow later chapters in this book, I note that pleasure and happiness are certainly of great interest to positive psychology but are more complex than whatever is conveyed by a smiley face. Positive psychologists study positive traits

2. A not well known story is that the smiley-face icon was created for a life insurance company in 1964 by a Massachusetts graphic artist, who was paid $45 for his creation. Neither the insurance company nor artist Harvey Bell copyrighted the symbol, which has—perhaps as a result—become extremely popular.

and dispositions—characteristics like kindness, curiosity, and the ability to work on a team—as well as values, interests, talents, and abilities. They study social institutions that can enable the good life: friendship, marriage, family, education, religion, and so on.

I cannot resist noting that not all smiles are created equal. Researchers have long distinguished among types of smiles, arguing that some are more genuine than others. A so-called Duchenne[3] (1862/1990) smile involves one's whole face and is sincere because it cannot be faked. Contrast it with a flight attendant's smile, a forced grimace that involves only one's lower face.

What Is the Relationship of Positive Psychology to Humanistic Psychology?

In one of the early discussions of positive psychology, Marty Seligman and Mike Csikszentmihalyi[4] (2000) tersely distanced this new field from humanistic psychology, one of psychology's venerable perspectives that was particularly popular in the 1960s and 1970s and still has many adherents today. In very general terms, **humanism** is the doctrine that the needs and values of human beings take precedence over material things and, further, that people cannot be studied simply as part of the material world. Humanists argue that scientific psychologists miss what is most important about people by focusing on the supposed causes of behavior, as if people were simply billiard balls, doing poorly or well depending on what other billiard balls happen to have ricocheted into them.

Well-known psychologists within the humanistic tradition include Abraham Maslow (1970) and Carl Rogers (1951). Both emphasized that people strive to make the most of their potential in a process called **self-actualization.** Self-actualization can be thwarted by various conditions, but if these conditions are changed, then the potential within each individual will necessarily unfold.

This is a very different way of thinking about human nature than that embodied in psychoanalysis or behaviorism, dominant perspectives within psychology during the 20th century. Humanistic psychology stresses the goals for which people strive, their conscious awareness of this striving, the importance of their own choices, and their rationality. The attention of psychology is thereby directed away from mechanical causes and toward fundamental questions about existence and meaning.

Humanistic psychology often overlaps with another venerable viewpoint: **existentialism.** The critical idea of existentialism is that a person's experience is

3. Guillaume-Benjamin Duchenne (1806–1875) was a French neurophysiologist who pioneered ways of describing and measuring facial expressions. He was the teacher of noted French neurologist Jean Charcot (1825–1893), perhaps best known for his studies of hysteria and his then-controversial argument—now universally accepted—that hysteria is a psychological malady and not a physical one. Charcot in turn was the teacher of Sigmund Freud (1856–1939), famous for so many contributions.

4. Pronounced *cheeks-sent-me-high.*

primary. To understand any individual is to understand him or her subjectively, from the inside out. There is no other way.

Existentialists see people as products of their own choices, and these choices are freely undertaken. To use their phrase, existence precedes essence, with essence understood to mean a person's particular characteristics. Existentialists stress that there is no fixed human nature, only the sort of person that each unique individual becomes by the way she chooses to define herself.

As applied specifically to psychology, these humanistic and existential viewpoints have several emphases (Urban, 1983):

- the significance of the individual
- the complex organization of the individual
- the capacity for change inherent in the individual
- the significance of conscious experience
- the self-regulatory nature of human activity

Implicit here is an impatience with "scientific" psychology as it is typically conducted, because it does not always deal with what is most important about people (Maslow, 1966).

Humanists and existential theorists believe that psychologists must pay more attention to an individual's way of seeing the world, and here they join ranks with yet another intellectual movement, **phenomenology**, which attempts to describe a person's conscious experience in terms meaningful for that individual. Described so starkly, phenomenology has a superficial resemblance to cognitive approaches within psychology (H. Gardner, 1985), in that both are concerned with thoughts and thinking, but this is a misleading similarity. Cognitive psychologists specify the terms with which to describe thinking and then try to use this theoretical language to describe the thoughts of all people. In contrast, phenomenologists start with the experience of a specific individual and then attempt to describe it.

In light of this background, why did Seligman and Csikszentmihalyi say that positive psychology was different? They made two arguments. First, positive psychology regards both the good and the bad about life as genuine, whereas humanists often—but not always—assume that people are inherently good. Second, positive psychology is strongly committed to the scientific method, whereas humanists often—but again not always—are skeptical of science and its ability to shed light on what really matters.

As points of relative and occasional contrast, I agree with the arguments of Seligman and Csikszentmihalyi, but as positive psychology has evolved and more carefully examined allied perspectives, the wholesale dismissal of humanistic psychology now seems glib and mistaken. Certainly, most existentialists would agree that each person has the capacity for good and bad, just as positive psychology assumes. That the good life is simply a matter of choice seems to go too far, given the well-documented barriers to thriving posed by external circumstances like pestilence, poverty, and prejudice, but positive psychologists nowadays acknowledge that notions of choice and will are indispensable ones (Peterson & Seligman, 2004).

Many humanistic psychologists, from decades ago (e.g., Rogers, Gendlin, Kiesler, & Truax, 1967) to the present (e.g., Deci & Ryan, 2000), are as committed to science as any positive psychologist. The deeper issue is what one counts as legitimate science. I have a relaxed and inclusive conception of the scientific method: the use of evidence to evaluate theories. There are multiple sources of useful evidence—each with its own pros and cons—and science should *not* privilege one source over another. Scientific psychology can learn much from carefully controlled laboratory experiments, but so too can it learn much from case studies of exceptional individuals, from interviews and surveys of the general population, and from analyses of historical information.

The aforementioned billiard ball conception of psychology is a caricature that applies nowadays to very few psychologists of any stripe. Like humanistic researchers, positive psychologists believe that people are appropriately studied by talking to them about things that most matter and seeing how their lives actually unfold (Park & Peterson, in press a).

In sum, positive psychology and humanistic psychology are close relatives. In some instances, their features are identical, and in some other instances, they can be distinguished. No good purpose is served by wrangling over which provides a better overall perspective, a debate that likely has no resolution. In any event, science is always about particulars, and some empirical studies undertaken from a humanistic perspective will shed light on the good life, as will some empirical studies undertaken from a positive psychology perspective.

Is Positive Psychology Anything More Than What Sunday School Teachers Know?

Some of the findings of positive psychology (and humanistic psychology, for that matter) seem commonsensical once articulated. So, other people matter mightily. Money cannot buy happiness. Those with a reason to live do so, and do so rather well. "I knew that," says the skeptic, which leads to another frequently asked question about the field: Does it add anything to what we already know about the good life and how to achieve it?

I am sure that you are familiar with Robert Fulghum's (1986) popular book *All I Really Need to Know I Learned in Kindergarten* and its numerous spin-offs. It seems only a matter of time before someone asserts that everything that positive psychology has to teach was already taught to most of us in kindergarten, in Sunday school, on our grandmother's knee, or on the *Lizzy McGuire Show*. How do I respond to this criticism?

Well, for starters, it is wrong. Common sense and obviousness can always be asserted after the fact. Suppose I had pointed out—contrary to the actual evidence—that positive psychology has shown that we need not be concerned with what other people think or do, that "he who dies with the most toys wins," and that a ceaseless quest for the meaning of life is a fool's errand. "I knew all that as well," says the same skeptic, which leaves us with an obvious need for evidence that will allow us to sort through the contradictory things that we all seem to know so well.

As you read this book, you can judge for yourself which of the findings of positive psychology are surprising. But when they are not especially surprising, I urge you to ask further, "So what?" Psychology makes too much of its counterintuitive findings, showing for example that people may be unaware of what influences their judgments and actions (e.g., Nisbett & Wilson, 1977), that our memory of events—even vivid ones—is rarely if ever literal (cf. Brown & Kulik, 1977), and that there are limitations to people's rationality (e.g., Kahneman & Tversky, 1973). This celebration of the counterintuitive often takes the form of highlighting the shortcomings of people and in effect saying, "Look at how stupid we all are." Research like this can be important for correcting common sense, but not if it leads to the conclusion that people are hopelessly flawed and inadequate. Then we have the scientific equivalent of shock journalism.

Remember the basic premise of positive psychology: that human goodness and excellence are as authentic as are human flaws and inadequacies. Too much attention to the counterintuitive leads us to ignore what people do well and results in a strange view of the human condition. Some of the true miracles of human activity receive scant attention from psychologists. For example, consider that most automobile drivers most of the time negotiate interstate highways without accident, all at more than 70 miles per hour. Consider that most people who give up smoking are successful on their own without professional help. Consider that almost all children learn language without explicit instruction. Consider that most people who experience a traumatic event recover from its effects.

In chapter 4, I describe research showing that people are often unable to predict how long they will be happy or sad following important life events. So, most young people predict that being dumped by a girlfriend or boyfriend will produce a state of despair that will last for months, if not years. It turns out that the typical person is sad for a much shorter period, and then he or she gets on with life (Gilbert, Pinel, Wilson, Blumberg, & Wheatley, 1998). This is an interesting and even important finding, especially because people seem not to learn from repeated experience that their emotional forecasts are wrong (Wilson, Meyers, & Gilbert, 2001), but it should not be taken to mean that people are complete ignoramuses. This research did not show that a romantic breakup makes somebody happy—*that* would be a counterintuitive finding!

We expect that the larger culture should know something about the conditions for the good life. How could this not be the case? Accordingly, many of the findings of positive psychology will be unsurprising. But there will be important exceptions. Consider the widespread belief in the contemporary United States that "all you need are looks and a whole lot of money" in order to be happy. This may work for Paris Hilton (perhaps), but the relevant research shows rather clearly that this is a wrongheaded formula for most of as we pursue the good life (chapter 4). Positive psychology needs to sort through conventional wisdom, and this is where the scientific method proves indispensable.

Are Positive Psychologists Indifferent to Suffering?

Psychologists who study human problems have the best of intentions: They want to eliminate suffering. The unstated corollary of this good intention is that well-being can be taken for granted. Indeed, the study of people who are happy, healthy, and talented may be seen as a guilty luxury that diverts resources from the goals of problem-focused psychology. From the perspective of positive psychology, I suggest a different possibility, namely, that a better understanding of well-being will allow psychologists to help all people, troubled or not.

In chapter 4, I describe some of my own recent research showing that deliberate interventions can encourage lasting happiness. Part of this research entails the further demonstration that happiness interventions also alleviate symptoms of depression.

The ranks of positive psychologists are filled with people whose larger professional identities are as social psychologists—a subfield of psychology that has long studied such social problems as prejudice and aggression—or as clinical psychologists with explicit concerns with problems in living and how to remedy them. None of these positive psychologists sees a disconnect between his or her core identity and an interest in the good life. Rather, suffering and well-being are both part of the human condition, and all psychologists should be concerned with both.

Indeed, the link between suffering and well-being deserves study. Are there lessons to be learned from those who have grappled with the worst of what life has to offer? In chapter 6, I describe some research that suggests that at least some people emerge from crisis and trauma with an increased appreciation of what matters most in life. Furthermore, with rare exceptions, people's satisfaction with life is remarkably robust after a period of adjustment and accommodation to bad life events (chapter 4).

Psychologist Shelley Taylor (1985) described a research program that began as an investigation of depression that followed in the wake of a diagnosis of breast cancer, a terrible and serious life event. The problem with her research is that she had trouble identifying a sufficient number of cancer patients who were severely depressed. Instead, most were able to deal with the diagnosis by a process Taylor labeled *downward* social comparison—thinking of someone[5] who had it worse off than they did. "Sure, I have breast cancer, but it could be worse. . . . after all,

5. The fine print of this finding is that downward social comparison may be more effective when it is done hypothetically than vis-à-vis actual others (Taylor & Lobel, 1989).

I could be younger. . . . The surgery required is a lumpectomy rather than a mastectomy, a single mastectomy rather than a double mastectomy. . . . I can tolerate the side effects of chemotherapy better than most. . . . I have a supportive family" and so on. A previous generation of psychologists might have concluded that these women were in denial, but they were clearly open-eyed, lucid, and sober. The only thing they denied was despair, and Taylor (1989) foreshadowed the premises of positive psychology by concluding that this was an important aspect of human nature.

This is not to say that we should program traumatic events for our children in the hope that they will somehow benefit. I think of the Johnny Cash tune about the father who named his son Sue in order to toughen him up. But neither is this to say that once people suffer, we should write them off as permanently flawed and bounded in their achievement of the good life (Linley & Joseph, 2004a).

Isn't Life Tragic?

Despite the arguments I have been making, some skeptics still believe that positive psychologists miss the "obvious" point that life is tragic. We are born, and then we die. What happens in between is short, brutish, and cruel. Look at the history of humankind (or yesterday's evening news)—war, disease, and natural disasters galore. There is no good answer to this charge if one's debate opponent sticks to his philosophical grounds (Russell, 1930). But why would anyone want to do so? Perhaps a tragic view of life provides some odd comfort to a person who wishes never to be disappointed or who thinks that a tragic view is smarter or more sophisticated. "Realistic" is a frequently chosen adjective by those who espouse such a view.

I disagree but will not belabor the point except to note that tragedy admits to gradations. Even if everything sucks, some things suck more than others, an irrefutable fact given how people actually behave if not what they say. We prefer some outcomes rather than others, pursue some goals rather than others, and desire some emotional states rather than others. Whether we label these preferred circumstances "positive" or "less sucky" then becomes a matter of semantics.

Are Happy People Stupid?

Our common culture is replete with stereotypes linking happiness and stupidity. We call someone a Pollyanna if we want to dismiss hope as foolish (chapter 5). We call someone a grinning idiot if we want to say that happiness is naïve. We talk about fiddling while Rome is burning. More clever is Elbert Hubbard's (1927) definition of a pessimist as a person who has been intimately acquainted with an optimist. Or consider *The Devil's Dictionary*'s definition:

> OPTIMISM, n. The doctrine, or belief, that everything is beautiful, including what is ugly, everything good, especially the bad, and everything right that is wrong. It is held with greatest tenacity by those most accustomed to the mischance of falling into adversity, and is most acceptably expounded with the grin that apes a smile. Being a blind faith, it is inaccessible to the light of disproof—an intellectual disorder, yielding to no treatment but death. It is hereditary, but fortunately not contagious. (Bierce, 1911/1999, p. 137)

We can even find similar sentiments in the scientific literature, as in the conclusion that the sadder are wiser, a proposition I examine in detail in chapter 4 (Alloy & Abramson, 1979).

Part of this stereotyping results from the aforementioned view in some quarters that life is tragic and that the human condition is draped in doom and gloom. Freud (1927/1953c) takes some responsibility here by arguing that people are unaware of their true motives, which reduce to sex and aggression, and that anything positive or happy is a defense, at best a sublimation and at worst a delusion.

The evidence, however, points to the opposite conclusion. When researchers compare the characteristics of "happy" and "unhappy" people, as ascertained by their own reports as well as the presumably more-objective reports of those who know them well, the happy people almost always come out on top (Lyubomirsky, King, & Diener, 2005). They are more successful at school and at work; they have better relationships with other people; and they even live longer.

In research described in detail in chapter 4, positive psychologists have shown that the experience of positive emotions can actually pay intellectual benefits. In a positive emotional state, people are more flexible and creative.

What about IQ? Here the evidence is equivocal, showing at most a small association between measured intelligence and life satisfaction (Argyle, 1999). But it is a positive correlation, not a negative one. In any event, "stupidity" (if that is what a low score on an IQ test reflects) usually resides in no particular place along the spectrum of happiness and certainly not at the high end.

I acknowledge that extremely exuberant people can be annoying when they unleash their happiness on us at the wrong time. Haven't we all had the experience, after receiving some terrible bit of news, of running into someone who tells us to cheer up and look on the bright side? At that moment, there is no bright side, and the good cheer they urge upon us is unwelcome. These people may or may not be stupid, but they are insensitive. I stress, however, that not all happy people are so obtuse.

Is Positive Psychology a Luxury?

Another charge that I sometimes hear is that the concerns of positive psychology are a luxury only for the privileged in our society. Positive psychologists may have inadvertently contributed to this perception. When the field took form in the late

1990s, Seligman and Csikszentmihalyi (2000) speculated that such an endeavor was only possible within a society that was prosperous and at peace. Positive psychologists have since changed our minds. For starters, even in the United States of the 1990s, not everyone was prosperous or a full participant in society. But is it plausible to think that only rich people care about fulfillment or that only White Anglo-Saxon Protestants concern themselves with character? Whatever else is captured by the red-blue partition of U.S. states into Republicans and Democrats, it is not an interest in the psychological good life (Fiorina, Abrams, & Pope, 2005).

The terrorist attacks of September 11, 2001, on the World Trade Center in New York and on the Pentagon and their aftermath changed our thinking profoundly. Those of us in the United States are no longer so prosperous, and we are no longer so much at peace, but if anything, interest in positive psychology has grown. We had the momentary thought post-9/11 that Americans would hunker down and attend to grim basics, postponing the pursuit of the good life until they again felt safe. But this is not what happened, and we now realize that the good life at its core involves how one rises to the occasion.

We should have studied history more carefully. For good reason, the men and women who successfully mounted the World War II effort are spoken of as the best generation in the 20th century (Brokaw, 1998). Faced with a terrible crisis from which they could have turned, they instead embraced it. The Allies worked together not only to help win the war against fascism but also to usher in an era of unprecedented progress and innovation.

Now, in the aftermath of 9/11, there is another occasion to which to rise, and we have some evidence that Americans are doing just that. Our ongoing study of character strengths has found that post-9/11, people reported that they were more likely to display the theological virtues of faith, hope, and charity (love; Peterson & Seligman, 2003a). Whether these changes will be sustained for a generation or beyond is an empirical matter that we will track with interest, but in the meantime, we have revised our original view about the societal conditions that make positive social science possible. As already noted, crisis may be the crucible of character.

Is Positive Psychology Value-Laden?

The goals of positive psychology are description and explanation as opposed to prescription. The underlying premise of positive psychology is prescriptive in that it says that certain topics *should* be studied: positive experiences, positive traits, and enabling institutions. But once the study begins, it needs to be hard-headed and dispassionate. The routes to the good life are an empirical matter. Indeed, whether what seems positive is always desirable is also an empirical question.

My own research into optimism has documented many benefits of positive thinking (happiness, health, and success in various achievement domains) but one notable downside: Optimistic thinking is associated with an underestimation of risks (Peterson & Vaidya, 2003). Should someone always be optimistic? The empirically informed answer is certainly not if one is a pilot or air traffic controller trying to decide if a plane should take off during an ice storm (Seligman, 1991). Here, the data advise caution and sobriety—pessimism, as it were (chapter 5).

The task for positive psychology is to provide the most objective facts possible about the phenomena it studies so that everyday people and society as a whole can make an informed decision about what goals to pursue in what circumstances. Not all of the news will be upbeat, but it will be of value precisely because it provides an appropriately nuanced view of the good life.

Is the Rest of Psychology "Negative"?

Another stumbling block is the umbrella term itself—positive psychology—because many psychologists hear what they have been doing throughout their careers dismissed as negative psychology. This automatic juxtaposition is unfortunate, and positive psychologists intend no disrespect. I prefer the term *business-as-usual psychology* to describe work that focuses on human problems. As emphasized, business-as-usual psychology is important and necessary—and what I have spent most of my own career pursuing.

To call someone a positive psychologist is but a shorthand way of saying that he studies the topics of concern to the field of positive psychology. It does not mean that the positive psychologist is a "positive" (happy, talented, virtuous) person, and it certainly does not imply that other psychologists are "negative" people. After all, social psychologists may or may not be social, and personality psychologists may or may not display a scintillating personality.

What About Culture?

Positive psychology cannot be just a Western endeavor (Walsh, 2001). So, the 2002 Positive Psychology Summit in Washington, DC, had an explicit international emphasis, and the lessons to be learned about the good life from scholars around the world are rich indeed. My research team has been inspired to collect and study what we dub *culture-bound* states and traits reflecting strengths of character, like *gelassenheit* among Old Order Amish, *kuy guyluk* among Koreans, or *hao xue xin* among Chinese.[6]

Along these lines, positive psychologists should attempt to identify cultural practices from all parts of the globe that contribute to the good life within given societies (e.g., Sandage, Hill, & Vang, 2003). I remember speaking to my friend

6. These words roughly mean, in German, Korean, and Chinese, respectively, showing relaxed equanimity in the face of crisis; being able to shoulder the moral concerns of others; and melding the heart and mind in learning. All can be translated into English, and all can be grasped by English speakers, but none has a one-to-one translation.

and colleague Nansook Park, who grew up in Korea, about an exercise that Marty Seligman and I had devised for our American college students, asking them to write a letter of appreciation to their favorite high school or elementary school teacher (chapter 2). I was quite proud of our creativity in crafting a gratitude ritual that went beyond the saccharine messages of preprinted Hallmark cards. She politely heard me out, and then asked, "Do you mean that your students never did this before?" Apparently, in Korea, every schoolchild every year writes a letter of appreciation to her teacher.[7] How many other such cultural practices need to be documented and disseminated across national borders?

Is This a Paradigm Shift?

Let us turn from these skeptical FAQs to one that embodies an over-the-top compliment. Is positive psychology something so new and revolutionary that it reflects an altogether different way of going about psychological science? The term that gets applied is philosopher of science Thomas Kuhn's (1970) notion of a **paradigm shift**, which he introduced to describe radical changes in a scientific field. According to Kuhn, scientific progress is marked by periods of stability in which an overarching perspective dominates and dictates the particulars of scientific activity: theory, research, and application. To be sure, progress is made in these periods of so-called normal science, but it is incremental and entails fine-tuning the dominant paradigm.

Every once in a while, a new way of conceiving things is introduced that catches on and creates what Kuhn termed a *scientific revolution.* The old paradigm is displaced, and a new era of stability and incremental progress begins. Einstein's physics supplanted those of Newton, which had supplanted those of Copernicus. The theory of evolution introduced by Darwin (1859) similarly revolutionized biology. And so on.

Let us leave aside the fact that Kuhn himself wrote about the natural sciences and seemed to believe that the various social sciences—including psychology—did not fit his formula because they have never had a single overarching perspective to be displaced. Social scientists introduce new perspectives all the time and rail against old perspectives, as Max Wertheimer (1912) did in creating gestalt psy-

7. In Korea and other Asian nations infused by Confucian values, the scholar is among the most highly revered social roles, and teachers are accordingly given great respect. To be sure, in the contemporary United States, to be a teacher is a good thing, but not nearly to the extent as in Korea. For example, Korean marriage ceremonies can be performed by anyone, but the person of choice is invariably a former teacher of the groom or bride. Teachers' Day is one of the few national holidays in Korea. And when a South Korean president is elected, an obligatory ritual is a visit by the new president to the home of his favorite elementary or high school teacher, to whom he bows in gratitude. I suspect that if U.S. teachers were accorded this sort of respect, we would not hear that teaching is a dying profession or one that someone might pursue until she figures out what she really wants to do with her life.

chology or John Watson (1913) did in creating behaviorism. But what usually happens is that seating at the table of social science just becomes more crowded, and when old perspectives do die, it is a slow demise due to neglect rather than a quick death due to revolution.

Let us leave aside the ironic fact that self-proclaimed paradigm shifts fall remarkably flat. Scientific articles that immodestly trumpet a new contribution as a scientific revolution or a paradigm shift are by my own checking less frequently cited by subsequent scientists than those articles immediately adjacent to them in the same journals.

Simply put, the answer is a resounding no. Positive psychology is a refocusing of subject matter and not a revolution. Indeed, the notable strength of positive psychology is its continuity with tried-and-true psychological research methods and its belief that these can be used productively to study new topics—those that make life most worth living.

What About Bad Company?

The problem, as it were, of being involved in something popular is that it is popular. There is a huge bandwagon emerging around positive psychology, and sometimes I do not know if I am helping to lead the parade or simply keeping up with the stampede.

There is a long tradition, at least within the United States, of pop psychology books and articles and more recently audiotapes, DVDs, and Web sites that take a few ideas from psychology and expand them into maxims for living. At its best, pop psychology succeeds in "giving psychology away" (Miller, 1969), and some of these endeavors are certainly valuable for the general public. But sometimes what emerges is a caricature of psychology that serves no good purpose besides entertainment. There is something amiss when the best-known psychologists in the world today are Dr. Joyce Brothers and Dr. Phil, not to mention Dr. Ruth or Dr. Laura, who were not to my knowledge ever trained as mental health professionals but who—like Bob Newhart and Kelsey Grammar—simply play the part of one. This is like confusing Judge Judy with Justice Thurgood Marshall or Britney Spears with Maria Callas.

Positive psychology's bad company includes any and all people who are mangling—note that I did not say "popularizing"—the theories and findings that are emerging from our careful studies and presenting them to an eager public as simple truths as opposed to tentative generalizations. A visit to the psychology section at Barnes and Noble or Borders will give you ample examples. Beware of any book titled something like *Five* (or *Seven* or *Nine*) *Easy Steps to Lasting Happiness* (or *Career Success* or *Physical Fitness* or *Scratch Golf*).

Bad company is not defined by celebrity or the intrusion of the profit motive. After all, I hope that you bought this book, and I will gladly cash whatever royalty checks I may receive. But I also hope that you read this book not only for what it says but also for what it does not. Earlier in this chapter, I promised food for thought and a tentative action plan, which may or may not work for you and in any event will require hard work to enact.

The bad company of positive psychology may not have bad motives. I assume that many of these folks simply like the positive and wish it for others; their only sin is overlooking the science except when it suits them. It is therefore important to emphasize that positive psychology is not an ideological movement nor a secular religion. It is not a get-rich scheme nor the mantra of an inspirational speaker. Our world has enough of these. To be sure, many provide insights into the good life that positive psychology should explore. I happen to be impressed with Oprah Winfrey and Tony Robbins, among others, and their ideas about the human condition. But to call something positive *psychology*, the emphasis needs to be on the exploration of these insights with the tools of psychological science to see which ideas square with the facts of the matter and which do not.

The bad company against which I am warning threatens to bring down positive psychology—or at least tarnish its credibility—by running far ahead of what the evidence actually shows, promising what cannot be delivered, and glossing over the real problems that many people face. More insidiously, glib popularizations run the risk of making unhappiness seem to be simply a matter of choice and will (and of course not buying a given book). Social scientists have long been aware of the dangers of unfairly blaming the victim (W. Ryan, 1978). The positive psychology flipside of this is unfairly congratulating the winner.

Do You Have to Be Happy to Be a Positive Psychologist?

This question may not be posed to all positive psychologists, but it is one I frequently hear from my friends and colleagues, who know me as a somewhat dour individual. I do my share of complaining, and I roll my eyes much more frequently than I smile. Am I drawn to this endeavor because at some level I simply do not get it? Said another way, what does a gloomy guy have to convey about positive psychology that anyone else should take seriously?

I think the answer is quite a lot. As already mentioned, positive psychology is not all about ebullience. And indeed, "authentic" happiness entails more than just positive feelings (Seligman, 2002). With my typically straight face, I can say that I am happy because I love what I do and because I am fiercely loyal to my family and friends. I am a teacher who comes into daily contact with the best and the brightest young people in the world. I lose myself in my work, and I can look myself in the mirror every morning and be highly satisfied with what I do—although a few cups of coffee certainly help this affirmation.

Positive psychology is much too important a field to trust its study only to the most cheerful among us.

What's Missing?

Although still a new field, positive psychology has attracted psychologists from many other established fields, notably social psychology, personality psychology, and the applied subdisciplines of clinical psychology and organizational psychology. For reasons not clear to me, positive psychology is not well populated with folks from developmental psychology, community psychology, or cultural psychology, fields of obvious pertinence if our goal is to understand the good life. To date, there is only a smattering of representation from "hard" (natural science) psychology—those who study cognitive and biological processes. As a result, there are gaps in positive psychology and unfortunately in this book as well.

And as has been pointed out to me, always by someone with a twinkling eye, there is no positive psychology of human sexuality. Maybe the field's leaders are a bunch of prudes or on the wrong side of middle age, or maybe we are dubious about obtaining federal funding in the current political climate to do research on "good" orgasms (as if there were other types). But maybe there does not need to be an explicit field devoted to the subject. From the *Kama Sutra* to Alex Comfort's (1972) *The Joy of Sex*, sexuality has rarely been discussed or pursued with the assumption that "good enough" is good enough.

The Pillars of Positive Psychology

Sexuality aside, within the framework of positive psychology (Seligman & Csikszentmihalyi, 2000), one can find a comprehensive scheme for describing and understanding the good life. We can parse the field into three related topics: (a) positive subjective experiences (happiness, pleasure, gratification, fulfillment), (b) positive individual traits (strengths of character, talents, interests, values), and (c) positive institutions (families, schools, businesses, communities, societies). A theory is implied here: Positive institutions facilitate the development and display of positive traits, which in turn facilitate positive subjective experiences (Park & Peterson, 2003).

The word *facilitate* deliberately avoids strict causal language. It is possible for people to be happy or content even in the absence of good character, and people can have good character even when living outside the realm of positive institutions. The example of apartheid's demise in South Africa shows that citizens can do the right thing even in the face of oppressive historical precedent. The example of whistleblowers shows that employees do not always conform with workplace norms. And the example of excellent students from underfunded school districts shows that intellectual curiosity is not always stamped out by educational mediocrity.

But matters are simpler when institutions, traits, and experiences are in alignment (Gardner, Csikszentmihalyi, & Damon, 2001). Indeed, doing well in life probably represents a coming together of all three domains, and that is why I discuss each at length in this book.

Chapters 3 and 4 cover the first pillar, positive subjective experiences; chapters 5 through 9 focus on the second pillar, positive traits of the individual. Chapter 10 begins the discussion of the third pillar—enabling institutions—by looking at interpersonal relationships (friendship and love), and the discussion of these institutions is continued on a more macro level in chapter 11. The concluding chapter is a brief look at the possible future of positive psychology. In the next chapter, I discuss ways to apply the ideas of positive psychology to your own life.

As you may know, psychology textbooks are often accompanied by an instructor's manual and a student study guide that contain exercises and applications. In the best of all pedagogical worlds, the content in these supplements is well integrated with the textbook and facilitates its study and mastery. Whether or not this typically occurs, I do not know, but in the case of positive psychology, exercises and applications are too essential to be relegated elsewhere for students to blow through the night before an exam.

Indeed, the philosophical underpinnings of positive psychology demand an experiential component to solidify learning. Those who have thought about the inculcation of good habits, from Aristotle to the present, agree that doing so requires both theory and practice (Park & Peterson, in press d). Theory is important because we need labels for what we are doing and a scheme for relating the specifics to one another. Practice is important because we best learn when we see the relevance of abstract information to the concrete, and if the concrete happens to be our own life, so much the better.

Every chapter in this book therefore contains a suggested exercise along with a rationale in terms of the ideas presented in the chapter. I urge you to try these out. These are not canned demonstrations. They may or may not work exactly as intended and should be approached in the spirit of experimentation. I would love to hear from you about your reactions. You can contact me at chrispet@umich.edu and tell me how these exercises worked for you.

Also note that each chapter ends with a glossary of important terms and their definitions. I also suggest further readings, some academic and some popular. Web sites are also suggested. I additionally recommend some films that can provide the bases for papers or discussions. Finally, because I have spent as much of my life listening to music as doing psychology, I note some popular songs that embody the themes in a given chapter. Some of us who teach positive psychology courses play one of these songs to signal the beginning of a class. (A much more civilized strategy than pounding on a table or trying to talk over the chitchat of students.) I show my age in most of these suggestions. I was born in 1950 and came of age in the 1960s, and I believe that the 20th century's greatest poets were John Lennon and Smokey Robinson. I would be happy to hear more-contemporary suggestions from readers.

EXERCISE *Writing Your Own Legacy*

Remember that I started this chapter by asking you to imagine the final moments of your life and how you might take stock of how you had lived. This exercise formalizes the request. Think ahead to your life as you would like it to be and how you would like to be remembered by those closest to you. What accomplishments would they mention? What personal strengths would they enumerate? In short, what is your legacy?

This is not the occasion to be modest or flip. But neither is this the occasion to indulge in a fantasy. Hopes and dreams have a way of not coming true unless we do something to make them happen. Look back over what you have written, and ask yourself if you have a plan that will bring about your legacy that is realistic and within your power. And more to the point, are you enacting this plan in your present life?

Psychologist Howard Gardner has been studying professional journalists and is interested in what he calls "good work" on their part, stories that blend professional competence and moral excellence (e.g., Gardner, Csikszentmihalyi, & Damon, 2001). Journalism is a field with a clearly articulated code of ethics, but most would agree that this code has eroded in recent years. One reason is the intrusion of big money into the news business. Journalists have always competed to break stories, but now the competition involves enormous monetary stakes, which can override ethical values.

Gardner interviewed young journalists, all of whom acknowledged the importance of ethics in their field and none of whom had any confusion about the right way to cover a story. But they also lamented that they could not "afford" to do good work early in their careers. When they were more established—with their own byline, a corner office, a good salary, and a loosely monitored expense account—*then* they would do good work.

I heard Gardner describe this research at a psychology conference, and everyone in the audience chuckled at the foolishness of these young journalists. But we soon stopped chuckling when we saw the larger point that of course applied to all of us, in our professions as well as in our everyday lives. "Good work" is not a faucet we can turn on when we eventually are moved to do so. Rather, it is the result of a lifetime of developing appropriate talents and habits, which include a moral sense.

Like many academics, I spent my young adult years postponing many of the small things that I knew would make me happy, including reading novels for pleasure, learning to cook, taking a photography class, and joining a gym. I would do all of these things when I had time—when I finished school, when I had a job, when I was awarded tenure, and so on. I was fortunate enough to realize that I would never have time unless I made the time. And then the rest of my life began.

That is the realization I am urging upon you as you think about your legacy and how you will make it happen.

Put aside what you have written, but do not lose it. Read it again a year from now, or 5 years from now. Have you made progress toward your goals? And feel free to revise it if new goals have emerged. It is, after all, *your* legacy.

Here is a legacy written by one of my college students:

> He was a good man.
>
> He was a good husband. He deeply loved his wife. Like all couples, they had their disagreements, but no matter what, he focused on the good.
>
> He was a good father. His children were a priority, and he was always patient, supportive, and fair. They never doubted his love because they never had reason.
>
> He was a good worker. He did his job well, not because he loved it, but because it was the right thing to do. When he retired, there was an outpouring of appreciation from friends, colleagues, and supervisors.
>
> He was a good citizen. He always lent a helping hand. As a young man, he spent his weekends working with a community outreach program that repaired low-income housing. Later on, he became more active in his church, and as long as he could, he led backpacking trips for troubled teens.
>
> All in all, he was a man who loved life. And life in turn loved him.

GLOSSARY

existentialism: doctrine that a person's experience is primary

humanism: doctrine that the needs and values of human beings take precedence over material things and, further, that people cannot be studied simply as part of the material world

paradigm shift: radical change in a scientific field

phenomenology: description of a person's conscious experience in terms meaningful for that individual

positive psychology: scientific study of what goes right in life

self-actualization: inherent tendency of people to make the most of their potential

RESOURCES

Books and Journals

Seligman, M. E. P. (2002). *Authentic happiness.* New York: Free Press.

Snyder, C. R., & Lopez, S. J. (Eds.). (2002). *Handbook of positive psychology.* New York: Oxford University Press.

American Psychologist. Special issue (January 2000).

American Psychologist. Special issue (March 2001).

Review of General Psychology. Special issue (March 2005).

Time. Special issue (January 17, 2005).
Journal of Positive Psychology

Articles

Seligman, M. E. P., & Csikszentmihalyi, M. (2000). Positive psychology: An introduction. *American Psychologist, 55,* 5–14.
Sheldon, K. M., & King, L. (2001). Why positive psychology is necessary. *American Psychologist, 56,* 216–217.
Peterson, C., & Park, N. (2003). Positive psychology as the evenhanded positive psychologist views it. *Psychological Inquiry, 14,* 141–146.
Gable, S. L., & Haidt, J. (2005). What (and why) is positive psychology? *Review of General Psychology, 9,* 103–110.

Web Sites

http://www.positivepsychology.org. This is the Web site of the Positive Psychology Center at the University of Pennsylvania, which "promotes research, training, education, dissemination, and the application of positive psychology."
http://www.authentichappiness.org. This Web site is associated with Martin Seligman's (2002) trade book on positive psychology, *Authentic Happiness,* and contains many positive psychology surveys that can be taken on-line.
http://www.apa.org/about/division/div17.html. The Society of Counseling Psychology (Division 17 of the American Psychological Association) has a section devoted to positive psychology.

Films

It's a Wonderful Life (1946)
Schindler's List (1993)
The Family Man (2000)
About Schmidt (2002)
American Experience: Partners of the Heart (2003)
Hotel Rwanda (2004)
Montana PBS: "Introducing Positive Psychology: Signature Strengths, Flow, and Aging Well" (2004)
Millions (2005)

Songs

"All You Need Is Love" (Beatles)
"Big Yellow Taxi" (Joni Mitchell)
"Cat's in the Cradle" (Harry Chapin)
"Here Comes the Sun" (Beatles)
"Oh, What a Beautiful Morning" (from *Oklahoma)*
"The Secret of Life" (Faith Hill)
"Time in a Bottle" (Jim Croce)

2

Learning About Positive Psychology: Not a Spectator Sport

If I study, I seek only the learning that . . . instructs me in how to die well and live well. —MICHEL DE MONTAIGNE (1580)

Positive psychology courses have only been offered since the 1990s,[1] which means that I know something about their short history and how they have changed over the past few years. Among the very first such courses were small seminars for undergraduate and graduate students offered by Marty Seligman at the University of Pennsylvania. Taking a leave from my position at the University of Michigan, I joined him in September 2000 and co-taught these courses over the next 3 years. Early on, these were conceived as typical seminars—assigned readings, discussions in class, and written papers.

But Seligman (2004) hit upon a way to begin these courses that we have come to call *serious introductions.* Most seminars begin by the students introducing themselves like this: "My name is Jennifer. I am a sophomore studying psychology because first-year premed courses killed me and my GPA. I grew up in Cherry Hill, New Jersey. I am taking this particular course because it fits my schedule." The instructor may say something similar, probably mentioning where he went to school and what his current scholarly interests are.

1. The Positive Psychology Teaching Task Force, headed up by Randy Ernst, has for several years collected useful resources for teaching positive psychology (syllabuses, reading lists, exercises) and made them available at http://www.positivepsychology.org. For some thoughtful discussions on teaching positive psychology, see Baylis (2004) and Fineburg (2004).

Introductions like these are so familiar to college students as to be clichéd. But Seligman started one of the first positive psychology courses with a different sort of introduction, which has come to be known as the "Nikki Story," after his then 5-year-old daughter and a pivotal encounter he had with her one afternoon.

For years, Seligman was a self-proclaimed grouch—urgent about time, task oriented, and incapable of small talk. His wife, Mandy, and their children are lively, cheerful, and attuned to others, making Seligman a "walking nimbus cloud in a household radiant with sunshine" (Seligman, 2002, p. 28).

One afternoon, he was in the garden weeding, doing it like he did everything—seriously. Little Nikki was helping him, which took the form of throwing weeds in the air, dancing, and singing. That may strike many of you as a perfectly reasonable way to weed a garden, but it distracted Seligman, who yelled at his daughter. She walked away but returned in a few minutes.

> "Daddy, I want to talk to you."
>
> "Yes, Nikki."
>
> "Daddy, do you remember before my fifth birthday? From when I was three until when I was five, I was a whiner. I whined every day. On my fifth birthday, I decided I wasn't going to whine any more. That was the hardest thing I've ever done. And if I can stop whining, you can stop being such a grouch." (Seligman, 2002, p. 28)

At that moment, Seligman had a realization. Actually, he had two. First was a personal insight: Raising children is not about correcting their weaknesses and fixing whatever is wrong with them. Rather, it is about identifying and nurturing their strengths. In Nikki's case, these strengths included a precocious will to improve herself and the ability to challenge her grumpy father to find that same will within himself.

Second was a professional insight that led to positive psychology: Psychology as it existed had little to say about these remarkable strengths. Where do they originate? How can they be encouraged? To describe Nikki as *not* whiny is to miss her essence by a country mile. To describe anyone in terms of the weaknesses and shortcomings they do or do not have is to ignore half of the human condition—the good half, obviously, that makes life worth living. And yes, the garden was eventually weeded, and yes, Seligman became less of a grouch. Nikki remains delightfully herself, even as the teenager she has since become.

In telling the Nikki Story to students in his first positive psychology course, Seligman's intent was just to put a face on a subject matter that seemed at odds with what he had spent his life studying and teaching: depression, despair, and disorder. But embedded here was a serious introduction, not just to the subject matter but to himself and his family. Here was a father who cared enough about his child to take her advice about life seriously. Here was a child who made a decision to be a better person. Here was a story about people at their best. What a good way to frame all subsequent interactions. Even when Seligman would relapse into grouchiness, his students would remember Nikki and know that there was more to their teacher than his sobriety and absence of small talk.

In every positive psychology course we have since taught, all students are asked to tell an analogous story about an event in their lives that showed themselves at their very best. We have learned to preface this request by a small sermon on modesty, a virtue in many circumstances but not if it is at odds with the truth. And we say that we are not interested in achievements or performances but rather in strengths of character. As instructors, we tell our own stories, and mine goes like this:

> A friend of mine at another university was preparing a new course to teach and discovered that her school library did not have any films or videotapes pertinent to the course. Showing such tapes would help bring the course material to life, so what was she to do? I offered to help, because my own university has lots of audiovisual resources. I went to the library and checked out a number of relevant tapes that were in the public domain. I bought blank videotapes and spoke to a colleague at Michigan who had a fancy videotape duplicating machine in her laboratory. I explained what I wanted to do. She told me I could use the machine and gave me a brief lesson. I sat down and started to make copies, a process that went on for hours. Every once in a while, my colleague would walk by and see that I was still at it. Finally she stopped and said, "This is taking you forever. Why don't you ask one of your students to do this for you? After all, your friend won't know that you didn't do it yourself." "True enough," I responded. "But I would know."

That was me at my best, and I am proud when I am able to act this way. Mind you, this is not me in every venue of my life. No one would confuse me with Mother Teresa of Calcutta, but it was a good day—tedious, boring, and frustrating when I would push the wrong button and undo what had been accomplished. Indeed, it was a very good day.

This story has a postscript that concerns my Michigan colleague who had chided me for wasting my time. Several times, I had to leave her lab for a few minutes to use the bathroom. I was confused that the repetitive process of inserting and removing tapes was apparently not delayed by my periodic breaks. At first, I assumed that I had so automated the steps that I was simply unaware of my progress. But then I noted that the identifying labels attached to the new tapes had a different handwriting than my own. My colleague was coming by during my breaks and helping. Although I now knew what was going on, I never said a word to her. In keeping with my own lesson, I thought it enough that *she* knew what she was doing.

In a class of 15–20 students, these serious introductions can take several hours and may stretch over several class periods, but we believe that it is time well spent. As mentioned, they frame how we all think about one another for the rest of the semester and thereafter. With apologies to my readers from the Garden State, it is much better to know that Jennifer once went against the social currents to befriend an ostracized classmate in junior high school than to know that she grew up in New Jersey and had failed chemistry.

We have also learned that we need to tell students about appreciative listening, how to listen carefully to what is said and then to respond in a way that builds on what has been conveyed as opposed to disagreeing with it or dismissing it. Once I told my story without this preface, and one of my students—meaning well—said, "I think that is a terrible use of your time. You are a professor and very busy." I responded as gently as I could, "And that is why the giving of my time means something."

Positive psychology has become for us a course in rhetoric—not just one in reading and writing, but one in speaking and listening (Seligman, 2004).

Something powerful goes on during these serious introductions. During at least a third of the introductions, one of the listeners is moved to quiet tears. With or without tears, strong bonds are forged. No one sits in the corner of the classroom working a crossword puzzle. Baseball caps and sunglasses are removed without prompting. A cell phone has *never* rung. Students even drop the annoying conversational hedges "like" and "you know" from what they say because they are speaking from the heart and not just filling time. Everyone can see the principles of positive psychology in action, and this is heady stuff indeed.

Contrast this with typical classroom demonstrations. They may work in physics and chemistry, but woe be it to the psychology instructor who tries to demonstrate psychological principles in class. At best they work in the aggregate, where their effects cannot be apprehended without stopping to compute some statistical average. Even so, they often fall flat.

Positive psychology seems to be different, and we realized that we could assign exercises—inside and outside the classroom—that compellingly illustrated the ideas on which we focused each week. As our positive psychology course evolved, we accumulated, tried out, and polished different exercises. Some of the very best were suggested by our students.

Skeptics might worry that the field is too new to inspire interventions, but I have a different opinion. I agree with social psychologist Kurt Lewin's (1947) sentiment, expressed decades ago, that the best way to understand a psychological phenomenon is to try and change it. By this view, intervention research is not something that follows basic research at a polite distance but instead is its inherent complement (Linley & Joseph, 2004b).

Being "Cool" as the Enemy

In an ongoing project, my colleagues—Angela Duckworth, Tom Geraghty, Jane Gillham, Karen Reivich, Barry Schwartz, Martin Seligman, and Tracy Steen—and I have packaged together exercises like these into a positive psychology course that is being taught by regular classroom teachers to ninth-graders in a high school in suburban Philadelphia. In keeping with our view of positive psychology courses as rhetoric, these are part of the language arts curriculum—not social sciences. Our eventual goal is to evaluate the effect of such a course on student well-being and achievement, and to this end, we are also looking at comparable students *not* enrolled in the course. This project fits under the rubric of character education but—we hope—goes beyond sloganeering to take a rigorous look at the long-term consequences of learning about the psychological good life (Berkowitz & Bier, 2004).

We believe that one can best learn about the good life by engaging in it, and weekly exercises done outside of class by these ninth-graders are therefore a critical component. Remember my earlier point that the best way to understand a psychological phenomenon is to try and change it? We have since learned that if you *really* want to understand something, try and change it among young adolescents.

Our ninth-grade students are bright and capable, and their school is an outstanding one. Critical thinking is constantly encouraged and frequently displayed, and students are given a great deal of autonomy. These are all good things, but they contain as well a downside that threatens the whole rationale for the course. Indeed, there is a general lesson here about any exercise in positive psychology for any group of people.

If one approaches these exercises with cynicism or half a heart, then of course they cannot work, and at least some of the students in our study do exactly this. The critical thinking honed throughout their education manifests itself as automatic criticism. They are skeptical and seemingly afraid to try something that is not only new but also on the face of it corny.

Barry Schwartz has described this barrier to positive psychology exercises as being "cool," and although "cool" is no longer adolescent jargon, it remains an apt description of a stance of skeptical distance. Point out what is wrong in someone else's ideas rather than what is right. Do not show enthusiasm. Do not do anything that would leave you open to ridicule. This describes much of academics, even or especially at good schools, but it is exacerbated by the peculiar features of the adolescent mind.

We all survived adolescence, but if you are like me, you have painful memories of being scrutinized and judged by "them" even if we could not put a finger on just who "they" were. Adolescence is a time of mushrooming intellectual and emotional growth, and it results in an acute self-awareness unprecedented for the young person (Strauch, 2003). It is not surprising that while experiencing these changes, the adolescent believes that no one else understands—especially teachers and parents—although of course all adults do understand because they too went through this themselves once upon a time. As adolescents, we believe that our peers are more together and less troubled simply because they are no more likely to talk about their doubts and insecurities than we are. Victor Raimy (1976) even gave a name to this phenomenon—he called it the *special person misconception*—and it contributes to coolness.

Many of the exercises we have devised for our ninth-graders involve opening themselves up to their peers, teachers, and parents. What are their long-term goals? What do they value in themselves and others? We even ask them to talk to "old" people (i.e., those over 30 years of age). These activities make them extremely self-conscious and as a result reticent. Because they are good students, they go along with our requests but at an emotional arm's length. In sum, they are too cool to try something that might make them happy.

In an unpleasant exchange I had with one of the ninth-grade students in a debriefing session one summer, I sat patiently while he regaled me for 30 minutes about my evil intents to brainwash him. He concluded, "You can't make me happy if I don't want to be!" And I blurted out, "Fine. You can be as miserable as you want to be." I was immediately embarrassed, but I admit that it felt good.

We can call this teen *angst* or adolescent *sturm und drang,* but I think that is an overinterpretation (cf. Arnett, 1999). Instead, I think kids (and most adults) want their happiness to be spontaneous, to happen rather than to be deliberately created. In a stint as a clinical psychologist, while doing therapy with couples, I encountered a similar sentiment:

> "Tell your spouse what you want. Tell him what would make you happy."
>
> "I don't want to do that."
>
> "Why?"
>
> "It wouldn't be real when he did it."
>
> "But maybe he doesn't know what you really want."
>
> "Well, he should know."
>
> "Why?"
>
> "He just should."

I suppose the divorce rate would be lower if we all were the mind readers that our spouses assume us to be (chapter 10). But we are not. A couple that is unhappy enough and committed enough to their marriage will eventually try out some of the standard couples-therapy exercises and usually to good effect. But there is a lingering suspicion that spontaneity has been subverted and that love deliberately given is somehow less genuine than love that just happens.

I have a different point of view. Love (or, for that matter, happiness) is not reserved "only for the lucky and the strong" but instead is hard work that may entail careful deliberation and awkward action. Happiness as positive psychology conceives it is not for sissies. I like Erich Fromm's (1956) point that our ideal should not be to "fall in love" but rather to "stand in love"—love and happiness are not heedless freefalls that just happen when gravity is on our side.

Contrast the experience with the adolescents with the experience we have had with adult volunteers to whom we have offered these exercises as a possible way to lead more fulfilling lives (Seligman, Steen, Park, & Peterson, 2005). They are eager to learn, and when they try them out, they go the extra mile, elaborate them, and take them very seriously. They do not worry about being cool. Many are restless and somewhat unhappy. They know something is missing in their lives, and they are willing to try and change things.

So, there is a paradox here. There is every reason in the world to expect that positive psychology exercises will be most effective for those who are already happy[2]—remember that this was one of Seligman's original premises, that positive psychology should be concerned with fulfilling the lives of "normal" people—but it may be that someone needs to be a bit discontented to try something out of the comfortable ordinary.

Some Examples

Mind you, not all positive psychology exercises work as intended, but enough do that the failures are not discouraging but intriguing, and they can teach us as much as the successes. For example, let me contrast an exercise that worked with one that failed.

Gratitude Letters Versus Forgiveness Letters

American society seems to lack gratitude rituals: formal ways of expressing thanks to those who have done well by us. Think of all the people—parents, friends, teachers, coaches, teammates, employers, and so on—who have been especially kind to you but have never heard you express your gratitude. This exercise tells us to write a gratitude letter to one of these individuals, describing in concrete terms why you are grateful. If possible, deliver it personally and have the person read the letter in your presence. If this is not possible, then mail or fax the letter and follow it up with a phone call.

Here is a letter sent by one of my colleagues to her favorite college teacher (L. M. Christie, personal communication, August 3, 2005):

> Dear Ms. Carter:
>
> It was back in 1979, and yet I still remember when you first walked into the classroom to teach Southern Literature. You were ten minutes late. You sat down, lit a cigarette, poured yourself some coffee from a thermos, and apologized for the delay. You couldn't find your car keys. Then you couldn't find the syllabus in the pile of papers in front of you. I thought: "This course is a bust. I'm going to have to see if I can transfer into that Shakespeare class down the hall." And then it all fell away. You started to talk about the joy of studying great literature. You had

2. The basis for this assertion is the belief among psychotherapists that therapy is most helpful for those who are the least troubled (Schofield, 1964). Although there is less room for improvement, there is less baggage to bog down the trip and more skills and assets with which to make the journey.

> been teaching this particular course for seven years, and you never tired of it. You couldn't wait to hear our impressions of William Faulkner, Harper Lee, and Eudora Welty, among others. Your enthusiasm was infectious. I wanted to delve right in. You went on to say that you were not going to waste our time on the plot and character development of each book. Granted, they were critical elements, but you'd rather focus on the universal themes of human emotion, thought, and experience. These were the most valuable aspects of the written word. Lastly, you welcomed complete honesty in the classroom. What did we love or hate about a particular author's work and why? Should you, as the teacher, choose different books that better represented that person's body of work next time around? (So much for first impressions. I wasn't going anywhere, even for Shakespeare.)
>
> The following year, I took two more courses with you. I was always impressed with the breadth and depth of your knowledge. Clearly, you loved being a teacher, and you had so much to offer your students. I particularly appreciated your open door policy when it came to office hours. You'd say: "If I'm there, come in. If I'm not, go be somewhere else." I loved your humor and directness. And I loved how you challenged me to work on my writing. You were never critical, always balanced in your critique of my papers, and it made me want to do better.
>
> Before I graduated, I made an appointment with you to express my appreciation. You were late, and that made me smile. I'd grown fond of your idiosyncrasies and couldn't imagine you without them. When you finally came into the office, I thanked you for all of your support and guidance. And I thanked you for deepening my love of literature and spurring me to continue my studies. With my speech behind us, you graciously accepted my gratitude and started fishing through the mound of papers on your desk. You had written me a letter of recommendation in hopes that I could use it for future employment. I hadn't asked for one. I was deeply touched by your kindness.
>
> I read in the alumni newsletter that you retired in 2004. You surely had a rich and distinguished career. I couldn't attend your retirement party, but I heard through a friend that you entertained your guests with a dead-on impersonation of Truman Capote. I wish I'd been there, but I'm sending this letter in lieu of hugs and congratulations. Thank you again, for everything. You are a gifted teacher, Ann Carter. And you are an accomplished scholar. I know that I am not alone in saying you are sorely missed in the English Department. But above all else, you are a good person.

In our experience with many dozens of gratitude letters like these, they "work" 100% of the time in the sense that the recipient is moved, often to tears, and the sender is gratified as well. Letters are sent to mothers or fathers, friends or spouses, teachers or bosses, brothers or sisters. (Interestingly, college students rarely send them to their boyfriends or girlfriends. Perhaps the gratitude is obvious, or perhaps this is a lingering symptom of adolescent coolness.) The only hesitation we encounter is someone worrying that if he expresses his gratitude to his mother, then his father might feel slighted by implication. This does not happen, though, and Dad is always happy when Mom is thanked.

In chapter 4, I describe our more-formal attempts to evaluate this and other positive psychology exercises, and the evidence is clear that the good feelings (happiness) produced by sending a gratitude letter are reliably created (Seligman, Steen, Park, & Peterson, 2005). However, the effects on happiness of a gratitude letter dissipate after a few weeks, which is neither surprising nor disappointing if you think about it. A gratitude letter is a dramatic event but not a life-changing one unless of course you make a point to send such a letter once a week forever; then, you have changed your life and might expect permanent changes so long as you do not run out of recipients. Certainly, we know that the habitually grateful among us are happier than those who are not (McCullough, Kilpatrick, Emmons, & Larson, 1999; Park, Peterson, & Seligman, 2004; Vaillant, 2002).

Encouraged by our experience with gratitude letters, I designed an analogous exercise that entailed another positive emotion—forgiveness (McCullough, Pargament, & Thoresen, 2000). Forgiveness undoes our own hatred and frees us from the troubled past. Indeed, forgiveness has been described as the queen of virtues—that is, those who forgive are much more serene than those who do not and display many other positive strengths. Forgiveness can be difficult, though, and despite its benefits, someone may have strong reasons not to forgive, which must be respected.

Accordingly, when I asked my students to craft a forgiveness letter, I told them to do so tentatively and not to send it unless they really wanted to do so and only if their forgiveness were sincere. Otherwise, the instructions paralleled those for the gratitude letter:

> Think of the people who have wronged you in the past whom you have never explicitly forgiven, although you desire to do so. Write a forgiveness letter to one of these individuals describing in concrete terms why you forgive him or her and what if anything you hope will happen between you in the future.
>
> By the way, has this individual ever apologized? If so, how did you react?
>
> Please do not send this letter unless you really want to do so and are sincere in your forgiveness. Regardless, bring the letter to class and be prepared to discuss it.

This exercise was thoroughly unsuccessful because almost all of the students felt that delivering the letter to an individual who had never requested forgiveness would create more bad feelings than good ones. Upon reflection, they believed that in many cases they themselves had contributed to the hurt (e.g., painful romantic breakups) and that "forgiving" the other party would imply that they had been but innocent victims as opposed to co-conspirators. The 1 student out of 20 who delivered the letter reports that she has yet to be forgiven for doing so.

This unsuccessful exercise was nonetheless informative and led to a spirited discussion of the nature of forgiveness. One consensus reached is that forgiveness is a dance that best begins with an apology. Accordingly, a more-fruitful exercise—which I have not yet tested but plan to in some future class—is to have my students write an apology letter.

One of my students made the wise observation that there are good apologies and bad apologies (Lazare, 2004; C. D. Schneider, 2000). Consider a typical apology—a bad one—made by public figures who have done something distasteful: "I apologize to anyone who was offended." This sort of apology on the surface sounds good and may even be sincere, but it contains an implicit message that all but undoes the apology: "But you should not have been offended." In contrast, a good apology is one that says more simply: "I am sorry." Along these lines, a good apology contains no excuses phrased in terms of youthful indiscretions, legalistic qualifications ("I didn't inhale"), or wardrobe malfunctions. It is up to the recipient of an apology to excuse the transgression, or not.

My colleague Karen Reivich has evolved the forgiveness letter exercise into a letting-go-of-grudges exercise. You can imagine the form that it takes. Letting go of grudges is a necessarily internal activity. You cannot—or at least should not—tell someone that he no longer annoys the hell out of you. You can only tell this to yourself—and then act differently if you really mean it.

Fun Versus Philanthropy

One of the solid findings of positive psychology is that an orientation to the welfare of others is in the long run more satisfying than an orientation to one's own pleasure (chapter 4). To illustrate this, Marty Seligman devised an exercise that he calls "fun versus philanthropy," and it usually succeeds in making the point, even in the short run. The conclusion is inevitable that a lifetime of altruism will replicate this lesson over and over again.

This exercise is introduced in class with a brief discussion of things that most people would agree to be pleasurable (fun)—hanging out with friends, watching a movie, or eating a hot fudge sundae—and things that most people would agree to be helpful to others (philanthropy), like shoveling the snow for elderly neighbors, helping a younger family member with his schoolwork, or doing the family laundry. Which sort of activity would students prefer doing? Everyone chuckles, because of course fun is more fun.

Regardless, they are asked in the next week to pursue one pleasurable activity of their own choice and one philanthropic activity of their own choice. (We have learned, by the way, that it is prudent when asking our young and even not-so-young students to do such exercises to be explicit that they should *not* do anything physically dangerous, illegal, or exploitative of others—some fun activities can border on the dark side.) Flip a coin to decide which one to do first, and spend the same amount of time at each activity. Students are asked to write a brief paper comparing and contrasting their reactions to each activity.

With few exceptions, this exercise works in suggesting some lessons for life. Fun is pleasurable in the moment, but it is a fleeting pleasure. Philanthropy in contrast lingers. One of our students told us of a marathon long-distance call in which she tutored her younger nephew in algebra. Not a mathematics whiz herself, she found the task extremely difficult. She was not even sure that she had been helpful, but regardless, she felt wonderful for having given to him the gift of her time and concern: "I had a spring in my step. I felt more mellow that day. Things did not bother me."

Marty Seligman (personal communication, September 12, 2000) loves to repeat the story told by one of his students enrolled in the prestigious University of Pennsylvania Wharton School of Business (Donald Trump's alma mater), who found this exercise to be life altering.

> I don't particularly like my economics and accounting courses. I actually hate them. But I have always told myself that I am in Wharton so I can get a job with a great salary. Then I can do and buy things that will be fun. And then I will be happy. It never dawned on me that I can be happy right now and that high-priced fun is overrated and at its core really selfish. I felt wonderful just helping someone else.

I have asked you to approach these exercises in the spirit of experimentation, and part of experimentation is an even-handed look at what the results of an exercise might actually mean. Can we really take at face value the apparent lesson of the fun-versus-philanthropy exercise, or did we inadvertently bias the conclusions that our students fed back to us? Even 5 minutes into our positive psychology course, our students know that it is not like being at the Playboy Mansion. Maybe our students are closet hedonists but are smart enough not to out themselves to their instructors.

Maybe, although here is why I think we can take the results at face value. First, our students are never shy about saying what they mean, whether or not we approve, an apparently increasing trend (Twenge & Im, 2005). All the time, I read stories about college students across the nation who feel oppressed by teachers for their political opinions, and I marvel at what it would be like to have students who actually could be cowed by what I happen to believe. Oh well.

Second, more-rigorous research shows that philanthropy is associated with long-term fulfillment. In chapter 10, I describe longitudinal studies on charitable giving and volunteering, and the benefits for the giver (if not always the recipient) are indeed real.

Third, one of the defining features of pleasure (fun) is that it is fleeting because the psychological apparatus responsible for its experience is governed by a principle of adaptation (chapter 3). Contrary to the behaviorist notion that we repeat—endlessly—those actions that produce reward (aka reinforcement) is the experiential fact that all such actions lose their zing, sometimes rather quickly. Years ago, I purchased a Nintendo game and played *Space Invaders* for 8 straight hours, undaunted by the cramps produced along the way. The next day, I played for 3 hours. Then an hour on the third day. And then not at all. Just the other week, I found the Nintendo game in the back of my closet where it had resided for decades. I could only shake my head. So, if our fun-versus-philanthropy exercise does no more than teach a lesson about adaptation to pleasure, then that is a valid and valuable lesson (chapter 3).

I acknowledge that we need to do a more-rigorous evaluation of the fun-versus-philanthropy exercise. In the meantime, you can try it yourself and arrive at your own honest reaction.

Although the exercise is presented as an X-versus-Y one, this only means a comparison and contrast of the pure forms of the two experiences. In real life, we do not need to choose exclusively between fun and service to others. In chapter 4, I introduce the notion of a full life and suggest the possibility that at least some activities can be both philanthropic and pleasurable.

Gift of Time

Remember the me-at-my-best story from earlier in the chapter? I have elaborated this into an exercise that I call the "gift of time." What is the most valuable gift we can bestow on those we love?

In my positive psychology classes, I introduce this exercise by recounting O. Henry's (1906) short story "The Gift of the Magi," in which a young husband and wife give to each other a present made possible only by the sacrifice of that which was personally most dear.[3] Social scientists debate whether there really is such a thing as altruism, if by that is meant activities that *only* benefit others and that pay no personal dividend in the moment. I find this a tedious debate because it fails to go out into the real world and find examples that would resolve it. Sure, we can stand on our heads and argue—for example—that Christians who sheltered Jews in Nazi Europe, putting themselves at risk for death, "really" were rewarding themselves in some non-obvious way. But is this as scientifically parsi-

3. If you do not know the story, here is a synopsis. This is a young couple of very modest means facing Christmas without the ability to purchase any presents whatsoever for one another. The husband's most-prized possession is his expensive pocket watch. His wife's most valued possession, so to speak, is her long beautiful hair. So, planning to surprise his wife, the husband sells his watch to buy combs for her hair. And the wife sells her hair to a wigmaker to buy her husband a watch fob. A sad story? Hardly.

monious as concluding that they were simply doing the right thing given how they had been raised (Oliner & Oliner, 1988)?

Many of us are not in a position to put our lives on the line for a stranger. But we all have a gift to give that is infinitely precious because it is thoroughly nonrenewable. That gift is our own time. When I think of my best teachers or my best friends, common to them all is that they gave of themselves *over time*. It was never what they gave to me that mattered but how they did it. Indeed, a few years ago, I wrote my own gratitude letter, and it was not until I was writing this section that I realized I was grateful to a very dear friend in large part because she gives to me her time:

> I am grateful that you are never too busy and that our friendship has never been put on hold while crises run their course. . . . It is said that what is seen lies only in the eye of the beholder. But nothing good about you is in my eye; it is all in you and how you live and what you give, and I am grateful to be a participant in this life so well lived.

A final frame for this exercise is to think about the yuppie expression *quality time*, used to describe the 15 minutes per day that harried parents try to spend with their children. Without meaning any disrespect, I suggest that quality time is at best an oxymoron and that a brief encounter with one's child, no matter how genuine, cannot substitute for being there most, if not all, of the time.

The actual exercise is simple to describe:

> Think of a person about whom you care. What might you be able to do for this person that entails nothing more than the giving of your time and indeed that takes time? Certainly, there are acts of kindness that entail gifts of money or goods, but in this exercise, time is of the essence, as it were. Plan a gift of time for this person and give it, whether it means doing something with them or something for them on your own. Spend as much time as needed to do the favor well and do not take any shortcuts. You might even consider taking off your wristwatch. Regardless, do not tell the recipient of your gift how much time you spent. Let the gift speak for itself.

This exercise has had checkered success. If it can be carried out according to the instructions, then most feel great about doing the favor. But all too often, the enemy is time itself: Someone does not have enough time to give time. Or in giving time in one arena of life, another arena necessarily suffers. One of my colleagues gave the gift of time to one of her children—spending an afternoon in a room without a clock with her older daughter and a coloring book. But she felt guilty about neglecting her younger daughter. Maybe she should have done something with the two of them, but then she would have worried that she was neglecting her husband. And so it goes.

We cannot create time out of thin air. I can remember complaining once to a friend that I had too many things to do. "So," said my friend, playing psychologist, "you have a time management problem." "No," I countered, "I manage my time perfectly well. What I have is a time problem—not enough of it!" I suppose this is really the point of the exercise, and it means we need to choose carefully how we deploy a resource for which deficit spending is not an option.

Three Good Things

Several different research groups have investigated the effects of asking people to stop and reflect on those things for which they are most grateful (Emmons & Crumpler, 2000; Emmons & McCullough, 2003; Lyubomirsky, Sheldon, & Schkade, 2005; Seligman, Steen, Park, & Peterson, 2005). The details of this intervention differ across studies, but the results are always the same: Counting your blessings on a regular basis makes you happier and more content with life.

We call our own version of this exercise "three good things" because it entails writing down at the end of each day three things that went well (Seligman, Steen, Park, & Peterson, 2005). We experimented with these instructions and discovered—for example—that asking people to list ten good things did not work as well as asking for three and further that asking them to count their blessings at the beginning of the day was not nearly as effective as asking them to do so at the end of the day. Irving Berlin was onto something when he advised us to count our blessings instead of sheep.

We also ask people to briefly explain why each event was a good one, and our rationale here is simply that people may not be especially mindful about good events, even when they enumerate them (chapter 5). For most people, "competence requires no comment" (Ryle, 1949), which means that we usually assume that good things are our due. Accordingly, we do not think much about them and miss the potential benefits of thoughtful (conscious) gratitude. Asking for an explanation leads to "deeper" thought.

Here are the instructions for this exercise:

> At the end of each day, after dinner and before going to sleep, write down three things that went well during the day. Do this every night for a week. The three things you list can be relatively small in importance ("My husband picked up my favorite ice cream for dessert on the way home from work today") or relatively large in importance ("My sister just gave birth to a healthy baby boy"). After each positive event on your list, answer in your own words the question "Why did this good thing happen?" For example, you might speculate that your husband picked up ice cream "because he can be really thoughtful" or "because I remembered to call him from work and remind him to stop by the grocery store." When asked why your sister gave birth to a healthy baby boy,

you might explain, "God was looking out for her" or "She did everything right during her pregnancy."

In our own investigation of this exercise, we found that counting one's blessings increases happiness and decreases symptoms of depression for up to 6 months of follow-up. The fine print of this finding is that the long-term benefits occurred for participants who continued the exercise beyond the suggested 1 week. This apparently was easy to do, because 60% of the participants in the study reported that they were still counting their blessings 6 months later. Some of our participants told us that they had made this a new routine in their marriage—sharing their blessings with their partner at the end of the day. If you go to sleep happy, you are probably apt to wake up happy as well. And if you go sleep next to someone else who is happy, that is good, too.

Being a Good Teammate

Here is an exercise that underscores the importance and satisfaction of being a good teammate and more generally the satisfaction of social responsibility and citizenship. At least in the contemporary United States, we are encouraged to be leaders but not followers, to heed our own drummer, and to follow our own hearts. Loyalty and teamwork may be labeled as conformity or obedience and thereby marginalized if not condemned (Asch, 1956; Milgram, 1963). What results, however, is a society which, at its worst, pits each against all (Hobbes, 1651/1982) and at its best is quietly empty at the center (Hardin, 1968). We are more likely as a people to bowl alone than to work for a common cause (Putnam, 2000), despite ample evidence that well-developed social interest benefits not just the group but the individual in the group (Peterson & Seligman, 2004).

How do we work against these trends and build good citizenship? One way to do so is by encouraging participation in groups by young people. Such early experiences—not necessarily as a leader but as a follower—set the stage for a lifetime of civic participation (DeMartini, 1983; Flanagan et al., 1998; McAdam, 1989).

Citizenship and teamwork can be rather abstract, but as a teacher I have approached them at a concrete and presumably interesting level by asking my students to think of their best teammates or favorite group members. What do these people do that makes them notable? Are any lessons able to be abstracted from their examples?

Or I ask them to think about Michael Jordan, the greatest basketball player of our generation and the winner of six professional titles during the 1990s. National Basketball Association and Nike marketing strategies notwithstanding, Jordan did not win these titles by himself but instead as a member of a team that included the ultimate sidekick, Scottie Pippen. In the 1990s, it was common to hear Pippen's basketball skills dismissed with the observation that he never won anything without Jordan. But in hindsight, it is just as true to observe that Jordan won little without Pippen.

Few of us can be "like Mike" in any of our own venues, but it is not so far-fetched to aspire to be a Pippen. Accordingly, here is an exercise I have asked my students to carry out:

> Choose one of the ongoing groups to which you belong but of which you are not a leader. Without fanfare, resolve to be the best group member (teammate) during the next month that you can be. The characteristics of the group will dictate the details of how you should act, but one would think that being a good teammate requires:
>
> - showing up, literally and metaphorically
> - not whining or being disruptive or feeling jealous
> - doing more than your share
> - volunteering without being prompted
> - spreading praise[4]
> - helping the leader—and of course the group—accomplish goals
>
> Keep track of what you did, and how it made you feel.

A teachable moment occurs when students find themselves at odds with the group or the group leader. This exercise does not require blind obedience or participation in stupid and wrong activities. Rather, good teammates dissent or disagree when appropriate, although they do so as a good group member. Consider the notion of *comity* (civility in discourse and disagreement) and the equally quaint political term *loyal opposition.*

This exercise has always worked well among my students, who report that it is not only novel but invigorating to think first of the team and how to advance its goals. Some of my students chose a discussion class as their group and worked to make discussions "good" ones. Others chose their part-time jobs, where they volunteered for the unpopular shifts. One of my students was the captain of her cheerleading squad, and she—with admitted reluctance—let a junior member choose the cheers.

4. A related exercise is called "letting someone else shine." So much of what we do in life is done in conjunction with others, and when we are done, we like to get credit and acclaim. But studies summarized by Leary and Forsyth (1987) should give us all pause because a common finding is that participants in a group project assign themselves more credit than others assign to them, so that the sum of attributed effort (from the viewpoint of each participant) always adds up to much more than 100%. This of course cannot be, no matter how mathematically challenged you are. In the letting-someone-else-shine exercise, regardless of your private opinion, you should assign your fellows all of the public credit following a group task or project. Let them make the final report or presentation. Thank them publicly, and praise them profusely. Say that you were along for the ride (in some cases, you probably were). In other words, step back and let them shine. Parents are usually pretty good about this vis-à-vis their own children and so are teachers who have achieved a certain maturity vis-à-vis their own students. I think the exercise is worth trying in other arenas of life as well.

In many cases, my students' embracing of Pippen-hood was acknowledged and appreciated by their teammates, but in a few other cases not. Even so, most of these students said that it did not really matter that their efforts had been overlooked, because there had been a clear payoff for them in the form of group success, solidarity, and morale. As the cheerleader captain said, knowing of my fascination with Kirsten Dunst, it was great that someone else was able to "bring it on."

Honey Versus Vinegar: Being Nice as a Way to Cut Institutional Red Tape

One of the striking changes brought about by the modern world is the increased mobility of its citizens. Whereas previous generations were born in a given place and lived out their lives there, people today make lots of moves. In the contemporary United States, for example, as many as 30% of adults have moved from one state to another within the previous 5 years. Particularly likely to move frequently are young adults and those with a college education. Even more frequent are local moves, within the same town or state. When I was in college and graduate school, I moved in September of every year and had eight different addresses between 1968 and 1976.

Moving can be an adventure, but it also has a downside. You need to shut off the electricity, the gas, and the garbage pickup at the old place. You need to start them up at the new place. You need to change your driver's license. Get a new license plate. Change your checking account. Get a new automated teller card. Change your phone—local and long distance. Get a new cell phone. Change your Internet provider. Stop your mail. Forward it. Oops—magazines are not automatically forwarded, so you need to contact each distributor separately. Oh yes, and then you need to do all of this again when mistakes are made.

Even if you do not move frequently, you still have to battle bureaucracies on an ongoing basis, at the Department of Motor Vehicles, the college registrar's office, or the return desk at Talbot's. And although I hope you grow old with grace, independent means, and perfect health and that you never need to deal with Medicare, Medicaid, Social Security, assisted living, a pension fund, a will, or inheritance taxes, none of that is likely to happen, so your battles with bureaucracies will continue to death and beyond.

Accordingly, here is a positive psychology exercise devised by Marty Seligman that may help. The next time that you go to red-tape war, take a deep breath and resolve to be cheerful. Whether you are confronting a bureaucrat face to face or on the phone (after 20 minutes of working yourself through the automated telephone "help" system), start out by asking the person how her day has been. What's the weather like in Bombay? Marvel at his patience. Say that it must be great to be in a position to help other people. As Patrick Swayze's character in *Roadhouse* advises the bar bouncers under his tutelage: "Be nice . . . be nice . . . be nice." Treat the bureaucrat as a person, and perhaps the favor will be returned.

You will probably be more successful in getting what you want if you use honey rather than vinegar. The "bureaucrat" after all is a person, and being on the receiving end of constant consumer anger can take a toll (Rupp & Spencer, in press). If you are nice, you may cheer up the person, and we know that good moods facilitate helpfulness (Cunningham, 1979). If nothing else, *you* might at least feel better.

You can do this exercise as a true experiment. Flip a coin before each encounter. Heads: Be nice. Tails: Kick some bureaucratic butt. After a few dozen trials, tally up the results, and draw a conclusion.

I alert you to two threats to being nice. First, some people—especially on the telephone—are on the clock, which means that they will be penalized for taking too long to resolve a request or dispute. You can figure this out pretty quickly, and in these cases, you need to be nice in a concise way. Indeed, to be concise *is* to be nice to someone on the clock. Second, some people may respond so well to your niceness that the two of you go off on some conversational tangent and neglect the actual reason for your encounter. For example, the last time I changed my long-distance provider, I had a wonderful conversation with "Fred" at AT&T about Allen Iverson of the Philadelphia 76ers and was so distracted that I forgot to ask when the service would begin, and my new friend forgot to tell me. I only discovered this when I received the next month's phone bill, the first half of which charged me $1 million a minute (approximately) for my calls. Oh well.

One more objection. Are you being a phony? This question could be asked about any of the positive exercises I have described and is one to which I have already alluded in describing people's desire to have their happiness spontaneously happen rather than deliberately occur. (Never mind that we also want to "deserve" our happiness, which would seem to entail doing something to bring it about; Nozick, 1974.) All things being equal, we want to be true to our real self, but the dilemma is when our real self—at least at that moment—is an angry and resentful self. Is it disingenuous to suppress these feelings and "be nice"?

Obviously, there is no simple answer. But a phone call to a customer service agent is hardly the best occasion to be true to your most righteous self. I believe that niceness should be regarded as part of the social script for such encounters and that following this script does not make you a phony any more than deliberately using your turn signals while driving makes you a phony.

There is a saying in Alcoholics Anonymous: "Fake it until you can make it." One of the best ways to change the inner person is to change the outer person. What starts out as phony may end up being genuine (Kelly, 1955). It would be wonderful to be spontaneously cheerful with bureaucrats, but is it really so evil to feign some good cheer until the day when you might be able to do this more routinely?

EXERCISE *Have a Good Day*

This chapter contained a number of positive psychology exercises. Here is one more that invites you to design an exercise tailored to your own self. I especially hope that you try this one and that you let me know how it worked.

"Have a good day" is a conversational gambit we hear all the time, but suppose we take the embedded wish seriously. What might we actually do to have a good day? Different people will have different answers, and thus there are two steps to this exercise. First, you need to determine what makes a good day for *you.* Here you need to be a careful observer of your own days, the good ones as well as the not-so-good ones, to see if you can identify the relevant features. Second, assuming that you can identify these, how can you change your future days to maximize the enabling factors and minimize those that detract?

There is a simple assumption here about what makes a good day to which I call your attention because it is at odds with the premise of much of the positive psychology research described in this book. The good life is often discussed in terms of the psychological states, traits, and habits that enable it, as well as the social and institutional settings in which these states, traits, and habits are most readily manifest.

But there is another route to the good life, and that is our mundane daily activity—our behaviors, as it were—regardless of our states, traits, habits, and larger settings. To be sure, these all affect what we do and indeed are probably how they affect our happiness and well-being. But in this exercise, I am suggesting that you go straight to the concrete activities. If you can determine, for example, that a good day is one during which you talked to your mother on the phone (or not) or exercised or wrote in your journal, then there is a very practical lesson to be learned: Have more days in which you do these things and fewer days in which you do not. Duh.

What rescues this exercise from the banal is that we may never have stopped and thought about what makes for a good day, and even if we have reflected on this in the abstract, our answers may not be the right ones in the concrete (Kahneman, Krueger, Schkade, Schwarz, & Stone, 2004). So, get a notebook or a pad of paper or create an Excel spreadsheet and keep track of what you do during a day. Some people find it easy to journal on an hour-to-hour basis, whereas others prefer to parse their day in terms of its dominant activities. Regardless, at the end of the day, write down an overall rating:

10 = it was one of the best days of my life
9 = it was an outstanding day
8 = it was an excellent day
7 = it was a very good day
6 = it was a good day
5 = it was an average or typical day

4 = it was a subpar day
3 = it was a bad day
2 = it was a terrible day
1 = it was one of the worst days of my life

Do this for at least 2 weeks and preferably a month.[5] Do not review your record until you are done, but then go back and look for the pattern across the days and weeks. Compare the good days with the bad days in terms of what you were doing (or not) on those days. Everyone who has done this exercise reports that a pattern is readily apparent, and in some cases, it was one that surprised them. In my own case, I discovered that a good day was one in which I finished something that had been nagging at me, either at work (e.g., sending off letters of recommendation for a student applying to law schools) or at home (e.g., vacuuming my living room). Mind you, these activities did not spiral me into ecstasy, but they clearly contributed to a good day. In contrast, bad days were ones in which I finished nothing, no matter what else was going on or how many praiseworthy projects I had begun.

I resolved, therefore, to finish something every day, and that strategy has done well for activities that could be finished on a frequent basis. But I have been writing this book for the past few months and of course I cannot finish it in one day or on every day. But I can write 500 words a day, almost every day, and that is exactly what I have been doing, and I have had a lot of very good days as a result, including this one.

I doubt that your own formula for a good day will be as task oriented as my own, but that is the point of this exercise: to find your own formula and to devise your own strategy based on it. Once you find these, change your typical day, tempered of course by common sense. A glass of wine with dinner may contribute positively to your assessment of a good day, but there is no reason to think that two liters in one sitting will make future days proportionately better. Similarly, a good night's sleep might make for a good day, but that does not mean you should resolve to sleep your life away.

Have a good day!

RESOURCES

Books and Journals

Linley, P. A., & Joseph, S. (Eds.). (2004). *Positive psychology in practice.* New York: Wiley.

5. Saturdays and Sundays are "good" days for many of us, for obvious reasons, which means you should not limit your assessment to weekends (Egloff, Tausch, Kohlmann, & Krohne, 1995; Larsen & Kasimatis, 1990). The goal here is to find a pattern in terms of your activities—over which you have control—and not the calendar, over which you have none.

Norcross, J. C., Santrock, J. W., & Campbell, L. F. (2000). *Authoritative guide to self-help resources in mental health.* New York: Guilford.

Krieger, E., & James-Enger, K. (2005). *Small changes, big results: A 12-week action plan to a better life.* New York: Crown.

Albom, M. (1997). *Tuesdays with Morrie: An old man, a young man, and life's greatest lesson.* Garden City, NY: Doubleday.

Articles

Seligman, M. E. P. (2004). Can happiness be taught? *Dædalus, 133*(2), 80–87.

Rosen, G. M. (1987). Self-help treatment books and the commercialization of psychotherapy. *American Psychologist,* 42, 46–51.

Web Sites

http://www.reflectivehappiness.com. Requiring a paid subscription, this Web site provides exercises like those described in this chapter.

http://www.positivepsychology.org/teachingpp.htm. This Web site provides a variety of resources for anyone teaching or studying positive psychology.

http://www.casel.org/home/index.php. The Collaborative for Academic, Social, and Emotional Learning (CASEL) "synthesizes the latest empirical findings and theoretical developments and provides scientific leadership to foster progress in [social and emotional learning] . . . research and practice."

http://www.actsofkindness.org. This is the Web site of the Random Acts of Kindness Foundation, "established in 1995 as a . . . resource for people committed to spreading kindness . . . [and providing] . . . a wide variety of materials . . . including activity ideas, lesson plans, project plans, teacher's guide, project planning guide, publicity guide, and workplace resources."

http://www.payitforwardfoundation.org. This is the Web site of the Pay It Forward Foundation, "established in . . . 2000 to educate and inspire young students to realize that they can change the world, and provide them with opportunities to do so."

http://www.kindnessproject.com/home.php. "The Kindness Project aims to prove that you can have an exponential effect on the spread of kindness around the world. It's simple—when someone does or says something kind, no matter how small, you give them a token. Taking a few seconds to pass on the token empowers you to brighten someone's day. The tokens are passed from person to person, again and again, turning the world into a kinder place." Tokens can be purchased from this Web site.

Films

My Fair Lady (1964)
Dead Poets Society (1989)
Mr. Holland's Opus (1995)

Songs

"Reach Out of the Darkness" (Friend & Lover)
"The Rose" (Bette Midler)
"What a Wonderful World" (Louis Armstrong)
"What a Wonderful World" (Sam Cooke)

3 Pleasure and Positive Experience

He must see life not as a vale of tears but as a happy time;
He must take joy in his work, without regarding it as the end and all of living;
He must be an alert man, an aware man, a man of taste, a man sensitive to pleasure,
A man who—without acquiring the stigma of the voluptuary or dilettante—can live life to the hilt.

Think about this characterization of the psychological good life, and guess who proposed it. Not Aristotle. Not Confucius. Not Maslow, Seligman, or Csikszentmihalyi.

Rather, it was Hugh Hefner, who in 1956 articulated it as part of his *Playboy* philosophy. Many readers probably think that *Playboy* is silly in its obsession with naked young women. But these assertions are still a great way to begin this chapter because they mention many of the topics studied by contemporary positive psychologists as they address positive experiences: happiness, joy, alertness, and pleasure. Living life to the hilt is what we mean by zest, exuberance, and vitality, and whether the hilt centers around breasts or something else is not the point.

That some of you find Hugh Hefner's specific formula for pleasure to be off-putting is worth comment as well, because it underscores the ambivalence many of us have about the senses and their so-called indulgence. Some pleasures simply seem wrong to most of us, and all pleasures seem wrong to at least a few of us. The seven deadly sins specified centuries ago share a core of pleasure, even if draped in shame or guilt.[1]

1. The seven deadly sins are anger, envy, gluttony, greed, lust, pride, and sloth (laziness), and their relationship to the Seven Dwarfs of Disney's *Snow White* is the topic of another book. Once upon a time, there was an eighth deadly sin—*acedia*, or neglect of one's spiritual duties—which fell

In this chapter, I discuss pleasure and related positive experiences, and I invite you to keep in mind the moral context of the psychological states that feel good. Positive psychology can be criticized for its ostensible focus on happy feelings, which is one of the reasons I went to such lengths to say that positive psychology is a broader field than hedonism or happiology (chapter 1). Pleasure nonetheless deserves to be studied, although in doing so, we have to ask if this leads to the sanctioning of selfishness or a celebration of the shallow (Wallach & Wallach, 1983).

I start with a discussion of sensory pleasure and move to positive emotions—more protracted and complex than immediate good feelings but still with identifiable beginnings and endings. Then I consider the stable disposition to experience positive emotions (called *positive affectivity*). And I close by looking at yet another positive subjective state—flow or engagement—that shares a family resemblance with these other topics but is arguably nonconscious.

Pleasure

Pleasure encompasses a family of subjective positive psychological states that range from the "raw feels" of the body (Ryle, 1949) produced by perfumes or back rubs to the "higher" pleasures of the mind occasioned by Beethoven's Ninth Symphony or the denouement of *The Usual Suspects* to the pleasures of accomplishment produced by the victory of a favorite political candidate or local football team (Dunker, 1941). Pleasure can be intense, aroused, and sharp—we call it joy or ecstasy in this case—or it can be quiet, mellow, and diffuse, and then we call it contentment or serenity. Contrast the experience of orgasm with the contemplation of a sunset on the Pacific Ocean. Regardless, pleasure *feels* good, and if we do not seek it relentlessly, at least most of us appreciate it greatly when it occurs, trying to maintain it or enhance it.

Rozin (1999) observed that the raw pleasures associated with sensations are generated along the skin[2] and specifically center on or about our body's orifices—mouth, nostrils, genitals, and anus—all of which are involved with the exchange of material substances between the outside and inside of the body. He speculated that

---

to the wayside as the Western world became more secular (Jackson, 1986). At least in the modern world, which so celebrates celebrity and self-esteem, pride may be on its way to the moral scrap heap as well.

2. Not exactly fitting this formula are the pleasures associated with the distance senses—vision and hearing (Kubovy, 1999). These of course produce pleasure in the form of sights and sounds that strike us as pleasing or harmonious, but it is not quite correct to call these visual or auditory pleasures. In any event, one important point about pleasure as we actually encounter it in the real world is that it is usually compound, simultaneously involving several sensory systems as well as more-complex cognitive processes.

these orifices are explicitly ambiguous in terms of their bodily location—are they inside or outside?—and perhaps pleasure arose as a way to monitor, index, and even guide the ongoing transaction between the person and the environment. So, pleasure serves survival and perhaps even existence itself.

The higher pleasures are not so easily explained from a functional perspective. Why should we have the capacity to enjoy music or sunsets, riddles or games? As psychologist Barbara Fredrickson (1998) phrased it, "What good are positive emotions?" Answers are emerging from the work of Fredrickson and other positive psychologists, and they converge on the possibility that the higher emotions signal safety and provide the opportunity to build and consolidate psychological skills that can later be used to good effect (Nakamura & Csikszentmihalyi, 2002).

This hypothesis was foreshadowed decades ago by the theorizing of ethologists (biologists who study animals in their natural environments) about the function of play among the young of many mammalian species (Symons, 1978). The specific behaviors that these youngsters rehearse and perfect in their rough-and-tumble play are precisely those they later use as adults to hunt, to escape predators, and to establish a dominance hierarchy. Although we have been taught as objective scientists not to attribute human motives to our animal cousins, it is nonetheless difficult to watch kittens or puppies gambol about without concluding that they are having "fun" in the process. Suffice it to say that *we* derive pleasure from watching them.

With occasional exception, pleasure has been ignored by psychologists over the years, but those who do grapple with it are almost always drawn to a position that emphasizes its role in the biological evolution of our species (Buss, 2000). So, if positive psychology is the study of what makes life most worth living, then the study of pleasure may additionally be the study of what makes life possible. Consider the important survival tasks faced by our ancestors: eating, mating, and raising offspring. It cannot be just a coincidence that these activities provide pleasure, making our ancestors more likely to do in the short run what they needed to do in the long run to survive and thrive as individuals and as a species (chapter 10).

This is not to say that pleasure is just biology. Our physical bodies evolved, but so too did our capacity for culture, which means that human beings are at their essence social beings and participants in a shared culture that is transmitted across generations by processes of socialization. We should not be surprised that our culture has something to say about a phenomenon as biologically potent as pleasure, just as it does about other biologically potent occurrences like birth and death. These pronouncements will differ across cultural groups, and the range of cultural scripts is wide indeed. At one end, we have a wholesale distrust of pleasure and its enthusiastic renunciation, as among the Greek stoics and various ascetic traditions (Bell, 1985). At the other end, we have the Greek hedonists and epicureans, the Haight-Ashbury generation of the 1960s, and the over-the-top pleasure seekers celebrated in Robin Leach's "Lifestyles of the Rich and Famous."

Pleasure is so much a part of the human landscape that the handful of people who are incapable of experiencing it have earned their own label—*anhedonic*—and a research literature has grown up around these folks (Chapman, Chapman, & Miller, 1982). Although the mechanisms responsible for anhedonia are not well understood,[3] what is clear is that people who do not experience pleasure fail to engage in a range of activities that other people pursue because they do not find anything to be rewarding.

The semantic antonym of pleasure is pain, although the psychological opposites of pleasure encompass as rich a set of feelings as pleasure itself, including of course pain but also anxiety, guilt, shame, and boredom. In keeping with a basic premise of positive psychology, pleasure is not simply the absence of its opposites, whatever these may be. Accordingly, when positive psychologists approach pleasure, they do so on its own terms and in its own right.

Here is some of what we know about pleasure (Rozin, 1999). For starters, pleasure is an experiential quality *and* an experiential quantity. That is, there are different types of pleasures, each of which admits to degrees. Psychologists are often chided for asking research participants to rate everything in the world along 7-point scales. In some cases, these are difficult if not impossible distinctions for people to make, but few of us have any trouble rating experiences along a dimension of more versus less pleasurable. This is a natural way to think about pleasure.

Pleasure is multidimensional. Even though people can readily offer summary judgments of pleasure, it is also true that we can simultaneously experience positive and negative feelings. Bittersweet describes a taste both bad and good and is an apt metaphor for many of our experiences. Indeed, sometimes the interplay between the positive and the negative produces a higher-order experience, which we label as especially positive or especially negative. Why are sad songs so appealing or "tastes of honey" so tragic?

Pleasures can result from adding a stimulus or subtracting it. Contrast eating a cheeseburger with emptying your bladder. Both produce pleasure but of different sorts. Some term the latter pleasures those of **comfort**, and they tend to be more conspicuous in their absence. You may be old enough to remember the days when air conditioning was not routinely available and what a great feeling it was on a hot and humid day to enter an air-conditioned room. Nowadays many of us take air conditioning for granted, except of course when it is on the fritz. It has morphed from an explicit pleasure to a mere comfort.

Although we often focus on pleasure in the here and now, we also experience

3. Research suggests that anhedonia runs through families in such a way as to imply genetic influence, and the biological basis of this inability may center in the left frontal lobe of the brain and/or involve deficiencies in the neurotransmitter dopamine (Berenbaum, Raghavan, Le, Vernon, & Gomez, 1999).

pleasure with respect to the past (in terms of memories) and with respect to the future (in terms of hopes). Is it too farfetched to propose that most of the pleasure we experience is not in the here and now but instead in the form of recollection or anticipation (Rozin, 1999)? An orgasm involves only a few seconds of "online" pleasure,[4] but how many of us spend more than mere seconds a day thinking about sex?

When we think about past pleasures, our memories are influenced by the intensity of the immediate experience as well as how it ended, a formula dubbed **peak-end theory** by its originator, psychologist Daniel Kahneman (1999). What peak-end theory reflects is the fact that our recollection of pleasure is *not* a faithful summary of its individual moments.

Research participants have been studied in a variety of brief situations, some pleasant (e.g., watching a funny movie) and some unpleasant (e.g., undergoing a painful medical procedure). While the experience is occurring, the participants evaluate its pleasantness versus unpleasantness on an ongoing basis; they also offer a summary evaluation when it is over. The consistent findings from studies like these support peak-end theory: People's summary evaluations closely reflect an average of the experience's most-extreme rating and how it was rated just before it ended (Fredrickson & Kahneman, 1993; Kahneman, Fredrickson, Schreiber, & Redelmeier, 1993; Redelmeier & Kahneman 1996; Varey & Kahneman, 1992). Essentially overlooked is how long the experience—pleasant or unpleasant—lasted. Kahneman (1999) called this phenomenon **duration neglect**, and it is a recurring theme in psychology's study of positive experience.

Peak-end theory reminds me of another line of research that investigates how people think about and navigate physical spaces. Landmarks are critical (Kaplan & Kaplan, 1982). When we think of the city where we live, we do so in terms of its particular buildings, streets, and monuments. They are regarded as especially prominent in size and distinctiveness, even if this is not entirely accurate. Landmarks are also used to estimate distance. If point A and point B have no landmarks between them, the distance is seen as shorter than the distance between point C and point D, with numerous landmarks in between, even if the two distances are the same. The peak of pleasure and how it ends can be regarded as the landmarks of positive experience and thus determine how we remember and think about it.

There is an interesting implication of peak-end theory borne out by appropriate studies. Kahneman et al. (1993) had some people keep their hand in ice-cold water—unpleasant but not dangerous—for 60 seconds. Other research participants were asked to keep their hand in the same water for the same amount of

4. For those of you who find numerical facts interesting: The orgasms of men and women are each accompanied by rhythmic muscle contractions occurring at the exact same rate, every 0.8 of a second. Men's orgasms last between 5 and 10 seconds, whereas those of women are usually longer in duration—10–30 seconds—and more variable (Darling, Davidson, & Jennings, 1991).

time and then to leave their hand immersed for an additional 30 seconds. During this extra time, without the research participants being told, the water's temperature was raised 1 degree, making it marginally less painful. Several minutes later, when rating the overall experience, individuals in the second condition (90 total seconds of cold) rated it as less unpleasant than did those in the first condition (60 seconds of cold) because the experience ended differently and more pleasantly for them.

Kahneman (1999) called these results "discouraging" in the sense of showing people's retrospective evaluations of experiences to be erroneous. But they are erroneous only if one believes—as does Kahneman—that true pleasure resides in the moment and that overall pleasure must be the sum of these moments. As will be discussed in chapter 4, this is known as a bottom-up approach, and while it makes a great deal of sense, there is no reason to think that it necessarily exhausts what pleasure and happiness mean. People live in the moment but also in the past and the present. Pleasure exists in all of these temporal domains and apparently does so in different psychological terms. This is not discouraging but instead interesting.

The practical implication of these findings is that we should build in high points and good finales with respect to our pleasures, so that when we think about them later, our memories will be "biased" (if that is the right word) in a particularly favorable direction. If these are the features that matter most in memory, then they deserve more attention than those that do not—like the sheer duration of the experience. Think about how you might plan a vacation or a meal in light of peak-end theory.[5] Use some common sense, because a 20-minute vacation or a 60-second meal—regardless of their peaks and ends—are probably not going to be all that enjoyable. And in the sexual domain, "duration neglect" has a different and decidedly dysfunctional definition.

Let us turn from the memory of pleasures to their anticipation. With respect to future pleasures, research shows that we are not perfectly accurate in our predictions. This is an important practical finding because we base many of our choices about how to act in the here and now on predictions concerning our happiness in the there and then. Indeed, economists have created an entire science around such predictions, although what I am calling *anticipated happiness*, they more soberly term *expected utility*. Regardless, decisions are made in light of the expected psychological payoffs of different options. What car should I purchase?

5. As implied in chapter 2, one can object that this strategy is phony, that pleasures should be experienced as they occur in the here and now without any thought to how they might later be remembered. I will concede this point to anyone who has never taken a photograph on a trip, who has never purchased a souvenir, or who has never described to a friend a pleasant experience from the day before. In short, I concede the point to no one. Some events are remembered more pleasantly than others, just as some events are experienced in the moment more pleasantly than others. Why not plan the events in our lives with both considerations in mind?

What long-distance telephone provider should I choose? Where should I go to school? What career should I pursue? Which job should I take? Whom should I marry? Many if not all of these decisions are based on a judgment of how an option will make us "feel" in the future, a judgment that may prove fallible.

In reviewing the research literature on the prediction of pleasure, George Loewenstein and David Schkade (1999, p. 86) acknowledged:

> The great majority of predictions of feelings are reasonably accurate. People know they will feel bad if they lose their job, get rejected by a lover, or fail an examination; that they will be stressed on the first few days of a new job; and that they will experience a post-jog "high."

Keep this point in mind—that people are not completely clueless about future pleasure (chapter 1)—but still appreciate that people make systematic errors in predicting how they will feel at a later date.

In some cases, these errors reflect psychological influences on pleasure of which people are simply not aware. For example, the **mere exposure effect** refers to our tendency to "like" objects to which we are frequently exposed, even if this exposure takes place subliminally (at levels below conscious awareness). In a classic demonstration, psychologist Robert Zajonc[6] (1968) flashed abstract stimuli on a screen more quickly than his research participants could consciously discern them. However, when later asked to rate how much they liked these stimuli, the research participants gave higher ratings to those they had "seen" more frequently. Accordingly, familiarity breeds liking and not contempt, even if we are not aware of the process.

The **endowment effect** refers to our tendency to like objects given to us, even if we did not especially want or value them in the first place (Thaler, 1980). Studies show that individuals given an object like a coffee mug or a ballpoint pen want to be paid more money for selling it back to the experimenter than other individuals merely given a choice between receiving the object or some amount of cash (Kahneman, Knetsch, & Thaler, 1991). No one predicts this phenomenon, which is obviously silly from an objective perspective.

Such influences show that people's predictions about future pleasure can be wrong, but they also suggest that people are pleased with what they have and with what is familiar. Maybe that is for the net good. In chapter 4, I will emphasize that most people most of the time are happy, and perhaps processes like these contribute to the typical life satisfaction that researchers observe.

One of the best-documented mistakes that people make in predicting future pleasure is with respect to how long good feelings will last—another instance of duration neglect. I already mentioned this phenomenon in chapter 1. Daniel Gilbert, Timothy Wilson, and their colleagues have conducted a series of studies of people before and after important life events—like the breakup of a romance,

6. Pronounced *zy-unce*; rhymes with science.

receiving tenure (or not) at a university, a gubernatorial election in which they had a favored candidate, applying for a job they wanted, and so on (Gilbert, Pinel, Wilson, Blumberg, & Wheatley, 1998; Wilson, Meyers, & Gilbert, 2001; Wilson, Wheatley, Meyers, Gilbert, & Assom, 2000). The details of each study reflect the particular event upon which they are focused, but in general terms, research participants are asked to forecast how they will feel pending the desirable or undesirable outcome in each case and how long these feelings will last. Their actual reactions are then ascertained after the event has occurred, allowing forecasts to be checked against what really happened.

Results are clear and consistent across the studies. Although participants of course get it right in the sense of knowing that desirable outcomes will make them happier than undesirable outcomes, they consistently overestimate how long their reactions will last. The bad feelings do not last as long as they had expected, and neither do the good feelings. Think about your own life and the very good things and the very bad things that have occurred during the last year. Which of these events are still front and center in your mind and affecting your current mood, and which have been put aside by other life events?

Duration neglect may occur simply because people do not acknowledge yet another well-documented phenomenon about pleasure: We adapt to it. When we repeatedly encounter the same pleasure-producing stimulus, we experience increasingly less pleasure in response. **Adaptation** is a familiar experience for all of us, even when it takes us by surprise. Perhaps we hope that *this* pleasure will show no adaptation.[7] Adaptation to pleasure is so widespread that theorists have proposed that we live on a **hedonic treadmill**, meaning that we continually adapt to improving circumstances to the point that we always return to a point of relative neutrality (Brickman & Campbell, 1971).

One of the most frequently cited studies of adaptation is an investigation reported some years ago by Phillip Brickman, Dan Coates, and Ronnie Janoff-Bulman (1978). These psychologists were then at Northwestern University in Evanston, Illinois, and the state of Illinois had started to run a lottery. The researchers interviewed 22 state lottery winners, each of whom had received at least $50,000 during the past year and some as much as $1 million. The winners were asked to rate their past, present, and future (expected) happiness on scales from 0 (= not at all happy) to 5 (= very happy), as well as the pleasure they took in mundane activities like talking with a friend, hearing a joke, and reading a magazine, again on 0–5 scales. Brickman and his colleagues also interviewed a group of 58 individuals who had not won the lottery but lived in the same neighborhoods as the winners. The results showed that lottery winners were scarcely more happy

7. The evidence is sketchy, but Frederick and Loewenstein (1999) speculated that there are a small number of positive experiences to which at least some people do *not* adapt, and they cited in particular having cosmetic surgery and looking at erotic pictures. Interesting, and I am sure that Hugh Hefner would approve.

than the comparison research participants in terms of their present happiness (4.00 versus 3.82) and future happiness (4.20 versus 4.14). And winners found *less* pleasure in everyday activities than did nonwinners (3.33 versus 3.82).

These researchers also interviewed 29 individuals who in the preceding year had suffered an accident that left their limbs permanently paralyzed. Their present life satisfaction was rated as 2.96, lower than that of the lottery winners (4.00) but probably not as low as one might have predicted. And their expected future happiness and their pleasure in everyday activities were slightly *higher* than that of the lottery winners (4.32 versus 4.20 for future happiness and 3.48 versus 3.33 for everyday pleasure).

These results imply that adaptation occurs both among those with good fortune and among those without.[8] But why do we adapt? Wouldn't it be nice if pleasure-producing stimuli always had the exact same effect, if honeymoons never ended, and if we only had to purchase one Gameboy cartridge?

Two related answers are plausible. First, adaptation protects us from being overwhelmed by the external stimuli that produce our sensations. Pleasure can be as distracting as pain, and it is good—survival-wise—that these experiences are brief and tempered and allow us to get back to the rest of life (Barkow, 1997).

Second, adaptation makes us especially sensitive to *changes* in our environment, where the survival action is apt to be found. Indeed, many of our sensory systems show adaptation, not just those that produce pleasure and pain. For example, we all adjust rather quickly to the illumination level in a room, to its background noise, and so on.

As you of course know, adaptation does not permanently alter our ability to experience a given pleasure. If it did, we would only want to eat one cookie, read one poem, and see one sunset in our lifetime. Obviously, we keep coming back for more, once a sufficient amount of time has passed. "Sufficient" here will vary greatly and idiosyncratically depending on the pleasure and the person, but as a rule of thumb, spreading out our pleasures over time maximizes the satisfaction that each produces, whereas bunching them up does not.

Let me close with one more comment about pleasure, a joke recounted by Frederick and Loewenstein (1999, p. 307): "Sex is like pizza: when it is good, it is really good, and when it is bad, it is still pretty good." The point is that many experiences are intrinsically pleasant and experienced as such in their own right, regardless of what has come before. Processes of adaptation of course influence our

8. Let me get on a scientific soapbox for a second. This study is sometimes reported in the popular media as showing that paraplegics and lottery winners are *equally* happy with life, which is not what the actual data show. The real results are provocative enough, and we should not gloss over the difficulties faced by individuals with spinal cord injuries and the toll that these difficulties can take on life satisfaction. One of the common consequences of spinal cord injury is severe depression (Cushman & Hassett, 1992; Elliot & Frank, 1996; Kemp, Krause, & Adkins, 1999). It may not be the injury per se that produces depression but instead the resulting unemployment (Chapin & Kewman, 2001).

experience of pleasure but not to the point of abolishing it. Kahneman (1999) observed that breakfast is almost always pleasant, no matter how routinized it has become, whereas shaving cuts remain unpleasant even as we nick ourselves time and time again.

Positive Emotions

Psychologists have distinguished a whole family of positive feelings, from pleasurable sensations like those just discussed, to affects, emotions, moods, and so on. The specific categories depend on the theorist, but all agree that feelings differ with respect to how long they last, their attachment to specific stimuli or situations, and their complexity—that is, the degree to which few or many psychological processes are involved in their experience (Larsen & Fredrickson, 1999). Pleasures are often brief, tied to specific stimuli and indeed specific sensory systems, and are rather simple; no one needs to learn that sugar is sweet.

Psychologists regard **emotions** as more complex in that they involve not just subjective feelings but also characteristic patterns of physiological arousal, thoughts, and behaviors. The word *emotion* comes from the same root as *motion*, conveying the idea that emotions move through us and perhaps drive us. Emotions have beginnings and endings, but they are more prolonged than fleeting sensations.

Scientific interest in emotions has long been guided by the perspective taken by naturalist Charles Darwin. In his 1872 book, *The Expression of the Emotions in Man and Animals*, Darwin drew parallels between animals and people in their emotional reactions to events. For example, dogs, cats, monkeys, and humans all bare their teeth when threatened (Brothers, 1990). Darwin suggested that emotions increase chances for survival because they are appropriate responses in the situations where they are experienced. For example, fear accompanies the avoidance of danger. It is obviously adaptive to be afraid when we are threatened, as opposed to indifferent, and so fear is experienced in threatening situations. As mentioned, fear shows itself not simply as a feeling but also in terms of arousal of the sympathetic nervous system, threat-relevant thoughts ("here there be danger!"), and specific behavior tendencies—fight or flight.

This approach still marks much of psychology's approach to emotions, leading theorists and researchers to focus on negative emotions like fear, sadness, disgust, and anger, the dangers to which they alert us, and the reactions they produce (Plutchik, 1962, 1980). Theorists in this tradition also follow Darwin's lead by emphasizing how people display emotions in their facial expressions.[9] Human be-

9. Other theorists reverse this argument, proposing that our facial expressions *determine* the emotions we experience (Cappella, 1993). When people are asked to smile or frown, they indeed report emotions appropriate to their expressions (Hess, Kappas, McHugo, Lanzetta, & Kleck, 1992; Ohira & Kurono, 1993; Sun & Meng, 1993). An elegant demonstration was devised by Larsen, Kasimatis,

ings are social creatures, and there is an obvious survival advantage in being able to communicate our feelings to others (Fridlund, 1991). Research finds that people around the world recognize basic emotions expressed in facial photographs of people from cultures other than their own (Izard, 1994). Even though cultures differ greatly in the words used to describe emotions (Mumford, 1993), facial expressions across cultures are similar (Ekman, 1993).

What about positive emotions? Theorists who catalog basic emotions usually include one or two positive ones—e.g., joy and sometimes surprise or curiosity—but their focus is mainly on the negative (Fredrickson, 2004; Watson, 2002). Part of the reason for neglecting positive emotions is the problem-focused nature of psychology in general; after all, "emotional problems" is a synonym for "psychological disorders" (chapter 1). A more specific reason is that emotion theorists have usually tried to explain emotions per se, and because they started with negative emotions like fear and anger, positive emotions were squeezed in after the fact. As it turns out, the fit is not a particularly good one.

A typical definition of an emotion is that it is linked to a specific behavioral predisposition; the jargon used here is *specific action tendency*. Fear makes us want to run; anger makes us want to attack; and disgust makes us want to spit up. In contrast, positive emotions are not linked to such specific action tendencies. Positive emotions like joy may activate us, but in a much more vague and diffuse way.

Another dissimilarity is that negative emotions are experienced in life-threatening situations, whereas positive emotions of course are not. In making evolutionary sense of emotions, then, it is difficult to find the survival payoff of a positive emotion in the here and now (Nesse, 1990).

Yet another dissimilarity is that researchers to date have been unable to distinguish among the different positive emotions with respect to their underlying physiological mechanisms. Again, a typical definition of an emotion is that it is associated with a given pattern of physiology, and positive emotions have eluded this characterization (Tomkins, 1962, 1963, 1982).[10] Along these lines, the facial ex-

---

and Frey (1992), who subtly altered the facial expressions of their research subjects. They glued golf tees on the foreheads of subjects and asked them to move these tees while also holding a pen in their mouths. In effect, they were requiring people to make a sad face without asking them to do so. When the research participants reported their emotions, they described greater sadness than did those in a comparison group.

10. Ongoing research by Richard Davidson (1984, 1992, 1993, 1999) implicates the left hemisphere of the brain as responsible for positive emotions, whereas the right hemisphere is responsible for negative emotions. Accordingly, left brain damage results in depression, fear, and pessimism, and right brain damage produces indifference or even euphoria (Derryberry & Tucker, 1992). And in another interesting study, Hatta, Nakaseko, and Yamamoto (1992) asked research subjects to handle identical objects with their right and left hands and report the emotional tone of the resulting sensations. Objects in the right hand (the nerves from which lead to the left hemisphere) were described in more positive terms than those in the left hand. Does this mean that if you hold your sweetheart's right hand in your left hand (or vice versa), one of you will be happier than the other?

pressions associated with various positive emotions are not nearly so distinct as those signifying the various negative emotions (Bruyer, 1981). "Having a dopey grin on one's face" seems to signal positive emotion, but which one in particular?

Finally, the Western world has long mistrusted emotions—consider the opposition of reason and emotion that dates at least to Aristotle—which means that we have often overlooked the possibility that there might be something positive about emotions other than the seductive sensations sometimes associated with some of them.

Psychology's interest in positive emotions has been sparked by psychologist Barbara Fredrickson's (1998, 2000, 2001, 2004) recent theorizing. Rather than trying to fit positive emotions into the negative emotion scheme, she has argued that positive emotions like joy, interest, contentment, and love should be looked at in their own right. Positive emotions not only feel different but function differently. As emphasized, negative emotions alert us to danger. When we experience a negative emotion, our response options narrow, and we act with haste to avoid whatever danger is signaled. In contrast, positive emotions signal safety, and our inherent response to them is not to narrow our options but to broaden and build upon them. The evolutionary payoff of positive emotions is therefore not in the here and now but in the future. Perhaps it is advantageous to experience positive emotions because they lead us to engage in activities that add to our behavioral and cognitive repertoires.

Research participants induced in the laboratory to experience a positive emotion show cognitive changes in accord with these predictions, e.g., broader attention, greater working memory, enhanced verbal fluency, and increased openness to information. In a representative study, Fredrickson and Branigan (2005) showed to college students brief film clips known to produce different emotions: amusement, contentment, anger, or anxiety. Then they tested these research participants with a global-local visual-processing task which required them to match abstract stimuli with one another; they could attend to local features (small details) or global features (large patterns). See Figure 3.1 for an example. The induction of positive emotions led to broadened attention (i.e., greater attention to large patterns). In a second study, following the same sort of induction, these researchers found that participants led to experience positive emotions answered more diversely in response to an open-ended "20 questions" task.

Positive emotions undo the physiological effects of negative emotions (Fredrickson & Levenson, 1998; Fredrickson, Mancuso, Branigan, & Tugade, 2000; Tugade & Fredrickson, 2004). College students were given just 1 minute to prepare a brief speech on "why you are a good friend" that would—so they were told—be videotaped and evaluated by their peers. They did so while being hooked up to psychophysiological recording devices which ascertained their heart rate, peripheral vasoconstriction, and blood pressure—all indices of anxiety and specifically arousal of the sympathetic nervous system. Following this prepara-

Figure 3.1. Local Versus Global Features Matching Task
Research participants are asked to "match" the top figure with one of the bottom figures. They can do so by attending to and emphasizing local details (the shapes of the individual figures); then, they match the top figure with the one on the bottom right. Or they can attend to and emphasize the global configuration (the arrangement of the individual figures); then, they match the top figure with the one on the bottom left. As the text explains, individuals experiencing positive emotions are more likely to categorize in global terms.

tion time, research participants saw one of four different films: Two produced positive emotions (joy or contentment); one produced feelings of sadness; and the last one was emotionally neutral.[11] Interestingly, none of these films in and of itself had an effect on sympathetic arousal. However, following the speech preparation exercise, research participants who then saw either of the positive emotion films showed more rapid cardiovascular recovery (return to "normal") than did those who saw the sad film or the neutral film. In other words, the experience of positive emotions undid the anxiety that had been induced in the research participants.

Laboratory experiments like these represent the most powerful strategies that researchers have for identifying possible causes. The specific film clip seen by a research participant was determined randomly, which means that there were no differences among participants in the four conditions except for the film that was shown. Accordingly, the differences observed in cardiovascular recovery times were *caused* by the films.

11. The actual film clips viewed were: (a) joy (puppy playing with a flower); (b) contentment (waves slowly breaking on a beach); (c) sadness (boy crying as his father dies); and (d) neutral (abstract display of colored shapes; Fredrickson & Levenson, 1998).

The standard question about laboratory experiments is whether their results apply outside the lab (Mook, 1983). In the present case, it seems that they do, because Fredrickson's experimental results converge well with studies of coping in "real" situations that document the benefits of experiencing positive emotions during stressful times (e.g., Folkman, 1997; Folkman & Moskowitz, 2000). Indeed, a century earlier, Freud (1905/1953a) talked about the phenomenon of gallows humor and how people use humor in the most dire circumstances to bolster their spirits. Fredrickson's research spells out a physiological mechanism for how this coping strategy might work (e.g., Fredrickson & Joiner, 2002; Fredrickson, Tugade, Waugh, & Larkin, 2003).

Fredrickson (2001, 2004) alliteratively calls her approach the **broaden-and-build theory**, and it has attracted attention inside and outside of positive psychology circles. Broaden-and-build theory is notable for drawing explicit attention to the positive and showing that insights result when we do something more than simply look at the absence of the negative. At the same time, Fredrickson's work is respectable in scientific circles because of its reliance on laboratory experimentation and psychophysiological assessment.

Finally, although Fredrickson herself has not undertaken interventions, broaden-and-build theory provides a ready rationale for them. Indeed, broaden-and-build theory has been embraced by all sorts of practitioners interested in doing something beyond the elimination of the negative.

I also suspect that broaden-and-build theory strikes a special chord among those of us who were told during school or maybe yesterday at work not to have so much fun. This is, after all, serious business. Whatever. As a teacher, I try to be playful and make my classes enjoyable for students. I know that some of my colleagues look down on me behind my back, as if the fun classroom I try to create must necessarily be a brainless one. Broaden-and-build theory gives me the last laugh, implying that a grim classroom produces a grim student unlikely to acquire the sorts of skills needed for the serious business of life.

I do have several questions about broaden-and-build theory that I hope will be answered in the years to come. First, in the laboratory work to date, different positive emotions are treated as equivalent at least insofar as their broadening and building potential. But can distinctions be made among various positive emotions, like those that are more aroused (e.g., joy) and those that are more quiet (e.g., contentment)? Do they build different resources or the same ones through different processes?

Second, what about emotions that feel good but seem to do quite the opposite of broaden and build, at least for most of us. Consider lust. Being turned on sexually feels great, but sexual feelings narrow our attention and limit our repertoire, sometimes drastically so. Ditto for the more public forms of pride. Are the seven deadly sins the seven important exceptions to broaden-and-build theory?

Third, broaden-and-build theory has been investigated most thoroughly in the laboratory under the assumption that positive emotions are equally available to all given the appropriate circumstances: Just show them the right film clip. Outside the lab, we of course differ in the emotions readily available to us. In some cases, we can program how we feel by changing the music on our Walkman or our iPod, but in other cases, we tend to experience some emotions rather than others, and eventually broaden-and-build theory needs to make contact with theories of personality that address habitual individual differences. In the next section, I describe a line of personality research that dovetails very nicely with broaden-and-build theory.

Positive Affectivity

Like many essential human traits, exuberance is teeming in some and not to be caught sight of in others. For a few, exuberance is in the blood, an irrepressible life force. It may ebb and flow, but the underlying capacity for joy is as much a part of the person as having green eyes or a long waist. . . . Not so for most others. . . . The nonexuberant lack fizz . . . they need to be lifted up on the enthusiasm of others; roused by dance or drugs; impelled by music. They do not kindle of their own accord.
—KAY REDFIELD JAMISON (2004)

The term *mood* sometimes refers to an attenuated emotion—"I was in the mood for it"—but an additional and more substantive meaning of **mood** emphasizes its role as a barometer of general well-being. We speak about people being mellow or crabby, merry or cranky, good-natured or irritable, and we apply these terms to their entire personality. To use psychological jargon, moods in this sense are trait-like, whereas emotions are state-like. Moods are less likely to have a specific object or meaning associated with them and less likely to be front and center in consciousness. However, moods are more long-lasting than emotions, and they color all of what we think, feel, and do.

Psychology has probably given us more words to describe bad moods than good moods, but consider terms like zest, vitality, ebullience, enthusiasm, and exuberance. These terms describe our very best moods, when we are literally cheer-full. Good moods infuse not just our minds but our very bodies. They put a spring in our step and a twinkle in our eye. In a good mood, we feel alive and enthusiastic about any and all activities. We describe people in perpetual positive moods as vigorous and energetic, bright-eyed and bushy-tailed, bouncy and perky, peppy and high on life. They have joie de vivre. These sorts of good moods are not to be confused with hyperactivity, nervous energy, tension, or mania.

Rather, good moods are experienced as fulfilling as they are brought to bear on life's worthy activities.

Here is the by-now-familiar refrain in this book: When psychologists studied mood in decades past, their attention was on the bad moods: irritability, boredom, generalized anxiety (aka neuroticism), chronic depression (aka dysthymia), and so on. A turning point, however, was the suggestion by Paul Meehl (1975, p. 299) that "Clinicians and theoreticians ought to consider seriously the possibility that not only are some people born with more cerebral 'joy-juice' than others but also that this variable is fraught with clinical implications."

Meehl dubbed the ability to experience positive feelings **hedonic capacity** and further suggested that it was a stable individual difference rooted in genetics. He further hypothesized that hedonic capacity was linked to the personality trait of *extraversion*—being outgoing and oriented to others. Finally, he argued that hedonic capacity was largely distinct from the experience—habitual or not—of negative emotions like anger and anxiety.

Subsequent research has supported most of Meehl's theorizing about hedonic capacity—now referred to as **positive affectivity**—the extent to which an individual experiences positive moods like joy, interest, and alertness (Watson, 2002). Making this research possible was the development of simple questionnaires like the PANAS, an acronym for Positive and Negative Affect Schedule (Watson, Clark, & Tellegen, 1988). Respondents are presented with words describing positive moods (e.g., inspired) and negative moods (e.g., ashamed) and asked to rate each according to the extent that it describes them. Instructions vary; they may ask for a rating right now, or over the past few days, or simply in general. Regardless, the ratings are averaged separately across the positive mood words and across the negative mood words.

Positive affectivity so calculated is independent of negative affectivity, meaning that people can be high or low on one dimension whether they are high or low on the other. Positive affectivity and negative affectivity prove highly stable across weeks, months, years, and even decades (Costa & McCrae, 1992). Grumpy old men may well have been testy young men, petulant youth, whiny toddlers, and difficult babies.

Another way to look at stability is to compare positive affectivity ratings across situations, and here again there is a great deal of convergence (Diener & Larsen, 1984). People who are in good moods when alone are also in good moods when with others, and conversely. An interesting wrinkle about positive affectivity is not only that its mean level for an individual is consistent across time and situation, but so too is its variability. That is, some folks show more of a range in their good moods than do other folks, and they do so consistently (Larsen, 1987; Watson, 2000). In other words, their moods are more labile and—simply put—more moody.

As suggested by Meehl, positive affectivity is indeed more likely to be observed among extraverted individuals, equally so among men and women (Watson, 2000). In general, people high in positive affectivity are socially active. They have more friends; they have more acquaintances; and they are more involved in social organizations. Negative affectivity is unrelated to these indicators of social behavior.

People high in positive affectivity are more likely than those who are low to be married—especially happily so—and also to like their jobs. Stated so simply, these are chicken-and-egg findings; it is unclear what causes what. However, studies that follow people over time suggest that positive affectivity foreshadows marital and occupational satisfaction and does not simply reflect it (e.g., Staw, Bell, & Clausen, 1986; Watson, Hubbard, & Wiese, 2000).

People who describe themselves as religious or spiritual score especially high on positive affectivity (Clark & Watson, 1999). Here the more informative longitudinal investigations have not been conducted, so we do not know whether positive affectivity leads one to religion or if it results from the sense of purpose and meaning and/or the social communion that religions provide (chapter 11).

What about the genetic basis to positive affectivity hypothesized by Meehl? Psychologists show that a characteristic is influenced by genetics by comparing the characteristic among identical twins (who have in common 100% of their genes) and fraternal twins (who are no more similar genetically than ordinary siblings—that is, 50% overlap). To the degree that pairs of identical twins are more similar to one another (both twins high, both medium, both low) than are pairs of fraternal twins, one can argue for genetic influence. A further refinement is made when these twins are divided into those raised together (presumably in a similar environment) and those raised apart (presumably in dissimilar environments).

The degree to which identical twin similarity exceeds fraternal twin similarity is quantified as the **heritability** of the characteristic in question: the proportion of its variation due to genetic factors. The more a characteristic's variation in a group of individuals is due to genetic factors, the greater its heritability (see Figure 3.2). For example, people's intelligence shows moderate heritability, meaning that differences among people in measured IQ reflect differences in their genes. As you would imagine, height and weight are highly heritable.

Do not equate heritability with any simple notion of inherited. I did not say that intelligence is inherited, passed directly from parents to children, and I did not say that height and weight are directly inherited. Heritability is a more-abstract concept, referring to a group of people, not to any individual. It refers to the *variation* in a characteristic across these people, not to the level of the characteristic for a given person. A greater than zero heritability estimate does not identify the genes responsible for a characteristic, and it does not preclude the influence of the environment or learning.

According to twin studies, positive affectivity proves heritable—influenced by genetics—less so than intelligence but to about the same degree as most per-

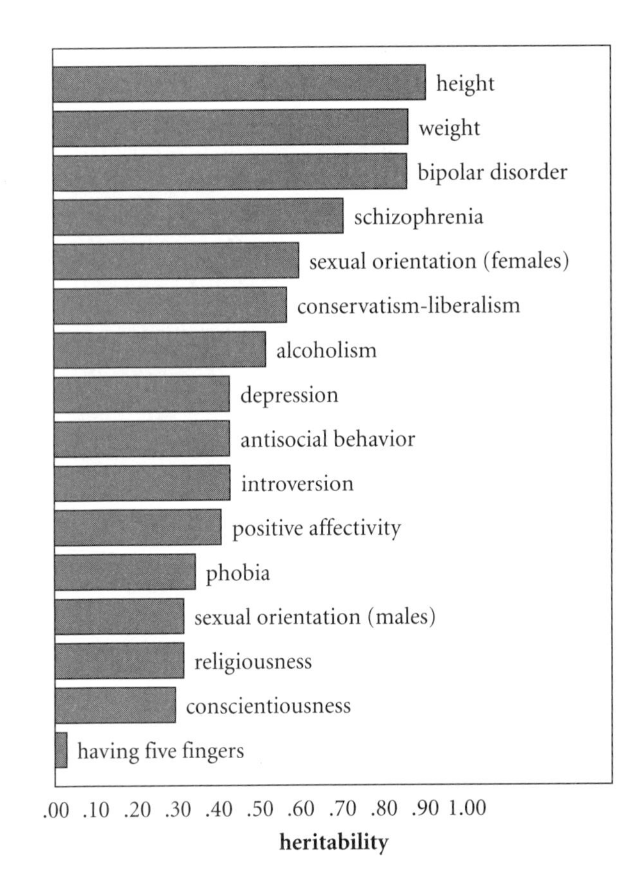

Figure 3.2. Heritability of Different Characteristics
From multiple sources, but chiefly Bouchard (2004). Within a group of people, heritability is the proportion of a characteristic's variation that is due to genetic factors (see text). Heritability estimates range from .00 (no genetic influence whatsoever) to 1.00 (only genetic influence). Note that the number of fingers that people have has near-zero heritability because the variation in this characteristic is almost entirely due to accidents and injuries, which are nongenetic factors.

sonality traits (Finkel & McGue, 1997; Jang, McCrae, Angleitner, Riemann, & Livesley, 1998; Tellegen et al., 1988). This is an interesting finding[12] and an important one as we ponder how to cultivate the good life.

Everyday people may hear the phrase *genetic influence* and think "inevitable," but this is not what the data actually mean. Heritable does not mean

12. High heritability need not mean that the characteristic has a basis in the evolutionary history of a species (Rowe & Osgood, 1984). Evolution usually minimizes variation within a species, so that members of a species come to resemble each other in ways that further survival. When variability does exist, theorists must grapple with the question of why. Several answers are possible (Tooby

immutable—fixed forever at the moment of conception—and it certainly does not mean unchanged by life events. As already noted, intelligence is heritable, but intelligence nevertheless increases with good health, good nutrition, and educational opportunities and decreases in their absence. Depression is more heritable than positive affectivity but readily changed by therapy. Indeed, political attitudes are more heritable than positive affectivity but also quite changeable, sometimes before our very eyes.

Thus, the moderate heritability of positive affectivity does not mean that we have a permanently fixed mood. According to the world's leading expert on affectivity, David Watson (2002, p. 116), "The genetic and biological data should not induce a fatalistic resignation; we still are free to increase our positive affectivity." Watson speculated that if we wish to improve our habitual mood, we should be more attentive to our actions than to our thoughts, that we should appreciate that striving toward goals creates more good cheer than actually achieving these goals, and that knowledge about moods and how they work can only help.

Flow

I have met many interesting people through my association with positive psychology, and one of my favorites is psychologist Mihaly (Mike) Csikszentmihalyi. Born in Hungary in 1935 and coming of age in wartorn Europe, Mike moved to the United States in the late 1950s. He went to school at the University of Chicago and then taught there for many years before moving in 1999 to the Claremont Graduate School.

Thoroughly unassuming, he is one of the most creative and productive people I have ever met. I remember a few years ago meeting with some of my fellow travelers in positive psychology. We had not seen each other in a year, and we went around the table catching each other up on our respective research activities. We all described the three or four projects that were consuming our time. Mike described seven or eight, which I knew was typical. It was only later that he offhandedly mentioned that *his* projects were books under contract that he was writing. The rest of us had described circumscribed research projects that might—operative word, *might*—result someday in a 15-page journal article.

& Cosmides, 1990). One is that the well-being of a group as a whole is served by variation in characteristics across individuals. Variation guarantees maximum flexibility in adapting to different environments and thereby promotes the fitness of an entire species (Buss, 1991). Another possible explanation is that personality characteristics, at least within normal ranges, are irrelevant for survival and so have never been selected against. A third possibility is that variation in personality is a consequence of other biological characteristics of people, such as the structure or function of the nervous system; natural selection produced these other characteristics, and what we mean by personality merely came along for the evolutionary ride (Gould, 1991).

When I speak to other psychologists about Mike, some of them do not know about whom I am talking. They of course have seen his name but never knew how to pronounce it. Hence they cannot recognize it. I have learned to say, "You know, the flow guy," and they immediately know whom I mean. **Flow** is his term for the psychological state that accompanies highly engaging activities (Csikszentmihalyi, 1990).

He first became intrigued by flow while studying highly creative painters (Csikszentmihalyi, 1975/2000). When these artists were working on a painting, and their work was going well, they were oblivious to hunger, fatigue, and discomfort. Once the painting was complete, however, they lost interest in it and moved on to another project. Csikszentmihalyi was struck by the **intrinsic motivation** that was behind the product. Painters did not paint with the external product in mind and certainly not with the thought of any extrinsic reward when they were done.

Although other researchers at that time were interested in intrinsic motivation and the inherent satisfaction associated with competent performance, none had taken a close look at the subjective phenomenology of intrinsically motivated skillful activity (Deci, 1975; White, 1959). Accordingly, Csikszentmihalyi's studies of flow began with interviews of people who cited "enjoyment" as their primary reason for pursuing some activity. He talked to chess players, rock climbers, and dancers, among many others. What emerged was a characterization of engagement that was highly similar across different activities. This characterization is what we now mean by flow.

During flow, time passes quickly for the engaged individual. Attention is focused on the activity itself. The sense of the self as a social actor is lost. The aftermath of the flow experience is invigorating. Flow is not to be confused with sensual pleasure. Indeed, flow in the moment is non-emotional and arguably nonconscious. People describe flow as highly and intrinsically enjoyable, but this is an after-the-fact summary judgment, and joy is not immediately present during the activity itself.

Here is a description by professional basketball player Ben Gordon of the Chicago Bulls of how it feels to be "in the zone" while playing:

> You lose track of the time, what quarter it is. You don't hear the crowd. You don't know how many points you have. You don't think. You're just playing. Offensively everything is instinctive. When the feeling starts going away, it's terrible. I talk to myself and say, C'mon, you gotta be more aggressive. That's when you know it's gone. It's not instinctive anymore. (Kennedy, 2005, p. 29)

Flow can be described as the experience of working at full capacity (Nakamura & Csikszentmihalyi, 2002), which is why the concept figures prominently in positive psychology. Flow of course has existed for as long as there have been people (Csikszentmihalyi, 1988), but it took the genius of Csikszentmihalyi to put a label on the experience, to articulate its phenomenology, and to investigate its enabling conditions and consequences. Unlike many positive psychology concepts, flow has been extensively investigated, using an experience sampling method—also known as the beeper technique—which asks research participants to carry a pager that goes off at random intervals (e.g., Larson & Csikszentmihalyi, 1978). They are then asked to describe what they are doing and how they are feeling at the time.

From numerous studies of this sort, psychologists have learned that flow is most likely to occur when there is an optimal balance between skill and challenge (Moneta & Csikszentmihalyi, 1996). In other words, flow represents the coming together of a person and an environment. The good news is that one need not be an expert in a domain to experience flow. All that matters is that the presented challenge meets one's skills, and vice versa. Too much challenge disrupts the process, as does too little skill. The bad news is that the challenge of the flow activity necessarily changes as one's skills improve. All of us know how initially engaging activities eventually lose their magic unless the bar is raised to meet our changes in expertise.

Flow can be experienced in all sorts of activities, at work or play, but usually among those activities perceived as voluntary (Kleiber, Larson, & Csikszentmihalyi, 1996). For example, homework for most schoolchildren strikes a balance between challenge and skill, but because homework is regarded as coerced, it rarely produces the flow state. Indeed, flow is rarely experienced by youth during *any* school activity. The other common activities of adolescents in the United States—watching television or hanging out with friends—also fail to produce flow, because they fail to meet one or another of its enabling conditions.

Thus, we have a paradox unanswered to date by research: Why do people so infrequently engage in the activities that they know will produce flow, even as they acknowledge the experience of flow as desirable? Why do we skim trashy novels rather than pore over great literature? Why do we chatter casually with our friends rather than talk about things that really matter? Why do we take the easiest path rather than the ones filled with challenge?

One possible resolution is provided by another experience that all of us can acknowledge—so-called junk flow or faux flow—with video games, reality TV shows, and idle gossip as prime examples. These have some of the elements of flow (engagement and absorption), but they are not especially challenging, and they certainly do not leave us feeling invigorated or satisfied. (For those readers energized by *Survivor* reruns, bless you, but I believe you are the exception and not the rule.) One may be seduced by the ease of experiencing junk flow and thereby distracted from the more difficult but ultimately more rewarding experience of real flow.

We do know that people differ greatly in the frequency with which they have flow, for reasons not well understood,[13] and that young people who experience more flow during adolescence show long-term desirable consequences, such as achievement in creative domains (e.g., Rathunde & Csikszentmihalyi, 1993). They may even be healthier (Patton, 1999, cited by Nakamura & Csikszentmihalyi, 2002).

This phenomenon has been described as the building of psychological capital, and perhaps we can wed flow research to positive emotions research to speculate that the aftermath of flow—positive emotions—is how psychological resources are created which are later deployed to good effect (Moneta & Csikszentmihalyi, 1996; Shernoff, Csikszentmihalyi, Shneider, & Shernoff, 2003).

Flow has attracted the attention of numerous practitioners, from product designers at Nissan and Volvo to teachers at Montessori schools to architects to football coach Jimmy Johnson (Nakamura & Csikszentmihalyi, 2002). In some interventions, the environment is reshaped to foster flow for all—or at least to make it less obstructed. In other interventions, an individual is helped to find flow. What are his skills? Where can they be deployed in an appropriately challenging way?

Flow principles have even been used in the context of psychotherapy (Massimini & Delle Fave, 2000). An individual's daily life is restructured to allow more flow experiences. Common to many psychological problems is a routinization of what is done, and if the routine is a rut, then one is apt to stay in it. Consider watching television versus performing volunteer work. Do we ever hear anyone say, "Damn, I'm getting good at watching TV! I can't wait until tomorrow to perfect my technique." But something like volunteer work can be challenging when it requires a whole host of skills that must be developed on an ongoing basis. Is it any surprise that a depressed or anxious person who spends more time helping others than watching television shows a reduction in symptoms (Delle Fave & Massimini, 1992)?

I also raise the possibility that psychological disorders—especially depression—might make it difficult for someone to initiate a challenging activity, so it may not be enough to provide the opportunity for challenge (Allison & Duncan, 1988). One must also teach individuals how to rise to the occasion and meet the challenge. Well-established clinical lore holds that otherwise-depressed people who manage to keep busy—e.g., go to work or sustain a close relationship—are not troubled by their symptoms as long as they are engaged. If this is a valid principle, it is worth our effort to figure out how to formalize it in an intervention.

Many discussions of flow, by Csikszentmihalyi and others, use examples like artistic creation or rock climbing, which make flow seem most common among

13. The predisposition to experience flow may be forged in families that can be described as complex, providing both challenge in the form of high-skill activities and support (Rathunde, 1988, 1996). Another influence may be early schooling experiences which lead children to identify and develop their interests and skills (Whalen, 1999).

solitary activities. But there is nothing in the concept that limits its experience to moments alone, and indeed, many of the most familiar examples of flow are explicitly social—good conversations, playing ensemble music or a team sport, coordinated efforts with others at work, and so on. Shared flow deserves more study, as does the phenomenon that Csikszentmihalyi (1975/2000) described as microflow, very short duration activities that produce flow and may well have benefits for restoring attention. Doodling is just one example (see Figure 3.3).

EXERCISE *Savoring*

Savoring refers to our awareness of pleasure and our deliberate attempt to make it last. Loyola University psychologist Fred Bryant (2003) discussed what psychologists know about savoring and contrasted it with the psychology of coping.

Figure 3.3.
Doodle done by Mike Csikszentmihalyi, January 7, 2004.

In *coping*, we experience a bad event that produces negative feelings—anxiety, sadness, and the like—and attempt to "deal with" these feelings in a variety of ways (Lazarus & Folkman, 1984). We may try to change the event itself or its consequences, or we may try to change ourselves so that the negative impact of the event is decreased (chapter 9).

A poor evaluation at work makes any of us feel upset. We ask what is at stake, and it may be our continued livelihood, the respect with which we are treated by our fellow workers, and our own sense of competence. One way to cope is to ask our work supervisor for advice about how to do better in the future, and we channel our efforts in this direction. Or we may look for another job. We may decide that the job is not that important to us and that we should spend more time with our family and friends. We may resolve to start each workday with 5 minutes of meditation. Perhaps we pray to God for help. Or we may distract ourselves from the hassles at work with drugs and alcohol, certainly not an effective strategy in the long run but perhaps so in the short run. All of these are ways of coping.

Suppose instead that we receive an excellent evaluation at work accompanied by a pat on the back, a merit raise, and our name permanently etched on the employee-of-the-month plaque in the office lobby. How do we "cope" with this event, its aftermath, and the good feelings produced? I hope you smiled at this question, because coping is not the right word, because why would we want to minimize or undo something good?

The answer is that some of us in effect do cope with life's triumphs and pleasures. We may trot out an adage learned years ago that reminds us that pride goeth before the fall and thereby rein in our happiness. We may worry that others will resent us. We may conclude that we are lucky or that our supervisor is lenient and that her praise means little. We may worry that we have now set a standard impossible to maintain.

Not everyone is so quick to undo the good, and Bryant (2003) has determined that our habitual predisposition to savor or not is a relatively stable characteristic that can be reliably measured with a survey that asks people how frequently they derive pleasure through such strategies as anticipating positive events in the future, relishing them in the moment, and reminiscing about those in the past. Contrary to the worries of those who cope with the positive, those who habitually savor are indeed happier and more satisfied in general with life (chapter 4), more optimistic (chapter 5), and less depressed (chapter 9) than those who do not savor.

The conclusion follows that savoring is a good thing. So what can those of us who are low on the savoring dimension do to add this useful habit to our psychological repertoire? We have developed the following exercise, based on Bryant's (2001, 2003, in press) discussion of specific techniques that promote savoring.

In a classroom, we introduce this exercise with an example from our colleague Joe Veroff about how he reads letters from his children, who now live far away:

> I find a quiet moment when I can linger a bit with them, and read them in order and let the words roll very slowly over me like a long warm gentle shower. I read each one slowly. Sometimes they are highly sentimental, and I can't hold back the tears. Sometimes they are profoundly insightful about what has been happening to them and the world around them, and I am amazed. I can almost feel the children gathered in the room in which I am reading.

We analyze what Veroff is doing to enhance the pleasure produced by these letters, and our students with little prompting identify his strategies. He takes his time to read the letters, and he does so without distraction. No multitasking here. He identifies how he is feeling, and he lets these feelings emerge. Although he does not explicitly say so, we suspect that he keeps these letters in a special place and rereads them frequently. We also suspect that he talks about the letters to his wife, and the two of them share their pride in the children they have raised so well.

This all seems obvious and the right way to read a welcome letter, an eagerly anticipated e-mail message, or a surprise birthday card. But don't some of us miss the obvious by skimming letters from our loved ones as we walk from the mailbox to our living room, by looking at the same time at the bills and junk mail we received, and by tossing the rapidly read letter into our recycle bin? Maybe we turn on the television set while reading, or maybe we gobble down some leftovers. Maybe we take a phone call: "What's new?" "Not much. Same old, same old."

We ask our students to stop and notice the next time something good—pleasurable—occurs. It can be a letter or praise at work, but it can also be a good grade on a paper, a great meal, an engaging conversation, or a spontaneous adventure. Regardless, we ask the students to savor this event, and we suggest the following strategies:

- Sharing With Others: You can seek out others to share the experience. If that is not possible, tell others how much you valued the moment.
- Memory Building: Take mental photographs or even a physical souvenir of the event and reminisce about it later with others.
- Self-Congratulation: Do not be afraid of pride. Tell yourself how impressed others are and remember how long you have waited for this to happen.
- Sharpening Perceptions: Focus on certain elements of the experience and block out others.
- Absorption: Let yourself get totally immersed in the pleasure and try not to think about other matters.

A few months before the writing of this chapter, I gave a brief talk to a group of undergraduate psychology students at Michigan who were being recognized for their academic achievements, and I challenged them to use as many of these techniques as possible to savor the honor they were receiving. Many of them were accompanied by friends and parents. That was good, at least if one thought to sit next to them during the ceremony. For those who showed up alone, I suggested that they call their parents on the phone or—how quaintly retro—write them a letter and describe what had happened. They could take a copy of the program home with them and look at it. They could give themselves an internal high-five. Bragging to others may be unattractive, but you after all are the only one inside your head. I even asked them to focus on my talk (which was very brief) and the praise it contained for their years of productive study. In particular, I told them not to think about the football game they were missing in order to attend the ceremony or the term paper they were not at that moment writing or whether their parking meter would run out before that damn professor would stop yapping about savoring. In short, I urged them not to be a kill-joy, because it would only be their own joy that they were killing.

My experience in asking people to do this exercise is that it invariably works as intended, whether or not someone is high or low on positive affectivity. Pleasure is available to almost all, and so too is the ability to enhance it. The real challenge is to make savoring a habit and not just something done on a one-time basis following a prompt like this exercise. To this end, I suggest being proactive and anticipating pleasures and how you will respond to them. I offer a provocative hypothesis, one I have not tested formally but that seems worth an experiment. Do not stack up your pleasures and try to experience them simultaneously. Have them one at a time, and relish each in its own right.

Think about weddings and honeymoons: an affirmation of love, a blessing by a higher power, a gathering of friends and families, beautiful bridesmaids wearing really ugly dresses about which they cannot complain, gifts, wonderful food, toasts, a limousine ride, three days in a Caribbean resort, and—if you are not stressed out by everything that has come before—some moments of physical intimacy. And then the honeymoon ends.

Is it heresy to propose that this is a terrible way to begin married life because it violates everything that we know about how to savor pleasure by jamming together so many good things that nothing in itself can be all that good?

I doubt anyone will hire me as a wedding planner, so let me end with a more modest suggestion about the next occasion in which gifts are exchanged, whether it is Christmas, a birthday, a wedding anniversary, or a retirement celebration. Give one gift only, and receive one gift only, and savor it.

If even this idea is not modest enough, try this one the next time you go out to a nice restaurant. Do not order a wonderful appetizer, a wonderful entrée, a wonderful wine, and a wonderful dessert. Choose one and only one to be the focus of your meal and savor it without flooding your taste buds with all the others. If nothing else, your wallet and waistline will be especially happy, but so too might you.

GLOSSARY

adaptation: after repeated exposure to the same emotion-producing stimulus, the tendency to experience less of the emotion
broaden-and-build theory: theory that positive emotions broaden psychological and behavioral repertoires and build psychological resources
comfort: positive subjective experience more conspicuous in its absence than its presence
duration neglect: tendency of people in thinking about an emotional event to overlook how long it lasts
emotion: psychological state defined by subjective feelings but also characteristic patterns of physiological arousal, thoughts, and behaviors
endowment effect: tendency to like objects given to us, even if we did not especially want or value them in the first place
flow: psychological state that accompanies highly engaging activities
hedonic capacity: ability to experience positive feelings
hedonic treadmill: continual adaptation to emotional circumstances, resulting in an ongoing return to a point of relative neutrality
heritability: proportion of variation in a characteristic due to genetic factors; roughly, "influenced by genetics" as opposed to "inherited"
intrinsic motivation: undertaking of activities because of their own appeal and not because of external rewards or punishments
mere exposure effect: tendency to like objects to which we are frequently exposed, even if this exposure takes place subliminally
mood: general emotional state of an individual
peak-end theory: theory of how emotional experiences are remembered, as a joint function of their greatest intensity and how they end
pleasure: positive subjective experience
positive affectivity: extent to which an individual habitually experiences positive moods like joy, interest, and alertness
savoring: awareness of pleasure and deliberate attempts to make it last

RESOURCES

Books and Journals

Kahneman, D., Diener, E., & Schwarz, N. (Eds.). (1999). *Well-being: The foundations of hedonic psychology.* New York: Russell Sage.
Jamison, K. R. (2004). *Exuberance: The passion for life.* New York: Knopf.
Csikszentmihalyi, M. (1990). *Flow: The psychology of optimal experience.* New York: Harper & Row.
Guiliano, M. (2005). *French women don't get fat: The secret of eating for pleasure.* New York: Knopf.

Articles

Fredrickson, B. L. (2003). The value of positive emotions. *American Scientist, 91,* 330–335.

Brickman, P., & Campbell, D. T. (1971). Hedonic relativism and planning the good society. In M. H. Appley (Ed.), *Adaptation-level theory* (pp. 287–305). New York: Academic.

Web Sites

http://www.authentichappiness.org. This Web site is associated with Martin Seligman's (2002) trade book on positive psychology, *Authentic Happiness*, and contains happiness surveys that can be taken on-line.

http://webscript.princeton.edu/~psych/psychology/research/kahneman/index.php. This is the Princeton University Web site of psychologist Daniel Kahneman, the 2002 Nobel Prize–winner in economics and a central figure in the study of pleasure and pain.

Films

Cocoon (1985)
Groundhog Day (1993)
La Vita è Bella (*Life Is Beautiful*) (1997)
ABC News's *20/20*: "Chocolate" (1999)
Chocolat (2000)

Songs

"59th Street Bridge Song" (Simon & Garfunkle)
"December 1963 (Oh What a Night)" (Four Seasons)
"Do You Believe in Magic" (Lovin' Spoonful)
"Good Vibrations" (Beach Boys)
"I Dig Rock and Roll Music" (Peter, Paul, & Mary)
"I Feel Good" (James Brown)
"Joy to the World" (Three Dog Night)

4 Happiness

Pleasure usually comes when called, but not happiness.
—MASON COOLEY (1990)

Happiness is of concern to positive psychology because it is of concern to people in general (King & Napa, 1998). The U.S. Declaration of Independence proclaims that all are entitled to life, to liberty, and to the pursuit of happiness. We tell our children, our friends, and ourselves that what counts most is to be happy with the choices made and avenues pursued. Happiness is what philosophers call an *ungrounded grounder*, a rationale that requires no further rationale.

Let me nonetheless ground happiness by describing two recently reported studies, both of which began many years ago. Each implies that happiness has striking long-term consequences for well-being.

The first study looked at yearbook photos from Mills College, a private school for women in Oakland, California. Like many high schools and colleges, Mills College every year publishes a yearbook containing pictures of graduating seniors. If you are like me, you dreaded your high school or college yearbook picture but comforted yourself with the thought that it did not mean all that much. Think again.

Berkeley psychologists Lee Anne Harker and Dacher Keltner (2001) analyzed 114 pictures from the 1958 and 1960 yearbooks. All but 3 of the young women were smiling, but the smiles varied. Remember from chapter 1 the notion of a Duchenne smile: a genuine, full-faced expression of happiness indexed by the degree to which the muscles surrounding one's eyes are contracted—crinkled, as it were. On a 10-point scale reflecting the Duchenne-ness of these yearbook smiles, the average rating was 3.8.

The researchers chose these particular pictures for analysis because the women in them were participants in a long-term study of important life events (Helson, 1967). Specifically, the researchers knew—decades after their yearbook photos—whether the women were married and if they were satisfied with their marriages. As it turns out, the Duchenne-ness of their yearbook smiles predicted both of these outcomes. Young women who expressed positive emotions (happiness) in yearbook photos, and presumably in other venues of their lives, as middle-aged women had better marriages.

The skeptic might wonder if these results reflect the operation of some confound like physical attractiveness. Leaving aside the fact that physical beauty is not much of a route to happiness for people in general (Argyle, 2001), prettiness did not account for the results in this particular sample. Harker and Keltner rated how attractive the pictures were, and this rating—largely independent of the Duchenne-ness rating—did not predict who had a satisfying marriage.

So, what can you tell from a picture? If you focus on the happiness expressed, you can tell whether someone will have a good life.

The second study analyzed the emotional content of autobiographical essays written by nuns in the American School Sisters of Notre Dame, a U.S. teaching order. In 1930, each sister had been asked by her Mother Superior to write a short autobiographical essay about her childhood, the schools she had attended, her religious experience, and her reasons for taking vows. These were only several hundred words long and are analogous to the personal statement you may have written if you applied to college. Like your yearbook photo, you probably agonized at the moment you were crafting your personal statement but then put it out of your mind as not all that important. Once more, think again.

The brief autobiographies by the nuns were no doubt read at the time they were written but then were filed away for decades. In the meantime, their order committed itself to helping the scientific community and specifically to assisting researchers in unraveling the mysteries of Alzheimer's disease. They opened their lives, their records, and—literally[1]—their brains to investigators, and much has been learned from the generosity of these women (Snowdon, 2001). Catholic nuns are good research subjects from the viewpoint of medical and psychological science because so much about their lives is constant: income, diet, education, access to health care, habits (no pun intended), and the like. Psychological influences on health can emerge unmasked by other considerations.

Deborah Danner, David Snowdon, and Wallace Friesen (2001) at the University of Kentucky read the essays of 180 sisters born before 1917 and scored them for

1. The nuns consented to autopsies following death, which allows the most reliable way to diagnose Alzheimer's disease.

emotional content simply by counting the number of sentences in each essay that contained positive emotion words and the number of sentences that contained negative emotion words. Here are examples (p. 806). The first is largely descriptive and neutral in its emotional tone, whereas the second is brimming with happiness.

> Sister 1. I was born on September 26, 1909, the eldest of seven children, five girls and two boys. . . . My candidate year was spent in the Motherhouse, teaching Chemistry and Second Year Latin at Notre Dame Institute. With God's grace, I intend to do my best for our Order, for the spread of religion and for my personal sanctification.
>
> Sister 2. God started my life off well by bestowing upon me a grace of inestimable value. . . . The past year which I have spent as a candidate studying at Notre Dame College has been a very happy one. Now I look forward with eager joy to receiving the Holy Habit of Our Lady and to a life of union with Love Divine.

By the 1990s, about 40% of the sample had died, and the researchers investigated whether the emotional content of the essays written 6 decades earlier had any relationship to survival. Positive emotional content (happiness) was strikingly related to longevity, whereas negative emotional content was unrelated. The happier nuns (those in the upper 25% of the essay writers) lived on average 10 years longer than their less-happy counterparts (those in the bottom 25%). For context, whether or not one smokes yields a 7-year difference in life expectancy, a substantial period of time to be sure but obviously less than the effect of happiness.

So, what can you tell from a personal statement? If you focus on the happiness expressed, you can tell whether someone will have a long life.

Neither of these studies is fine-grained, so we do not know the process which led from the apparent happiness of the young women to their long and satisfied lives. We can suspect that these effects were not wrought by magic but rather by their mundane day-to-day activities, with the happy women slowly building good lives one smile and one word at a time. The unhappy women just as gradually failed to do this, and their lives went slip-sliding away.

Then again, maybe happiness is irrelevant to these results, a misleading by-product of some third variable—perhaps one rooted in genetics—that is itself responsible for how one's life unfolds. The way the game of science is played, however, is for skeptics to do more than object to the interpretations put forth by researchers. The burden of proof shifts to the skeptics to show—with their own evidence—that the interpretations they favor are more-reasonable ones. Accordingly, I will take the Mills College investigation and the nun study at face value until I have reason to do otherwise. I will conclude that happiness is not just a feeling in the moment but an important influence on the future. In sum, these studies ground the ungrounded grounder.

The Meanings of Happiness

Happiness matters, but what does happiness mean? There is a casual tendency to equate happiness with pleasure in the moment, to the tickling of our senses by chocolate or caresses. Pleasure as discussed in chapter 3 is certainly part of happiness, but philosophers over the millennia have carefully examined the meaning of happiness and arrived at an impressively broad conception that often goes beyond fleeting feelings (Guignon, 1999; Russell, 1930, 1945). Often they propose a sovereign principle to be followed in order to be happy.

The doctrine of **hedonism**—maximizing pleasure and minimizing pain—was articulated thousands of years ago by Aristippus (435–366 BCE), who championed immediate sensory gratification (J. Watson, 1895; chapter 3). Hedonism was elaborated by Epicurus (342–270 BCE) into the edict of *ethical hedonism*, which holds that our fundamental moral obligation is to maximize our experience of pleasure. Early Christian philosophers denounced hedonism as inconsistent with the goal of avoiding sin, but Renaissance philosophers such as Erasmus (1466–1536) and Thomas Moore (1478–1535) argued that it was God's wish that people be happy, so long as they did not become preoccupied with "artificial" ways of achieving pleasure.

Later, British philosophers like David Hume (1711–1776) and Jeremy Bentham (1748–1832) used the doctrine of hedonism to lay the foundation for *utilitarianism*, which was ushered into psychology as the underpinning of psychoanalysis and all but the most radical of the behaviorisms. Hedonism is alive and well today in the name of a new field: *hedonic psychology* (Kahneman, Diener, & Schwarz, 1999). At least in the modern Western world, the pursuit of pleasure is widely endorsed as a way to achieve satisfaction: "Don't worry, be happy."

Standing in contrast to hedonism is another venerable tradition that can be traced to Aristotle's (384–322 BCE) notion of **eudaimonia**—being true to one's inner self (demon). According to this view, true happiness entails identifying one's virtues, cultivating them, and living in accordance with them (Aristotle, 2000). Aristotle considered sensual pleasure as touted by the hedonists to be vulgar. Similar positions were advanced by John Stuart Mill (1806–1873) and Bertrand Russell (1872–1970) and undergird more modern psychological notions such as Rogers's (1951) ideal of the fully functioning person, Maslow's (1970) concept of self-actualization, Ryff and Singer's (1996) vision of psychological well-being, and Deci and Ryan's (2000) self-determination theory. Uniting eudaimonic emphases is the premise that people should develop what is best within themselves and then use these skills and talents in the service of greater goods—including in particular the welfare of other people or humankind writ large. Again, in the modern world, the pursuit of a meaningful life is widely endorsed as a way to achieve satisfaction: "Be all that you can be," and "Make a difference."

As implied, different psychological traditions have addressed these two principles of achieving satisfaction. Often these traditions have proceeded independently from one another, with confusion introduced by the tendency of those working within each tradition to claim "happiness" as a label for their subject matter and to deny—if only implicitly—its use by those in the other camp. Sometimes the debate becomes explicit, and we see investigators playing off the merits of pleasure and eudaimonia as routes to the psychological good life (e.g., Compton, Smith, Cornish, & Qualls, 1996; Ryan & Deci, 2000; Waterman, 1993).

Some of our own recent research suggests that eudaimonia can trump pleasure as a predictor of life satisfaction (Huta, Park, Peterson, & Seligman, 2005; Peterson, Park, & Seligman, 2005b). Using different samples and different methods, we found that those who pursue eudaimonic goals and activities are more satisfied than those who pursue pleasure. This finding is robust, occurring across the adult years, for males and for females, and for residents of the United States, Canada, and other nations. He who dies with the most toys may or may not win, but he will not do so as happily as he who dies after a life of helping others.

This is not to say that hedonism is irrelevant to life satisfaction, just that all things being equal, hedonism contributes less to long-term happiness than does eudaimonia. However, one need not always choose between them. Indeed, I believe that the full life is characterized by both and further that these orientations can be synergistic with respect to life satisfaction. The whole can sometimes be greater than its parts. At the same time, the whole can also be less than the sum of its parts; individuals who are neither hedonistic nor eudaimonic in their pursuits are dramatically dissatisfied with their lives.

The bottom line appears to be that people need at least one route to happiness in order to be satisfied. Seligman (2002) recounted the story of his friend "Len," who illustrates this point. In the language of chapter 3, Len was extremely low on positive affectivity, and he seldom laughed, smiled, or teased. Although sensitive to others, he still came off as cold. Len had a career that he had pursued with dedication and success, and he was financially very well off. He also had hobbies that engaged him—like playing bridge and following sports. He had several good friends. According to Seligman, Len was handsome and considered by all a nice guy.

Good for Len, but he had a long-standing problem because women did not find him attractive. Len was not a fun guy, and who wants to be with someone who never acts like he is enjoying himself? You could take it personally and think that *you* are unattractive because you cannot rouse Len from his chilly state. Actually, so the story goes, it was women from the United States who found Len unattractive. Women from Europe, with different notions of what makes a man attractive, saw beyond his emotional restraint to his substantive characteristics, all of which were laudable. Len eventually married a woman from Europe—and happily, I might note.

What is the lesson of Len? Not that he needed therapy or medication. Nothing about him needed to be "fixed." He simply was low on positive affectivity and as a result did not present himself as a bubbly hedonist. This route to well-being was not open to him. He had other pathways available, though, and for him, the good life was achieved by following them.

The more-general point, which the half of you who are below average on positive affectivity can well appreciate, is that your life can be quite a good one except insofar as other people nag at you to cheer up, to have fun, and to smile more. I have been on the receiving end of such comments, and if nothing else, theorizing and research about eudaimonia arms me against the thought that there is something wrong with me when I fail to bounce down the sidewalk.

Hedonism and eudaimonia may not exhaust the routes to happiness. Consider yet another orientation: the pursuit of **engagement**. Remember Csikszentmihalyi's (1990) writings on flow, the psychological state that accompanies highly engaging activities (chapter 3). Flow differs from hedonism, in which positive emotional experience is front and center (Csikszentmihalyi, 1999). At least at any given point in time, flow and pleasure may even be incompatible. And although the pursuit of a eudaimonic life can at times produce flow for some individuals—e.g., those volunteering in a hospice or a soup kitchen—not all flow-producing activities are meaningful in the sense of connecting an individual to a greater good (consider playing bridge or Scrabble), and not all meaningful activities entail the total absorption that defines flow.

More recently, Marty Seligman (January 21, 2005, personal communication) has suggested to me that yet another possible route to happiness entails the pursuit of **victory**—winning at whatever matters most to us, whether these be literal contests (sports and games) or more metaphorical ones (work and love). I am not yet convinced that a life of victory belongs with the lives of hedonism, eudaimonia, and engagement just discussed. It may not be as widely recognized or celebrated (McClelland, 1961), and it may not be fully distinct from the other routes. But it is undeniable that at least some people constantly compete and measure themselves—and their own well-being—on the scorecard of life. Whether the pursuit of victory is linked to life satisfaction and whether it is more or less important than the other orientations are questions we are in the process of exploring.

Whatever we discover, happiness and its pursuit will remain complex. Seligman, Steen, Park, and Peterson (2005) acknowledged this complexity by suggesting that *happiness* is best reserved as the name of a field within positive psychology, just as cognition or motivation are names of fields within business-as-usual psychology. One cannot study happiness per se but only particular manifestations of it, defined in specific ways and measured accordingly.

Explaining and Measuring Happiness

Positive psychologists are thus concerned not only with abstract definitions of happiness but additionally with how it can be ascertained in the concrete, thereby making research possible. How can we tell that one person is happier than another, or that one group of people is happier than another group? How can we tell if happiness is increasing, decreasing, or holding steady for the same individual?

In thinking about how to measure happiness, the following distinctions are useful, drawn from a discussion of approaches to explaining happiness by Seligman and Royzman (2003). They distinguished three traditional theories of happiness. Each has its own assessment implications.

Traditional Theories of Happiness

The first has already been mentioned: hedonism. It holds that happiness entails raw feelings front and center in our conscious experiences. A happy life is one in which the good feelings (pleasure) are maximized, and the bad feelings (pain) are minimized. By this view, happiness is the sum over the lifetime of all of these specific feelings, what Kahneman (1999) has described as a bottom-up approach to explaining happiness. To be sure, there are some needed subtleties. The pattern of pleasure and pain across one's life certainly matters (Velleman, 1991). "We can imagine two lives that contain the same exact amount of momentary pleasantness, but one life tells a story of gradual decline (ecstatic childhood, light-hearted youth, dysphoric adulthood, miserable old age), while another is a tale of gradual improvement (the above pattern in reverse)" (Seligman & Royzman, 2003).

Think high school quarterback versus revenge of the nerds.

Think of the old joke: "Other than that, Mrs. Lincoln, how did you enjoy the play?"

Or think about the studies by Kahneman and his colleagues described in chapter 3 that support peak-end theory: What matters in how we remember hedonic episodes is how they end.

There are two methodological implications of this bottom-up view of happiness and its needed qualification. First, one excellent way to measure happiness is in the moment—on-line—and here positive psychologists favor the **experience sampling method** (ESM; Larson & Csikszentmihalyi, 1983), mentioned briefly in previous chapters. Research participants are given an electronic device not much larger than a pack of cigarettes. They carry it around with them, and at randomly determined intervals, it gives off a signal—beep! Then they complete a questionnaire, describing where they are, what they are doing, how they are feeling, and what they are thinking. The most high-tech version of experience sampling allows research participants to respond by entering responses on a tiny keyboard, but a pencil and paper usually suffice.

For instance, Harlow and Cantor (1994) used experience sampling to map out how concern with academic activities by college students could spill over into their social activities. This phenomenon usually took the form of a student asking her friends for reassurance about academic pursuits. If done too frequently, individuals report lower social satisfaction, because not all of their friends provide the desired reassurance, and indeed some may become frustrated with them.

ESM avoids problems with memory (Stone, Shiffman, & deVries, 1999). Research participants need not think about what they usually do; they need only report what is going on at the moment. The immediacy of the procedure allows the researcher to make conclusions about everyday thoughts, feelings, and actions. Another benefit of experience sampling is that it allows the researcher to take the participant's immediate surroundings into account. Current thinking in psychology accords great importance to the setting in which our behavior occurs. ESM gives the researcher a glimpse at the subject's environment, although beepers do not work too well in swimming pools, nightclubs, churches, or neighborhoods in which police officers are patrolling on the lookout for drug sales (Hormuth, 1986).

Second, just as important as bottom-up assessment is asking people for an overall summary of the trajectory and pattern of their lives. Not to do so would miss the forest for the trees and ignore the critical sequencing of momentary pleasures. For an extreme example, consider the life of noted philosopher Ludwig Wittgenstein. By all accounts, for all of his brilliance, he was highly self-critical and relentlessly dysphoric. But at the very end of his life, as he lay dying in Cambridge, his final words were reportedly, "Tell them I have had a wonderful life" (Monk, 1990).

A second theory of happiness is **desire theory**, which holds that happiness is a matter of getting what you want, whether or not it involves pleasure (Griffin, 1986). Again, the best way to ascertain happiness according to this view is to ask the person, because what a person wants is left up to him to define. Desire theory and hedonism often agree, because we may desire more pleasure than pain, but they part company when we are indifferent to pain or—indeed—are attracted to it for whatever reason. Moreover, pleasure and pain do not exhaust what we might desire.

Philosopher Robert Nozick (1974) proposed the following thought experiment. Imagine that an experience machine has been invented that allows you to spend your entire life safely immersed in a tank, your brain wired to a device that allows any experience you desire to take place by stimulating whatever parts of your brain might be responsible for it. These experiences are vivid, intense, prolonged, pleasurable if you wish, and indistinguishable in the moment from "real" ones. The prospect of such an experience machine sounds intriguing, and I can only assume that Microsoft is working feverishly to create one. But according to Nozick, people reject these hypothetical experiences because they want to "earn" their pleasures by virtue of their actions and character—just as the protagonists in *The Matrix* movies reject the computer simulation that most people unknowingly experience as reality. Critical to what we desire is a life with integrity as opposed to one created by illusions of brain chemistry.

Suppose what we want strikes others as shallow or inconsequential? A third approach to explaining happiness has therefore emerged known as **objective list theory** (Nussbaum, 1992; Sen, 1985). By this view, there really are truly valuable things in the world, and happiness entails achieving some number of these: freedom from disease, material comfort, a career, friendships, children, education, knowledge, and so on. Consider thugs and hooligans who are relentless pleasure seekers and get much of what they want—cheap thrills in the form of promiscuous sex, drug highs, and the casual exploitation of suckers. Most of us would not want to say that these folks are "really" happy, although they perfectly meet the criteria set forth by hedonism and desire theory.

The methodological implication of objective list theory is that we need to ascertain whether these truly valuable things have been attained by an individual. The problem is of course deciding what these things are. I believe there is more consensus than a strict relativist might assert, but there are still gray areas and difficult tradeoffs among the items on anyone's list of what is objectively good.

Consider education, valued in virtually all circles within the United States and elsewhere (M. C. Waters, 1990). As a faculty member at a big-time academic school as well as a big-time sports school, I frequently hear debates about our student-athletes and the tradeoffs they are forced to make between schoolwork (getting a degree) and sports (preparing for a lucrative career as a professional athlete). A less-than-elite athlete has no objective conflict and should always opt for education because a professional career is a pipe dream. But what about a truly skilled college athlete participating in a money sport?

Some years ago, a student of mine who was a football star for the Wolverines asked me what would happen if he skipped the final exam for our course. I checked his grades and found that if he took the exam and did minimally well, he would pass the course, receive credit, and—so he informed me—earn his degree and make his mother very happy. If he did not take the exam, he would not pass the course.

Why would he even consider missing the exam? He had an unavoidable conflict with a National Football League testing combine, which if he attended and then performed to his ability, would improve his draft position and make a literal difference of a million dollars in his salary over the next few years. One would think that might make his mother happy as well. So what is the objective good here? Getting his college degree or financially setting up his family and himself for life? The best he could do was score one out of two. The point is that objective list theory is not foolproof as an explanation of happiness, and it also requires us to return to an individual's own overall evaluation of his feelings and wishes.

This story may be too unusual to provide a compelling objection to objective list theory. Ponder, therefore, the following patterns in the United States and indeed the world as a whole. By any and all criteria, objective goods have increased for the typical person over the decades. Literacy rates are higher; life expectancy is longer; information is more available; and material goods that provide safety and comfort are much more abundant. But self-reported happiness has not increased in pace with these objective goods. According to survey research, people in the United States today are no happier than their counterparts 40 or 50 years ago.

Gregg Easterbrook (2003) has dubbed this phenomenon the *progress paradox*, and David Myers (2000) drew the same conclusion in arguing that we have lost our spiritual bearings as we have accumulated more objective goods (Jung, 1933).

Perhaps there is no paradox: In reporting happiness, people are simply offering a relative and not an absolute judgment, which means that we should not expect an ever-increasing trend toward more happiness. As I will discuss shortly, this is part of the resolution, but there is more afoot than how survey respondents react to numerical scales. For reasons not well understood, severe depression has also increased dramatically over the past half century, in the United States as well as in other industrialized nations, so that younger adults today may be 10 times more likely to have a full-blown depressive episode at some point in their lives than were their parents or grandparents—who not only had fewer objective goods but also lived through the Great Depression and World War II (Robins et al., 1984). Clinical depression is not simply how someone responds to a survey.

Objective list theory requires that we dismiss what people say about their happiness if it is at odds with their objective goods. What counts is what they have, but this makes no sense in the face of the epidemic of depression.

The best theory may be one that somehow combines these different explanations of happiness. The best assessment of happiness would rely on a battery of measures, some completed by the individual and others by informed and objective observers. No such battery exists at present, although Ed Diener and his colleagues are working to create one and encourage its use to gauge the psychological well-being of entire nations (Diener, 2000; Diener & Seligman, 2004).

In the meantime, researchers usually measure by surveying or interviewing people and taking what they report at face value. This approach to measuring happiness as a subjective experience has much to recommend it because it resonates with how most of us think about happiness. Happiness is a personal experience and indeed an idiosyncratic one. We may find it bizarre that folks are happy with how they pursue their lives—as stamp collectors, as fans of the Chicago Cubs, or as interstate truck drivers—but we allow that happiness is after all their business, and who are we to say that they are not happy? We would in turn object if they vetoed our own conception of happiness.

The following terminology has emerged among researchers (Diener, 1984). **Quality of life** is an overarching label that includes all of the emotions, experiences, appraisals, expectations, and accomplishments that figure into the good life. **Subjective well-being** is a more-specific notion usually defined as relatively high levels of positive affect, relatively low levels of negative affect, and the overall judgment that one's life is a good one. This latter appraisal is often identified as **life satisfaction**.

These terms are often used interchangeably in the research literature, and in more popularized presentations, **happiness** is introduced as an everyday synonym of this family of concepts (e.g., Argyle, 2001; Baker & Stauth, 2003; Lykken, 2000; Myers, 1993; Seligman, 2002). Researchers have often preferred measures of life satisfaction because these tend to be stable over time but still sensitive enough to capture changes in life circumstances (Pavot & Diener, 1993; Schuessler & Fisher, 1985). However, there is a growing trend to identify all of these as subjective well-being or even happiness measures (Diener & Seligman, 2002), and the empirical fact is that different measures—whatever their labels—usually agree rather substantially.

Researchers are attracted to self-report surveys and interviews for an additional reason: They make measurement simple and straightforward, not to mention inexpensive.[2] One need merely ask people a handful of standardized questions to ascertain whether or not they are happy. Usually a time period is specified—right now, during the past 4 weeks, or "in general"—and research proceeds accordingly. Most of the research described in this chapter and elsewhere in this book concerning happiness and well-being uses this strategy of measurement.

The objection to this approach, despite its popularity, is twofold. First, self-report is not always foolproof, even about subjective experience. Although positive psychologists do not automatically distrust what people say about themselves, neither do they treat all self-reports as infallible (Park & Peterson, in press a). Depending on the context in which assessment occurs, someone may shade their answers—deliberately or inadvertently—in one direction or another. Consider these extreme examples. A plaintiff in a personal injury lawsuit will emphasize his pain and suffering and minimize his reports of feeling well and doing well. An employee speaking to her boss about a merit raise will mention the things she loves about the job. More subtly, especially in the United States where being happy is so highly valued, research participants with no explicit incentive to exaggerate their well-being may still end up doing so because this is an expected and socially desirable response (Diener & Suh, 2000).

Some years ago, one of my students always made me shake my head. When I would ask her, as a conversational gambit, "How are you doing?" she would *always* respond with an enthusiastic "great" or "wonderful" or "spectacular." To be sure, this made her a low-maintenance individual because she never needed soothing, but because I knew her well, I did not always believe her. When she was ill, or having problems with her boyfriend, or being thwarted in her work, she was still doing great, no better than in other circumstances but never any worse, all of which led me not to take her self-reports too seriously.

Was she deliberately dishonest? I think not. This was who she was, but I still believe that late at night, when she was alone with her thoughts, she admitted to some gradations in her subjective experience. But she would never reveal these to anyone else, or at least not to me.

Where does this leave a researcher? If my student is a typical person, not in a good place, because it means that self-report questionnaires about happiness pro-

2. Although ESM is touted as a good method for measuring well-being, the fact remains that this is an expensive research strategy. The paging devices can cost as much as $100 each (batteries not included), and some number are lost or damaged by research participants.

duce studies of social scripts as opposed to investigations of more deeply rooted psychological characteristics.

Schwarz and Strack (1999) wrote an interesting piece on what people actually do when they respond to surveys that ostensibly measure happiness or global life satisfaction. They argued that people are not literally introspecting on some stable thing within themselves that we can call happiness. Instead, they are making a judgment at that particular point in time, and like any judgment, this one results from psychological processes susceptible to numerous influences, some quite annoying from the perspective of a researcher.

All things being equal, wrote Schwarz and Strack, people base their judgments of overall life satisfaction on how they are *feeling* at the present moment. Flushed with a momentary triumph or thrown for a loop by a recent setback, people may accordingly report that life per se is good or bad. More generally, these writers argued that a happiness judgment is based only on the information readily available to people at the moment the judgment is solicited, and what is salient at the moment is easily manipulated. So, if a survey asks young adults about their dating frequency, and then follows immediately with a question about their overall life satisfaction, the correlation is quite high (Strack, Martin, & Schwarz, 1988). People who indicate that they date a lot—and thus have this "fact" front and center in their minds—go on to report that overall they have a good life. And the converse is true for people who have just reminded themselves that they do not date a lot. If these questions are simply reversed, so that a reminder of one's dating frequency is not so recent, the correlation with life satisfaction becomes much smaller (although it still remains positive).

I am drafting these paragraphs in January 2005, as stories abound in the media of the terrible devastation wrought by the tsunami in the Indian Ocean. There is dirty snow on the ground outside; I have a sore throat; and I am not fully prepared for the beginning of the winter semester (in 90 minutes), but I think my life is pretty good. It is very salient to me that I live in Ann Arbor and not Sumatra. Absent the tsunami, my overall judgment would be more muted and might well reflect the local hassles just mentioned.

Furthermore, according to Schwarz and Strack, respondents to survey questions about life satisfaction are rendering a *relative* judgment. How does that vaudeville joke go?

> How's your wife?
> Compared to what?

The joke may not be all that funny, but it conveys a deeper truth that we often make judgments by comparing. In the case of well-being, we have lots of candidates for comparison. We can compare our lives to what is, to what was, or to what will be. We can even compare our lives to what is not—so-called counterfactual thinking, as exemplified by the downward social comparison of cancer patients mentioned in chapter 1. None of these influences on judgment makes the process of assessing well-being capricious, but together they introduce problems of interpretation if we overlook them.

Asians tend to report lower levels of life satisfaction than people in other parts of the world (Diener, Suh, Smith, & Shao, 1995). This is a robust phenomenon that admits to different explanations, but perhaps the simplest is in terms of the Asian norm of not standing out from one's peers. According to a Japanese proverb, "The nail that stands up gets pounded down." (In the United States, the nail that stands up gets its own television show.) Perhaps an Asian respondent to a survey does not want to say that his life is better than anyone else's life; hence, he uses the middle of the rating scale.

This explanation does not trivialize the result, by the way, because if such a norm is operating, it is not at work just when people respond to surveys. Perhaps Asians across the board hold themselves more in check vis-à-vis happiness, its expression, and perhaps even its experience.

Schwarz and Strack (1999) described numerous studies of other influences on well-being judgments, ostensibly trivial factors that nonetheless have demonstrable impacts. So, if a researcher simply includes a general well-being question on the same page as other questions about life, answers to these influence the well-being answer (and vice versa). People may follow the norm to provide "new information" in the context of a sustained conversation. If we ask someone about his marital satisfaction, and then about his overall life satisfaction, he may construe the latter question as "Other than your marriage, how is your life going?" If these two questions are on separate pages of the survey package, in what seem to be separate questionnaires (because they are formatted differently), the answers do not spill into or play off one another to the same degree.

As you might suspect, Schwarz and Strack concluded that general happiness measures are not valid because of all these influences. They recommended instead the use of ESM, measuring happiness on-line and aggregating responses.

I take their arguments seriously, but I do not fully buy them. First, this critique assumes that people are really stupid, even about a topic as important and as transparent as their own well-being and life satisfaction. As explained in chapter 1, this negative view of human nature is a philosophical stance and not one compelled by the data. To be sure, people's judgments can be shoved around by appropriate variations of the phrasing and formatting of questions, but the robustness of such manipulations is debatable (Eid & Diener, 2004; Schimmack, Boeckenholt, & Reisenzein, 2002).

Second, if the business of measuring global life satisfaction and well-being by self-report is so fraught with problems, why are the resulting scores reliable and stable? Why are they related to so many objective life outcomes, like in the yearbook study and the nun study? Why are these scores demonstrably heritable (influenced by genetics)?

Third, for every demonstration that global judgments are influenced by bottom-up processes, there is another demonstration that specific judgments are influenced by top-down processes (Fiske & Taylor, 1984). Schwarz and Strack argued that one's judgment of overall well-being can be determined by how one feels at the moment. True enough, but how one feels at the moment can be determined by one's overall well-being (Schimmack, Diener, & Oishi, 2002). With some colleagues, I did a study of optimism among college students and how they viewed their ongoing lives. Optimistic students saw their daily lives filled with challenges and opportunities, whereas pessimistic students saw their lives filled with hassles and frustrations (Dykema, Bergbower, & Peterson, 1995). The same event—for example, having to take care of a neighbor's cat over a weekend—could be a source of amusement for an optimist but a looming disaster for a pessimist.

In any event, that self-report measures of well-being are flawed does not mean that they are hopelessly flawed.

How's your measure of well-being?
Compared to what?

One of the ways that self-report surveys of general life satisfaction have been validated is by seeing how well they agree with ESM results. The agreement is substantial (Sandvak, Diener, & Seidlitz, 1993). Perhaps the most important way to judge the adequacy of a measure is to see where it leads us in terms of research results. Are they coherent, sensible, and interesting? You be the judge as I turn next to some of these results.

Self-Report Measures of Happiness

Psychology's interest in happiness and well-being goes back almost 100 years (Angner, 2005). The earliest self-report measures were single items included in surveys (e.g., Bradburn, 1969; Campbell, 1981; Campbell, Converse, & Rodgers, 1976; Cantril, 1965). Some of these survey items ask for judgments about life in general, and others are called *domain-specific measures* because they ask people to describe their happiness in a given venue of life: work, health, family, leisure activities, and so on. Often the general and specific measures line up. People who are satisfied with one domain of life are satisfied with other domains and with life in general, but the agreement is not so high as to imply complete redundancy. Thus, we can ask about the differential contributions of satisfaction with various venues to overall life satisfaction.

For example, Park and Huebner (2005) did such a study among adolescents in the United States and Korea. In both nations, satisfaction with one's family was strongly and equally linked to overall life satisfaction, not a surprising finding. But in the United States, satisfaction with the self was more strongly associated with general life satisfaction than in Korea, whereas satisfaction with school contributed more to overall life satisfaction among Korean youth than among U.S. youth. These patterns make sense in terms of the different cultural values and emphases that prevail in these nations.

Along these lines, Diener and Lucas (2000) also reported cross-national comparisons about domain-specific life satisfaction measures and overall life satisfaction. In the United States, the best predictor of overall satisfaction is how one judges the domain in which one is *most* satisfied. One may be unhappy with one's work, with one's marriage, and with one's physical health. But one's children are great, and therefore overall life is splendid. In Japan, a different pattern is found. Overall satisfaction is best predicted by the domain with which one is *least* satisfied. So, work, marriage, and health may all be going well, but if the children are wretched, so too is overall life.

These are broad generalizations to which exceptions certainly exist, and each of you has your own life satisfaction calculus. Some of you may be the sum of your parts. Others of you may be less than the sum (the Japanese pattern) or more than the sum (the U.S. pattern).

Contemporary researchers use a variety of measures of general well-being, life satisfaction, and happiness (e.g., Fordyce, 1977; Lyubomirsky & Lepper, 1999; Peterson, Park, & Seligman, 2005b; Seligman, Steen, Park, & Peterson, 2005). One especially popular measure is the Life Satisfaction Scale (Diener, Emmons, Larsen, & Griffin, 1985). It contains the following five items rated on 7-point scales, from 1 (= strongly disagree) to 7 (= strongly agree). Answers are summed and range from 5 to 35.

______In most ways my life is close to my ideal.
______The conditions of my life are excellent.
______I am satisfied with my life.
______So far I have gotten the important things I want in life.
______If I could live my life over, I would change almost nothing.

If you answer these questions (please do *not* think about your dating frequency) and then add up your responses, here is a rough interpretation suggested by the creators of the measure: 31–35 = extremely satisfied, 26–30 = satisfied, 21–25 = slightly satisfied, 20 = neutral, 15–19 = slightly dissatisfied, 10–14 = dissatisfied, 5–9 = extremely dissatisfied.

There are well-being measures suitable for children and adolescents (e.g., Park, 2004b) and even for very young children, who are asked to point to the face that expresses how they are feeling:

Regardless of the measure, each assigns a quantitative score to someone reflecting "how much" happiness or satisfaction they report. These are measures of what psychologists call *individual differences,* and the key word is *differences.* Measures that do not vary across people are not especially useful for this sort of research.

To evaluate the adequacy of measures of individual differences, psychologists determine each measure's **internal consistency** or **reliability** (do different questions ostensibly measuring the same notion yield answers that agree for a respondent) and its **stability** or **test-retest reliability** (does the same person score the same across periods of time). By both of these criteria, measures of happiness and subjective well-being fare quite well and are certainly as consistent and as stable as measures of creativity, values, political attitudes, and basic personality traits like extraversion and conscientiousness.

The thornier but even more important issue has to do with the **validity** of these measures, a matter already touched upon in my discussion of the annoying influences on self-report. Do happiness surveys truly measure what they intend to measure? If there were an objective measure of happiness, we could simply check the surveys against this criterion and see if they agree. Then we would know if the survey questions were valid or not.

In medicine, measures of an illness based on the self-report of symptoms can often be checked against laboratory tests determining the presence (or not) of the relevant germ. When this is possible, we speak of having a **hard diagnostic test**, although a moment's reflection tells you that even in medicine there is no such thing in an ultimate sense because even the hardest of tests is imperfect. There are inevitable mistakes and errors. Regardless, matters are much more challenging in psychology research because there are rarely even candidates for hard tests.

I suspect that for many psychological characteristics, hard diagnostic tests may not exist even in principle. If they did exist, they would presumably take the form of checking the psychological characteristics against an objectively measured biological or physical characteristic. Suppose someone touts a hormonal assay or a given neuroimaging pattern as *the* hard measure of happiness. Suppose that in most cases, self-report surveys agree with this test. There would still be some exceptions. Some people would satisfy the hard criterion but still say that they are unhappy, whereas other people would not meet the criterion but nonetheless say they are happy. Would we want to say they are wrong, as we would in the case of people who believe they have cancer or AIDS when all lab tests point to the opposite conclusion? I think not. The more general point is that psychological characteristics are best measured at their own level of meaning because they are not reducible to another level.

In the absence of hard diagnostic tests against which to check their measures, what psychology researchers must do to evaluate validity is painstaking. They must use a measure in research along with other measures and then look for overall patterns (Campbell & Fiske, 1959). Do the (theoretically) expected associations occur? And just as important but sometimes overlooked, do (theoretically) expected lack of associations *not* occur? It may take many years and hundreds of studies to arrive at a judgment concerning the relative validity of a given measure. And the theory behind the measure must be a reasonable one, because it determines the ground rules for this judgment (MacCorquodale & Meehl, 1948).

Measures of happiness and well-being have been studied frequently enough to allow the conclusion that they have at least a modicum of validity. Different tests tend to agree with one another rather well. And the story they tell in terms of their patterns of association with other variables is a coherent one, to which I now turn. Indeed, the story is coherent enough that even surprising findings are not used to dismiss the measures but rather to correct our intuitions and theories about happiness.

Who Is Happy?

Probably the most striking and consistent finding from happiness research is that the majority of people are rather happy (Diener & Diener, 1996). Regardless of the measure, and regardless of the sample of research participants, most folks live somewhere north of neutral—above the scale midpoint. I wish that my colleagues who believe that life is so tragic and that people are so miserable would grapple with this fact about happiness (chapter 1).

Happiness surveys have been conducted in many nations, and the results are usually presented to highlight differences (Diener, Diener, & Diener, 1995; Inglehart & Klingemann, 2000). Differences are interesting,[3] but they should not obscure the essential happiness of most people, whether they are multimillionaires in the United States (Diener, Horwitz, & Emmons, 1985) or pavement dwellers in Calcutta (Biswas-Diener & Diener, 2001).

Because subjective well-being research began with surveys of the general population, it stands apart from psychology's other lines of studies, which have relied on young adults enrolled in university courses. The range of people studied by well-being researchers is much wider, and thus they know a great deal about who is more versus less happy.

Given a sample of potential research participants, the studies are simple to do: Include a measure of well-being or life satisfaction in a survey along with other questions, and then see what goes with what. Across different studies using different measures, a consensus has emerged, not only of the factors linked to happiness (life satisfaction, subjective well-being) but also those that are not. Table 4.1 summarizes this consensus, based on reviews by Argyle (1999, 2001); Diener (1984, 1994); Diener, Suh, Lucas, and Smith (1999); Myers (1993); Myers and Diener (1995); and W. Wilson (1967).

I have organized these findings in terms of the strength of the correlation be-

3. For example, rich nations have citizens who are on the average happier than those from poor nations, a finding not to be confused with one that I report shortly, namely, that *within* a nation, income has but a small association with individual happiness. The unhappiest people are from former communist nations in Eastern Europe, and the happiest are from the Protestant nations of Northern Europe. Those from Asian nations are less happy than we would predict from their affluence, whereas those from South America are more happy.

Table 4.1. Positive Correlations With Happiness and Life Satisfaction

Zero to Small	Moderate	Large
age	number of friends	gratitude
gender	being married	optimism
education	religiousness	being employed
social class	level of leisure activity	frequency of sexual intercourse
income	physical health	percent of time experiencing positive affect
having children	conscientiousness	test-retest reliability of happiness measures
ethnicity (majority versus minority)	extraversion	happiness of identical twins
intelligence	neuroticism (negative correlation)	self-esteem
physical attractiveness	internal locus of control	

tween the factor in question and the well-being measure. A **correlation coefficient** (usually abbreviated as *r*) is a quantitative index of the degree to which two variables, if graphed, fall along a straight line. *Positive correlations* range from 0 to 1 and describe scatter plots in which a high value for one variable is associated with a high value for the other variable. *Negative correlations* range from 0 to –1 and describe scatter plots in which a high value for one variable is associated with a low value for the other variable. The larger the magnitude of the correlation (the further it is from 0), the greater the association between the two variables. *Zero correlations* occur when there is no association, and the scatter plot looks like buckshot.

The magnitude of a correlation coefficient does not have an intuitive meaning (Estepa & Sánchez Cobo, 2001). We readily grasp what is meant by a correlation coefficient of 0 and just as readily what is meant by a correlation coefficient of ± 1. But in practice, researchers never encounter correlations this stark. Instead, the strongest correlation found among psychological variables is usually about 0.3, and over the years, there has been spirited debate about whether correlations of this magnitude are worth taking seriously.[4]

Some decades ago, Walter Mischel (1968) published an influential critique of personality research hinging on his assumption that a correlation of 0.3 was

4. Setting an upper limit on the magnitude of a correlation between two variables is the fallibility (less than perfect reliability) of their measures. Furthermore, most psychological phenomena are complex, with many influences and determinants that often operate independently of one another. The greater the number of these independent influences, the smaller correlations can be (Ahadi & Diener, 1989). Consider happiness, which is linked to genetics, to personality, to culture, to specific life circumstances—to all sorts of considerations which can be independent of one another. No single influence can be expected to be a large correlate of happiness; that would be to deny the other influences.

trivial in size. This argument occasionally resurfaces (e.g., Doris, 2002; Ross & Nisbett, 1991), but current thinking is that a correlation of 0.3 is worth taking seriously (Peterson, 1992). The problem is more one of perception; a correlation of 0.3 does not *seem* like an impressive association because it is closer to 0 than to 1.

Suppose you have a serious medical condition that results in death in 65% of the cases. Now suppose that there is a treatment available that reduces your chances of dying to 35%. Would you want to receive this treatment? Of course you would, and the likelihood of its success—while not a guarantee—is not exactly in the ballpark of desperation or a miracle. The point is that if you recast this hypothetical example as a correlation between receiving the treatment (or not) and recovering from the illness (or not), the resulting coefficient is exactly 0.3 (Rosenthal & Rubin, 1982). Or consider the following familiar associations expressed as correlation coefficients (Meyer et al., 2001):

- aspirin and reduced risk of death by heart attack: $r = 0.03$
- chemotherapy and survival with breast cancer: $r = 0.03$
- smoking and lung cancer: $r = 0.08$
- antihistamine use and reduced nasal congestion: $r = 0.11$
- college grades and job performance: $r = 0.16$

We take all of *these* correlations quite seriously. If we are at risk for a heart attack, we swallow a daily aspirin. If we have breast cancer, we seek aggressive treatment. If we smoke, we know that we should stop. If we have a congested nose, we reach for antihistamines. If we are hiring a recent college graduate, we want to know her grade point average. As Meyer et al. concluded, a correlation approaching 0.3 is something about which a researcher should be pleased and not dismayed.

In describing the magnitude of correlation coefficients, researchers often use the following verbal labels. A "small" correlation is between 0 and ±0.2; a "moderate" correlation is in the ballpark of ±0.3; and a "large" correlation exceeds ±0.5. I repeat that a moderate correlation is usually as robust as it gets in the social sciences.

Look at Table 4.1, which I have organized in terms of small, moderate, and large correlations as just explained. Let me summarize for you. First, demographic factors like age, gender, ethnicity, education, and income—usually strong determinants of how people live their lives—are all associated with happiness but at low levels. One way to make sense of these findings is to conclude that happiness is available to all.

Second, among the more-robust determinants of happiness are social or interpersonal factors—number of friends, marriage, extraversion, and gratitude. Other more-robust correlates include religiousness, leisure activities, and employment (although not income per se), which often have the effect of bringing people into contact with others.

Other people matter, and there may be no happy hermits (chapter 10). In support of this conclusion, Diener and Seligman (2002) compared happy people to very happy people, a different comparison than those reflected in Table 4.1, which are correlations along the full happiness-unhappiness continuum. What Diener and Seligman found is that even the more-robust correlates in Table 4.1 fell away at the upper end of the happiness scale, with one striking exception: good relationships with other people. Of the very happy people in their sample, *all* had close relationships with others. Psychology research documents very few necessary or sufficient conditions for anything, but it looks like good social relationships may be a necessary condition for extreme happiness.

Third, several personality traits—optimism, extraversion, conscientiousness, self-esteem, internal locus of control (believing that you have control over what happens to you)—have moderate to strong correlations with avowed happiness, as do low scores on neuroticism. One possible explanation is that these correlations reflect a way of talking or presenting oneself—what researchers call a *common methods factor*: Happy people attribute other positive characteristics to themselves, whereas unhappy people do not. I suspect this accounts for some of the results, but they still are obtained when "personality" is measured in ways other than self-report, like by observer rating. I think these results show that happiness can be a product of the person and his outlook.

Some further qualifications are in order about the correlations summarized in Table 4.1. Many of the factors listed are themselves linked with one another, which means that in making sense—for example—of the correlation between religiousness (measured, let us say, by church attendance) and well-being, we need to remember that physical health may be dragged into the finding: Seriously ill people after all may have difficulty attending church. Those in the lower economic classes have less education, less access to health care, and fewer opportunities for leisure. And so on.

Some of these relationships are small ones when expressed as a linear (strictly straight-line) correlation, but become more robust with a closer look. Consider the correlation between income and happiness, overall associated weakly but much more robustly if we look only at the lower end of income. There, the correlation becomes a larger one, which of course makes sense. One must meet basic needs to be happy. Beyond that, income does not much matter.

So What? The Consequences of Happiness

The most important qualification about Table 4.1 is that it presents correlations, and one of the truisms in social science research is that *correlation does not imply causation*. That is, two variables may be associated without any causal link between them.

Nonetheless, when we see correlations like those in Table 4.1, we want to interpret them in causal terms. In some cases, we want to conclude that these factors "cause" happiness, and in other cases, we may want to conclude that happiness leads to these factors. Up to a point, common sense helps us sort through different interpretations. After all, happiness cannot cause age, but it is plausible to wonder if happiness leads to marriage, friendship, or good health or if these lead to happiness. Or there could be what social scientists call **third variables** afoot—pesky confounds in the research that are unmeasured but responsible for the apparent association between two variables that are measured.[5]

Lyubomirsky, King, and Diener (2005) grappled with this chicken-and-egg problem by reviewing specifically two sorts of studies of happiness: those that measure variables across time (longitudinal studies) and those that deliberately manipulated positive moods and ascertained the consequences (experimental studies; see also Argyle, 2001). These sorts of studies strengthen the inference that happiness does (or does not) actually lead to an outcome with which it is correlated.

They concluded that happy individuals experience later success in many domains of life, including:

- marriage
- friendship
- employment
- income
- work performance
- mental health
- psychological health

In later chapters of this book, I will describe many of the specific studies that they summarized. Suffice it to say that happiness is not just a marker of the good life but may also be one of its causes.

I do want to comment, however, on one study that implies just the opposite. My colleagues Lauren Alloy and Lyn Abramson (1979), while graduate students at the University of Pennsylvania, did a series of laboratory experiments investigating what has come to be known as **depressive realism**. They recruited college students—some mildly depressed and others not—and gave them a simple task. In front of each research participant was a button to be pressed and a green light that flashed on and off. Participants were asked to determine the relationship between pressing the button and the flashing of the light. In one of the experimental conditions, there was no relationship—the light flashed regardless of the button pressing—but the participants were not told this.

5. Here is my favorite example of a third variable. Consider that a positive correlation exists across the decades between the stork population in the Netherlands and the birth rate in this country (Georgia Skeptic, 1993). More storks → more babies; fewer storks → fewer babies. So, do storks bring babies? Of course not. Babies are found in cabbage patches, although rumor has it that fathers figure into the process as well. As a seafaring nation, the Netherlands is hugely influenced by prevailing weather patterns, a potent third variable affecting not only the relative presence of storks in the port cities but also the amount of seamen in these cities (pun intended).

The intriguing finding is that the depressed students more accurately apprehended the lack of any relationship than did the nondepressed students. In other words, the depressed research participants were more apt to say correctly that nothing they did mattered. The nondepressed participants in contrast advanced complex but incorrect hypotheses: "The light flashed when I pressed the button twice—first for 2 seconds and then for 5 seconds."

These results have attracted a great deal of attention because they are at odds with theories holding that depressed people are irrational and out of touch with reality (Beck, 1967; Jahoda, 1958). Alloy and Abramson (1979) published their studies in an article subtitled "Sadder but Wiser," and their conclusions have been widely reported and—indeed—widely generalized beyond the details of their experimental procedure.

In the present context, such generalization leads to the conclusion that happy people are stupid and that if we want to know about the real world, we should not trust what happy people have to say about it. These conclusions fly in the face of the results I have been discussing, which imply that happiness has all sorts of benefits.

What is the resolution? I do not quarrel with the basic findings of Alloy and Abramson (1979), but we can ask how widely we want to generalize them (Ackermann & DeRubeis, 1991; Haaga & Beck, 1995). Implying that their studies addressed wisdom does not mean that they really did, and indeed, no theories of wisdom reduce this complex phenomenon to the ability to detect patterns between pressing buttons and flashing lights (Baltes & Staudinger, 2000; Sternberg, 1998).

That depressed individuals more readily entertain the possibility of their own ineffectuality is a conclusion closer to the data, and when the situation in which depressed individuals find themselves happens to be one in which ineffectuality is the correct answer, then of course they are more likely than the nondepressed to be accurate. This remains a provocative finding,[6] but we should not overlook its necessary qualifications. Even stopped clocks tell the right time twice a day. If we happen to consult them only on those occasions, we might be led to the conclusion that stopped clocks are preferable to those that are consistently a few seconds slow or fast.

In sum, the evidence that sadness is associated with more-realistic perceptions of reality is bounded and does not argue against the conclusion that happiness is often associated with highly desirable outcomes in a variety of life's venues.

6. Further research using the paradigm of Alloy and Abramson suggest that depressive realism as originally demonstrated does not occur among more severely depressed individuals (e.g., Dobson & Pusch, 1995). Furthermore, when depressive realism is apparent, it involves the accurate detection of noncontingencies but not the accurate detection of contingencies (Carson, 2001). In other words, when the right answer is "I do have control over what is happening," nondepressed individuals are more realistic.

Boosting Happiness

Given that happiness has many desirable consequences, can we boost it in a lasting way? Here, there is a lot of pessimism, and researchers often point to the hedonic treadmill as setting a limit on what an intervention might do. Or they point to the heritability of happiness to argue that there is a genetically determined **set-point** for happiness, above which one cannot rise. For example, Lykken and Tellegen (1996) did a twins study of happiness and found evidence for substantial heritability. In presenting their findings, they touched on the issue of boosting happiness and offered the dour conclusion[7] that "[t]rying to be happier is as futile as trying to be taller" (p. 189).

Let me leave aside the fact that some components of happiness (like positive affectivity) are more heritable than others. Let me leave aside the fact that the hedonic treadmill is a metaphor that explains hedonic inertia and is not a biological fact.[8] Let me simply repeat the point made in chapter 3 that high heritability does not mean immutability.

Lyubomirsky, Sheldon, and Schkade (2005) offered the following heuristic for thinking about the determinants of happiness:

happiness = set-point + life circumstances + volitional activity

I have mentioned the notion of set-point, which if we take seriously is a constant for a given individual. Table 4.1 lists many of the life circumstances relevant to happiness. *Volitional activity* is the interesting part of the equation, and it echoes a point that I made in chapter 1 that positive psychology converges with humanistic approaches in acknowledging at least some role of will and choice. Happiness is not solely the product of will, but will is a component at least insofar as it leads us to do things that will result in more versus less happiness.[9]

This is the premise behind the have-a-good-day exercise described in chapter

7. In a later publication, Lykken (2000) "recanted" (his word) this conclusion and now believes that happiness can be changed, if only because most of us live below the set-point of what is possible. He cited the following as frequent "thieves" of happiness: depression, fear, shyness, anger, and resentment. If we lock up these thieves, happiness will necessarily increase.

8. Longitudinal studies of life satisfaction suggest that certain life events—like unemployment for men and divorce for women—have extremely long-lasting effects on well-being, even if a person finds another job or another spouse (e.g., Lucas, Clark, Georgellis, & Diener, 2003, 2004). Proponents of set-point theory would say that the set-point has been reset by these events, but we could just as simply conclude that there was no fixed set-point in the first place.

9. Fleeson, Malanos, and Achille (2002) asked introverted and extraverted college students to keep a careful diary for 3 weeks of their activities and moods. Both introverts and extraverts were happiest when doing extraverted things, implying that anyone who musters the will to be outgoing will be happy as a result. It is not what we are predisposed to do that matters but what we actually do, and here is where volition enters the picture.

2: Identify those situations or circumstances that make for a good day—I assume that for most of us, a good day is a happy day (King & Napa, 1998)—and deliberately create more of these situations (Buss, 1987). At least some of the factors in Table 4.1 are matters we can choose to pursue.

So, we can make more friends, and we can spend more time with them (chapter 10). We can find leisure activities that engage us, and we can find a job that lets us do what we do best (chapter 11). We can embrace a religion if we are so inclined (chapter 11). We can improve our health and fitness (chapter 9). We can experience more pleasures (chapter 3). We can see a therapist to help us banish anxiety or depression (chapter 9). We can become more optimistic (chapter 5).

If these possibilities seem too daunting, here are some very simple activities that entail—literally—doing nothing. Do *not* fret over your attractiveness or how much education you have. If you are able to pay your bills, do *not* fret over your salary. Do *not* fret about getting older.

There have been relatively few scientific attempts to boost happiness, but when researchers have occasionally mounted such efforts, they seem to work rather well (e.g., Argyle, 2001). It is interesting that the success of happiness interventions receives little publicity, whereas studies of the heritability of happiness receive massive media attention. Regardless, let me end this chapter by mentioning some research I did at the University of Pennsylvania that investigated whether happiness could be increased in a lasting way (Seligman, Steen, Park, & Peterson, 2005).

Notable about our research, I believe, is that it used 50 years of lessons learned from psychotherapy research about how to answer the question about the effectiveness of an intervention. Decades ago, one could read that therapy was ineffective—indeed even harmful (Eysenck, 1952). The problem back then was that research methods were not sophisticated enough to give the matter a fair test. Over the years, researchers have added one methodological refinement after another to their repertoire—e.g., formal diagnosis of participants, comparison groups, placebo controls, random assignment of participants to conditions, "objective" assessment of outcomes, long-term follow-up, calculation of the robustness of effects—and now we can say with certainty that psychotherapy is effective (Nathan & Gorman, 1998, 2002).

Happiness intervention research need not go through the same 50-year process because these refinements can be applied just as well to studies that try to increase happiness as to studies that try to decrease anxiety and depression.

Our initial interest in boosting happiness was sparked by our experience teaching positive psychology courses and our fortunate discovery that exercises could have apparently powerful effects on the satisfaction and fulfillment of our students (chapter 2). As intriguing as these effects seemed to be, they were suggestive but not definitive. So, we set about more rigorous examination. First, we collected interventions suggested over the centuries, from the Buddha through Tony Robbins (1992), which claimed to increase happiness. Where possible, we distilled them into replicable and teachable forms. Which really worked, and which were at best placebos, capitalizing on a participant's expectation of effectiveness as opposed to any inherent value?

For initial testing, we focused on five exercises, each of which took 1 week. Briefly, these exercises were:

- Gratitude Visit (write and deliver a letter of gratitude; see chapter 2)
- Three Good Things (every day for a week, write down three things that went well that day and explain why; again, see chapter 2)
- You at Your Best (write a story about an event that brought out the best in you; review this story every day for a week)
- Identifying Signature Strengths (take our on-line measure of strengths of character and note your highest scores; use these strengths more in the following week; chapter 6)
- Using Signature Strengths in a Novel Way (take our on-line measure of strengths of character and note your highest scores; use these strengths "in novel ways" during the following week; again, see chapter 6)

Participants were recruited from the Internet through a link identified as "Happiness Exercises." They were told they would be assigned to one condition only, which might or might not have an effect on them. They were told as well that they might receive an inert (placebo) exercise. Each exercise took 1 week to do. Participants completed measures of happiness and depression before and after the exercise, and up to 6 months later. All of this was done via the Internet (Prochaska, DiClemente, Velicer, & Rossi, 1993).

We created a plausible placebo control exercise: asking participants to write in detail for a week about their early memories. We had no reason to think that doing so would make people happier, but given everyday stereotypes about psychotherapy and its great interest in childhood events, we thought that research participants would accept this request as the sort of thing that psychologists ask of people.

Research participants were randomly assigned to one of the six conditions (five exercises plus placebo). This random-assignment placebo-controlled design that we used is considered the royal road for answering questions about the effectiveness of medication or psychotherapy, and in the present case, it led to some clear answers about boosting happiness.

First, relative to the pretest, the placebo exercise increased happiness (and decreased depression), but only in the extreme short term, immediately after the exercise was done. Second, the largest overall effect on happiness resulted from the gratitude visit, but this effect all but vanished after 1 month. As noted in chapter 2, this is not a surprising effect. Third, lasting effects on happiness—evident at 6 months of follow-up—were found for three good things and for using signature strengths in novel ways. Fourth, the lasting effects of these exercises were in particular reported by those people who continued to use them beyond the initial

1-week period. Fifth, the strength of these effects is what statisticians term "moderate" and are at least as robust as the effect sizes of psychotherapy and medication for the reduction of psychological problems.

I want to underscore the finding that continued use of an exercise led to its continued success. This repeats the important lesson about weight loss through dieting: The real challenge is not taking weight off—almost any diet will do that—but in maintaining weight loss. The more bizarre the diet in the first place, the harder it is to stay on it for the rest of one's life. Ditto for doing things to be happier. To have a lasting effect, these must be integrated into one's life. Counting one's blessings and using one's signature strengths in new ways seem to have this property. To return to Lyubomirsky et al.'s (2005) happiness equation, the results of our study suggest that their volitional activity should be expanded to read *sustained* volitional activity, which is enabled to the degree that the activity fits one's life circumstances.

Although 6 months is far from "happily ever after," our results suggest that enduring happiness might be possible even outside fairy tales. An important question left unanswered by our research to date is whether more is better when it comes to happiness interventions. Given that several exercises were individually effective, does it make sense to assign them all to the same person who wishes to be happier? And if so, is there an optimal sequence?

EXERCISE *What Is Your Happiness Profile?*

In this chapter, I described four possible routes to happiness: through pleasure, through engagement, through meaning, and through victory. Here is a questionnaire that measures each of these four possible ways to be happy (Peterson, Park, & Seligman, 2005b).

Instructions

All of the questions reflect statements that many people would find desirable, but answer only in terms of whether the statement describes how you actually live your life. Please be honest and accurate.

1. My life serves a higher purpose.
   - ☐ Very much like me
   - ☐ Mostly like me
   - ☐ Somewhat like me
   - ☐ A little like me
   - ☐ Not like me at all
2. Life is too short to postpone the pleasures it can provide.
   - ☐ Very much like me
   - ☐ Mostly like me

- ☐ Somewhat like me
- ☐ A little like me
- ☐ Not like me at all

3. I seek out situations that challenge my skills and abilities.
   - ☐ Very much like me
   - ☐ Mostly like me
   - ☐ Somewhat like me
   - ☐ A little like me
   - ☐ Not like me at all
4. I keep score at life.
   - ☐ Very much like me
   - ☐ Mostly like me
   - ☐ Somewhat like me
   - ☐ A little like me
   - ☐ Not like me at all
5. Whether at work or play, I am usually "in a zone" and not conscious of myself.
   - ☐ Very much like me
   - ☐ Mostly like me
   - ☐ Somewhat like me
   - ☐ A little like me
   - ☐ Not like me at all
6. I am always very absorbed in what I do.
   - ☐ Very much like me
   - ☐ Mostly like me
   - ☐ Somewhat like me
   - ☐ A little like me
   - ☐ Not like me at all
7. I am rarely distracted by what is going on around me.
   - ☐ Very much like me
   - ☐ Mostly like me
   - ☐ Somewhat like me
   - ☐ A little like me
   - ☐ Not like me at all
8. I have a responsibility to make the world a better place.
   - ☐ Very much like me
   - ☐ Mostly like me
   - ☐ Somewhat like me
   - ☐ A little like me
   - ☐ Not like me at all
9. My life has a lasting meaning.
   - ☐ Very much like me
   - ☐ Mostly like me

☐ Somewhat like me
☐ A little like me
☐ Not like me at all

10. No matter what I am doing, it is important for me to win.
☐ Very much like me
☐ Mostly like me
☐ Somewhat like me
☐ A little like me
☐ Not like me at all

11. In choosing what to do, I always take into account whether it will be pleasurable.
☐ Very much like me
☐ Mostly like me
☐ Somewhat like me
☐ A little like me
☐ Not like me at all

12. What I do matters to society.
☐ Very much like me
☐ Mostly like me
☐ Somewhat like me
☐ A little like me
☐ Not like me at all

13. I want to accomplish more than other people.
☐ Very much like me
☐ Mostly like me
☐ Somewhat like me
☐ A little like me
☐ Not like me at all

14. I agree with this statement: "Life is short—eat dessert first."
☐ Very much like me
☐ Mostly like me
☐ Somewhat like me
☐ A little like me
☐ Not like me at all

15. I love to do things that excite my senses.
☐ Very much like me
☐ Mostly like me
☐ Somewhat like me
☐ A little like me
☐ Not like me at all

16. I love to compete.
☐ Very much like me
☐ Mostly like me

☐ Somewhat like me
☐ A little like me
☐ Not like me at all

Scoring

Assign 5 points for a "very much like me" response, 4 points for a "mostly like me" response, and so on, through 1 point for a "not like me at all" response. Your Orientation to Pleasure score is the sum of points for questions 2, 11, 14, and 15; your Orientation to Engagement score is the sum of points for questions 3, 5, 6, and 7; your Orientation to Meaning score is the sum of points for questions 1, 8, 9, and 12; and your Orientation to Victory score is the sum of points for questions 4, 10, 13, and 16.

Interpretation

What is the highest score of the four? (See Figure 4.1.) This is your dominant orientation. And what is the configuration of your scores? That is, are you "high" (>15) on all four orientations? If so, you are oriented toward a full life and are likely to be highly satisfied. Or are you "low" (< 9) on all four orientations? If so, you may have a more empty life and are likely to be dissatisfied. You might consider doing something different—anything!—in your life. And if you are high on one or two orientations, chances are that you are satisfied with life, although you might seek further opportunities for pursuing your signature way of being happy.

Figure 4.1. My Own Happiness Profile
Scores on each orientation to happiness can in principle range from a low of 4 ("not like me at all") to a high of 20 ("very much like me"). As can be seen, I am high on orientations to meaning and victory and especially high on an orientation to engagement, but I am quite low on an orientation to pleasure.

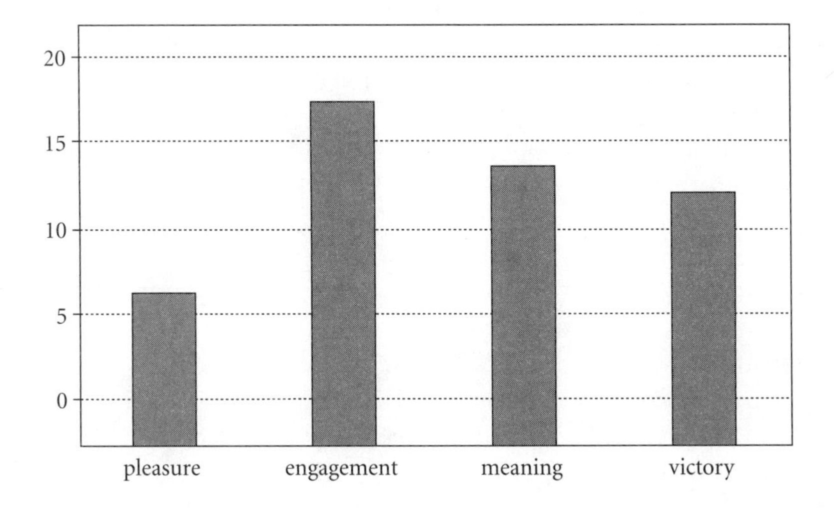

GLOSSARY

correlation coefficient (r): quantitative index of the degree to which two variables, if graphed, fall along a straight line.

depressive realism: theory proposing that depressed people see the world more accurately

desire theory: theory that happiness is a matter of getting what one wants, whether or not it involves pleasure

engagement: involvement in activities that produce flow

eudaimonia: idea that true happiness entails identifying one's inner self (demon), cultivating one's strengths and virtues, and living in accordance with them

experience sampling method (ESM): research method that uses an electronic beeper to signal research participants at random intervals, indicating that they should stop whatever they are doing, describe it, and respond to questions

happiness: everyday synonym for subjective well-being, life satisfaction, and the like

hard diagnostic test: foolproof measure, like for a disease

hedonism: doctrine emphasizing the maximizing of pleasure and the minimizing of pain

internal consistency (reliability): degree to which different measures of the same notion yield answers that agree

life satisfaction: overall cognitive appraisal that one's life is a good one

objective list theory: theory that happiness entails achieving objectively good things in the world, e.g., freedom from disease, material comfort, a career, friendships, children, education, knowledge, and so on

quality of life: overarching term for the emotions, experiences, appraisals, expectations, and accomplishments that figure into the good life

set-point (for happiness): genetically determined level of happiness, to which one returns after positive or negative emotional experiences

stability (test-retest reliability): degree to which a measure administered at different points in time yields answers that agree

subjective well-being: relatively high levels of positive affect, relatively low levels of negative affect, and the overall judgment that one's life is a good one

third variables: unmeasured factors that produce apparent but spurious associations between two variables

validity: degree to which a measure actually ascertains what it purports to measure

victory: winning at whatever matters most

RESOURCES

Books and Journals

Myers, D. G. (1993). *The pursuit of happiness.* New York: Avon.

Magem, Z. (1998). *Exploring adolescent happiness: Commitment, purpose, and fulfillment.* Thousand Oaks, CA: Sage.

Lykken, D. (2000). *Happiness: The nature and nurture of joy and contentment.* New York: St. Martin's.

Argyle, M. (2001). *The psychology of happiness* (2nd ed.). East Sussex, England: Routledge.

Cloninger, C. R. (2004). *Feeling good: The science of well-being.* New York: Oxford University Press.

Journal of Happiness Studies

Social Indicators Research

Articles

Diener, E., & Diener, C. (1996). Most people are happy. *Psychological Science, 7,* 181–185.

Myers, D. G., & Diener, E. (1995). Who is happy? *Psychological Science, 6,* 10–19.

Csikszentmihalyi, M. (1999). If we are so rich, why aren't we happy? *American Psychologist, 54,* 821–827.

Ryan, R. M., & Deci, E. L. (2000). On happiness and human potentials: A review of research on hedonic and eudaimonic well-being. *Annual Review of Psychology, 52,* 141–166.

Peterson, C., Park, N., & Seligman, M. E. (2005). Orientations to happiness and life satisfaction: The full life versus the empty life. *Journal of Happiness Studies, 6,* 25–41.

Web Sites

http://www.nunstudy.org. "The Nun Study is a longitudinal study of aging and Alzheimer's disease funded by the National Institute on Aging. Participants are 678 American members of the School Sisters of Notre Dame religious congregation who are 75 to 106 years of age."

http://www.authentichappiness.org. This Web site is associated with Martin Seligman's (2002) trade book on positive psychology, *Authentic Happiness*, and contains life satisfaction surveys that can be taken on-line.

http://www.eur.nl/fsw/research/happiness. "The World Database of Happiness is an ongoing register of scientific research on subjective appreciation of life. It brings together findings that are scattered throughout many studies and provides a basis for synthetic studies."

http://www.psych.uiuc.edu/~ediener. This is the University of Illinois Web site of Ed Diener, one of the world's leading investigators of life satisfaction and happiness.

http://www.cob.vt.edu/market/isqols. This is the Web site of the International Society for Quality-of-Life Studies, "an international society whose purpose[s] are to promote and encourage research in the field of quality-of-life (QOL) studies."

Films

A Christmas Carol (1951)

Dr. Seuss's How the Grinch Stole Christmas (1966)

Gandhi (1982)

Fast, Cheap, and Out of Control (1997)

ABC News Special: "The Mystery of Happiness: Who Has It . . . How to Get It" (1998)

Songs

"Don't Worry, Be Happy" (Bobby McFerrin)

"Girls Just Want to Have Fun" (Cyndi Lauper)

"Memories Are Made of This" (Dean Martin)

"Oh Happy Day" (Edwin Hawkins Singers)

"Walking on Sunshine" (Katrina & the Waves)

"With a Little Bit of Luck" (from *My Fair Lady*)

5 Positive Thinking

The difficult is done immediately; the impossible takes just a little longer.
—UNOFFICIAL MOTTO OF THE U.S. MARINE CORPS

It is time to move from an examination of how we feel to how we think. The topics of hope and optimism have been of interest to positive psychologists from the beginning and helped to set the stage for this new field. For many years, my own work as a psychologist focused on the consequences of positive (and negative) thinking. Let me describe two of the studies I conducted.

The first began in the mid-1980s, when I flew from Roanoke, Virginia, to Boston to Hanover, New Hampshire. My destination was Dartmouth College and, more specifically, the research archives of psychiatrist George Vaillant.[1] Vaillant for years had been responsible for guiding a unique investigation: the Harvard Study of Adult Development. It began in the late 1930s when researchers received funding from the Grant Foundation to study people who are well and who do well (Heath, 1945). Such a goal was as unusual then as it would have been anywhere until just a few years ago when positive psychology arrived on the scene to make a generic argument in favor of such investigations.[2]

This chapter is an updated and elaborated version of C. Peterson (2000), The future of optimism, *American Psychologist, 55*, 44–55.

1. Pronounced in Anglicized—not French—fashion: *val-yunt.*

2. It is not surprising that George Vaillant has become one of the leaders of positive psychology, and his many contributions are mentioned throughout this book.

Through the matchmaking of our mutual colleague Marty Seligman, I was fortunate enough to be invited by George Vaillant to use the study archives to investigate how styles of thinking early in life might be related to physical health later in life. There is plenty of speculation about such relations, and *mind-body interaction* has today reached clichéd status as something that "everyone knows" (chapter 9). But in the mid-1980s, as I gritted my teeth for my airplane flights, it was not so obvious that such relations existed or that they could be documented. If they were to be found, however, the Harvard Study archive was the best place to look.

The original researchers were at Harvard University, and they turned to the college deans to nominate the best and the brightest of the young men attending their elite school. Approximately 3% passed this test, and they were given extensive batteries of psychological and physical tests. They were interviewed about their childhoods. Information was carefully recorded.

These men have been followed ever since, with an attrition rate of essentially zero except for death. Although one can lament that the original sample was not more diverse—Harvard of the 1930s and 1940s after all had no female students and little demographic variety among its young men, who were mostly WASPs from the northeastern United States—the fact remains that there are almost no other prospective studies of how life unfolds over the adult decades. The Harvard Study has been a unique source of information about coping, wisdom, aging, mental health, and spirituality, among many other topics (e.g., Vaillant, 1977, 1983, 1995, 2002).

Almost all of the participants served in the U.S. armed forces during World War II. Some finished college first, and others interrupted their college studies to ship out to Europe or the Pacific. Regardless, most returned alive at the end of the war. In 1945, each responded to a questionnaire asking him to describe in his own words the "difficult wartime experiences" he had encountered.

It was these essays that I wanted to analyze because they were exactly the sort of written material that would allow me to describe the writer as more versus less optimistic. I read the essays of a randomly selected 99 young men—which were usually several hundred words long, uniformly sincere, often eloquent, and (I must say) highly legible—on the lookout for descriptions of bad events: setbacks, failures, frustrations, and disappointments. Everyone of course reported such events, but my attention was directed at how each writer explained their causes.

Did he do so by pointing to inherent flaws within himself and to factors that were chronic and pervasive? If so, I scored his essay at the pessimistic end of thinking. "I was not happy in the service [because of my] . . . intrinsic dislike for the military." Or did he explain bad events by distancing himself from their causes and circumscribing them? "I was in danger during the military attack [because] . . . I was not assigned a specific task that kept me in a single position." If so, I scored his essay at the optimistic end of thinking. Appreciate that these ratings capture whether a person believes that the future is something that can be different from the negative past (optimism) or simply its relentless reincarnation (pessimism).

For days, I sat alone in a room reading and coding these essays. I knew nothing else about the research participants, although this information was of course available to Vaillant, who later combined my ratings (after verification by my own research team back in Virginia) with his ratings of the health of the essay writers based on physical exams conducted every 5 years by the individuals' own doctors.

The results were straightforward and quite exciting. Thinking "good" as a young adult predicted being "well" 35 years later. The more optimistic young men were more likely to be in good health decades later (Peterson, Seligman, & Vaillant, 1988). The correlation between optimism and good health was not immediately evident, appearing first when the men were 40 years old and reaching its most-robust level at age 45 ($r = 0.37$).

This study was my initial foray into positive psychology. It convinced me that attention to the positive—in this case, positive thinking—could provide insight into life and more specifically that people who were optimistic (cheerful, hopeful, sanguine) were not buffoons but people who might have figured out something important about how to live the psychological good life (Peterson & Bossio, 1991).

My second foray into positive psychology solidified these conclusions. This was a research project headed by Harold Zullow at the University of Pennsylvania (Zullow, Oettingen, Peterson, & Seligman, 1988; Zullow & Seligman, 1990). The study was carried out as the U.S. presidential race of 1988 was heating up. In case you do not remember, this election pitted Vice President George H. Bush against Massachusetts governor Michael Dukakis.

The question of interest was whether the professed optimism of a presidential candidate would influence voters and the outcome of an election. At this point, we were thinking that optimism was often a beneficial stance for an individual, so this particular study promised to be intriguing because it tested whether optimism was contagious (in a good way) throughout society. We coded as optimistic or pessimistic the acceptance speeches by all major candidates at their party conventions in the previous presidential elections throughout the 20th century, as well as the degree to which negative events were a focus in these speeches. From 1900 (McKinley versus Bryan) through 1984 (Reagan versus Mondale), the candidate who focused less on negative events and expressed more optimism won 18 out of the 22 elections.

Honesty compels me to say that we did the same coding for Bush the Elder versus Dukakis, and we predicted before the election—based solely on our ratings—that Dukakis would win. So, make that 18 out of 23 elections won by the more-optimistic candidate. This is still a striking pattern that attracted a great deal of attention including I suspect from those who manage presidential campaigns. I have no inside information, but conspicuous about Bill Clinton circa 1992 was his upbeat and optimistic message to the American public:[3] "I'm from a place called Hope." In 1996, Bob Dole tried to counter with his own message: "I'm Bob Dole, and I'm the most optimistic man in America," but hopefulness rolled easier off Clinton's tongue.

Our attempts to distinguish presidential candidates based on their professed optimism has since been a total failure (e.g., Peterson & Lee, 2000). Each loudly proclaims himself to be an optimist and certainly more of an optimist than his opponent. Each says the sorts of things in speeches that end up being scored by us as hopeful. Again, I wonder if the results of our earlier study had anything to do with this new way of campaigning. Regardless, the conclusion follows that all things being equal, U.S. voters prefer an optimist over a pessimist as their leader, a conclusion consistent with the results of many other studies of everyday people leading their lives (Peterson, Maier, & Seligman, 1993).

Cognitive Psychology

Let me place research on optimism in a broader context within psychology, starting with some terminology and a little history. **Cognitive psychology** is the field that studies how people acquire, retain, transform, and use knowledge (Sternberg & Smith, 1988). Among its central concerns are processes like attention, perception, learning, memory, judgment, decision making, and problem solving. Over the years, psychology has flip-flopped with respect to the importance it has accorded cognition. The very first psychologists defined psychology as the study of the mind—an inherently cognitive endeavor. But the influential approach of behaviorism dismissed the importance of cognition and made psychology lose its mind (J. B. Watson, 1913).

Cognitive psychology is alive and well today because psychologists could not escape the importance of cognition. It is impossible to speak about human beings without referring to their capacity for knowledge. Even the simplest habits have mental aspects. Cognition underlies much of what we regard as uniquely human: language, personal identity, and culture. These processes help us cope with the demands of the world in various ways.

Cognition regained a prominent place within psychology during the 1960s, so forcefully that its reemergence has been dubbed the **cognitive revolution** (H. Gardner, 1985; Hilgard, 1987). Many place the beginning of modern cognitive psychology in 1967, when Cornell University psychologist Ulric Neisser published his groundbreaking *Cognitive Psychology.*

Even someone as brilliant as Neisser did not invent a field from scratch, and

3. Not far from Ann Arbor where I now live is the little town of Hell, Michigan. I would love to see the day when a presidential candidate from this town opens his stump speech by proclaiming, "I'm from a place called Hell."

as modern cognitive psychology took form, it fell into a way of describing the mind that had existed in the Western world for thousands of years, at least since the Athenian philosophers. Many believed that the mind was composed of a small number of rather independent faculties (e.g., memory, judgment, logic), each of which operated according to its own general principles regardless of the specific content or subject matter.[4] So, when psychologists studied learning and memory, they asked research participants to memorize and recall lists of nonsense syllables; when they studied judgment, they asked for opinions about trivial matters. If content is irrelevant, then why not make it simple?

There is one problem with this approach: Content does matter. Cognitive psychologists today believe there to be few content-free or content-independent psychological processes. Instead, the mind is composed of numerous cognitive modules each linked to a specific content and obeying its own sorts of rules (Tooby & Cosmides, 1989). For example, the processes responsible for memory differ according to the type of information to be recalled—faces, odors, or narrative sequences—and also how and when the information was initially encountered.

I am providing this background to explain why positive thinking has only recently received serious attention from research psychologists. Whether the content of thought was positive, negative, or neutral was not deemed to be relevant—thinking was simply thinking—and thus researchers often studied how people thought about innocuous (neutral) topics. However, one of the most important properties of the content of thought is whether it concerns positive or negative matters, pleasant or unpleasant stimuli, good or bad topics. Even when researchers did not go out of their way to find such effects on cognition, a huge number of findings nonetheless accumulated showing that the hedonic tone of thought is a potent determinant of all sorts of cognitive processes.

The Pollyanna Principle

In 1978, Margaret Matlin and David Stang summarized findings like those presented in Table 5.1. As you can see, positive versus negative is a pervasive way of organizing the content of thought and guiding cognitive processes. Often the positive seems to be the default. Apparently, in our minds, we are all residents of Lake Woebegone, where everyone and everything is above average.

Matlin and Stang termed this striking positive selectivity in thought the Pollyanna Principle, elevating Boucher and Osgood's (1969) earlier "Pollyanna hypothesis" to a full-blown law of the mind in recognition of the ubiquity of such

4. Here we find a rationale for why students are told to study academic disciplines that seem remote to their eventual lives: topics like geometry, Latin, and logic. It has long been believed that whatever lessons are learned in such courses strengthen the relevant cognitive faculty and generalize to other domains of life. Psychologists have shown that this is an altogether false assumption, but it is still a common justification in educational circles (Lehman & Nisbett, 1990).

Table 5.1. Evidence in Support of the Pollyanna Principle

- People seek out positive stimuli and avoid negative stimuli.
- People take longer to recognize what is unpleasant or threatening than what is pleasant and safe.
- People report that they encounter positive stimuli more frequently than they actually do.
- People believe that good events are more likely to occur than negative events, even when the objective probabilities are the same.
- Pleasant stimuli are perceived as larger in size than unpleasant or neutral stimuli, even when they are not.
- People communicate good news more frequently than bad news.
- In English, pleasant words have higher frequencies of use than negative words.
- In English, the positive member of an antonym pair (e.g., optimism) entered the language before the negative member (e.g., pessimism).
- The positive member of antonym pairs is likely to be linguistically more basic.
- In free association (when one is asked to say whatever comes into one's mind in response to a cue), people are more likely to respond with a positive word than a negative one.
- When making lists of items—spewing them out—pleasant items appear before negative ones. For example, if we are asked to list people we know, we list our friends before our enemies.
- In such lists, people list more positive items than negative ones.
- People are more accurate in recalling positive events than negative events.
- People are more accurate in learning and recalling positive words than neutral or negative words.
- As time passes, events are remembered as increasingly pleasant.
- People make the judgment "good" more rapidly to pleasant items than the judgment "bad" to unpleasant items.
- People believe that most of the events in their lives are positive ones.
- Most people believe that they are above average on positive traits like intelligence, driving ability, sense of humor, attractiveness, and optimism.
- In general, people render positive judgments about most individuals, groups, topics, things, and circumstances. Even distilled water, which has no chemicals to trigger taste buds, is rated by most people as being "rather pleasant" in its taste.

From Matlin & Stang, 1978

findings. Whether this is really a principle is beside the point. Suffice it to say that pleasantness predominates in thought.

Selective Attention to the Negative

The predominance of the positive in cognition per se should not be confused with another "principle" of thought: the selective attention to the negative that often characterizes consciousness. Psychologists usually define consciousness as awareness of one's current environment and mental life. A precise definition is elusive because awareness after all is a synonym for consciousness. Most theorists nevertheless agree that consciousness includes awareness of particular sensations, perceptions, needs, emotions, and thoughts. Cognition in contrast is a more-inclusive term that includes those thoughts of which we are aware at any moment but also all of the processes that underlie our thoughts, some of which can be brought into awareness and some of which cannot (Nisbett & Wilson, 1977).

Ornstein (1988) called consciousness the front page of the mind. Like a newspaper, consciousness contains what is new, surprising, and important to us. In normal waking consciousness, each of us monitors our ongoing experience. When something notable occurs, we bring it front and center into awareness. Not everything makes it into consciousness, however, and normal waking consciousness is therefore characterized by *selective attention* (Johnston & Dark, 1986). Many of the tasks we perform during the day are automatic, and we perform them without being fully aware. Consider driving your car down an interstate highway. You drive perfectly well, but you are not attending to everything going on about you. Oops, watch out! There is an abandoned car on the shoulder up ahead. Suddenly your consciousness is engaged. There is a problem to be solved. You check your rearview mirror, put on your turn signal, and swing into the passing lane. The potential crisis is averted, and you return to what you were thinking about—which may have been nothing.

The appeasement of doubt is the motive for thought, wrote philosopher Charles Peirce (1878) more than a century ago, meaning that consciousness is engaged when something puzzling occurs. Many of these puzzling occurrences are negative and indeed urgent. Dennett (1991) followed this line of reasoning to sketch how the capacity for consciousness might have evolved in the first place. Imagine an animal that focused its sensory systems on threats and then mobilized its resources to deal optimally with them. Natural selection would presumably favor such orientation and mobilization, not just to specific stimuli but more generally. An animal that provided itself with occasional updates about its environment and internal state would have a survival advantage over an animal that did not. Periodic vigilance of this sort would eventually give rise to regular exploration of the outer and inner worlds, obtaining information for its own sake, because it might someday be valuable.

What has resulted in the modern human being is a creature much more aware of what is going wrong or could go wrong than what is going well. Another philosopher, Gilbert Ryle (1949), observed that competence requires no comment. We do not frequently stop and make the conscious observation that things are as they should be. Meanwhile, the default to the positive plays itself out on a nonconscious level and is shown in all the ways described by the Pollyanna Principle. Perhaps our selective attention to the negative explains why positive psychology is not such an obvious field and why some people think that life is tragic and that most individuals are flawed (chapter 1). Think about it.

In the rest of this chapter, I discuss positive thinking—optimism and hope—but keep in mind the tension in thought that I have just sketched. If by positive thinking we mean thoughts that are front and center in consciousness, positive thinking often shows itself about negative topics. To study optimism and hope, it is often useful to see how people think and respond in the wake of challenge, setback, and failure.

What Is Optimism?

Over the years, optimism as a style of thinking has had at best a checkered reputation. From Voltaire's (1759) Dr. Pangloss, who blathered that we live in the best of all possible worlds, to Porter's (1913) Pollyanna, who celebrated every misfortune that she and others faced, to contemporary celebrities who spin embarrassing news into something wonderful, so-called optimism has often given thoughtful people pause. Connotations of naïveté and denial have adhered to the notion. In recent years, thanks to research by positive psychologists, optimism occupies a more respected position, even among the sophisticated.

Indeed, as exemplified in the Harvard Study described earlier, optimism has demonstrable benefits, and pessimism has drawbacks. Optimism, conceptualized and assessed in a variety of ways, has been linked to positive mood and good morale; to perseverance and effective problem solving; to academic, athletic, military, occupational, and political success; to popularity; to good health; and even to long life and freedom from trauma. Pessimism, in contrast, foreshadows depression, passivity, failure, social estrangement, morbidity, and mortality. These lines of research are surprisingly uniform, so much so that an optimism bandwagon has been created, within positive psychology and among the general public. There is growing interest in how optimism can be encouraged among the young and how pessimism can be reversed among the old.

Let me start with a review of what we have learned about optimism, but my eventual purpose here is to discuss its future both as a research interest of positive psychologists and as a social value. I believe that these futures are entwined. Optimism as a research topic began to flourish in the contemporary United States precisely when people in general started to become more hopeful about the future.

The danger of this coupling is twofold. First, some of the documented benefits of optimism—at least as typically studied—may be bounded. In some circumstances, it can have costs, although contemporary researchers rarely look for these qualifying conditions. Second, even if it needs to be contextualized, optimism as a research topic deserves to be more than a fad. A sophisticated optimism can be most beneficial to individuals in trying circumstances, and it behooves psychologists to learn as much as possible about the topic right now, so that these lessons can be deployed in other times and places where they can do the most good.

A useful definition of optimism was offered by anthropologist Lionel Tiger (1979): "a mood or attitude associated with an expectation about the social or material future—one which the evaluator regards as socially desirable, to his [or her] advantage, or for his [or her] pleasure" (p. 18). An important implication of this definition, one drawn out by Tiger himself, is that there can be no single or objective optimism, at least as characterized by its content, because what is considered optimism depends on what the individual regards as desirable. Optimism is predicated on evaluation—on given affects and emotions, as it were.

Contemporary approaches usually treat it as a cognitive characteristic—a goal, an expectation, or a causal attribution—which is sensible so long as we remember that the belief in question concerns future occurrences about which individuals have strong feelings. Optimism is not simply cold cognition, and if we forget the emotional flavor that pervades optimism, we can make little sense of the fact that it is both motivated and motivating. People may well *need* to feel optimistic about matters. We should not be surprised that optimism and pessimism can have defensive aspects as well as ego-enhancing ones (Norem, 2001; Norem & Cantor, 1986).

Along these lines, we can ask whether people can be generically optimistic, that is, hopeful without specific expectations. Although at odds with conventional definitions, the possibility of free-floating optimism deserves scrutiny. Some people readily describe themselves as optimistic yet fail to endorse expectations consistent with this view of themselves. This phenomenon may merely be a style of self-presentation, but it might additionally reflect the emotional and motivational aspects of optimism without any of the cognitive aspects. Perhaps extraversion or positive affectivity is related to this cognitively shorn version of optimism.[5]

Optimism as Human Nature

Discussions of optimism take two forms. In the first, it is posited as an inherent part of human nature, either to be praised or decried. Early approaches to optimism as human nature were decidedly negative. Writers as diverse as Sophocles and Nietzsche argued that it prolongs human suffering: better to face the hard facts of reality. This negative view of positive thinking lies at the heart of Sigmund Freud's influential writings on the subject.

In *The Future of an Illusion*, Freud (1927/1953c) decided that optimism was widespread but illusory. For Freud, optimism helps to make civilization possible, particularly when institutionalized in the form of religious beliefs about an afterlife. But it comes with a price: the denial of our instinctual nature and hence the denial of reality. Religious optimism compensates people for the sacrifices neces-

5. It is interesting and relevant here that the word *optimism*, when translated into Chinese or Korean, is usually rendered not as *positive expectation* but as *cheerfulness*.

sary for civilization and is at the core of what Freud termed the "universal obsessional neurosis" of humanity.

Freud proposed that optimism is part of human nature but only as a derivative of the conflict between instincts and socialization. Some individuals—Freud mentioned the educated and, in particular, neurologists—did not need the illusion of optimism, although the masses were best left with their "neurosis" intact and the belief that God was a benevolent father who would shepherd them through life and beyond. Only with this belief and its associated fear that God would retaliate against them if they transgressed would people be law abiding. According to Freud, a rational prohibition against murder is not compelling to the masses. It is more persuasive to assert that the prohibition comes directly from God.

As psychodynamic ideas became popular, Freud's formula equating (religious) optimism and illusion had widespread impact. Although no mental health professional asserted that extreme pessimism should be the standard of health—pessimism of this sort was presumably due to fixation at an early psychosexual stage—most theorists pointed to the *accurate* perception of reality as the epitome of good psychological functioning: "The perception of reality is called mentally healthy when what the individual sees corresponds to what is actually there" (Jahoda, 1958, p. 6). Similar statements were offered by the entire gamut of influential psychologists and psychiatrists from the 1930s through the 1960s: Allport, Erikson, Fromm, Maslow, Menninger, and Rogers, among many others (see Snyder, 1988, and S. E. Taylor, 1989, for thorough reviews).

Never mind that one cannot know what is "actually there" in the future until it happens, and never mind that Freud acknowledged that an illusory belief was not necessarily a false one. "Reality testing" became the hallmark of the healthy individual, and psychotherapists took as their task the need to expose people to reality, however painful it might be. This is reasonable as far as it goes, especially when applied to here-and-now reality, but the twist is that only the most modest expectations about the future could pass muster as realistic, and anything else was regarded as denial (Akhtar, 1996).

Matters began to change in the 1960s and 1970s in light of research evidence showing that most people are not strictly realistic or accurate in how they think. Cognitive psychologists documented an array of shortcuts that people take as they process information (Kahneman & Tversky, 1973). And as already described, Matlin and Stang (1978) surveyed hundreds of studies showing that language, memory, and thought are selectively positive.

The skeptical fan of a harsh reality might dismiss these findings as demonstrating only how widespread optimistic illusions are, but it proved more difficult to dismiss results showing that psychologically healthy people in particular showed the positivity bias. Richard Lazarus (1983) described what he called "positive denial" and showed that it can be associated with well-being in the wake of adversity. Aaron Beck (1967) began to develop his influential cognitive approach to depression and its treatment, a cornerstone of which was the assertion that depression was a cognitive disorder characterized by negative views about the self, experience, and the future—that is, pessimism and hopelessness.

At least early in the course of his theory development, Beck was still influenced by the prevailing view of mental health as grounded in the facts of the matter because he described depressives as illogical. By implication, nondepressives are logical—i.e., rational information processors—although there was no good reason for this assumption. Part of cognitive therapy is the design of experiments to "test" negative views, but the procedures are geared to guaranteeing the results of these experiments. Furthermore, cognitive therapists never attempt to falsify the occasionally positive view that a depressive might bring to therapy (Beck, Rush, Shaw, & Emery, 1979). In any event, Beck (1991) later modified his theory by acknowledging that nondepressed individuals were not necessarily "logical" in their thinking, because they can bring a positive bias toward their ongoing experiences and expectations for the future.

Anthony Greenwald's (1980) statement likening human nature to a totalitarian regime was another turning point in how optimism was regarded by psychologists. According to Greenwald, the self can be regarded as an organization of knowledge about one's history and identity. This organization is biased by information-control strategies analogous to those used by totalitarian political regimes. Everyone engages in an ongoing process of creating and revising her own personal history (McAdams, 1993). The story each of us tells about ourselves is necessarily egocentric: Each of us is the central figure in our own narratives. Each of us takes credit for good events and eschews responsibility for bad events. Each of us resists changes in how we think. In sum, the ego maintains itself in the most self-flattering way possible, and it has at its disposal all of the psychological mechanisms documented by Matlin and Stang (1978).

Yet another turning point in the view of optimism was Shelley Taylor and Jonathan Brown's (1988) literature review of research on positive illusions. They described a variety of evidence showing that people in general are biased toward the positive, the exceptions being those who are anxious or depressed. Taylor (1989) elaborated these ideas in her book *Positive Illusions*, where she proposed that the pervasive tendency to see oneself in the best possible light is a sign of well-being. She distinguished optimism as an illusion from optimism as a delusion: Illusions are responsive, albeit reluctantly, to reality, whereas delusions are not (Taylor, Collins, Skokan, & Aspinwall, 1989).

The strongest statement that optimism is an inherent aspect of human nature is found in Tiger's (1979) book *Optimism: The Biology of Hope.* He located optimism in the biology of our species and argued that it is one of our most defining and adaptive characteristics. Tiger proposed that optimism is an integral part of human nature, selected for in the course of evolution, developing along with our cognitive abilities and indeed the human capacity for culture.

Tiger even speculated that optimism drove human evolution. Because it entails thinking about the future, it first appeared when people began to think ahead. Once people began to think ahead, they could imagine dire consequences, including their own mortality. Something had to develop to counteract the fear and paralysis that these thoughts might entail, and that something was optimism. By this view, optimism is inherent in our makeup, not a derivative of some other psychological characteristic. Tiger went on to characterize optimism as easy to think, easy to learn, and pleasing—what modern evolutionary psychologists describe as an "evolved psychological mechanism" (Buss, 1991, 1995).

Optimism as an Individual Difference

At the same time that optimism as human nature was being discussed in positive terms by theorists like Lazarus, Beck, Taylor, and Tiger, other psychologists who were interested in individual differences began to address optimism as a characteristic which people possess to varying degrees. These two approaches are compatible. Our human nature provides a baseline optimism, of which individuals show more versus less. Our experiences further influence the degree to which we are optimistic or pessimistic.

There are numerous treatments of optimism as an individual difference. A definitive history of their antecedents is beyond the scope of this chapter (see Peterson & Park, 1998), but certainly I should acknowledge several intellectual precursors, starting with Alfred Adler's (1910/1964, 1927) "fictional finalism," which is based on Vaihinger's (1911) "as-if" philosophy. Kurt Lewin's (1935, 1951) field theory and George Kelly's (1955) personal construct theory provided influential frameworks for understanding how beliefs—optimistic, pessimistic, or whaever—channeled people's behavior. Julian Rotter's (1954, 1966) social learning theory and especially his generalized expectations (locus of control and trust) legitimized an approach to personality in terms of broad expectancies about the future.

Also important was the waning of traditional stimulus-response (S-R) approaches to learning and their replacement with cognitive accounts which emphasized expectancies (Peterson, Maier, & Seligman, 1993). According to S-R accounts, learning entails the acquisition of particular motor responses in particular situations. Learning by this view entails the forging of associations between stimuli and responses, and the more closely these are linked together in experience (contiguity), the more likely learning is to occur. Under the sway of behaviorism, learning was thought to have no central (cognitive) representation.

Arguing against S-R views of learning were findings that the associations acquired in conditioning are strengthened not by contiguity per se but by contingency: the degree to which stimuli provide new information about responses (Rescorla, 1968). S-R theory stresses only temporal contiguity between the response and the reinforcer, viewing the individual as trapped by the momentary co-occurrences of events. If a response is followed by a reinforcer, it is strengthened even if there is no real (causal) relationship between them. In contrast, the contingency view of learning proposes that individuals are able to detect cause-effect relationships, separating momentary noncausal relationships from more enduring true ones (Wasserman & Miller, 1997).

So, learning at its essence entails the discovery of "what leads to what" (Tolman, 1932). Because learning of this sort necessarily extends over time, it is sensible to view it in central (cognitive) terms. Although there is disagreement about the fine details of these central representations, it is clear that contingency learning is a critically important psychological process, linked to subsequent motivation, cognition, and emotion. Most theorists in this tradition have opted to regard the representation of contingency learning as an expectation, in order to explain how it is generalized across situations and projected across time. As I will explain shortly, most approaches to optimism as an individual difference adopt this approach, regarding optimism as a generalized expectation that influences psychological processes in which learning is involved.

I will now briefly survey several of the currently popular approaches to optimism as an individual difference. Not by coincidence, each has an associated self-report questionnaire that allows efficient research. The correlates of these cognates of optimism have therefore been extensively investigated. Optimism, however measured, is usually linked to desirable characteristics, like happiness, perseverance, achievement, and good health.

Most studies are cross-sectional, but the demonstrated correlates are usually interpreted as consequences of optimism (chapter 4). Researchers have paid relatively little attention to the origins of this individual difference and in particular to the possibility that its putative outcomes are alternatively or additionally its determinants. They have also paid little attention to the larger web of belief in which optimism resides (Quine & Ullian, 1978). And the same lack of attention is evident with respect to why optimism has such a wide array of correlates. Indeed, optimism is what I call a "Velcro construct." Everything sticks to it for reasons that are not always obvious.

Dispositional Optimism

Psychologists Michael Scheier at Carnegie-Mellon University and Charles Carver at the University of Miami (1992) have studied a personality variable that they identify as dispositional optimism: the global expectation that good things will be plentiful in the future and bad things scarce. Scheier and Carver's overriding perspective is in terms of how people pursue goals, defined as desirable values. To them, virtually all realms of human activity can be cast in goal terms, and people's behavior entails the identification and adoption of goals and the regulation of actions vis-à-vis these goals. They therefore refer to their approach as a "self-regulatory model" (Carver & Scheier, 1981).

Optimism enters into self-regulation when people ask themselves about impediments to the achievement of the goals they have adopted. In the face of difficulties, do people nonetheless believe that goals can be achieved? If so, they are optimistic; if not, pessimistic. Optimism leads to continued efforts to attain the goal, whereas pessimism leads to giving up.

Scheier and Carver (1985) measure optimism (versus pessimism) with a brief self-report questionnaire called the Life Orientation Test (LOT). Representative items, with which respondents agree or disagree, include:

1. In uncertain times, I usually expect the best.
2. If something can go wrong for me it will. (reverse-scored)

Positive expectations are usually combined with (reverse-scored) negative expectations, and the resulting measure is investigated with respect to health, happiness, and coping with adversity (e.g., Carver et al., 1993; Carver & Scheier, 2003; Scheier & Carver, 1987, 1992; Scheier, Carver, & Bridges, 2001; Scheier et al., 1989, 1999; Strack, Carver, & Blaney, 1987). Results show that dispositional optimism is moderately linked to desirable outcomes and in particular to active and effective coping (Scheier, Weintraub, & Carver, 1986).[6]

Explanatory Style

With my colleagues, I have approached optimism in terms of an individual's characteristic **explanatory style**—how one explains the causes of bad events (Buchanan & Seligman, 1995). As detailed earlier when I described the Harvard Study of Adult Development and the presidential election study, people who explain bad events in a circumscribed way—with external, unstable, and specific causes—can be described as optimistic, whereas those who favor internal, stable, and global causes can be described as pessimistic.

The notion of explanatory style emerged from the attributional reformulation of the learned helplessness model (Abramson, Seligman, & Teasdale, 1978). Briefly, the original helplessness model proposed that following experience with uncontrollable aversive events, animals and people become helpless—passive and unresponsive—presumably because they have "learned" that there is no contingency between actions and outcomes (Maier & Seligman, 1976). This learning is represented as a generalized expectancy that future outcomes will be unrelated to their responses. It is this generalized expectation of response-outcome independence that produces later helplessness.

Explanatory style was added to the helplessness model to better account for the boundary conditions of human helplessness following uncontrollability. When is helplessness general, and when is it circumscribed? People who en-

6. Remember that a moderate correlation in psychological research is worth taking seriously (chapter 4).

counter a bad event ask "why?" Their causal attribution determines how they respond to the event. If it is a stable (long-lasting) cause, helplessness is chronic. If it is a pervasive (global) cause, helplessness is widespread. If it is an internal cause, self-esteem suffers.

All things being equal, people have a habitual way of explaining bad events—an explanatory style—and this explanatory style is posited as a distal influence on helplessness following adversity (Peterson & Seligman, 1984). Explanatory style can be measured with a self-report questionnaire called the Attributional Style Questionnaire (ASQ), which gives respondents hypothetical events involving themselves and asks them to provide "the one major cause" of each event if it were to happen to them (Peterson et al., 1982). Respondents then rate these provided causes along dimensions of internality, stability, and globality. The ratings are combined, separately for bad events and good events. Explanatory style for bad events is usually independent of explanatory style for good events. Explanatory style based on bad events usually has more robust correlates than explanatory style based on good events, although correlations are typically in the opposite direction (Peterson, 1991).

A second way of measuring explanatory style is with a content analysis procedure—the CAVE (an acronym for Content Analysis of Verbatim Explanations)—that allows written or spoken materials to be scored for naturally occurring causal explanations (Peterson, Schulman, Castellon, & Seligman, 1992). Researchers identify explanations for bad events, extract them, and present them to judges, who rate them along the scales of the ASQ. The CAVE technique makes possible longitudinal studies after the fact, so long as spoken or written materials can be located from early in the lives of individuals for whom long-term outcomes of interest are known.

Remember that the generalized expectation of response-outcome independence is hypothesized as the proximal cause of helplessness, even though research in this tradition has rarely looked at this mediating variable. Rather, researchers measure explanatory style and correlate it with outcomes thought to revolve around helplessness: depression, illness, and failure in academic, athletic, and vocational realms. Invariably, an optimistic explanatory style is associated with good outcomes (Peterson & Park, 1998), with one apparent exception: Relative to pessimists, those with an optimistic explanatory style underestimate the likelihood of future bad events[7] (Peterson & Vaidya, 2001). Optimists believe that they can forestall such events through their own actions, and—as other research shows—sometimes they are right (Peterson & de Avila, 1995).

As explanatory style research has progressed and the theory has been modi-

7. Even this exception is called into question by the research of psychologist Lisa Aspinwall and her colleagues, who have shown that optimists can be quite accurate in their use of diagnostic information when they see it as personally relevant and when it allows them to choose among alternative courses of action (e.g., Aspinwall & Brunhart, 1996; Aspinwall & Richter, 1999).

fied, the internality dimension has seen less emphasis. It has more inconsistent correlates than do stability or globality; it is less reliably assessed; and there are theoretical grounds for doubting that it has a direct impact on expectations per se (Peterson, 1991). Indeed, internality may well conflate self-blame and self-efficacy, which would explain why it fares poorly in empirical research. In a modification of the helplessness reformulation, Abramson, Metalsky, and Alloy (1989) emphasized only stability and globality.

The most important recent chapter in helplessness research was the reframing of explanatory style by Marty Seligman (1991) in his book *Learned Optimism*, in which he described how his lifelong interest in what can go wrong with people changed into an interest in what can go right (Seligman, 1975). Research on helplessness was flipped into an interest in what Seligman called optimism, although he could have called it mastery, effectance, or control. His terminology is justified by the central concern in helplessness theory with expectations, but it is worth emphasizing yet again that these expectations tend not to be explicitly studied. The Nikki Story notwithstanding (chapter 2), perhaps the real origin of positive psychology dates to Seligman's reframing of explanatory style years earlier.

Peterson, Maier, and Seligman (1993) asserted that everything learned about helplessness (pessimism) informs what we know about optimism, but this statement is glib and at odds with positive psychology as we have since articulated it. Optimism is *not* simply the absence of pessimism, and well-being is *not* simply the absence of helplessness. Research on learned optimism (i.e., optimistic explanatory style) will not be as substantial as it might be if it remains closely tied to helplessness theory. I will return to this point later in the chapter.

On one level, the Scheier and Carver approach is congruent with our approach. LOT correlates and ASQ/CAVE correlates are strikingly similar, and measures of the two constructs tend to converge when they are—rarely—examined together in the same study. However, a closer look reveals some critical differences. The LOT is a pure measure of expectation—very close to the dictionary definitions of optimism and pessimism. An optimistic expectation leads to the belief that goals can be achieved, although it is neutral with respect to how this will happen. In contrast, the ASQ measures perceived causality, so it is additionally influenced by people's beliefs about *how* goals are brought about. Said another way, optimistic explanatory style is more infused with agency than is dispositional optimism.

Hope

These two visions of optimism—expectation and agency—are integrated in a third approach, studies of hope by psychologist Rick Snyder (1994) at the University of Kansas. Snyder traced the origins of his thinking to the earlier work of Averill, Catlin, and Chon (1990) and of Stotland (1969), in which hope was cast in terms of people's expectations that goals could be achieved. According to Snyder's view, goal-directed expectations are composed of two separate components. The first is *agency*, and it reflects someone's determination that goals can be achieved. The second is identified as *pathways*: the individual's belief that successful plans can be generated to reach goals. The second component is Snyder's novel contribution, not found in any other formulation of optimism as an individual difference.

Hope so defined is measured with a brief self-report scale (Snyder et al., 1991). Representative items, with which respondents agree or disagree, include:

1. I energetically pursue my goals. (agency)
2. There are lots of ways around any problem. (pathways)

The responses are combined by averaging, and scores have been examined with respect to goal expectancies, perceived control, self-esteem, positive emotions, coping, and achievement. The typical results show that hope is beneficial, as expected (Snyder, 2000, 2002).

Issues in Optimism

Let me turn to the future of optimism, focusing on issues that deserve attention both by positive psychologists and by people in general. To set the stage for this discussion, let me introduce a distinction between two types of optimism (Tiger, 1979).

Little Optimism Versus Big Optimism

Little optimism subsumes specific expectations about positive outcomes: "I will find a convenient parking space this evening." **Big optimism** refers—obviously—to larger and less-specific expectations: "Our nation is on the verge of something great." The big versus little optimism distinction reminds us that optimism can be described at different levels of abstraction and that it may function differently depending on the level. Big optimism may be a biologically given tendency filled in by culture with a socially acceptable content; it leads to desirable outcomes because it produces a general state of vigor and resilience. In contrast, little optimism may be the product of an idiosyncratic learning history; it leads to desirable outcomes because it predisposes specific actions that are adaptive in given situations.

Said another way, the mechanisms linking optimism to outcomes might vary according to the type of optimism on focus. For example, one of the striking correlates of optimism is good health. This link seems to reflect several different mediators, including immunological robustness (Kamen-Siegel, Rodin, Seligman, & Dwyer, 1991; Scheier et al., 1999; Segerstrom, Taylor, Kemeny, & Fahey, 1998; Udelman, 1982), absence of negative mood (Weisse, 1992), and health-promoting behavior (Peterson, Seligman, Yurko, Martin, & Friedman, 1998). The big versus little distinction helps us to understand which pathways are involved in given instances of well-being (Peterson & Bossio, 1991). The trajectory of severe illnesses such as AIDS or cancer may be better predicted by big optimism working through the immune system and mood, whereas the onset of disease and the likelihood of traumatic injuries might be more influenced by little optimism working through behavior and concrete lifestyle (Peterson et al., 2001).

What exactly is the relationship between little and big optimism? Empirically, the two are no doubt correlated, but it is possible to imagine someone who is a little optimist but a big pessimist, or vice versa. It is also possible to imagine situations in which big optimism has desirable consequences but not little optimism, or vice versa. The determinants of the two may be different, and encouraging them therefore requires different strategies.

Researchers need to approach the big versus little distinction more deliberately. On the face of it, the dispositional optimism measure of Carver and Scheier and the hope measure of Snyder tap big optimism because they ask people to respond to generalizations about the future. In contrast, measures of explanatory style—especially the CAVE technique—tap a smaller optimism because the focus is on specific causal explanations for concrete events. Studies to date have rarely included more than one optimism measure at a time, and those that do have been more interested in how measures agree than with the possibility that they have different patterns of correlates.

Again, What Is Optimism?

In addition to the little-big distinction, there are other theoretical issues that need to be addressed. Let me repeat that optimism is not just a cognitive characteristic; it has inherent emotional and motivational components (Carver & Scheier, 1990). Researchers often seem to regard emotion and motivation as outcomes that are separate from optimism per se. At least in the case of big optimism, this assumption may not be warranted.

We ask different questions if we see emotion and motivation as part of big optimism. How does optimism *feel* (Peterson, 1999)? Is it happiness, joy, mild mania, or simply contentment? Is the optimistic person in flow, actively engaged in what she is doing but not self-consciously mindful (chapter 3)? Positive psychologists have argued that positive emotions broaden a person's cognitive and behavioral repertoire (chapter 3). Is this true as well for big optimism? We know that optimism is linked to perseverance, but is it associated as well with a good choice of goals, those that lend themselves to pursuit and eventual attainment? As Ryan, Sheldon, Kasser, and Deci (1996) discussed, not all goals are of equal merit for different individuals, given their particular psychological makeup and context. Is optimism therefore associated with the choice of goals that facilitate authenticity in this sense?

There are probably activities that satisfy a person's need to be optimistic but are—ultimately—pointless, the psychological equivalent of junk food. Are video games, the Internet, mystery novels, gambling, and collecting thimbles or matchbooks analogous to empty calories, activities whose pursuit consumes time and energy because they engage optimism but eventually leave us with nothing, individually or collectively?

Optimism and Pessimism

Another issue has to do with the relationship between optimism and pessimism. They are usually regarded as mutually exclusive, but surprisingly there is evidence that they are not. For example, the optimism and pessimism items in Scheier and Carver's LOT prove somewhat independent of one another. This lack of correlation can be regarded as a methodological nuisance, but it is worth considering the possibility that some people expect both good things *and* bad things to be plentiful. Such individuals could be described as having hedonically rich expectations as opposed to misbehaving on a questionnaire. Are they living life fully, or are they ambivalent and confused? Distinguishing between optimism and pessimism allows an intriguing question to be investigated: Are there effects of optimism above and beyond those of the absence of pessimism (Robinson-Whelen, Kim, MacCallum, & Kiecolt-Glaser, 1997)?

Along these lines, as I have already noted, explanatory style derived from attributions about bad events is usually independent of explanatory style based on attributions about good events. The former is usually identified as *the* optimistic explanatory style, in part because the correlates are stronger, but a step back reveals this to be curious. Attributions about bad events (presumably linked to expectations about such events) are identified as optimistic or pessimistic, whereas attributions about good events are not. One would think it should be just the opposite, a point made by Snyder (1995) when he described explanatory style as a strategy of excuse making. This criticism is blunted—but only somewhat—when internality-externality is removed from the meaning of the construct.

The concern of helplessness theorists with attributions about bad events is explained by the outcomes of historical interest: depression, failure, and illness. Optimism is correlated with their absence, and pessimism with their presence. Explanatory style research has led to increased understanding of these problematic states. But appreciate that the zero point of these typical outcome measures signifies, respectively, *not* being depressed, *not* failing, and *not* being ill. If we want to extend findings past these zero points to offer conclusions about emotional fulfillment, achievement, and wellness, we may or may not be on firm ground. Perhaps explanatory style based on attributions about good events would then be more relevant. In any event, positive social science needs to study not just independent variables that pertain to strength but also appropriate dependent variables (chapter 1).

As you know, optimism research helped to usher in positive psychology, but perhaps it is time for positive psychology to shape how optimism research unfolds. Psychological well-being cannot be viewed simply as the absence of distress and conflict, any more than good health is the absence of disease (chapter 9). Discussions of what well-being entails are ongoing in various research and theoretical literatures (e.g., Barsky, 1988; Seeman, 1989; Vaillant, 2003), and these need to inform lines of inquiry concerned with optimism. I believe that big optimism might be a more potent influence on well-being than little optimism.

In the typical demonstration of learned helplessness, animals or people exposed to aversive events which they cannot control show deficits at problem solving relative to research subjects exposed to aversive events which they can control and to subjects given no prior experience with aversive events; these latter two groups do not differ from one another (Peterson, Maier, & Seligman, 1993). Prior experience with controllable events confers no apparent benefit. Perhaps this is because the baseline assumption is that control exists, or to say it another way, individuals are optimistic unless there is a reason not to be.

If the test tasks are changed, however, prior experience with controllable events does have a demonstrable effect: enhanced persistence at a difficult or unsolvable task. Theorists have discussed this opposite manifestation of learned helplessness under such rubrics as *learned hopefulness, learned industriousness, learned mastery, learned relevance*, and *learned resourcefulness* (e.g., Eisenberger, 1992; Mackintosh, 1975; Rosenbaum & Jaffe, 1983; Volpicelli, Ulm, Altenor, & Seligman, 1983; Zimmerman, 1990). Outcome measures have to allow the benefit to be manifest.

In choosing appropriate measures, it behooves optimism researchers to examine the literature on resilience (Anthony & Cohler, 1987). Here we see an interest in children growing up in dire circumstances who not only survive but thrive. Their resilience is only evident if we choose measures that reflect thriving. Resilience depends critically on a supportive relationship with another person. Could the same be true of optimism in the face of adversity? Much of the optimism literature is curiously asocial. Researchers do not even distinguish between private versus public (socially communicated) optimism, which would seem to be an important distinction. The emphasis is quite individualistic, but optimism may be as much an interpersonal characteristic as an individual one.

The Reality Basis of Optimism

One more important issue is the relationship between optimism and reality. Optimism can have costs if it is too unrealistic. Consider "unrealistic optimism" as described by Weinstein (1989) with respect to people's perceptions of their personal risk for illnesses and mishaps. When people are asked to provide a percentage estimate in comparison to their peers that they will someday experience an illness or injury, most underestimate their risks. The average individual sees himself as below average in risk for a variety of maladies, which of course cannot be.

This phenomenon is appropriately lamented because it might lead people to neglect the basics of health promotion and maintenance. More generally, optimism in the form of wishful thinking can distract people from making concrete plans about how to attain goals (Oettingen, 1996). Unrelenting optimism precludes the caution, sobriety, and conservation of resources that accompany sadness as a normal and presumably adaptive response to disappointment and setback (Nesse & Williams, 1996).

For another example, consider the personality variable of "John Henryism" (James, Hartnett, & Kalsbeek, 1983; James, LaCroix, Kleinbaum, & Strogatz, 1984). Inspired by the railroad worker of folklore, who won a contest against a steam hammer but died thereafter of a heart attack, this individual difference reflects the degree to which African Americans believe that they can control all events in their lives solely through hard work and determination. Individuals who score high on the John Henryism measure but are low in socioeconomic status are apt to be hypertensive (James, Strogatz, Wing, & Ramsey, 1987).

Constant striving for control over events without the resources to achieve it can take a toll on the individual who faces an objective limit to what can be attained regardless of how hard she works. If optimism is to survive as a social virtue, then the world must have a causal texture that allows this stance to produce valued rewards. If not, people will channel their efforts into unattainable goals and become exhausted, ill, and demoralized. Or people may rechannel their inherent optimism into attainable but undesirable goals.

Positive social science should not become so focused on optimism as a psychological characteristic that it ignores how it is influenced by external situations, including other people. This danger is clear in the case of little optimism, where we can easily decide that a given belief is wrong. It is less easy to see in the case of big optimism, but even here we can use the broader vantage of history or aggregate data to realize that some widely shared big goals are just as unrealistic as the expectation that someone can lead a life free of illness and injury.

Simply put, people should be optimistic when the future can be changed by positive thinking but not otherwise. This advice reflects what Seligman (1991) called a "flexible or complex optimism," a psychological strategy worth exercising when appropriate as opposed to a reflex or habit over which we have no control:

> You can choose to use optimism when you judge that less depression, or more achievement, or better health is the issue. But you can also choose not to use it, when you judge that clear sight or owning up is called for. Learning optimism does not erode your sense of values or your judgment. Rather it frees you to . . . achieve the goals you set. . . . Optimism's benefits are not unbounded. Pessimism has a role to play, both in society at large and in our own lives; we must have the courage to endure pessimism when its perspective is valuable. (p. 292)

Particularly in the case of little optimism, people need to undertake a cost-benefit analysis of the belief in question.

When there is room for doubt, people should fill the gap with hope. Big optimism can be more hopeful than little optimism, which has a greater press to be accurate. I assume that big and little optimism are redundant for many people. Positive psychologists should think about how to help people disaggregate the two in a useful way, to teach them how to have dreams but not fantasies—illusions without delusions. The prior question, of course, is what other psychological characteristics need to be in place for an individual to exercise flexible optimism?

The Cultivation of Optimism

Despite the cautions I have just raised, there is abundant reason to believe that optimism—big, little, and in between—is useful because positive expectations can be self-fulfilling. How can we set optimism in place for the young? Gillham, Reivich, Jaycox, and Seligman (1995) created an intervention—the Penn Resiliency Program (PRP)—using strategies from the cognitive-behavioral therapy realm to teach grade-school children to be more optimistic. Results to date suggest that this kind of training makes subsequent episodes of depression less likely. I point out again that the absence of depression should not be the only outcome that interests us. We also want to know if optimistic children end up happy and healthy, wealthy and wise, with rich social networks and rewarding pursuits.

If big optimism is truly part of human nature, then we need to be concerned with somewhat different matters. First, how can optimism be channeled in one direction rather than another? As I will discuss shortly, optimism in the United States has long been entwined with individualism. Is there any way to harness our inherent optimism to include a concern with the commons? Can optimism about one's neighbor ever be made as satisfying as optimism about oneself?

Religion can provide some answers. Indeed, Tiger (1979) argued that religions arose at least in part to tap the biologically given need of people to be optimistic. Religious thought lends itself particularly well to big optimism because of its certainty. Tiger observed, much as Freud (1927/1953c) did decades earlier, that religion is more amenable to optimism than is science, which is explicitly tentative and probabilistic in its pronouncements.

Secular social scientists interested in optimism often ignore the close link between optimism and religion, with the exception of an investigation by Sethi and Seligman (1993) which studied the causal explanations contained in religious texts. Across Christian, Jewish, and Muslim texts, conservative tracts were more optimistic than liberal ones. Can we generalize from this result, juxtaposing it with research on the benefits of optimism, and conclude that fundamentalists are better off than their reformed colleagues? This possibility deserves further investigation. We can only hope that researchers will be willing to follow the data where they might lead (Schumaker, 1992).

Second, how can we prevent optimism from being thwarted? Here there is no mystery. Stress and trauma of all sorts take their toll on optimism, and to the degree that people can lead less-terrible lives, optimism would be served. We do not want to create a life without challenge because perseverance can only be encouraged when people meet and surmount difficulties, but we need to make sure that difficulties can indeed be surmounted.

Also contributing to optimism is social learning. I assume that optimism can be acquired by modeling—vicariously, as it were—so we need to be attentive to the messages our children receive about the world and how it works. Explanatory styles of parents and children converge, and although part of the reason for this may be shared experiences or genetic predispositions, it could also reflect the wholesale transmittal of belief systems via modeling (Seligman et al., 1984). And what about messages from the popular media, which are as mixed vis-à-vis optimism as they are on any other subject? Rags-to-riches stories—unrealistic parables suggesting that anything and everything wonderful is possible—are juxtaposed on the evening news with stories about the horrors that lurk around every corner (Levine, 1977).

Third, what can we do to rekindle optimism that has been thwarted? We know that cognitive therapy as developed by Aaron Beck effectively targets pessimistic explanatory style in such a way as to alleviate depression and prevent its recurrence (Seligman et al., 1988). Again, studies like this need to be enriched by additional outcome measures. Does cognitive therapy merely get the person back to a nondepressed mode, or does it further enrich the individual? Does it affect big optimism as much as little optimism?

The human potential movement began in the 1960s by using "therapy" techniques with normal people in an attempt to make them supernormal (Tomkins, 1976). Whether this succeeded is debatable, but is there some equivalent here with respect to optimism training? What happens when cognitive-behavioral therapy is used with nonpessimistic people? Do superoptimists result, and what are they like? Are they the epitome of well-being or caricatures of positive thinking like Dr. Pangloss and Pollyanna? You can find out for yourself by trying the exercise at the end of this chapter.

Optimism and Society

Do cultures or historical eras differ in their characteristic optimism? The answer is probably no insofar as our focus is on the biggest optimism. Big optimism makes society possible, and a pessimistic civilization cannot survive for long. Indeed, societies make available to people countless ways of satisfying their need to be optimistic about matters:

> One of the recurrent themes of human culture has to do with contests—with play which is given an effortful structure and in which some more

> or less entertaining activity takes place but with an uncertain outcome. Countless humans affiliate with teams, boxers, billiard players, gymnasts, skaters, racers, runners, divers and cheer for them to win and feel despondent when they lose. . . . Contests have a great deal to do with the matter of optimism and they may well be one of the commonest expressions of a way of behaving which . . . is common anyway. Contests are usually optional. . . . Certainly no one is required to take the fan's role. (Tiger, 1979, p. 250)

But of course many of us do take on this role, and even fans of the Chicago Cubs find a way to be optimistic about next season, when of course everything will be different (McAdams, 2005).

Virtually all societies have contests, but striking differences exist across societies in terms of most other ways of feeling and being optimistic. As noted, the goals considered desirable will vary from person to person, group to group, culture to culture. Other than a nebulous belief in progress and some human universals like contests, there is considerable variation across cultures in the content of optimism (e.g., Chang, 1996; Heine & Lehman, 1995; Lee & Seligman, 1997). Here is another fruitful topic for examination by researchers and members of a given society. What are the goals that a society holds up as most desirable, and how optimistic are members of that society vis-à-vis those goals?

In the United States, the biggest goals of most people include individual choices, individual rights, and individual fulfillments. Americans are greatly occupied with what they can and cannot accomplish in their everyday lives and in particular with what they can acquire. In a capitalist society, people's acquisition of material goods and their concomitant fascination with the money that allows them to do so represent a socially sanctioned way of satisfying the optimistic force that organizes the entire culture. The downside of optimism satisfied in this way is the stranglehold of greed.

In the United States today, we live with shallow materialism (chapter 7). People even turn themselves into commodities. We want to be marketable, to keep our options open, to cash in on what happens to us, even our misfortunes. "Because it will look good on my resume" is a rationale I increasingly hear from my students as an explanation for why they are pursuing some seemingly selfless and good activity. No wonder people are alienated, and no wonder depression is on the rise among young adults (Robins et al., 1984).

Only the crassness of this rationale is new. There has long been a tradition in the United States of self-help books promising people success if only they think positively (Starker, 1989). As emphasized, though, optimism need not be attached just to selfish concerns, and it need not pertain just to individual agency (Wallach & Wallach, 1983). Collective agency—collective optimism, if you will—would seem a desirable goal to add to those associated with individual optimism (Snyder, Cheavens, & Sympson, 1997). A resurgence of traditional religion, volunteerism, or philanthropy would facilitate this change, so long as people do not ask what is in it for them (Seligman, 1988).

In his book *The Positive Thinkers*, Donald Meyer (1988) traced the history of a uniquely American brand of optimism by discussing its influential proponents: Phineas Quimby, Mary Baker Eddy, Dale Carnegie, Norman Vincent Peale, and Ronald Reagan, among others:

> The popular psychology of positive thinking . . . flourished among people able, for reasons of culture and politics, to imagine that the only thing wrong with their lives was within themselves. If they could learn how to manage their own consciousness . . . the world outside would prove positive in its response. Of course this world was always that of the United States, not of mankind, but the sense of God's abundance waiting only to be received . . . had always taken for granted the greater readiness of Americans, and hence America, for such grace. (p. 382)

What Meyer identified is a very big optimism, rich and fuzzy in its meaning. Numerous other isms adhere to this politically laden form of American optimism, notably capitalism, materialism, and individualism, as I have already discussed.

"Positive thinking" as examined by Meyer (1988) has additionally been defined by what it opposes: Catholics, women, minorities, the lower classes, intellectuals, homosexuals, and even government itself. Victim blaming is common (W. Ryan, 1978). And pessimists are singled out as especially objectionable: Some of you may remember former Vice President Spiro Agnew's alliterative attacks on the "nattering nabobs of negativism." It would be wise for positive psychologists to anticipate that segments of the general public may hear pronouncements about the importance of optimism in terms of these unfortunate political connotations, as an inadvertent code for exactly the opposite of what is being conveyed. I hope that I have made one point clear: Optimism and its benefits exist for all of us, as long as we approach it in an evenhanded way.

EXERCISE *Learning Optimism on the Hot Seat*

Although there are ample reasons to be optimistic, urging you to be more hopeful is as empty as telling you "don't worry, be happy." What you additionally need are strategies for putting this advice into action. In this chapter, I mentioned Aaron Beck's cognitive therapy, which teaches the depressed to be more optimistic in order to alleviate their depression, and the Penn Resiliency Program, which similarly teaches nondepressed children to be more optimistic in order to prevent depression in the future.

Each of these interventions takes place over an extended period of time—weeks or months—and is embedded in what clinicians call a "therapeutic alliance" with a trusted clinician or facilitator, who leads the individual through the necessary steps, devising and evaluating homework assignments in which various strategies for thinking more optimistically are perfected. Learning optimism is hard work and takes practice to perfect. The good news is that the pertinent techniques are well specified and demonstrably effective.

The following exercise presents you with one such technique that you might want to try out if you are the kind of person who gets thrown for a loop whenever you face failure or disappointment. Chances are that what spirals you into a bad mood or worse following a setback is a pessimistic style of thinking about the setback that you then carry into the future where it demoralizes you in other situations.

You need to interrupt your immediate reaction to a setback and then to think about it in a less-pessimistic way. Suppose your boss or teacher passes you in the hallway without saying hello or even acknowledging you. That of course makes you feel bad, but then what? A pessimistic person might start to ruminate:

> She hates me.
> I deserve to be hated.
> I am—after all—a complete loser, and she knows it.
> I am going to be fired (or flunked).
> If only I were smarter, this would not happen to me.
> I will never be able to support myself.
> I will die miserable and alone.

Let us leave aside the possibility that this is a realistic appraisal.[8] Let us assume that you have performed well enough in the past at work or at school that you are not a complete loser. What you need to do in this case is to head off your ruminative spiral before it goes too far. Are there different—more optimistic—ways to make sense of being ignored?

> She was having a bad day.
> She was in a hurry.
> She was thinking about something else.
> I like her, but what a space cadet!
> She wasn't wearing her glasses, which are really thick ones. Maybe she didn't see me.

8. Years ago, I spoke to a novice therapist, who described one of his new cases. The client's presenting problem was anxiety centering around her worry that her daughter's new boyfriend might be molesting her young granddaughter. "What's your plan?" I asked. "I'm not sure," he answered. "Maybe you can give me some advice. My first impulse is to help her stop worrying, maybe with a thought-stopping technique. That's pretty effective for unwanted thoughts, right?" I almost yelled, "Don't even think about it. She might be right, and you have a moral and legal obligation to get to the bottom of it immediately. Her anxiety is a red flag, not a symptom." It is fortunate that everything worked out just fine. I am mentioning this conversation to emphasize that pessimism sometimes is warranted and that the most adaptive way of thinking is to be flexible enough to recognize the situations that call for it.

I just got a radically different haircut.
I'm so good-looking that I intimidate people.

Maybe this last interpretation is as pathological as making a catastrophe out of the incident, but you get the general idea about how to reinterpret hurtful but ambiguous events so that they do not do psychological damage.

One of the PRP techniques is designed to help you offer benign (optimistic) interpretations in the moment (Reivich, Gillham, & Shatté, 2004; Reivich & Shatté, 2003). It is called the *hot seat technique* or, alternatively, the *rapid-fire technique*. Its purpose is to teach you how to dispute rapidly pessimistic thoughts. It is a powerful strategy for learning optimism but one that develops only through practice. No one is a natural disputer, and you will learn to do this with speed by trying it out.

You can practice the hot seat technique best if you enlist the help of a friend, but you can do it yourself if you have some index cards that you can shuffle. In either case, make a list of several dozen common events that push your buttons and bum you out. I chose the being-ignored-in-the-hallway example because it used to be something that would upset me for the rest of the day whenever it happened. Give the list to your friend, or write each event on a separate index card.

Then have your friend choose at random one upsetting event and present it to you, or pull out one of your index cards and read aloud what is written on it. Try to identify the immediate, automatic, and pessimistic thoughts that the event triggers. Then, as rapidly as you can, do *one* of these three things:

- evaluate the evidence for the pessimistic thought: "Am I going to get fired? Probably not, because I just got a good raise last week."
- think of an alternative explanation: "My boss is not one for small talk."
- put the thought in perspective: "The people I work with are not my family, and besides, my Mom really loves me."

Say out loud your response. Then do this again with a second event, and a third, and so on. Over time, you will get better at this technique, even to the point of making it automatic.

There are some caveats here. I have already stressed one: the possibility that your pessimistic reaction contains a kernel of truth. If your boss or teacher looks you square in the face and says, "You are a complete loser," reminding yourself that your Mom doesn't think so may not be the right response. Instead, you should ask for a more specific evaluation.

A related pitfall in developing and using this technique is that you may minimize the bad situation to the point that you deny its significance. Although part of optimistic thinking is not to catastrophize an event, there really are bad things in the world. You should not deny them or their import when they occur.

Finally, although many of the optimistic examples just offered appropriately turn the event back on other people or circumstances, being optimistic is not the same thing as shirking responsibility. Remember the point in this chapter that the internality (my fault) versus externality (their fault) of causal beliefs is not nearly as important as whether you generalize them over time and situations, so when you think of alternative explanations, try to think of circumscribed interpretations rather than externalized ones. In my case, I learned to handle the being-ignored-in-the-hallway event by thinking, "I didn't say hello first." Now, I greet people I know in a loud voice, and I receive a return greeting 100% of the time. No one ignores me in the hallway any more, because I don't let them.

GLOSSARY

big optimism: expectations about highly general—even vague—positive outcomes
cognition: thoughts of which we are aware at any moment as well as all of the processes that underlie our thoughts
cognitive psychology: field that studies how people acquire, retain, transform, and use knowledge
cognitive revolution: 1960s return to prominence within psychology of cognition
consciousness: awareness of one's current environment and mental life; particular sensations, perceptions, needs, emotions, and thoughts
dispositional optimism: global expectation that good things will be plentiful in the future and bad things scarce
explanatory style: tendency to believe that different events have the same sorts of causes
hope: determination that goals can be achieved coupled with beliefs that successful plans can be generated to reach goals
little optimism: expectations about specific positive outcomes
optimism: mood or attitude associated with the expectation of a desirable, advantageous, or pleasurable future
Pollyanna Principle: pervasive positive selectivity in thought

RESOURCES

Books and Journals

Tiger, L. (1979). *Optimism: The biology of hope.* New York: Simon & Schuster.
Taylor, S. E. (1989). *Positive illusions.* New York: Basic.
Seligman, M. E. P. (1991). *Learned optimism.* New York: Knopf.
Gillham, J. E. (Ed.) (2000). *The science of optimism and hope: Research essays in honor of Martin E. P. Seligman.* Radnor, PA: Templeton Foundation Press.
Peterson, C., & Bossio, L. M. (1991). *Health and optimism.* New York: Free Press.

Seligman, M. E. P., Reivich, K., Jaycox, L., & Gillham, J. (1995). *The optimistic child.* Boston: Houghton Mifflin.

Carver, C. S., & Scheier, M. F. (1981). *Attention and self-regulation: A control-theory approach to human behavior.* New York: Springer-Verlag.

Snyder, C. R. (Ed.). (2000). *Handbook of hope: Theory, measures, and applications.* San Diego, CA: Academic.

Piper, W. (1930). *The little engine that could.* New York: Platt & Munk.

Articles

Peterson, C. (2000). The future of optimism. *American Psychologist, 55,* 44–55.

Peterson, C., Seligman, M. E. P., & Vaillant, G. E. (1988). Pessimistic explanatory style is a risk factor for physical illness: A thirty-five-year longitudinal study. *Journal of Personality and Social Psychology, 55,* 23–27.

Zullow, H., & Seligman, M. E. P. (1990). Pessimistic rumination predicts defeat of presidential candidates, 1900 to 1984. *Psychological Inquiry, 1,* 52–61.

Web Sites

http://www.psy.miami.edu/faculty/ccarver and http://www.psy.cmu.edu/faculty/scheier. These two Web sites describe the studies of dispositional optimism by Charles Carver at the University of Miami and Michael Scheier at Carnegie-Mellon University, leading investigators of optimism and its consequences

http://www.positivepsychology.org/research.htm. This Web site describes our research on optimistic explanatory style.

http://www.psych.ku.edu/faculty/rsnyder/hoperesearch.htm. This is the Hope Research Web page at Kansas University and describes the work of C. Rick Snyder, one of the leading investigators of positive thinking.

http://www.wish.org. This is the Web site of the Make a Wish Foundation, which grants "the wishes of children with life-threatening medical conditions to enrich the human experience with hope, strength, and joy."

Films

Pollyanna (1960)
Rocky (1976)
Mask (1985)
Forrest Gump (1994)
The Shawshank Redemption (1994)
Apollo 13 (1995)
A&E *Biography*: "Thomas Edison" (2000)
ABC *Primetime*: "63 Reasons to Hope: The Babies of 9/11" (2002)
Seabiscuit (2003)
A Very Long Engagement (2004)

Songs

"I Will Survive" (Gloria Gaynor)
"My Future's So Bright, I Gotta Wear Shades" (Timbuk 3)
"This Night Won't Last Forever" (Sawyer Brown)
"Wishin' and Hopin'" (Dusty Springfield)

6

Character Strengths

Happiness is the aim of life,
[But] virtue is the foundation of happiness.
—THOMAS JEFFERSON (1819)

At the Positive Psychology Center at the University of Pennsylvania, my unofficial title is director of virtue, which sounds Orwellian. But the title should be taken at face value, because it refers to an ongoing project I have been conducting on character strengths and virtues—positive traits like curiosity, humor, kindness, leadership, and religiousness.

"How can we help youth to realize their full potential?" The project began with this question posed by representatives of the Mayerson Foundation. Positive psychology seemed an ideal perspective from which to answer it, given the field's concern with the promotion of what is best among people, as opposed to the prevention of what is most problematic (Seligman, 2002; Seligman & Csikszentmihalyi, 2000). As I have taken pains to explain (chapter 1), the past concern of psychology with human problems is of course understandable and will not be abandoned any time in the foreseeable future, but psychologists interested in promoting human potential need to pose different questions from their predecessors who assumed a disease model (Peterson & Park, 2003). Among the most critical tools for positive psychologists are a vocabulary for speaking about the good life and assessment strategies for investigating its components.

Under the auspices of Marty Seligman at the University of Pennsylvania, a conference was held in 1999, where youth development practitioners from around the United States described different programs designed to encourage healthy development. Despite the merits of these individual programs, it became clear that they lacked common ways of characterizing optimal development and agreed-upon strategies for assessing the effectiveness of their interventions. Without comparable concepts and measures, it was impossible to generalize across programs to identify active ingredients that could be deliberately embodied in further interventions. Critically needed was a common vocabulary as well as related measurement tools.

The Values in Action (VIA) Institute[1] was therefore created by the Mayerson Foundation in 2000 to provide the conceptual and empirical means of describing positive youth development. The decision was made to focus on good character in light of ongoing societal concerns with the topic (Hunter, 2000). What does "good character" mean, and how can it be measured?

These goals framed the VIA project from its very beginning, when I joined with Marty Seligman to assemble a team of social scientists to produce the **VIA Classification of Character Strengths** (Peterson & Seligman, 2004). We remain greatly interested in positive youth development (e.g., Park, 2004a, 2004b; Park & Peterson, 2004), but we now believe that our project has even wider applicability. It can guide program design and evaluation not only in the youth development field but in any arena in which optimal development is the goal (Peterson & Park, 2004). We further believe that the information provided by the research guided by the VIA project is worth taking seriously by philosophers interested in virtue (Darwall, Gibbard, & Railton, 1992).

At one time, psychologists were greatly interested in character—what it meant and how it could be cultivated (McCullough & Snyder, 2000). But the topic fell out of favor. First, there was a growing sophistication among psychologists about how personal values could unintentionally pervade "objective" research and theory. This made researchers shy away from pronouncements concerning the psychological components of the good life.

Second, Gordon Allport, the major personality trait theorist in 20th-century U.S. psychology, banished the term "character" from academic discourse concerning personality (Nicholson, 1998), arguing that character was a philosophical matter rather than a psychological one (Allport, 1921, 1927; Allport & Vernon, 1930). The traits he urged psychologists to study were presumably objective entities stripped of moral significance and linked to "adjustment" but not imbued with inherent value.

Allport's argument reflected the positivism sweeping social science and its rigid distinction between fact and value. *Fact* was the province of science, and *value*

1. Because sometimes I have too much time on my hands, once the VIA Institute was named, I went surfing on the Internet and discovered other VIA Institutes. Most seem to be home-grown militia groups—that's scary company. Several promote character education—that's much less scary. And my favorite VIA Institute, other than our own, is one that gives awards to convenience store clerks for bravery; maybe these are the employees who forget that only $25 in cash is on hand at any given moment.

was the province of philosophy. Traits were therefore part of psychology, whereas character was not. Although Allport's argument won the day, not all of his contemporaries agreed. John Dewey (1922/1998), in particular, thought that psychology's empirical methods could profitably inform discussions of character and value by philosophers. The VIA project falls squarely within the Dewey vision.

Basic Issues in Studying Good Character

For our work on the VIA project to begin, important issues needed to be resolved. First was how to approach good character. Is character defined by what someone does *not* do, or is there a more active meaning? Does character—however we define it—exist in degrees, or is it just something that one happens to have or not? Is character a singular characteristic of an individual, or is it composed of multiple aspects?

We decided to regard good character as a family of positive dispositions, characteristics like perspective, teamwork, kindness, and hope. To convey the plurality of good character, we took to calling its components **character strengths**. We assumed that the various character strengths are in principle distinct from one another, that a person can be high on one strength yet low or middling on others. We assumed that character strengths are trait-like in the sense of being individual differences with a modicum of stability and generality. However, we did not assume that they are fixed or necessarily grounded in immutable biogenetic characteristics. In keeping with a fundamental premise of positive psychology, we assumed that good character is more than bad character negated or minimized. Rather, character strengths must be defined and assessed in their own right.

Second, because good character and its components are morally esteemed, we worried that we were entering a domain so value-laden that our project was doomed from the start. Perhaps good character is little more than a social construction, existing in the eye of the beholder and functioning mainly as a projection of someone's idiosyncratic likes and dislikes. A less-extreme but still daunting objection is that the valued components of character are so thoroughly contextualized that generalizing across important social contrasts like age, gender, social class, national origin, and ethnicity is impossible. To handle these legitimate challenges, we reminded ourselves of the stance taken by positive psychology: that human goodness and excellence are as authentic (as "real") as distress and disease (chapter 1). If we are willing to regard problems as something more than a dysphoric world view, we should be just as willing to assume that strengths of character have bases in the actual conduct of people.

Once we accepted that character indeed exists in the world, it became an empirical question whether or which strengths of character are culturally bound. Some are of course recognized only in some settings; punctuality as a positive trait has no meaning in a culture that lacks widely available and reliable means of keeping time. But in other cases, the possibility that there may be universal values and virtues deserved to be taken seriously (e.g., Bok, 1995; Comte-Sponville, 2001; MacIntyre, 1984; S. H. Schwartz, 1994).

Our own surveys of widely influential religious and philosophical traditions (i.e., Confucianism, Taoism, Buddhism, Hinduism, Athenian philosophy, Judaism, Christianity, and Islam) found that certain core virtues were widely endorsed (Dahlsgaard, Peterson, & Seligman, 2005). Specifically, within these traditions, there was near-universal recognition and praise of the virtues of wisdom, courage, humanity, justice, temperance, and transcendence. Biswas-Diener (in press) confirmed in focus groups that the nonliterate Maasai (in western Kenya) and Inughuit (in northern Greenland) recognized and celebrated these same core virtues.[2] We were encouraged that a nonarbitrary classification of ubiquitously valued character strengths was possible.

A third issue we confronted was whether to wed our emerging classification to an a priori theory of good character, drawn from philosophy or psychology. We found Aristotle's (2000) account of virtue in *The Nicomachean Ethics* a powerful one, and we were similarly impressed by Jahoda's (1958) monograph on positive mental health and Erikson's (1963, 1982) well-known account of psychological maturity in terms of psychosocial virtues (chapter 9). Also intriguing were evolutionary accounts of "the moral animal," which is us (e.g., Wright, 1994). However, we decided not to adopt any given theory as our explicit framework because none of these could be fully evaluated in light of hard evidence. As I have already explained, our project was triggered in part by the lack of empirical tools.

We therefore labeled the project a classification as opposed to a taxonomy. The technical distinction is that a *classification* tries to be descriptive—demarcating a domain and describing its instances—whereas a *taxonomy* is based on a deep theory that explains relationships among these instances (Bailey, 1994). Positive psychology may someday produce a theory of good character that can undergird a classification like the one we created, just as Darwinian theory eventually was used to make sense of Linnaean classification, but this is a future goal.

A fourth issue we addressed was how detailed we wanted the entries in our

2. There were culture-specific nuances with respect to how strengths and virtues were manifest. So, a Maasai elder reported that bravery was recognized among his people, that it was celebrated when shown, and that there existed cultural rituals that nurtured it. A young man was considered brave once he single-handedly killed a lion. When asked if he himself were brave, the elder replied, "I once was brave, but I no longer need to be." When asked to elaborate, he explained, "My son has killed a lion." Apparently, among the Maasai, bravery is a characteristic not simply of the individual but of the individual's family. This account may seem esoteric to those of us in the West, but it corresponds to what we learned from interviews with award-winning firefighters (Peterson & Seligman, 2004). Despite being singled out for valor, all of them said that the award really belonged to the entire team with whom they had worked, including the captains who never entered burning buildings but instead stayed outside in constant radio contact to make decisions about how the firefighters inside should proceed. The team as a whole was brave.

classification to be. Our identification of core virtues suggested that we might opt for only six entries, but these proved too abstract given our measurement goals. Although these core virtues each define a coherent family of character strengths, there is acknowledged heterogeneity within each family. For example, the virtue of humanity includes character strengths that we identify as kindness and as love. We can imagine people who epitomize one strength but not the other. So, despite conceptual overlap, these distinctions are possible and important.

Along these lines, we found that people spontaneously talked about the components of good character in more-specific terms like curiosity, fairness, and religiousness and not in the more-abstract terms of core virtues (e.g., wisdom, justice, and transcendence). The "natural concepts" used to describe good character are strengths of character and not core virtues (Rosch, Mervis, Gray, Johnson, & Boyes-Braem, 1976). Finally, there already existed research literatures that addressed many of the strengths of character that we eventually included in the classification, and by focusing on this more-specific level, we were able to benefit from what had already been learned.

Identification of Character Strengths

After taking positions on these issues, we set about creating the entries for our classification. We reviewed pertinent literatures that addressed good character—from psychiatry, youth development, character education, religion, philosophy, organizational studies, and of course psychology—with the goal of identifying candidate strengths. We also looked at the character strengths explicitly mentioned in an array of cultural products: popular songs, greeting cards, bumper stickers, obituaries and testimonials, mottoes and credos, and personal ads in newspapers. We identified virtue-relevant messages in *Saturday Evening Post* covers by Norman Rockwell, graffiti, Tarot cards, the profiles of Pokémon characters, and the Hogworts residence halls in the Harry Potter books.

Our goal was to leave no stone unturned in assembling an exhaustive list of character strengths. From the many candidate strengths identified, we winnowed the list by combining redundancies and applying criteria like these. The character strength

- is ubiquitous: is widely recognized across cultures
- is fulfilling: contributes to individual fulfillment, satisfaction, and happiness broadly construed (chapter 4)
- is morally valued: is valued in its own right and not for tangible outcomes it may produce
- does not diminish others: elevates others who witness it, producing admiration, not jealousy (Keltner & Haidt, 2003)
- has a nonfelicitous opposite: has obvious antonyms that are "negative"

- is trait-like: is an individual difference with demonstrable generality and stability
- is measurable: has been successfully measured by researchers as an individual difference
- is distinct: is not redundant (conceptually or empirically) with other character strengths
- has paragons: is strikingly embodied in some individuals
- has prodigies: is precociously shown by some children or youth
- can be selectively absent: is missing altogether in some individuals (Peterson, in press)
- has enabling institutions: is the deliberate target of societal practices and rituals that try to cultivate it (Park & Peterson, in press d)

Space does not permit a strength-by-strength discussion of how these criteria are met, but you can find a detailed presentation in Peterson and Seligman (2004).

The VIA Classification of Character Strengths and Virtues

The VIA Classification contains 24 strengths of character organized under the six core virtues already described. Here are sketches of the virtues and the strengths.

Strengths of wisdom and knowledge include positive traits related to the acquisition and use of information in the service of the good life. In psychological language, these are cognitive strengths. Many of the strengths in the classification have cognitive aspects—e.g., social intelligence, fairness, hope, humor, and religiousness—which is why many philosophers concerned with virtue consider wisdom or reason as the chief virtue making all others possible. However, there are five character strengths in which cognition is especially salient:

1. *creativity*: thinking of novel and productive ways to do things; includes artistic achievement but is not limited to it
2. *curiosity*: taking an interest in all of ongoing experience; finding all subjects and topics fascinating; exploring and discovering
3. *love of learning*: mastering new skills, topics, and bodies of knowledge, whether on one's own or formally; obviously is related to the strength of curiosity but goes beyond it to describe the tendency to add systematically to what one knows
4. *open-mindedness*: thinking things through and examining them from all sides; not jumping to conclusions; being able to change one's mind in light of evidence; weighing all evidence fairly
5. *perspective*: being able to provide wise counsel to others; having ways of looking at the world that make sense to the self and to other people

Strengths of courage entail the exercise of will to accomplish goals in the face of opposition, external or internal. Some philosophers have regarded virtues as corrective because they counteract some difficulty inherent in the human condition, some temptation that needs to be resisted, or some motivation that needs to be checked or rechanneled. It is debatable whether all character strengths are corrective in one or more of these senses, but the following four strengths in the classification clearly are:

6. *authenticity*: speaking the truth but more broadly presenting oneself in a genuine way; being without pretense; taking responsibility for one's feelings and actions
7. *bravery*: not shrinking from threat, challenge, difficulty, or pain; speaking up for what is right even if there is opposition; acting on convictions even if unpopular; includes physical bravery but is not limited to it
8. *persistence*: finishing what one starts; persisting in a course of action in spite of obstacles; "getting it out the door"; taking pleasure in completing tasks
9. *zest*: approaching life with excitement and energy; not doing things halfway or halfheartedly; living life as an adventure; feeling alive and activated

Strengths of humanity include positive traits manifest in caring relationships with others, what Taylor et al. (2000) described as dispositions to tend and befriend. The entries in this virtue class resemble those identified as justice strengths, with the difference being that strengths of humanity are brought to bear in one-to-one relationships, whereas those of justice are most relevant in one-to-many relationships. The former strengths are interpersonal, the latter broadly social. Three of the strengths in the classification exemplify positive interpersonal traits:

10. *kindness*: doing favors and good deeds for others; helping them; taking care of them
11. *love*: valuing close relations with others, in particular those in which sharing and caring are reciprocated; being close to people
12. *social intelligence*: being aware of the motives and feelings of other people and the self; knowing what to do to fit into different social situations; knowing what makes other people tick

Strengths of justice are broadly social, relevant to the optimal interaction between the individual and the group or the community. As the group shrinks in size and becomes more personalized, the strengths of justice converge with the one-on-one strengths of humanity. We maintain the distinction by proposing that strengths of justice are strengths *among*, whereas those of humanity are strengths *between*, but the difference is perhaps more of degree than kind. Regardless, three of the positive traits included in the classification fit nicely under the virtue class of justice:

13. *fairness*: treating all people the same according to notions of fairness and justice; not letting personal feelings bias decisions about others; giving everyone a fair chance
14. *leadership*: encouraging a group of which one is a member to get things done and at the same time fostering good relations within the group; organizing group activities and seeing that they happen
15. *teamwork*: working well as a member of a group or team; being loyal to the group; doing one's share

Strengths of temperance are positive traits that protect us from excess. What are the types of excess of special concern? Hatred—against which forgiveness and mercy protect us. Arrogance—against which humility and modesty protect us. Short-term pleasure with long-term consequences—against which prudence protects us. And destabilizing emotional extremes of all sorts—against which self-regulation protects us.

It is worth emphasizing that the strengths of temperance temper our activities, rather than bringing them to a complete halt. We may be highly forgiving, but we can still defend ourselves while being pummeled. Modesty does not require falsehood—just authentic acknowledgment of who we are and what we do. A prudent course of action is still a course of action. Optimal self-regulation of emotions does not mean suspending our feelings, good or bad, but only taking charge of them.

16. *forgiveness/mercy*: forgiving those who have done wrong; giving people a second chance; not being vengeful
17. *modesty/humility*: letting one's accomplishments speak for themselves; not seeking the spotlight; not regarding oneself as more special than one is
18. *prudence*: being careful about one's choices; not taking undue risks; not saying or doing things that might later be regretted
19. *self-regulation*: regulating what one feels and does; being disciplined; controlling one's appetites and emotions

I could have included some or all of the strengths of courage under this virtue but did not do so because the strengths of courage lead us to behave in positive ways regardless of temptations to the contrary (e.g., fear, sloth, inauthenticity, fatigue), whereas the defining feature of temperance lies in tackling head on the temptation at hand. Strengths of temperance may therefore predispose strengths of courage, but they are still distinct.

Temperance strengths are defined in part by what a person refrains from doing, and they might be more apparent to observers in their intemperate absence than in their temperate presence. Indeed, in our attempts to measure this class of strengths, we have found that among people in the mainstream United States, strengths of temperance are infrequently endorsed and seldom praised. Perhaps in cultures in which the middle path of Buddhism or other teachings about balance and harmony are influential, these particular strengths are more frequently celebrated. Regardless, the strengths of temperance are important. They are included in virtually all philosophical and religious discussions of virtue, and they have a rich array of consequences for the psychological good life.

Strengths of transcendence may at first glance seem a mixed lot, but the common theme is that each allows individuals to forge connections to the larger universe and thereby provide meaning to their lives. Almost all of the positive traits in the classification reach outside the individual—character after all is social in nature—but in the case of the transcendence strengths, the reaching goes beyond other people per se to embrace part or all of the larger universe. The prototype of this strength category is spirituality, variously defined but always referring to a belief in and commitment to the transcendent (nonmaterial) aspects of life—whether they be called universal, ideal, sacred, or divine.

How do the other strengths classified approach this prototype? Appreciation of beauty is a strength that connects someone directly to excellence. Gratitude connects someone directly to goodness. Hope connects someone directly to the dreamed-of future. Humor—admittedly the most controversially placed entry—connects someone directly to troubles and contradictions in a way that produces not terror or anger but pleasure.

20. *appreciation of beauty and excellence*: noticing and appreciating beauty, excellence, and skilled performance in all domains of life, from nature to art to mathematics to science to everyday experience
21. *gratitude*: being aware of and thankful for the good things that happen; taking time to express thanks
22. *hope*: expecting the best in the future and working to achieve it; believing that a good future is something that can be brought about
23. *humor*: liking to laugh and tease; bringing smiles to other people; seeing the light side; making (not necessarily telling) jokes
24. *religiousness/spirituality*: having coherent beliefs about the higher purpose and meaning of the universe; knowing where one fits within the larger scheme; having beliefs about the meaning of life that shape one's conduct and provide comfort

I hasten to add that there are other positive traits that a positive psychologist might wish to study among people—ambition, autonomy, *gravitas*, and patience, to name but a few—and their absence in our classification reflects only our judgment that these do not meet the criteria set forth. They may not be as widely valued across cultural groups as the included entries; they may reflect blends of more-basic strengths; they may fail the test of a nonfelicitous opposite; and so on. The VIA Classification is but a descriptive tool.

The overall usefulness of this classification does not depend on exactly under which virtue each of its 24 strengths is classified, and I would not be surprised if a future grouping of character strengths is revised, expanded, or contracted. If appreciation of beauty is discovered to be the province mainly of the expert who has studied a given domain for years, then it probably belongs with other strengths of wisdom and knowledge. If gratitude and humor as character strengths play themselves out mainly between two people (and not between a person and the larger world), they probably belong with the other strengths of humanity. Or maybe humor will seek the company of vitality, among the strengths of courage.[3] I think that hope and religiousness will stay allied, given the strong historical link between them (Tiger, 1979).

It is worth noting that the entries in the VIA Classification overlap considerably with those in two other contemporary classifications arrived at in very different ways. First, French philosopher André Comte-Sponville (2001) surveyed classical and contemporary Western philosophical traditions for mention of the "qualities that constitute the excellence and essence of humankind" (book dustjacket). He included politeness and gentleness (which we did not because they seem prerequisites for more-substantive strengths) and excluded several of the VIA strengths (e.g., appreciation of beauty, curiosity, and zest), but otherwise there is substantial agreement.

Second, Marcus Buckingham and Donald Clifton (2001) of the Gallup Organization described "workplace themes" that emerged from focus groups with thousands of individuals about the traits that contribute to excellent performance at work (chapter 8). They included some strengths that are culturally bound (e.g., competition) as well as strengths that strike us as complex blends of more-basic strengths (e.g., communication), but again there is substantial agreement.

What About Talents?

To say that a strength is *morally* valued is an important qualification, because there exist individual differences that are widely celebrated, contribute to fulfillment, and qualify as signature characteristics, but still fall outside of our classification. Consider intelligence, perfect pitch, or athletic prowess. These talents and abilities are cut from a different cloth than character strengths like valor or kindness, but what is the difference?

We have devoted considerable thought to the distinction between character strengths and virtues, on the one hand, versus talents and the abilities, on the

3. A late addition to our classification, humor was added in part because of its universality and in part because our classification was too grim without it. "Too much seriousness, even about virtue, is somehow suspect and disturbing. . . . Humorless virtue thinks much of itself and is thereby deficient in virtue" (Comte-Sponville, 2001, p. 211). Among character strengths enumerated by philosophers and theologians, humor is rarely mentioned explicitly, although it lurks beneath the surface of many classical treatments of virtue. Lao-Tsu does not tell anyone to be humorous (an impossible edict in any event) but he himself is humorous in what he does convey. Ditto for Benjamin Franklin.

other[4] (chapter 8). Many talents and abilities on the face of it seem more innate, more immutable, and less voluntary than strengths and virtues. These of course are matters of degree. So, the talent of perfect pitch is always discussed as if it were more innate than the strengths of kindness or modesty, but the ability to read train schedules certainly is not. And suppose it turns out that the character strengths in the present classification prove to be heritable (chapter 4)? All other investigated individual differences seem to have some basis in genetic variation, so why not curiosity, for example, or even spirituality or leadership?

To be sure, no one will ever discover single genes that code for specific moral virtues, and any biogenetic account of character will ultimately be phrased in terms of heritable raw ingredients interacting with specific environments and experiences. But the same account already exists for many talents and abilities, so where is the distinction?

I am left, somewhat reluctantly, with the conclusion that character strengths differ from talents and abilities because they fall into the moral domain. This is a less-than-satisfactory conclusion because we must cede the designation of a character strength to the larger society and culture. During my early efforts in creating this classification, I worried that I would create a list of characteristics that reflected only my own take on the good life. I think that I have avoided this problem. I did not include characteristics valued only at the turn of the new century by an upper middle-class, agnostic, European American, male academic.

There are two further distinctions between character strengths and other dimensions of virtuosity. First is the role played by effort and will in the exercise of these characteristics. Basketball player Michael Jordan was revered for his athletic ability but also for his refusal to lose. In both cases, the innate talent/strength was practiced and nurtured, but those of us who are not delusional recognize that we can never soar through the air like Michael, with or without the shoes he endorsed. We can imagine, however, that we might arise from our sickbed to do our job as best we can, as Jordan did in a 1997 playoff game against the Utah Jazz, in which only his temperature (103°) exceeded his point total (38). This storied performance represented the melding of a talent with a character strength, yet it is the latter that we value morally.

This chapter is not the right forum for a discussion of free will and determinism, so I will just note in passing my strong suspicion that positive psychology, as the field evolves, will necessarily lead social scientists to grapple anew with the crucial role that choice plays in human activity. A morally praiseworthy action is

4. Hampering this distinction are Western intellectual trends to which we are heir. For example, the Greeks used the term *virtue* to include both moral character and talent, and the word *virtuoso* has survived in the talent domain (although, interestingly, not in the character domain). In Renaissance Florence, physical beauty and moral goodness were regarded as part and parcel of the same individual difference, at least for upper-class women (O'Neill, 2001), and we still seem to labor under the assumption that what is beautiful is good (Dion, Berscheid, & Walster, 1972).

chosen in a way that a merely skilled action is not. All people can aspire to have strong character in a way that they cannot aspire to be good-looking or physically resilient.

A second distinction between character strengths and talents is that the latter seem valued more for their tangible consequences (acclaim, wealth) than are the former. Someone who "does nothing" with a talent like a high IQ or musical skill courts eventual disdain. Witness the ridicule directed at Michael Jordan when he abandoned basketball to pursue a baseball career or the dismay we experience when extremely talented individuals like Judy Garland, John Belushi, Kurt Cobain, Elvis Presley, or Darryl Strawberry are overwhelmed by drug problems. In contrast, we never hear the criticism that a person did nothing with her wisdom or kindness. Said another way, talents and abilities can be squandered, but strengths and virtues cannot.

Assessment of Character Strengths

What distinguishes the VIA Classification from most previous attempts to articulate good character is its simultaneous concern with assessment, and I turn now to our measurement work. Some social scientists have responded with suspicion when they hear this goal, reminding me of the pitfalls of self-report and the validity threat posed by social desirability—the tendency of research participants to convey a positive impression of themselves whether or not it is strictly accurate (Crowne & Marlowe, 1964). I do not dismiss these considerations, but their premise is worth examining from the vantage of positive psychology. We seem to be willing, as researchers and practitioners, to trust what individuals say about their problems. With exceptions like substance abuse and eating disorders, in which denial can be an inherent part of the problem, the preferred way to measure psychological disorders relies on self-reports, through questionnaires or interviews. Why not ascertain wellness in the same way? Perhaps we accept self-reports about the negative but not the positive because we do not believe that the positive exists. That is the assumption that positive psychology urges us to reject (chapter 1).

Suppose that people really do possess moral virtues. Most philosophers emphasize that virtuous activity involves choosing virtue in light of a justifiable life plan (Yearley, 1990). In psychological language, this characterization means that people can reflect on their own virtues and talk about them to others. They may of course be mistaken, but virtues are not automatically beyond the realm of self-commentary (cf. Nisbett & Wilson, 1977). Furthermore, character strengths are not "contaminated" by a response set of social desirability; they *are* socially desirable, especially when reported with fidelity.

Consider the results of previous research that measured positive traits with self-report questionnaire batteries (e.g., Cawley, Martin, & Johnson, 2000; Greenberger, Josselson, Knerr, & Knerr, 1975; Ryff & Singer, 1996). In no case did a single methods factor emerge from the data. Different clusters of strengths were always apparent. External correlates were always sensible. These conclusions converge with what we have learned from our own attempts to measure the VIA strengths with self-report questionnaires. We acknowledge the possibility that some strengths of character lend themselves less readily to self-report than do others. Almost by definition, strengths like authenticity and bravery are not the sorts of characteristics usually attributed to oneself. But this consideration does not preclude the use of self-report to assess other strengths of character. And all of them can be assessed by asking about their behavioral indicators. Someone may be reluctant to describe herself as brave, but she will more readily say that she takes an unpopular public stance or that she endures chronic illness without complaint.

As a critical aspect of our project, we commissioned literature reviews by expert social scientists of what was known about each of the 24 strengths included in the classification (Peterson & Seligman, 2004). These experts followed a common format, touching upon definition, theory, enabling factors and causes, consequences, and correlates. Each expert also summarized previous efforts to assess each strength as an individual difference. Again, space does not permit a strength-by-strength summary of the assessment, so here are the major conclusions:

- In most cases, there exist reliable and valid ways of measuring each strength as an individual difference, not a surprising fact considering that we included strengths already of interest to psychologists.
- However, there are some exceptions. Modesty and humility have eluded reliable assessment, although nomination procedures have been used to identify modest/humble paragons. And there seem to be no extant self-report measures of bravery, although again nomination procedures have been used by previous researchers.
- In most cases, the assessment strategy of choice is a self-report questionnaire, although these existing measures are often lengthy and would not be practical to combine into an inclusive battery.

With these insights as a starting point, my colleagues and I set about creating our own measures that would allow the character strengths in our classification to be assessed among English speakers in the contemporary Western world: surveys, interviews, and informant reports (Peterson, Park, & Seligman, 2005a). We are also undertaking translations of our survey measures into some of the world's major language groups—e.g., Chinese, Spanish, Japanese, and German—but we began with English-language versions. Our first goal was to create face-valid and reliable measures; then we turned to the equally important matter of construct validity.

The assessment strategy we have most extensively developed to date entails self-report surveys able to be completed by respondents in a single session. We have devised separate inventories for adults and for young people (ages 10–17). These include scales that assess each of the 24 strengths.

The **VIA Inventory of Strengths (VIA-IS)** is intended for use by adults and has been completed in five different incarnations by almost 350,000 individuals from more than 200 different nations.[5] It is a face-valid questionnaire that measures the degree to which respondents endorse items reflecting the various strengths of character in the classification (from 1 = very much unlike me to 5 = very much like me). There are 10 items per strength (240 total). For example, the character strength of forgiveness is measured with items such as "I always allow others to leave their mistakes in the past and make a fresh start," "I believe it is best to forgive and forget," "I am unwilling to accept apologies" (reverse-scored), and "I hold grudges" (reverse-scored).[6]

Developed by Nansook Park, the **VIA Inventory of Strengths for Youth (VIA-Youth)** is intended for use by young people (ages 10–17; Park & Peterson, 2005, in press b). Like the VIA-IS, it is a face-valid questionnaire that measures the degree to which respondents endorse items reflecting each of the 24 strengths

5. The book describing the VIA Classification was written at the same time that the measures of the VIA strengths were being developed. I had asked experts to draft chapters describing the state-of-the-art research literature with respect to each of the character strengths, and I needed to wait some months for these drafts to be completed and sent to me. What I did in the meantime, simply as an exercise, was to place an early version of the VIA-IS on-line and direct my students and friends to it. I was hoping that a few hundred people would find their way to it and provide enough data for me to see if the scales were reliable. Then I intended to create the sort of paper-and-pencil questionnaire that has been the staple of survey researchers for decades.

A funny thing happened. The Web-based survey became incredibly popular and has proven so useful to us that I now do most of my survey research on-line. On any given day, hundreds of individuals may complete the survey. We do not pay any of these respondents, and there is little reason to believe that the same individual responds more than once to the survey. About 75% of the respondents are from the United States. About two-thirds of the respondents are women. The ethnic makeup of the U.S. sample approximates that of the country as a whole. The typical respondent is about 40 years of age, is married, is employed, and has completed some schooling post–high school, although there is great variation across all such contrasts. Given the need for computer literacy and access, respondents are of course not a perfect match to the United States or the world population, but they are arguably much closer than convenience samples otherwise obtained by psychology researchers (e.g., college sophomores enrolled in an introductory psychology course). The efficiency, economy, and scale of Web-based research seems to offset some of the concerns about the makeup of the samples (Gosling, Vazire, Srivastava, & John, 2004).

Why has the on-line VIA-IS been so popular? Immediately after respondents complete it—which usually takes 30–45 minutes—they receive individual feedback about their top five strengths, along with brief blurbs describing what the strengths mean. Over the years, I have been contacted by thousands of respondents saying that they found it uplifting to know that they had strengths of character and to be able to put a name to them.

6. A standard strategy in self-report surveys is to include items in a scale that are worded in opposite directions, to avoid confounding the substantive intent of the measure with a respondent's tendency to be agreeable (endorsing all items regardless of content) or contrary.

of character in the VIA Classification (1 = not like me at all, 5 = very much like me). The VIA-Youth was developed by writing age-appropriate items that reflected each of the strengths. The current version contains 5–9 items per strength (198 total), a smaller number of questions than in the VIA-IS to reduce the burden on our youthful respondents. The VIA-Youth has been completed by thousands of young people across the United States, both as a paper-and-pencil survey and as an on-line measure. In the latter case, parents or guardians need to contact us first to give permission for their child to help with our research.

Developed with the help of Tiffany Sawyer, the **VIA Structured Interview** identifies what we call "signature strengths" by talking to someone about the situations in which these strengths are most likely to be shown (Peterson & Seligman, 2004). Certain strengths are evident only when someone "rises to an occasion" that presents itself. One cannot be brave except in frightening circumstances. One cannot be forgiving unless trespassed against. In contrast, the other strengths can be displayed in a generic and ongoing way. So, except perhaps for the presence of other people, there are no special circumstances in which to display kindness or playfulness.

The VIA Structured Interview takes about 30 minutes to complete. The interviewer asks a respondent how he usually acts in a given setting vis-à-vis the character strength on focus; if appropriate, the setting is detailed, and in the case of tonic strengths, and otherwise, the situation is described as "everyday life." If people describe displaying the strength the majority of the time, follow-up questions ask: (i) how they name the strength; (ii) if the strength however named is really who they are; and (iii) whether friends and family members would agree that the strength is really who they are. Our studies to date show that adults usually have between two and five signature strengths. For these strengths, the corresponding VIA-IS scores are—not surprisingly—elevated.

The drawback of the structured interview, as I see it, is that it does not quantify an individual's character strengths, which is at odds with my conceptualization of strengths as existing along dimensions. The off-setting benefit is that the VIA Structured Interview allows us to say that a strength is (or is not) self-consciously owned by an individual. We have theoretical reasons for believing that owned strengths may be qualitatively different in their effects than non-owned strengths (Seligman, 2002). For example, I have some skill at transactional leadership—taking charge of a group and making sure that its trains run on time. But I do not enjoy these tasks, nor do I consider the strength of leadership part of my core identity. However successfully I complete the tasks, I am left exhausted and unfulfilled. In contrast, I gladly embrace other strengths, like humor and kindness, and when I exercise them, I feel exhilarated. We need additional research to test more systematically these speculations about signature strengths, and the VIA Structured Interview will be a crucial tool.

I want to describe one more way to assess strengths that relies on content analysis of spontaneous spoken or written descriptions of someone. Developed by Nansook Park, the **strengths content analysis** technique was originally intended to study the earliest precursors of character strengths among children too young to complete the VIA-Youth, which is sometimes able to be used with children as young as 8 years old but more typically requires that a respondent be at least 10 years old. In our initial study, hundreds of parents were asked to use several words to describe one of their children between the ages of 3 and 9 (Park & Peterson, in press c). These brief descriptions were rich in character language and readily able to be coded for mention or not of each of the strengths in the VIA Classification.

The starting point of the coding scheme was the strength names and their obvious synonyms. For example, the character strength of kindness was recognized of course as kindness but also as generosity, nurturance, care, compassion, or niceness. We elaborated the coding scheme to capture the ways that parents describe various strengths among their children. For instance, no one described a child as zestful, vital, or ebullient, but parents did describe their children as full of life, enthusiastic, a live wire, or "raring to go" every morning. These words and phrases were considered indicators of the character strength of zest. In some cases, the coding scheme was broadened to include behavioral trends that reflected the strength of concern. For example, parents rarely described their children as religious or spiritual, but they would say, "she loves her God," or "he says his prayers regularly."

In relying on "spontaneous" descriptions of children, we avoided putting words in the mouths of our parent informants. Regardless, the descriptions were simple to code. On average, three strengths were explicitly mentioned for each child. If it is possible to speak of a typical child, as seen by her parents, the typical child is one who is loving, kind, creative, humorous, and curious. Infrequently mentioned strengths—e.g., authenticity, gratitude, modesty, forgiveness, and open-mindedness—fit with theoretical speculation and common sense that some strengths of character require psychosocial maturation to be evident (Peterson & Seligman, 2004).

The research value of the strengths content analysis technique extends beyond the study of children. It can in principle be used to assess strengths of all sorts of people—the quick, the unwilling, and the dead—who are unavailable or unable to complete a survey or interview. All we need is some written or spoken record, by them or about them, that has been left behind. For example, my colleague Fiona Lee at the University of Michigan is using this technique to ascertain character strengths mentioned in obituaries and in popular songs, and Nansook Park (2005) looked at character strengths mentioned in the official citations of Medal of Honor recipients (Highland Publishers, 2002). Bravery is a given, granted the meaning of this award, but in a number of cases, character strengths of perseverance, self-regulation, teamwork, and leadership are evident as well. There is additional evidence that Medal of Honor recipients exhibit humility (Collier, 2003). Taken together, these findings provide a rich view of heroic bravery (Becker & Eagly, 2004). Bravery must be located in an immediate social context and typically involves the exercise of well-learned skills (Rachman, 1990).

Empirical Findings

Both the VIA-IS and the VIA-Youth are demonstrably reliable (i.e., items converge), valid (i.e., self-ratings of character strengths agree with reports by informed others), and stable over at least 6 months (e.g., Park & Peterson, 2005, in press b; Peterson, Park, & Seligman, 2005b; Peterson & Seligman, 2004). Here I wish to mention some of the empirical findings to date, which strike me as interesting and which illustrate the value of an empirically informed approach to good character.

First, my colleagues and I have discovered a remarkable similarity in the relative endorsement of the 24 character strengths by adults around the world and within the United States (Park, Peterson, & Seligman, in press). The most commonly endorsed ("most like me") strengths, in 54 different countries, from Azerbaijan to Zimbabwe, are kindness, fairness, authenticity, gratitude, and open-mindedness, and the lesser strengths consistently include prudence, modesty, and self-regulation (Figure 6.1). The correlations of the rankings from nation to nation are all very strong, usually in the 0.80+ range, defying cultural, ethnic, religious, and economic differences.

The same ranking of greater versus lesser strengths also characterized all 50 U.S. states—except for religiousness, which is somewhat more evident in the

Figure 6.1. Mean VIA-IS Scores in a U.S. Sample
(N = 83,576). Scores range from 1 (= very much unlike me) to 5 (= very much like me).

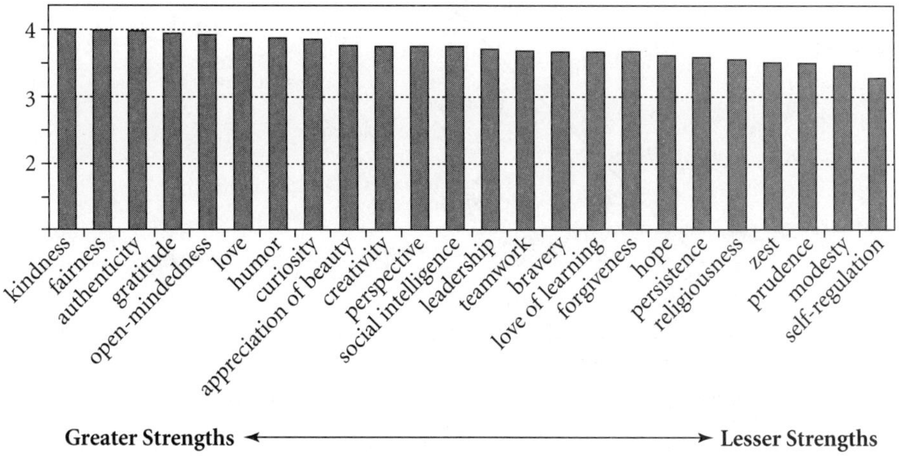

South—and held across the contrasts of gender, age, education, and whether one lived in a state that voted Republican or Democratic in recent presidential elections. These results may reveal something about universal human nature and/or the character requirements minimally needed for a viable society (Bok, 1995).

Second, a comparison of strengths profiles between U.S. adults and U.S. adolescents revealed overall agreement on ranking, yet a noticeably lower agreement than that found between U.S. adults and adults in any other nation we have studied (Park, Peterson, & Seligman, 2005). Hope, teamwork, and zest were more common among U.S. youth than among U.S. adults, whereas appreciation of beauty, authenticity, leadership, and open-mindedness were more common among adults (Figure 6.2). As our attention turns to the deliberate cultivation of character strengths, we should be as concerned with how to keep certain strengths from eroding on the journey to adulthood as with how to build others from scratch (Park & Peterson, in press d).

Third, although part of the definition of a character strength is that it contributes to fulfillment, strengths "of the heart"—zest, gratitude, hope, and love—are more robustly associated with life satisfaction than the more-cerebral

Figure 6.2. Strengths Profiles for Youth (*N* = 250) Versus Adults (*N* = 83,576) in the United States

Strengths are ranked from lowest (= 1) through highest (= 24).

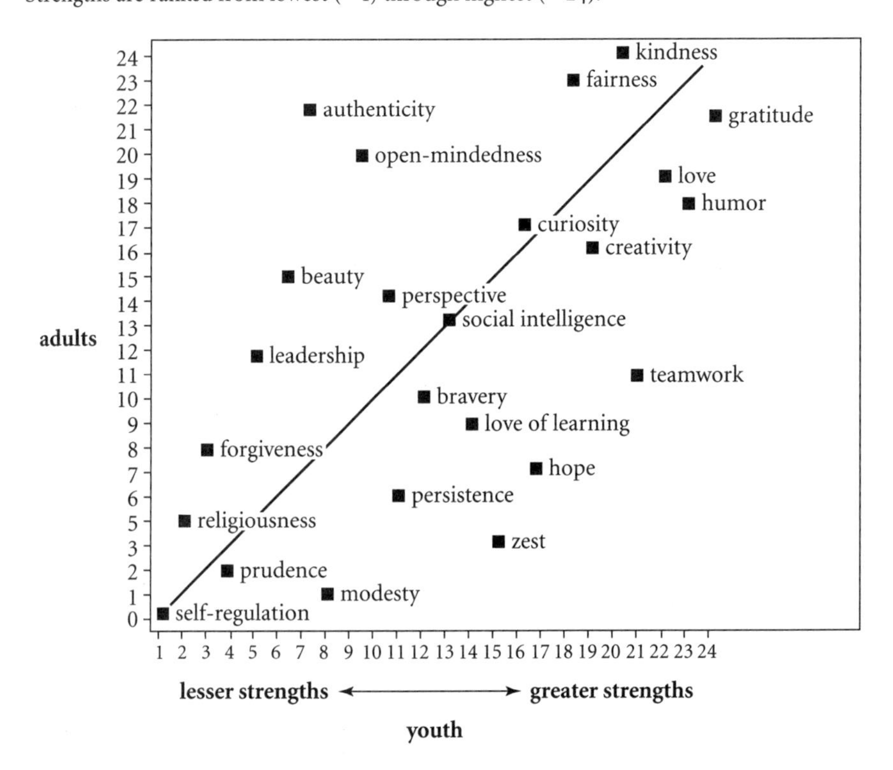

strengths like love of learning (Park & Peterson, 2005, in press b, in press c; Park, Peterson, & Seligman, 2004, 2005). We find this pattern among adults, youth, and even very young children as described by their parents.[7] We also have some longitudinal evidence that these heart strengths foreshadow subsequent life satisfaction (Park, Peterson, & Seligman, 2005). As we have seen in previous chapters, other people matter mightily. Character strengths that orient us toward others in turn make us happy.

Fourth, when VIA-IS scores for U.S. residents completing the survey on-line in the 2 months immediately post-9/11 were compared to those doing so before 9/11, the character strengths of faith (religiousness), hope, and love showed increases, a pattern not evident among European respondents (Peterson & Seligman, 2003a). These strengths comprise the theological virtues identified by Thomas Aquinas (1966) and sung about by Alan Jackson in his award-winning country music anthem about 9/11, "Where Were You?" One way to make sense of these data is with terror management theory, which holds that people "manage" the terror of their own mortality by increasing identification with culturally salient values (Greenberg, Pyszczynski, & Solomon, 1986).

Fifth, as initial steps toward studying people at their best, we did three parallel studies of adults with respect to good character and its correlates at work, love, and play (Peterson & Seligman, 2004). Rather than asking our respondents about current jobs, current relationships, and current recreational activities (the typical research strategy when these topics are of concern), we asked them to think of their most-fulfilling job, their truest love, their best friend, and their most-engaging hobby, whenever these were present in their lives. (We also gave respondents the option of saying "does not apply," which some small number of them, invariably young adults, exercised.)

Interestingly, respondents did not always describe their current jobs, relationships, or leisure pastimes. The clichéd standards by which people seem to judge and even to choose among options in these domains—like salary, status, or geographical location for jobs; good looks or financial security for relationships; and unalloyed sensory pleasure for leisure activities—did not characterize what our respondents reported as the best they ever had. Instead, what people most valued was a job, a relationship, and a hobby congruent with their own strengths of character. For instance, those with the character strength of kindness especially enjoyed jobs where they could mentor others; those with the character strength of curiosity preferred romantic partners who were "adventurous"; and those with the character strength of love of learning were happily found gardening in their spare time.

Sixth, we have begun some studies to look at the effects on character strengths of previous life crises (e.g., Peterson, Park, & Seligman, 2006). When positive psychology was first delineated, Seligman and Csikszentmihalyi (2000)

7. Parental descriptions were also coded for the "happiness" attributed to the child.

speculated that it was a field that made sense for a society that was peaceful and prosperous. Its goal was moving people not from –5 to 0 but from +2 to +6 (chapter 1). Accordingly, positive psychology would seem to have little to do with distress and pathology—the typical concerns of business-as-usual psychology (Peterson, in press).

The thinking of many positive psychologists has changed since the events of 9/11, which reminded us that what is best in people can be shown when they rise to an occasion (Brokaw, 1998). Crisis may or may not be the crucible of character, but it certainly allows the display of what virtue ethicists refer to as "corrective strengths of character" (Peterson & Seligman, 2004).

Anecdotal evidence is ample that such crises—at least when surmounted—leave a person with a fresh appreciation of what really matters in life and perhaps the readiness to act in accordance with this appreciation. More systematic research under the rubrics of resilience and posttraumatic growth documents that at least some people emerge from crises less damaged than typical theories might predict (e.g., Bonnano, 2004; Linley & Joseph, 2004a; Masten, 2001; S. E. Taylor, 1985; Tedeschi & Calhoun, 1995), but what remains unclear is the frequency with which people actually benefit from a difficult experience by finding or building strengths of character.

There are barriers to definitive conclusions. One is the common cultural script, at least in the United States, of redemption, which leads people to regard a bad experience retrospectively as a good one (McAdams, 1993, 2005). Self-definition as a survivor becomes an important aspect of one's identity and colors how one responds to direct questions about the aftermath of a crisis. I am not cynical enough to suggest that this identity is inauthentic, but I do believe that comparisons with people who have not experienced the crisis in question are needed to confirm the self-affirmation and rule out such mundane confounds as maturation.

Our research sidestepped these barriers. Although our studies had a retrospective design and relied on self-report, we did not ask about previous crises until the very end of the survey that we administered. Thus, our research participants were not explicitly primed to respond in terms of a survivor identity. We have done three such studies, first administering the VIA-IS to measure character strengths and then asking respondents about physical illnesses, psychological disorders, or traumatic events like assaults. In each case, those who experienced the crisis showed elevated levels of certain character strengths relative to those who had not experienced the crisis. For example, serious physical illness—if one had recovered from it—was associated with bravery, kindness, and humor. These strengths in turn were associated with higher life satisfaction. The ultimate implication of the present results is that deliberate interventions targeting these strengths may help people not only survive but flourish following a crisis.

A final line of research that I have just begun with Nansook Park takes a look at the previously unquestioned assumption that one can "have it all" in a character sense. That is, in our work to date, we have identified strengths of character, measured them, and started to map out their correlates and consequences, which—not surprisingly—are often positive in nature. The implication is that we should develop and use as many strengths of character as possible.

But is this really possible? Barry Schwartz and Kenneth Sharpe (in press) took the VIA Classification project to task for ignoring the tradeoffs that sometimes need to be made among character strengths as we live our everyday lives. "Do I look good in this dress?" is how they started their critique. Most of you are probably smiling because you know that those who ask questions like this often suspect that something is amiss. So, how does one respond to this question? Perhaps with kindness—as in "you look marvelous." Perhaps with honesty—as in "you look terrible." Or perhaps with prudence—as in "green is a good color."

There is no universally right solution to this dilemma, although Schwartz and Sharpe argued that social intelligence—which they dubbed "practical wisdom"—helps us to choose an answer in a concrete situation that takes into account all sorts of subtleties. Does she have time to change the dress? Does she even have another dress? And so on. The point is that sometimes someone cannot simultaneously be kind and honest. A tradeoff must be made.

We suspect that people make these tradeoffs in characteristic ways. All things being equal, some of us will tend to be kind, whereas others of us will tend to be honest. If this is the case, we would expect to see certain strengths of character as measured by the VIA-IS stand in a reciprocal relationship with one another—i.e., being high on one strength should be correlated with being low on others, and vice versa. The structure of these tradeoffs might reveal something about how the real world allows good character to present itself.

Using statistical procedures that allow these sorts of conclusions,[8] we indeed found tradeoffs among strengths as well as a simple interpretation. Figure 6.3 depicts the relationships among the strengths along two dimensions in a **circumplex model**, used by psychologists in different fields (like perception, emotion, and personality) to depict theoretical or empirical relationships among concepts in terms of their placement around a circle.

The X axis corresponds to a focus of the strength on the self (e.g., creativity, curiosity) versus others (e.g., teamwork, fairness), and the Y axis corresponds to strengths that entail intellectual restraint (e.g., open-mindedness, prudence) versus emotional expression (e.g., love, gratitude). Two strengths close together on the graph comfortably co-occur, but two strengths that are far apart are more likely to be traded off. These tradeoffs are not inevitable, of course, but they do imply that people display good character in habitually different ways.

8. To be technical, we standardized the VIA-IS scale scores within individual subjects in a large sample of adult respondents ($N = 12{,}758$) and conducted an oblique factor analysis from which two unambiguous factors emerged.

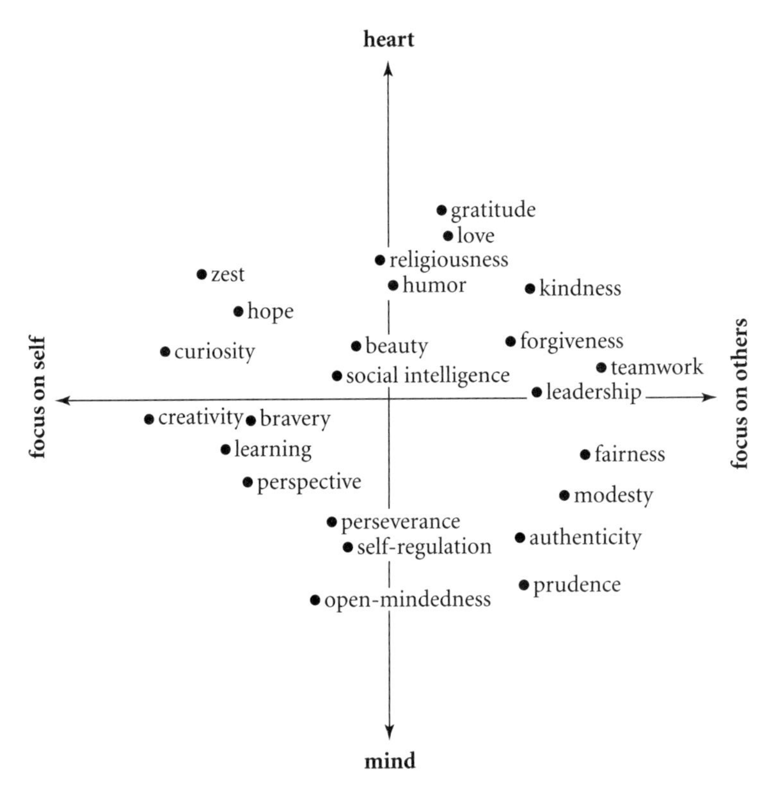

Figure 6.3. Tradeoffs Among Character Strengths
The farther apart are two strengths, the less likely it is that the same person habitually shows both.

EXERCISE *Using Signature Strengths in New Ways*

I believe that people possess **signature strengths** akin to what Allport (1961) identified decades ago as personal traits. These are the strengths of character that a person owns, celebrates, and frequently exercises. In our interviews with adults, we find that almost everyone can readily identify a handful of strengths as very much their own, typically between two and five. Here are possible criteria for a signature strength (Peterson & Seligman, 2004):

- a sense of ownership and authenticity ("this is the real me") vis-à-vis the strength
- a feeling of excitement while displaying it, particularly at first
- a rapid learning curve as themes are attached to the strength and practiced
- continuous learning of new ways to enact the strength

- a sense of yearning to act in accordance with the strength
- a feeling of inevitability in using the strength, as if one cannot be stopped or dissuaded from its display
- the discovery of the strength as owned in an epiphany
- invigoration rather than exhaustion when using the strength
- the creation and pursuit of fundamental projects that revolve around the strength
- intrinsic motivation to use the strength

My hypothesis is that the exercise of signature strengths is fulfilling, and these criteria convey the motivational and emotional features of fulfillment with terms like excitement, yearning, inevitability, discovery, and invigoration.

The purpose of this exercise is twofold. First, identify your signature strengths by taking the VIA-IS online at www.authentichappiness.org or at www.viastrengths.org. These Web sites provide instantaneous feedback about the strengths for which you scored highest. Look at your top scores in light of the criteria just described for a signature strength and decide which of the top strengths qualify as signature strengths—as the real you.

Second, take one of the signature strengths you have identified, and for the following week, use the strength in a new way every day. As you may remember from chapter 4, this is one of the interventions we have systematically tested and shown to have long-term positive effects on happiness (Seligman, Steen, Park, & Peterson, 2005). The critical ingredient is using the strength in a new way. You can probably think of new ways on your own, but here are some suggestions based on lists generated by Jonathan Haidt (2002) and by Tayyab Rashid and Afroze Anjum (2005):

- appreciation of beauty
  - visit an art gallery or museum with which you are unfamiliar
  - start to keep a beauty journal in which you write down every day the most beautiful things you saw
  - at least once a day, stop and notice an instance of natural beauty, e.g., a sunrise, a flower, a bird singing
- authenticity
  - refrain from telling white lies to friends (including insincere compliments)
  - think about your most important values and do something every day that is consistent with them (chapter 7)
  - when explaining your motives to someone, do so in a genuine and honest way
- bravery
  - speak up for an unpopular idea in a group
  - protest to the appropriate authorities about a clear injustice that you observe
  - do something that you ordinarily would not because of fear

- creativity
  - enroll in a pottery, photography, sculpting, drawing, or painting class
  - choose some object in your home and find another use for it rather than its typical use—no fair using your exercise bike as a clothes rack
  - send a card to a friend that includes a poem you have written
- curiosity
  - attend a lecture on a topic about which you know nothing
  - go to a restaurant featuring cuisine unfamiliar to you
  - discover a new place in your town, and learn about its history
- fairness
  - at least once a day, admit a mistake and take responsibility for it
  - at least once a day, give due credit to someone you do not especially like
  - hear people out without interrupting them
- forgiveness
  - let a grudge go every day
  - when you feel annoyed, even with justification, take the high road and do not tell anyone how you feel
  - write a forgiveness letter; do *not* send it (chapter 2), but do read it every day for a week
- gratitude
  - keep track of how many times you say "thank you" during the day, and increase the number every day for a week
  - at the end of every day, write down three things that went well (chapter 2)
  - write and send a gratitude letter (chapter 2)
- hope
  - think of a past disappointment and the opportunities it made possible
  - write down your goals for the next week, the next month, and the next year; then make concrete plans for accomplishing these goals
  - dispute your pessimistic thoughts (chapter 5)
- humor
  - make at least one person smile or laugh per day
  - learn a magic trick and perform it for your friends
  - make fun of yourself, if only by saying, "there I go again"
- kindness
  - visit someone in a hospital or nursing home
  - when driving, yield to pedestrians; when walking, yield to cars (this latter suggestion also counts as an act of prudence)
  - perform an anonymous favor for a friend or family member

- leadership
  - organize a social get-together for your friends
  - take responsibility for an unpleasant task at work and make sure that it gets done
  - go out of your way to make a newcomer feel welcome
- love
  - accept a compliment without squirming; just say "thank you"
  - write a brief note to someone you love, and leave it where it will be found during the day
  - do something with your best friend that he or she really enjoys doing
- love of learning
  - if you are a student, read something that is "recommended" but not "required"
  - learn and use a new word every day
  - read a nonfiction book
- modesty
  - for an entire day, do not talk about yourself at all
  - dress in a way that does not call attention to yourself
  - think of something that a friend does much better than you do, and compliment him or her about it
- open-mindedness
  - in a conversation, play the devil's advocate and take a position at odds with your private opinion
  - every day, consider some strong-held opinion, and think about how you might be wrong
  - listen to a radio show or read a newspaper that espouses the "other" political line
- perseverance
  - make a list of things to do, and do one thing on the list every day
  - finish an important task ahead of schedule
  - work for several hours straight without interruptions, e.g., no television in the background, no phone calls, no snacks, no checking e-mail
- perspective
  - think of the wisest person you know, and try to live one day as if you were that person
  - offer advice only if asked, but then do so as thoughtfully as you can
  - resolve a dispute between two friends, family members, or coworkers
- prudence
  - think twice before saying anything other than "please" or "thank you"

- when driving, stay 5 miles per hour *under* the speed limit
- before you eat any snack, ask yourself, "Is this worth getting fat for?"

- religiousness
  - every day, think about the purpose of your life
  - pray or meditate at the start of every day
  - attend a religious service of a faith unfamiliar to you
- self-regulation
  - start an exercise program and stick with it every day for a week
  - refrain from gossiping or saying mean things about others
  - when tempted to lose your temper, count to 10; repeat as needed
- social intelligence
  - make someone else feel at ease
  - notice when friends or family members do something that is difficult for them, and compliment them
  - when someone annoys you, understand his or her motives rather than retaliate
- teamwork
  - be the best teammate you can be (chapter 2)
  - spend 5 minutes every day picking up litter on the sidewalk and putting it in a trashcan
  - volunteer your time to a charitable group
- zest
  - every day for at least a week, go to sleep early enough that you do not need to set an alarm, and eat a nutritious breakfast when you do wake up
  - say "why not?" three times more frequently than you say "why?"
  - do something every day because you want to and not because you need to

GLOSSARY

character strengths: positive traits; individual differences such as curiosity, kindness, and gratitude

circumplex model: depiction of concepts around a circle according to their relative similarity or dissimilarity

courage, strengths of: positive traits entailing the exercise of will to accomplish goals in the face of opposition, external or internal

humanity, strengths of: positive traits manifest in caring relationships with others

justice, strengths of: broadly social positive traits relevant to the optimal interaction between the individual and the group or the community

signature strengths: positive traits that a person owns, celebrates, and frequently exercises

strengths content analysis: technique for identifying the 24 strengths in the VIA Classification from spoken or written text

temperance, strengths of: positive traits that protect us from excess

transcendence, strengths of: positive traits that allow individuals to forge connections to the larger universe and thereby provide meaning to their lives.

VIA Classification of Character Strengths: classification of 24 positive traits

VIA Inventory of Strengths (VIA-IS): self-report survey for adults that measures the 24 strengths in the VIA Classification

VIA Inventory of Strengths for Youth (VIA-Youth): self-report survey for youth that measures the 24 strengths in the VIA Classification

VIA Structured Interview: interview for determining which of the 24 strengths in the VIA Classification qualify as individual signature strengths

wisdom and knowledge, strengths of: positive traits related to the acquisition and use of information in the service of the good life.

RESOURCES

Books and Journals

Peterson, C., & Seligman, M. E. P. (2004). *Character strengths and virtues: A handbook and classification.* New York: Oxford University Press; Washington, DC: American Psychological Association.

Comte-Sponville, A. (2001). *A small treatise on the great virtues* (C. Temerson, Trans.). New York: Metropolitan.

Aristotle. (2000). *The Nicomachean ethics* (R. Crisp, Trans.). Cambridge: Cambridge University Press.

Buckingham, M., & Clifton, D. O. (2001). *Now, discover your strengths.* New York: Free Press.

American Behavioral Scientist. Special issue (December 2003).

Articles

Cawley, M. J., Martin, J. E., & Johnson, J. A. (2000). A virtues approach to personality. *Personality and Individual Differences, 28,* 997–1013.

Dahlsgaard, K., Peterson, C., & Seligman, M. E. P. (2005). Shared virtue: The convergence of valued human strengths across culture and history. *Review of General Psychology, 9,* 209–213.

Peterson, C., & Seligman, M. E. P. (2003). Character strengths before and after September 11. *Psychological Science, 14,* 381–384.

Park, N., Peterson, C., & Seligman, M. E. P. (in press). Character strengths in 54 nations and all 50 U.S. states. *Journal of Positive Psychology.*

Becker, S. W., & Eagly, A. H. (2004). The heroism of women and men. *American Psychologist, 59,* 163–178.

Web Sites

http://www.viastrengths.org. This is the Web site of the Values in Action (VIA) Institute and describes our ongoing research on strengths and virtues. Here you can take the VIA Inventory of Strengths and receive feedback about your signature strengths of character.

Films

The Wizard of Oz (1939)
The Diary of Anne Frank (1959)
Roots (1977)
The Elephant Man (1980)
Witness (1985)
Glory (1989)
The Hunt for Red October (1990)
Braveheart (1995)
Courage Under Fire (1996)
ABC News's *20/20*: "Emotional IQ" (1996)
PBS *Biography*: "Benjamin Franklin" (2002)
ABC News's *Nightline*: "Whistleblower" (2004)

Songs

"Abraham, Martin, and John" (Dion)
"True Colors" (Cyndi Lauper)
"The Wind Beneath My Wings" (Bette Midler)

7 Values

To know the good is to do the good. —PLATO (~360 BCE)

One of the questions raised about our work on character strengths is whether these strengths can be used for wrong purposes. Although a character strength is by definition morally valued, a despot can be an effective leader, a suicide bomber can be brave, and a bitingly sarcastic person can be humorous. None of these individuals exemplifies moral goodness, but the character strength is still apparent. Said another way, a trait can be a strength without the person who displays it being praiseworthy.

We need other considerations to deem a person good, and these include the larger goal to which his strengths of character are directed. So, one can muster leadership skills to organize hurricane relief or to amass a fortune by marketing violent video games. One can be brave by starting a fight or by walking away from one. One can be funny in bringing people together or in driving wedges between them. It is the aim of the behavior that ultimately determines its goodness.

Accordingly, part of the good life is the articulation and pursuit of those goals that we deem worthy; these are **values**. Values are often moral, religious, or political in nature, and they figure mightily in the lives that we lead or should lead. According to a 1999 survey by Public Agenda, adults in the United States cited not learning values as the most important problem facing today's youth, more so than drugs and violence.

In presenting most topics in positive psychology, I worry that my own preferences intrude to determine what I deem to be positive (chapter 1). The study of values is different because it starts with the perspective of what others deem worthy, and virtually all people have beliefs about these matters. It is the task of positive psychologists to study these beliefs and the roles they play in people's lives and to refrain from endorsing some of these values and not others.

Sometimes what we learn about values is surprising. For instance, the research by Swarthmore College psychologist Barry Schwartz (2004) shows what happens when an investigator follows the data to where they may lead. He concerned himself with *choice*, a value that most of us would regard as a virtual motherhood—an unalloyed good.

The way he tells the story, his interest was piqued by a visit to a clothing store to buy a pair of blue jeans, a purchase he had made every few years for decades. This had always been a simple enough chore: Remember his size, buy jeans in that size, break them in, and wear them for as long as they held together and probably a bit longer. But in between his last trip to purchase jeans and this one, the blue jeans industry had discovered choice, and what confronted him at the store were countless options besides size and Levi's versus Lee jeans: stonewashed, faded, loose fit, relaxed, boot cut, tapered, and so on and so forth. And "blue" jeans of course could now be black or green or gray, and maybe even teal or periwinkle or desert rose (to name a few colors that I am thoroughly unable to identify). Schwartz was overwhelmed with the options, and it took him a long time to buy a pair of pants. He fretted afterward that he had not made the right choice, all the while acknowledging that this was just a pair of jeans.

Choice and the freedom to make choices are bedrock values in much of the world and certainly in the United States, a country that from its very beginning has embraced individual rights and autonomy. Freedom to choose among religions, careers, residences, friends, and romantic partners is a cherished American right.

But Schwartz went beyond social consensus to summarize a series of experiments asking if choice has any downside, and the data confirmed his own experience buying jeans. As the number of options we confront increases, so too does the amount of time we spend making decisions, even trivial ones, as does our after-the-fact regret over what we chose. "What-ifs" intrude as choices increase. So, two or three options may be more satisfying than one, but there is little good gained—psychologically—when there are more than a handful.

According to further research by Schwartz and his colleagues (2002), many people show a consistent style in how they make choices when confronted with a variety of options. At one end, we find those who want to make the very best choice among alternatives; at the other end we find those who are content to make a good-enough choice. Borrowing terms from the Nobel Prize–winning theorist Herbert Simon (1956), Schwartz called the former people **maximizers** because their goal is to optimize whatever payoff presumably follows from a choice and the latter people **satisficers** because their goal is to make a choice that is satisfactory.

No one is a pure maximizer or a pure satisficer, of course, but people can be arrayed along the implied continuum according to their agreement with statements like the following (Schwartz, 2004, p. 80):

- I never settle for second best.
- No matter how satisfied I am with my job, it's only right for me to be on the lookout for better opportunities.
- When shopping, I have a hard time finding clothing that I really love.

People's responses predict how they make actual choices and the psychological aftermath. As we would expect, maximizers take longer to arrive at a decision, but more interestingly, they also experience less satisfaction with their decisions, even if these seem "better" than the quicker decisions made by satisficers.

Schwartz studied graduating college students as they looked for their first jobs. Maximizers took longer to settle on a job than did satisficers, but these jobs on average paid much better salaries. That might be a good tradeoff. However, follow-up with these graduates showed that the maximizers were less satisfied with their jobs than were the satisficers, despite the higher pay. In general, maximizers have lower life satisfaction than do satisficers (chapter 4). Hence the paradox of choice. We want it, and the more the better, but increased choices do not necessarily make us more happy.

You can ponder the further implications of this line of research by taking an objective look at yourself and how you make decisions. If you are a relentless maximizer, you might experiment by letting go of that style in minor consumer domains, as suggested in the exercise at the end of this chapter. But the take-home message from this discussion is that values can have both costs and benefits.

Functions of Values

Are values themselves valuable? There is the theoretical possibility of individuals or groups that function perfectly well without values (Scott, 1963). But they seem not to exist. Whether this is an arbitrary happenstance of social history or one rooted in a deep human nature, I do not know, but values are nearly universal (Wright, 1994). Most theorists use the ubiquity of values to argue for their functional significance at both the individual and the group level. All of these functions can contribute to the good life, although we should not automatically equate the good life with what is easy or pleasurable. We want to do the right thing—however we define it—because it is the right thing to do.

For the individual, values not only suggest goals of action but also the criteria by which these goals are evaluated (Williams, 1951). Values go beyond what we prefer to describe what we *should* prefer. As ideal standards, values are not always achieved, and we should not be surprised when people's concrete behaviors do not map neatly onto what they profess, although there is usually a modest empirical association between values and behaviors.

Indeed, an enduring research question asks: When are values and behaviors most likely to be congruent? Here is a summary of the circumstances in which we can expect someone's beliefs to be reflected in their actions (Peterson, 1997):

- *The circumstances under which a person originally acquires a value.* Values stemming from direct experience are more consistent with our behavior than those acquired secondhand.
- *The degree to which a value helps to define a person's self-image.* If who you are is tied up in a given value, then you usually act quite consistently.
- *Whether people are self-conscious while they are behaving.* Sometimes people need to reflect on their values before they behave consistently with them. People who are not thinking about the meaning of their actions—e.g., those who are mindlessly enacting social scripts—tend to behave inconsistently.
- *A person's evaluation of the particular behavior that supposedly reflects the value in question.* If there is a strong norm for or against acting in a particular way, one's value exerts little influence on behavior. Here the individual is not inconsistent with values so much as consistent with the expectations of others.
- *The generality of the value with regard to the behavior that is being examined.* Highly general values about beauty, for instance, do not predict given behaviors like returning aluminum cans as well as do more specific beliefs about the virtue of recycling.
- *The scope of the behavior relevant to the value.* The correlations between what one believes and how one acts are boosted considerably if behaviors are measured in various ways on repeated occasions. Said another way, behaviors are more likely to reflect values if we look at the total of what someone does.

When we do behave in accordance with some value, we liberate ourselves from the proximal causes of behavior in our environment or our biological makeup. Religious values, for example, may lead us to turn the other cheek when provoked or to refrain from certain foods or sexual activities regardless of our desires. Seen in this way, values allow us to sustain our activities against the immediate causal grain and to be independent.

Values are expressive. They tell the world—and ourselves—who we are and what is most important about us. We plaster value-relevant bumper stickers on our cars or tattoo value-relevant icons on our biceps. We have favorite mottoes that embody our values which we repeat to others and to ourselves (Burrell, 1997). Again, whether we always adhere to a motto is not the point; the motto is how we want to present ourselves. Nonetheless, we feel righteous when we live up to our values and shame or guilt when we do not even try. A final function of values is to provide justifications for what we do and feel (Kristiansen & Zanna, 1994).

Values also have social functions. People in the same group profess the same sorts of values, at least insofar as the values are relevant to the group's purpose. A shared sense of what is desirable may even be a defining characteristic of a viable group because it explains why the group exists in the first place, why people should join the group, and why the group should continue (chapter 11). So, the *New York Times*'s motto, "all the news that's fit to print," conveys all of these notions in one pithy phrase. Excellence in journalism is expected of reporters and promised to readers.

Shared values regularize behavior within a group in an efficient way by articulating a general rule that applies broadly, so group members are spared the ongoing reinvention of standards and their justifications. "The parents are always right" is a value held within many traditional families, and "the children are always right" is a value apparently held by many yuppie families, or at least those seated next to us in restaurants. Regardless, shared values reduce conflict within the group. "That's the way we do things around here; it's the right thing to do. If you don't like it, leave."

Shared values justify sanctions against deviants, and they help to muster the collective indignation of the group against an offender. Punishment becomes possible without arousing the sympathetic opposition of the group. Firing someone because he showed up to work 5 minutes late seems cruel and harsh, but firing him because he did not respect the rules or his fellow workers sounds much more reasonable, even if his specific infraction was showing up for work 5 minutes late.

Values held by group members also allow them to judge other groups—for better or worse—and to decide how to treat them. So, are Jews, Christians, and Muslims all children of Abraham, or are they locked in inherent conflict? The value someone holds about the breadth of the relevant moral circle—sometimes called *universalism*—dictates how this question is to be answered (P. Singer, 1981, 1993).

Like at the individual level, group values are a public statement. How does one's group want to be known to the world? Most U.S. states have mottoes (Burrell, 1997), and it is no coincidence that the mottoes of the 13 original states convey sentiments justifying the 1776 revolution against England. The New Hampshire slogan is "Live Free or Die," and the Rhode Island slogan is "Hope." In Delaware, we have "Liberty and Independence," and in New Jersey, "Liberty and Prosperity." In Pennsylvania, the motto is "Virtue, Liberty, and Independence." The Massachusetts motto is a mouthful that makes the same point: "By the sword we seek peace, but peace only under liberty." My own state of residence, Michigan, is a newer addition to the United States. Our motto has little to do with freedom and apparently more to do with tourism: "If you seek a pleasant peninsula, look around you." (The Michigan motto is more impressive when rendered in Latin: *Si Quaeris Peninsulam Amoenam Circumspice.*)

Shared values are not just a means of social control and a way to protect the status quo. Change is also possible because of values, and one of the rallying points for social activism of any stripe is to make some plan into a cause by phrasing it in the language of values.

The Peace Corps was established in 1961 to promote world peace, understanding, and friendship. Nowadays, the Peace Corps may also provide a way for young Americans to see the world, to learn a language other than English, and to decide what they want to do for a career, but these motives—not in themselves objectionable—do not provide the moral oomph to have sustained the efforts of more than 180,000 Peace Corps members over the decades.

I will now describe what psychologists have learned about values. What are they, and—just as important—what are they not? How can we identify and assess values? Is it possible to speak of universally recognized values? What are the tradeoffs among different values? Where and how do they originate? Is value change possible, and if so, with what effects?

What Are Values?

One hears a great deal about values—family values, American values, cultural values, and the like. In general terms, a *value* is an enduring belief that some goals are preferable to others (Rokeach, 1973, 1979). People and societies of course differ in their values, with important consequences for behavior.

Unlike many other topics of interest to positive psychology, values have long been the subject of research and indeed a focus within all social science disciplines, including anthropology, economics, political science, sociology, and of course psychology (F. Adler, 1956; Barth, 1993; Dukes, 1955; W. F. Hill, 1960; Hull, 1945; Kluckhohn, 1951; Scitovsky, 1993; Sherif, 1936; Vernon & Allport, 1931). Here I will privilege the study of values by psychology because of its concern with their underlying processes and meanings. Psychological approaches treat *value* not simply as a noun but also as a verb. How do we arrive at preferred goals (Rohan, 2000)?

One of my graduate school professors at the University of Colorado, William Scott (1963), extensively studied values and grappled with how they might be defined and measured. Professor Scott was very much an empirical scientist, and to study values, he started by talking to people (Scott, 1959). His interview strategy entailed establishing rapport with a series of warm-up questions and then cutting to the chase:

> Think about the various people you admire, and try to reflect on what it is about them that is admirable. Now consider the general question: What is it about any person that makes him [or her] good? What personal traits would you say are particularly admirable? . . . Please

> [think about] the traits you have mentioned. . . . Which ones do you think are inherently good, and should properly be regarded as good by all people? (Scott, 1963, p. 17)

Scott deliberately chose the word *admire* to capture what people valued without raising anyone's hackles by using more loaded terms such as *right* and *wrong*. However, as subsequent questions in the interview revealed, most people showed little hesitation in labeling admired traits morally right.

Scott used these open-ended descriptions to arrive at a fuller definition of a value as a preferred goal that one regards as (a) inherently good: being an ultimate goal; (b) absolutely good: holding in all circumstances; and (c) universally good: applying to all people. To be sure, there were individuals who offered more-qualified responses ("it depends"), but the majority regarded values in these terms. Indeed, most interview subjects believed that all right-minded people should see things as they did and therefore should have the same values.[1]

Although Scott's interview started with questions about admired traits and thus sounds like an investigation of character strengths like the one described in chapter 6, note the difference. He asked about characteristics we admire in others, whether or not we embody these characteristics in our own actions.

Scott's interview subjects were college students from two generations ago, and he did not suggest that the admired characteristics they identified were exhaustive or universal. Nonetheless, here are the values that emerged from his interviews, and you can see that they have a degree of generality:

- achievement
- creativity
- honesty
- independence
- intellectualism
- kindness
- loyalty
- physical prowess
- religiousness
- self-control
- social skills
- status

1. At least in the contemporary United States, political differences are increasingly being recast as moral differences or value divides. Given how most people regard values—goals that all reasonable people should prize—the nearly inevitable consequence of believing that your political opponents do not agree with your values is to conclude that they are stupid, evil, or both. This vilification of one's opponents occurs across the political spectrum, and if I may say so, it is simply not a good thing (e.g., Franken, 2003; Hannity, 2004). My perspective is that most political debates need reframing. What are called value differences are actually attitude or opinion differences—important, to be sure, but without sweeping implications about the moral character of one's opponents.

Most, if not all, of these values are ideals that everyone endorses, which illustrates another important point about values. They are usually regarded by most people as positive; all are found somewhere north of neutral. When we say that people have different values, the more precise statement is that people have different *value priorities*. We order our values and use this ordering to adjudicate conflicts as they arise (Tetlock, 1986). Yet another important point is that almost all of us have a *value system* composed of several values.

All things being equal, loyalty to one's group is a value that everyone endorses. Try to imagine a group not on a reality television show that celebrates treachery and fickleness. In the real world, though, loyalty may butt up against honesty, another widely endorsed value. Some folks resolve the conflict by being loyal (e.g., not criticizing the group even when the criticism is accurate), and others by being honest (e.g., saying that the emperor has no clothes). In neither case should we presume that the subordinated value is unimportant, just that it is less important at that time than the primary value.

Later in this chapter, I will discuss how psychologists measure values, and one of the problems posed by their general positivity is the creation of what researchers call **ceiling effects**. The endorsement of values usually bunches up at the higher end of a rating scale, which means that distinctions among them can be difficult to measure reliably or meaningfully.

I should emphasize again that values are also social. Groups can be described as sharing values (because their individual members tend to agree about what are desirable goals). Shared values are one of the defining characteristics of a group and serve to distinguish them from mere aggregations—collections of people who happen to be in the same place at the same time (chapter 11).

Scott (1963) showed, for instance, that many groups differ, as we would expect, with respect to their shared values. So, members of college thespian societies value creativity more than do undergraduates in general. Fraternity and sorority members especially value social skills and loyalty. Seminarians value religiousness. Honors students value academic achievement. Athletic and outdoorsy groups value physical prowess. And in a comparison that makes me smile, he studied members of a University of Colorado student group that prided itself on its deviance and found that they shared values of independence and nonconformity (but apparently not vis-à-vis one another).

Scott also showed that college students join groups that hold values congruent with their own, and further that group members are evaluated by their peers in terms of their similarity or dissimilarity to the shared values of the group. Interestingly, there was little evidence in his research that belonging to a college group moved any member over time to be more similar to the shared values, although it should be remembered that these were voluntary organizations, and there may have been little room for further movement. Later in this chapter, I discuss some of the origins of values, and theorists agree that social institutions such as the family and the larger culture create and shape values. The social context of values should always be kept in mind, even if it recedes into the background of a given discussion (Hitlin & Piliavin, 2004).

In sum, values are beliefs held by individuals and shared by groups about desirable ends; they transcend specific situations; they guide how we select actions and evaluate others and ourselves; and they are ordered by their relative importance (S. H. Schwartz & Bilsky, 1987). Furthermore, values are not held in a vacuum; they are part of someone's larger ideology about the world and how it should be (Maio, Olson, Bernard, & Luke, 2003).

What Are Values Not?

Most commentators observe that the term *value* has been used promiscuously to refer to all sorts of entities: interests, pleasures, likes, preferences, duties, moral obligations, desires, wants, goals, needs, and orientations. I have tried to be clear what values are, but given the sprawling use of the notion, it is also worth mentioning what they are not.

Values are *not* attitudes, although a slippery slope connects the two. Values are abstract ideals, whereas **attitudes** are favorable or unfavorable evaluations of a specific object or issue.[2] If we believe that people should be kind toward others, that is a value. If we believe that drivers should use their turn signals, that belief more closely resembles an attitude because it is much more specific. And if we despise drivers in SUVs who do not use their turn signals in heavy traffic, that is unambiguously an attitude.

Abstract values subsume specific attitudes, although the mapping is not perfect, and its details vary across people. The value of equality may translate itself into strong support for affirmative action programs, but it may also lead to equally strong opposition to such programs. Someone who values "life" may be opposed to abortion, but someone else who equally values "life" may be opposed to war or the death penalty. As you well know, at least in the United States, these someones are rarely the same people. The devil—or at least the attitude—is always in the details.

It is worth noting that those who champion a given value usually do so in the affirmative—echoing the premise of the Pollyanna Principle that the positive is more basic and memorable (chapter 5). So, those who favor the right to abortion describe their position as pro-choice. Those who favor the death penalty speak of

2. Even in the abstract, the value-attitude distinction is not always a clean one. Some people treat attitudes as values, elevating their evaluation of a specific group to a broad moral imperative and using it to guide all of their thoughts, feelings, and actions. Consider groups that revolve around opposition to Jews, or Blacks, or Catholics. The relevant attitudes are specific but lead to goals—the eradication of these sorts of people—that are regarded by those who hold them as inherently, absolutely, and universally desirable.

law and order and accountability. Those opposed to gay marriage say that their goal is to protect the traditional family.

There are further distinctions between values and attitudes. Most values are more central to an individual's self-concept than are most attitudes (Hitlin, 2003). "I hate Brussels sprouts" may be a strongly held attitude, but it will rarely define how a person thinks about herself (Hitlin & Piliavin, 2004). At the same time, abstract values are less related to specific behaviors than are specific attitudes (S. H. Schwartz, 1996). Those who hate Brussels sprouts probably do not eat them, but those who value hedonism may or may not eat Brussels sprouts, no matter how weird they taste. Finally, longitudinal research shows that values are more stable across the lifespan than are attitudes (Konty & Dunham, 1997).

Values are *not* traits, even though identical terms can be used to describe each[3] (chapter 6). **Traits** are dispositions to think, feel, and act in consistent ways, whereas values are beliefs about desirable goals which—as already noted—may not map neatly onto specific or consistent behaviors. Some traits are positive (e.g., kindness) and others negative (e.g., neuroticism), but many are simply neutral (e.g., introversion or extraversion). We use our own values but not our own traits to judge the conduct of others.

Values are *not* norms, although both embody a sense of oughtness (Marini, 2000). The difference is that **norms** are thoroughly situational—shared beliefs that one should act in certain ways in certain circumstances. Wedding guests *should* bring wrapped presents. Values, in contrast, cut across situations. People *should* be polite to everyone, including brides and grooms but also parking lot attendants, waiters, and limousine drivers.

Another difference, at least for some of us, is that we chafe under norms and feel that they constrain who we really are (R. H. Turner, 1976). "I do not want to buy a present for someone just because I am expected to do so." In contrast, we do not experience our values as constraining us. They are, after all, who we are, and it is when we fail to express our values in our actions that we feel discomfort or disappointment.

Values are *not* needs, although both influence how we behave. **Needs** have a biological connotation—e.g., hunger, thirst, sex—and function as motives. They move us to behave in ways to satisfy them. Values enter into the process by providing socially acceptable ways of articulating needs.[4] They dictate desirable or

3. Values and virtues (positive traits) may be used to explain the same morally praiseworthy behavior, but values are regarded as external standards and virtues as internal qualities (Holmes, 1998; Rachels, 1999).

4. Not all values direct biological needs, unless we want to stretch what we mean by a need to include any and all motives. Many motives do not behave like biological needs in the sense of impelling behavior to "satisfy" the need, after which the behavior ceases until the need returns. Hunger is a need in this sense: We are hungry; we eat; and then we are not hungry and do not eat. Many of the uniquely human motives do not show this pattern of arousal, consummation, and satiation. Consider the state of flow and our desire to experience it (chapter 4). Do we ever say, "Okay, enough of that"?

undesirable ways to gratify a given need. Sexual desire is rarely satisfied indiscriminately. Marriage is a valued institution revolving around the satisfaction of sexual needs (among other things), whereas prostitution is a crime revolving around the satisfaction of sexual needs (among other things).

I hope that I have distinguished values from attitudes, traits, norms, and needs. I should note as well that values are not mere tastes or idiosyncratic preferences. Personal interests are very important to us and have a place in positive psychology because we pursue them with vigor and use them to define who we are (chapter 8). But personal interests are simply that and carry with them little expectation that others should have the same interests. Indeed, we assume variation across people and probably prefer it, because variation serves our own sense of uniqueness. Some of us like Pepsi and others Coca-Cola. Some like the Chicago Cubs and others the White Sox. Some of us hang toilet paper over the top and others down the wall. We may tease one another about our respective tastes, preferences, and interests, and some of the "get a life" folks among us may turn them into larger moral issues. But for the most part we do not. Values are of course different. People on opposite sides of value conflicts are not known to chide each other gently nor to find the values of others a source of amusement.

Cataloging Values

The number of values we might espouse is finite but still potentially very large. How might we sift through them to arrive at a set big enough to capture the range of what people believe about desirable goals but small enough to be scientifically wieldy?

Some psychologists simply rely on their own intuitions, experiences, and hunches to identify a core of important values. Milton Rokeach (1973), one of the pioneering researchers in the study of values, relied largely on his own notions of what people value to distinguish what he called **terminal values**, beliefs about ideal states of existence:

- a comfortable life
- an exciting life
- a sense of accomplishment
- a world at peace
- a world of beauty
- equality
- family security
- freedom
- happiness
- inner harmony
- mature love

- national security
- pleasure
- salvation
- self-respect
- social recognition
- true friendship
- wisdom

Rokeach also articulated what he called **instrumental values**, beliefs about ideal modes of conduct that presumably aid and abet terminal values, but his instrumental-terminal distinction (means versus ends) does not hold up in practice (e.g., S. H. Schwartz, 1994).

Other psychologists, like William Scott, have been more systematic and use interviews or focus groups to identify people's values. And still others turn to existing theories to deduce a set of values that deserves study.

For example, an early and still influential catalog of values was proposed years ago by Harvard psychologist Gordon Allport and his colleagues (Allport, 1937; Allport, Vernon, & Lindzey, 1960; Vernon & Allport, 1931). Their starting point was an even earlier theory about the basic "types" of people (Spranger, 1928). Although contemporary psychologists do not so readily assume that people fall into discrete psychological clumps[5] (cf. Haslam & Kim, 2003), one can still make distinctions among their beliefs and then describe actual people in terms of how closely their beliefs resemble the prototypes captured by each distinction. Allport et al. followed this strategy in proposing six basic values:

- theoretical: valuing truth and its discovery
- economic: valuing what is useful and practical
- aesthetic: valuing what is beautiful and harmonious
- political: valuing power, influence, and renown
- social: valuing other people and their welfare
- religious: valuing transcendence and communion with the larger universe

Another example of a value catalog based on a previous theory is political scientist Ronald Inglehart's (1990) use of Maslow's (1970) **hierarchy of needs** to specify the goals that groups of people most value. As you may know, Maslow believed that human motives could be arranged in a hierarchy reflecting the order in which we attend to them.

5. This is not to deny the existence of actual people who perfectly exemplify personality or social types (Peterson & Seligman, 2004). There really are optimists in the world, and there really are mean girls. The issue is whether these sorts of categories exhaust the population. Does it make sense to say that there are only two types of people: optimists and pessimists (chapter 5)? If someone is not a mean girl, must she then be a nice girl (chapter 6)? Not necessarily, and we therefore talk about these categories as ideal types or as prototypes and recognize that people usually depart from prototypes in degree and not kind.

At the bottom are biologically based needs, such as hunger and thirst. We cannot leave these needs unsatisfied for too long, because our lives are at stake. Only when these needs are met does the need to be free from threatened danger arise. Maslow called this need one of safety—both physical and psychological. We need to believe that the world is stable and coherent. Next in the hierarchy is attachment, which leads us to seek out other people, to love, and to be loved. If we successfully satisfy this need for attachment, then we need to feel esteemed, by ourselves and by others. Maslow grouped our needs for knowledge, understanding, and novelty together as cognitive needs, and proposed that they are next in his hierarchy. Then we find aesthetic needs: the desire for order and beauty. Near the top of his hierarchy is self-actualization: "the full use and exploitation of [one's] talents, capacities, potentialities" (Maslow, 1970, p. 150). Maslow argued that we must satisfy lower needs before we seek the satisfaction of higher needs. The need for self-actualization is in particular difficult to achieve because it only becomes relevant when the needs that fall below it have been successfully addressed.

Although Maslow's theory is about needs and not values, Inglehart recast each need as an end state that people might regard as desirable, thereby arriving at a catalog of values. He distinguished between **survival values** (those corresponding to needs at the bottom of Maslow's hierarchy) and **self-expressive values** (those corresponding to needs at the top), and has been involved in research that measures instances of such values in a variety of nations around the globe. In keeping with Maslow's basic premise, nations that become more affluent over time usually show the predicted progression from survival to self-expressive values.

Another use of theory to deduce values is by philosopher Sissela Bok (1995), who tried to identify universally held values. Her insight was that the level of abstraction matters in deeming values to be universal or not. In very general terms, people in all times and places must endorse three sets of values: (a) positive duties of mutual care and reciprocity; (b) negative injunctions against violence, deceit, and betrayal; and (c) norms for rudimentary fairness and procedural justice in cases of conflict regarding positive duties and/or negative injunctions. Bok called these **minimalist values**—a term I do not especially like because it conjures up images of sparseness (think Yugos or generic cigarettes)—but her intended meaning is that these values embody the minimal requirements for a viable society. In the absence of even one of these values, it is difficult to imagine a society continuing.

There are also maximalist values, as it were, more numerous, extensive, elaborated, and culturally situated: e.g., the teachings of the Roman Catholic Church with respect to contraception and abortion. Any given cultural group of course endorses both minimalist and maximalist values and usually has no reason to distinguish between them. But if one wishes to speak across groups—like when members of the United Nations make pronouncements to the entire world about human rights—it behooves one to keep them straight.

A final example of the use of theory to demarcate important human values is found in the work of psychologist Shalom Schwartz and his colleagues (Schwartz, 1992, 1994, 1996; Schwartz & Bilsky, 1987, 1990; Schwartz & Sagiv, 1995). Like Bok, they started with a vision of what was universally required for individuals and groups to survive and thrive, pointing specifically to the (a) biologically based needs of the individual; (b) requirements for social coordination and interaction; and (c) institutional demands concerning group welfare. Into this scheme, they fit more specific values, relying to a large degree on the list of values proposed by Rokeach.

I note in passing that some theorists have proposed more-circumscribed value catalogs, intended to be relevant to given groups but not necessarily to others. So, William Scott (1963) studied U.S. college students and in particular social fraternities and sororities. Geert Hofstede (2001) concerned himself with values in the workplace. Given the meaning of a value as trans-situational, it is not surprising that the values included in even these deliberately focused endeavors are rather general and see use by theorists and researchers whose interest goes beyond Greek organizations or work sites.

As lists of values accumulated, the most typical strategy used to identify important values has been for a psychologist to consolidate, elaborate, and tweak these earlier efforts (e.g., Braithwaite & Law, 1985). Most psychologists agree, not surprisingly, that there are a dozen or so important values recognized by most people in most places.

The problem with this approach is that it fails to recognize the emergence of a new value among people because of its reliance on extant theorizing about old values. For instance, Timothy Kasser (2005) drew psychology's attention to an emerging value in some segments of the population that he called "time affluence": valuing a life in which there is enough time to do what one really wants to do. He juxtaposed and contrasted time affluence with the more-familiar value of material affluence,[6] finding in his research that they might be incompatible and further that time affluence is a more-robust predictor of well-being than is material affluence. Remember the finding cited in chapter 4 that one of the stronger correlates of life satisfaction is the amount of time one spends at leisure activities? Valuing time affluence may set the stage for a satisfied life and thus deserves more attention by positive psychologists. More generally, think of your own

6. Kasser's (2002) general research interest is materialism and its psychological costs. So, people who pursue expensive things—material goods—and the images they create are not as happy as those who pursue less-tangible goals like good relationships with others. Materialism is arguably sustained by our consumer culture, which promises happiness if we only purchase the right wristwatch, the right clothes, or the right car. In this context, think about a genre of contemporary ads in which young couples breathlessly recite to one another all the things they have to do in their lives and their insight that a given product will allow them to achieve everything in their otherwise impossible schedules. The subtext of these ads undercuts the value of time affluence because the possibility is never raised that one might simply put less on one's temporal plate.

group or society. Are there emerging values not captured in past and present value catalogs?

Measuring Values

Given some set of values that we think worthy of study, how do we actually go about this? As I have discussed in previous chapters, researchers must come up with concrete ways to assess the abstract concepts in which they are interested. Although there are occasional discussions of "unconscious" values[7] (S. Epstein, 1989), researchers for the most part have assumed that people know what they think is desirable and hence can report their values. By far the most typical way of measuring values relies on self-report[8] (Braithwaite & Scott, 1991). Within this strategy, though, there is considerable variation.

Some researchers ask respondents about specific attitudes and behaviors that presumably reflect a given value. From the pattern of responses, the value is inferred. So, we might conclude that you have a strong religious value to the degree that you report attending religious services regularly, pray on a daily basis, consult religious texts for guidance, and so on. I have already implied the problem with this strategy: Although behaviors and attitudes are of course related to more general values, the relationship is not one of perfect redundancy. You may attend church because of the social needs thereby satisfied, because it confers status in your community, or simply because there is no other game in town. Or you may attend church because you value religion. How do we know what is behind your behavior? We are clueless if we inquire only about these concrete and fallible indicators of religiousness (Allport, 1950). A related problem with this approach is that it makes it impossible to investigate the degree to which behaviors and attitudes are congruent with values or the circumstances that determine this congruence.

Earlier values researchers were of course mindful of these issues, and they opted for the indirect strategy of assessment only because they believed that gen-

7. Without deeming values to be unconscious and dragging along all that might mean, we can still recognize that people might not be entirely clear about what their values are or how they might be reflected in their behavior. Accordingly, there is a self-help approach known as **values clarification**, which provides ways to help people see what they value most, like asking them to list the things they most love to do, the places they most like to visit, the fictional characters with whom they most identify, and so on (Simon, Howe, & Kirschenbaum, 1995). One looks for common themes across exercises and thereby clarifies what one most values.

8. It cannot be a coincidence that most of the influential theorists discussed in this chapter are also known for devising a questionnaire measure of values that has seen widespread use, e.g., Allport, Scott, Rokeach, Inglehart, Hofstede, and S. Schwartz. There is some insight into psychological science provided by this fact, which recurs across subfields of the discipline: A psychologist becomes important not just by having good ideas but by providing concrete methods that allow others to investigate these ideas.

eral questions about abstract values might not be valid. More-recent researchers have found that people can offer abstract judgments about their values that prove scientifically useful—reliable and valid—so long as the questions do not stray too far into the stratosphere (S. H. Schwartz et al., 2001).

Given that people can be directly asked about their values, what do we ask them? Again, we find considerable variation. Some researchers ask for a simple yes-no endorsement of particular values. Other researchers ask for more fine-grained distinctions, using psychology's familiar 5-point or 7-point scales of agreement or endorsement. This has the benefit of spreading out responses although, as already mentioned, most values remain north of neutral.

In some approaches to value measurement, only one question per value is asked, a strategy that is efficient but suspicious. When researchers pose different questions about the same value, answers converge but not perfectly, implying the prudence of trying to measure the same notion in different ways and then combining answers.[9]

An altogether different approach to measurement asks respondents to rank order different values. The rationale for this strategy is that value ranking reflects how people actually use values in everyday life. Ranking builds into measurement the hierarchy thought to characterize value systems.[10] So, the Rokeach Value Survey provides research participants with the 18 values listed earlier and asks that they be placed in order. People are given separate cards or labels for each value and asked to rearrange them physically.

The ranking strategy yields what are known as **ipsative scores** for each individual: the position of each value held by the individual relative to other values (Cattell, 1944). With ipsative scores, we cannot make absolute comparisons across people. We can imagine a respondent whose ipsative rank for freedom is 1 who

9. The reliability (internal consistency) of a questionnaire is a function of the number of items it includes (chapter 4). A 10-item scale is more reliable than a 5-item scale, and a 50-item scale is more reliable than a 10-item scale (Cronbach, 1951). Accordingly, most measures of traits, attitudes, and values contain multiple items that try to ascertain the same concept with somewhat different questions. I often hear complaints from research participants in my own survey studies that "you are asking the same question over and over" or "you must be checking up on my memory for how I just answered." Up to a point, these complaints mean that the different questions I have devised—which by the way are never identical—are doing their intended job. But there is a line that a researcher does not want to cross, because research participants may become annoyed with what they think is busy work on a survey.

10. There is a minority opinion that values are not always traded off by people and that many of our activities can simultaneously reflect two or more values. Indeed, perhaps we prefer activities that embody our full value system and not just one value to the exclusion of the others we may hold dear. Someone who values religion and beauty, for example, may be drawn to worship in a majestic cathedral or to participate in a talented church choir. Does she value religion or beauty? The answer is both, and for her, there is no tradeoff. So why should tradeoffs be built into our theories and measures? Here we have an instance of the full life vis-à-vis values that is analogous to the full life vis-à-vis approaches to happiness that I discussed in chapter 4.

nonetheless values freedom in an absolute sense less than someone else whose ipsative rank for freedom is 2 or 3 or even lower.

Another drawback to the ranking approach is that it limits the number of items that can be considered by a research participant at the same time. Providing 18 different values to be rank ordered can be unwieldy. I have myself tried to use such an approach by giving people index cards to be physically arranged, and what results is sometimes more slapstick than science. My research subjects drop the cards or lose them; they bend, they fold, they spindle, and they mutilate. They create a big mess.

The good news is that ranking methods, at least when used by researchers more skilled than me, yield much the same results about the relative importance of values as those that rely on rating methods. This allows researchers to rely on the simpler strategy of rating. If ipsative scores are of theoretical interest, they can be calculated after the fact from ratings (Park, Peterson, & Seligman, 2004).

A Universal Structure of Human Values

I have noted that the value catalogs proposed by different psychologists over the years agree substantially. This conclusion is buttressed by the research of Shalom Schwartz, who set out deliberately to identify what he hoped to be universally recognized human values by studying value endorsement in dozens of countries around the world. His work is also notable because he addressed the relationships among different values—what he called their "structure"—and thus studied not just individual values but entire value systems.

This approach is scientifically laudable because it allows nuanced conclusions about the consequences of holding certain values rather than others. In emphasizing one value, we may be deemphasizing another, and it is not always clear what is responsible for a given empirical finding. So, Kasser (2002) found that materialists are unhappy, but is this because the pursuit of material goods in itself lowers life satisfaction or because materialistic individuals often do not value other people so much and as a result miss out on the interpersonal sources of happiness?

As mentioned, Shalom Schwartz started with the Rokeach list of terminal values, which he asked research participants to rank order in importance. He then had them go back to their ranks and fine-tune them by rating how similar or dissimilar two adjacently ranked values were in terms of personal importance. By using sophisticated statistical procedures, the details of which need not concern us here, Schwartz looked first at the values which people distinguished and second at how these distinguished values were related to one another. He and his colleagues went on to repeat these studies in 70 different nations, finding much the same results in each sample.

Ten different values are consistently distinguished around the world:

- achievement: personal success through the demonstration of competence in accordance with society's standards, e.g., ambition
- benevolence: preservation and enhancement of the welfare of others in one's immediate social circle, e.g., forgiveness
- conformity: restraint of actions that violate social norms or expectations, e.g., politeness
- hedonism: personal gratification and pleasure, e.g., enjoyment of food, sex, and leisure
- power: social status, prestige, dominance, and control over others, e.g., wealth
- security: safety, harmony, and stability of society, e.g., law and order
- self-direction: independent thought and action, e.g., freedom
- stimulation: excitement, novelty, and challenge in life, e.g., variety
- tradition: respect for and acceptance of one's cultural or religious customs, e.g., religious devotion
- universalism: understanding, appreciating, and protecting all people and nature, e.g., social justice, equality, environmentalism

These values are structured along two basic dimensions, as shown in Figure 7.1. This figure is another example of a circumplex model, discussed in the previous chapter in the context of tradeoffs among character strengths (p. 157). If two

Figure 7.1. Tradeoffs Among Values

The farther apart are two values, the less likely it is that the same person strongly endorses both.

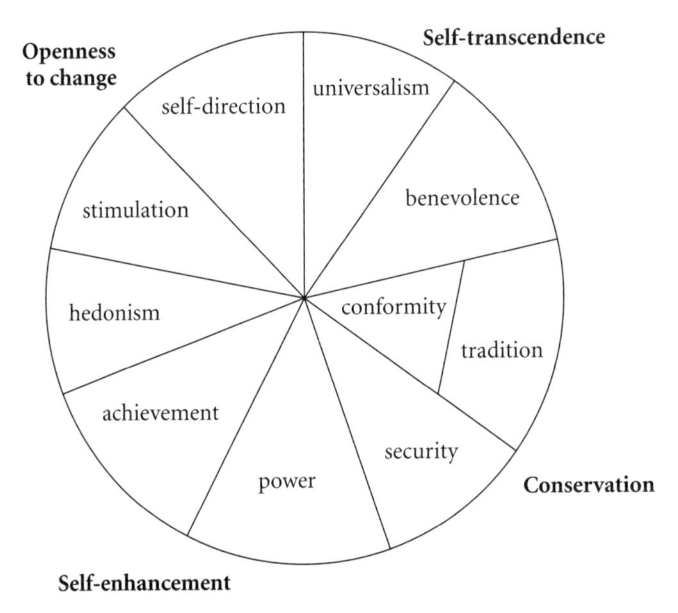

values are close to one another on the circle (like achievement and power), then they are compatible, and the same people tend to endorse both. If two values are on opposite sides of the circle (like benevolence and achievement), then they tend to be incompatible and *not* likely to be held by the same people. Remember, though, that all values lie north of neutral. These pronouncements about the relationships among values describe *relative* emphases—conclusions about value priorities. Someone who strongly values security does not believe, for example, that stimulation is a bad thing, just that it is less valuable than security. By the way, conformity and tradition are depicted as they are in Figure 7.1 because they are distinguished by people yet related similarly to other values, with tradition being more extreme than conformity.

A theorist tries to make further sense of a circumplex model by specifying its underlying dimensions. In the case of Schwartz's circumplex, these seem rather obvious. One dimension—as shown in Figure 7.1—is whether the values revolve around *self-enhancement* (achievement, power) or around *self-transcendence* (universalism, benevolence). We could also label this dimension self versus other, agency versus communion, individualism versus collectivism, or independence versus interdependence (Helgeson, 1994; Markus & Kitayama, 1991; Triandis, 1995). Or we could use Inglehart's distinction between survival values and self-expressive values. Each of these sets of labels has slightly different connotations, but together they capture the idea that people's value priorities can reflect an emphasis on what is good for themselves as individuals or an emphasis on what is good for other people and groups with which they have commerce.

The second dimension underlying the value structure in Figure 7.1 is anchored on one end by *conservation* (conformity, tradition, security) and on the other by *openness to change* (hedonism, stimulation, self-direction), a dimension which I could also label conservatism-liberalism if you promise not to interpret these terms in a narrowly political way. Another set of labels for this contrast is traditional versus secular (Baker, 2005), and Rohan (2000) suggested priority on organization versus priority on opportunity.

Whatever we call its two dimensions, Schwartz's circumplex model helps us to make sense of someone's value system as a whole and the tradeoffs that often result within it. Rohan (2000) gave the example of human rights activists, who presumably place a high value on equality, or universalism in Schwartz's scheme. We can expect that most activists value the adjacent value of self-direction. Because the power value is in direct opposition to universalism, we can further expect human rights activists to make few status distinctions among their ranks, to avoid staying at luxury hotels when at a political rally, and to react negatively to a show of police strength.

Similarly, think about other value-relevant events that attract attention and debate. I am drafting this paragraph amid news stories about Federal Communications Commission censorship, the privatization of Social Security, and the Terry Schiavo life-support case. Whatever your position with respect to any of these issues, you probably frame it in terms of some value of importance to you, and your related positions can likely be predicted from the circumplex model of Schwartz.

Origin of Values

Once we arrive at our values, we hold them rather tenaciously. But where do they originate? Theorists over the years have invariably pointed to processes of socialization and learning. The fine detail of their explanations reflect whatever psychological theory was prevailing at the time.

In the 1940s and 1950s, when reinforcement theories were popular in psychology, the acquisition of specific values was explained in terms of reward and punishment (Hull, 1945). A generation later, with the advent of social learning theory à la Rotter (1954) and Bandura (1969) and its emphasis on other people as the primary source of what we learn, the acquisition of specific values was explained in terms of **modeling**: emulating what influential others say and do. When the cognitive revolution swept through psychology (chapter 5), legitimizing cognitive explanations of any and all phenomena, values acquisition was explained in terms of inherent tendencies to be consistent in what one believes.[11]

From the vantage point of positive psychology, I speculate that people may also acquire values by a deliberate process of asking what is the right thing and choosing an answer which then becomes a value. This process does not reduce value acquisition to the automatic operation of reward, modeling, or consistency seeking. To be sure, the deliberate embracing of value priorities might be occasioned by events in our lives that trigger scrutiny. For instance, many people who have had a brush with death say that they now "know" what is most important. In my own studies of character strengths, I have found that people who have recovered from a life-threatening illness show elevated levels of appreciation of beauty, curiosity, fairness, forgiveness, gratitude, humor, kindness, love of learning, and spirituality, and as virtues slide into values, perhaps we have another instance of how values change (Peterson, Park, & Seligman, 2006).

11. A host of theories stressing cognitive consistency were at one time extremely popular in psychology (e.g., Abelson et al., 1968). Common to all was the assumption that our thoughts seek out emotional balance, harmony, concordance, or consistency. If you like Penny, and you also like Mary, then you want Penny and Mary to like one another (Heider, 1946). If this is not the case, you experience discomfort—Festinger (1957) dubbed it "cognitive dissonance"—and are motivated to resolve the inconsistency and reduce your discomfort. Maybe Penny is really not all that likable. Maybe Mary does not know the real Penny. Or maybe both of them are shallow and not worthy of your friendship. A major drawback to consistency theories is that most of us do a good job segregating our various thoughts and beliefs from one another, which means that contradictions may never consciously register. So, when psychologists use consistency theories as a basis for designing interventions to change attitudes or values, making salient what people believe is always a critical first step.

As I described in the last chapter, immediately after 9/11, Americans were more likely to emphasize behaviors reflecting core values of faith, hope, and love (Peterson & Seligman, 2003a). These changes were not permanent, and as lives more or less returned to normal, so too did the emphases on these values.

But in other cases, changes are more long-lasting. My own valuing of human equality was permanently forged during my college years as my circle of friends expanded beyond the suburban kids with whom I had grown up. Even as the larger society in general and social science in particular recognize and stress "diversity" among people, I still strongly believe that folks are more similar than they are different, and the implied value of equality infuses how I act.

A more-striking example of value conversion is the story of John Newton, an 18th-century ship captain involved in the trafficking of slaves. After a storm in which his ship was almost lost, he examined his life and became a minister and—by some reports—an abolitionist. Why do we know his story? Following his brush with death, Newton wrote "Amazing Grace," which two centuries later became one of the anthems of the U.S. civil rights movement:

> Amazing grace! How sweet the sound
> That saved a wretch like me!
> I once was lost, but now am found;
> Was blind, but now I see.
> —John Newton (1779)

All of these processes—reward and punishment, modeling, cognitive consistency, and self-examination—work in tandem to explain how we acquire given values. For instance, honesty is a value I learned as a child. Part of my learning was bottom-up in the sense that I was spanked for telling specific fibs and praised, after a fashion, for 'fessing up after specific misdeeds. From this pattern of discipline, I arrived at the conclusion that honesty was usually a good policy.

My parents were also excellent models for this value, not only because they themselves consistently told the truth but also because they endorsed honesty in more-general terms. "Always tell the truth so you do not have to remember what you said" was one of the wry family mottoes that I remember to this day. Rhetoric about generation gaps notwithstanding, parents and their children often profess similar values, implying that the modeling of values transcends superficial cohort differences in musical preferences, hairstyles, and the like (Alessandri & Wozniak, 1989; Kohn, 1983; Kuczynski, Marshall, & Schell, 1997).

Cognitive consistency entered the scene as I became a teenager and was bombarded with news stories that morally undressed people whom I thought were heroes. The only way I could rationalize these kinds of stories, which always left me feeling empty, was to recognize that all people have flaws, even my heroes, but that the ultimate flaw is false righteousness—lying about one's transgressions even when they are incontestable. Anyone who lied stopped being my hero. Honesty for me became a way of resolving what otherwise seemed to be impossible contradictions.

Honesty is a good policy but not always an easy one to enact, at least for me. I also have a strong value concerning benevolence, which means that I like to please other people. That often means telling them what they want to hear. Sometimes benevolence in these terms runs at cross-purposes to honesty, and on more than a few occasions, I have needed to take deliberate stock of how I interact with others and to speak the unpleasant truth as I see it.

Rokeach (1971) elaborated this strategy of **value self-confrontation** into a means of deliberately changing someone's values. Earlier in the chapter (see fn. 7, p. 179), I mentioned values clarification, based on the gentle premise that people may need help in recognizing the values they already hold. Rokeach's intervention has a bolder rationale: People may place insufficient emphasis on a particular value because they have not confronted the contradiction among their value priorities. His strategy entails confronting people with their value priorities, explicitly interpreting the contradictions, and seeing what happens. In the vast majority of studies testing value self-confrontation, change in the expected direction occurs (Grube, Mayton, & Ball-Rokeach, 1994).

Originally, Rokeach attributed value change to the operation of cognitive consistency, but later he made a slightly different argument in terms of people's desire to think well of themselves. That is, if someone believes that a morally competent person should hold value X, and if it is pointed out that she does not hold this value, then change occurs.

This sort of intervention has been tested in experiments, usually with two conditions. In the *value confrontation condition*, respondents are asked to rank their values, and the results are fed back to them. They are also shown how other groups of people rank the same set of values. A simple comment by the researcher directs the individual's attention to discrepancies. So, in the paradigm case of this intervention, done with U.S. research participants in the 1970s when the civil rights movement was at its height, college students were shown that their peers rated freedom very highly as a value but equality much lower. Their own ratings usually reflected a similar discrepancy. Then they were told, "It appears that college students in the United States value their own freedom more than they value the equality of others." The conclusion—unstated but presumably obvious—is that they themselves were espousing a contradiction, like the majority of their peers. In a *comparison condition*, other research participants were asked to rank their own values, but without any of the subsequent self-confrontation.

Follow-up showed that participants in the confrontation condition not only changed their value priorities but did so in lasting fashion. Furthermore, when later given the opportunity to display their values—like joining the National Association for the Advancement of Colored People—they were more likely to do so than those in the comparison condition.

Similar studies have been done with other values—e.g., about the environment—always with the same results. And in an audacious experiment, this intervention was even delivered on a television show in the northwestern United

States; viewers in different regions were assigned to different conditions, again with the same results (Ball-Rokeach, Rokeach, & Grube, 1984).

These studies seem almost too powerful to be true, and the skeptic within me wonders if demand characteristics had anything to do with what was found.[12] Counting against this criticism are the behavioral checks that validated the intervention. Another consideration is one provided by Rokeach himself in his observation that this technique only works with those predisposed to change their values in the implied direction (Rokeach & Grube, 1979). So, the value self-confrontation technique has not been used to encourage members of groups with long-standing antipathies to embrace each other: Turks and Armenians, Israelis and Palestinians, and the like. Increased emphasis on equality was successfully encouraged among college students but not Ku Klux Klan members.

Assuming that it actually works, is value self-confrontation Orwellian? Rokeach has stressed that this intervention is done with everyone's eyes wide open. There is no deception. Participants are told what the purpose of the experiment is, and it would probably not work if done in a sneaky way or indeed with the goal of moving values in arbitrary directions.

Let me switch the level of discussion. Given that psychological processes are at work when we acquire specific values, the question remains about the pool of possible values from which we learn to favor some over others. Our larger culture and its priorities set the table, and here the work by University of Michigan political scientist Ronald Inglehart and his colleagues is instructive. For years, they have worked on the **World Values Survey**, an ambitious study that periodically surveys people around the world with respect to their attitudes, beliefs, and values (Inglehart, Basanez, & Moreno, 1998). Questions range from the mundane ("Is throwing away litter ever justified?") to the sacred ("How often do you think about the meaning and purpose of life?").

The World Values Survey stands apart from related projects for the large number of nations sampled—81 different countries containing 85% of the world's population—and because the respondents in each nation are **representative samples**, that is, they represent the range of individuals across important contrasts like age, gender, education, occupation, and the like. Most samples studied by social scientists and certainly psychologists in contrast are **convenience samples**, recruited by the researcher from conveniently available individuals: students in a college course, surfers on the Internet, children at a local daycare center, and so on. The hope in each case is that the convenient sample somewhat resembles the larger population to which one wishes to generalize results, but this is an ideal more than

12. A "demand characteristic" refers to an inadvertent message to a research participant in a study that certain ways of responding are more desirable than others (Orne, 1962). Expected results are produced in response to the implied demand and not for the reasons deemed to be important by whatever theory is being tested.

an actuality.[13] If one is studying what are broadly human characteristics—like how our sensory organs work—a convenience sample is likely no different from a representative sample. But in other cases, a representative sample deserves to be taken very seriously.

Here is a summary of what Inglehart (1990, 1993) has learned about value priorities in different nations:

- The values emphasized in a nation are strongly associated with its political and economic institutions.
- As nations develop industrially, specialized and educated labor forces emerge, and these economically advantaged individuals value autonomy and self-expression in all spheres of life, including politics.
- Accordingly, with industrialization comes trends toward democracy and the endorsement of values that are liberal and secular.
- When a nation shows value changes, it is usually through a process called **generational replacement** and not because given individuals change what they value. That is, younger people who come of age under different circumstances than their parents or grandparents have different value priorities, and they eventually replace the older generation.[14]
- By the way, within nations, whether people hold traditional or secular values is unrelated to their reported happiness, but the value difference is reflected in what they say is most important in determining their own happiness (Inglehart & Klingemann, 2000).

One of the conclusions that emerges from the World Values Survey is that the United States is an anomaly: the most-affluent nation on the planet yet one that remains highly traditional in its value priorities, especially with respect to religion

13. In the United States, the "best" samples in the sense of being representative are those contacted by political pollsters with the resources to contact potential respondents from across the nation, each of whom has an equal and known chance of being included. Usually, pollsters employ a random-digit dialing procedure, in which phone numbers are randomly sampled and then called. At one time, when fewer people in the United States had telephones, this procedure did not yield a representative sample. The famous misprediction of the 1948 presidential election (in which Thomas Dewey was forecast as the winner over Harry Truman) is usually explained by its reliance on telephone sampling. This strategy led to an overrepresentation of wealthier individuals, who were more likely to have telephones and more likely to favor Dewey. Some pollsters today worry that telephone sampling has run its course, with the advent of the national do-not-call registry and the growing tendency, especially among young adults, to have only a cell phone. In both cases, millions of potential poll respondents are removed from the eligible population.

14. It is not surprising that the 1989 Tiananmen Square protests in China were spearheaded by young adults, just as the 1965 Freedom Marchers and the 1971 antiwar protesters in the United States were mainly young adults. I predict with confidence that future pushes for democracy in different parts of the world will represent the sentiments of younger and more-affluent generations eager to replace older generations: "Get out of the way if you can't lend a hand 'cause the times they are a'changing."

and nationalism. For example, other than citizens of mainline Islamic nations like Indonesia, Iran, and Pakistan, people in the United States are more likely to attend religious services regularly than people elsewhere. The most secular nations, according to their value priorities, are Japan, China, Germany, Sweden, and Norway.

Baker (2005) explained the anomalous value priorities of the United States in terms of the unique history of this nation and its settling by religious refugees from Europe. Virtually every other nation has a common language, a common history, and a common ethnicity to unite its citizens. The United States has only a common value system, which may explain the tenacity of traditional values. Indeed, as I mentioned earlier, there are few value differences across U.S. generations, unlike the cohort differences found in some other parts of the world. In other words, there is less generational replacement in the United States than elsewhere.

Although the United States may abound with cultural contradictions, I think it goes beyond the actual data to say that this country is the battleground for a cultural war. That would require discrete sides, and there is no good evidence that the nation is neatly divided. Most Americans share the same values and typically endorse moderate attitudes with respect to even the most contentious issues (Fiorina, Abrams, & Pope, 2005). Even when there are demonstrable disagreements, they do not map onto the red-blue (Republican/Democrat) state partition of which political pundits seem so fond (e.g., S. B. Greenberg, 2004; J. K. White, 2003). I think the "cultural war" metaphorically rages more within each individual American than it does between Americans.

Let me close by noting the ongoing societal debate about the role of the media—television, radio, movies, newspapers, and the like—in shaping values. Are the people featured in the media—athletes, Hollywood actors, teen idols, news anchors, generic celebrities—role models in the sense of displaying values that we the people then embrace as our own?

The issue obviously comes down to whether the media and its characters create our value priorities or merely reflect them. Should we regard MTV as the root cause of everything wrong in society or simply a sensitive barometer of what actually is wrong? Perhaps the truth is a little bit of both, with the specific answer depending on the value, on the person, and on a host of other considerations. Muddying any interpretation is the fact that people exercise considerable choice over the media and messages to which they expose themselves (Ball, 1976). Countless surveys show that people listen to news with which they already agree.

We do know something about media effects in the aggregate. For example, many social scientists today agree that exposure to media violence leads people *on average* to be more violent themselves and certainly *on average* to be more inured to violence (Eron, Huesmann, Lefkowitz, & Walder, 1972; Huesmann, Moise, Podolski, & Eron, 2003). But when a teenager takes a gun to school and shoots his classmates, we have no basis for saying that his specific actions resulted from a movie he saw or a video game he played. Neither can we say that the media had nothing to do with his actions. Sometimes the ability of social science to speak to the individual case is limited (Runyan, 1981). Regardless, the positive psychology perspective implies that the media should fairly represent the world, what is good about it, and what is less so, thereby supplying a range of embodied values to which to aspire (Cohn, 2004). In particular, violent role models should be balanced with those who can elevate and inspire us (Keltner & Haidt, 2003).

EXERCISE *Choosing When and How to Choose*

When I moved to Philadelphia in 2000, I sold my car and did not replace it because I could avail myself of public transportation. Upon returning to Ann Arbor in 2003, I needed a car, but without a car with which to look for a car, I was forced to make a quick and efficient purchase. In short, I was put in a position where I needed to be a satisficer, and that worked in my favor. I learned something and confirmed Barry Schwartz's (2004) ideas in my own life.

I took a taxi to a local car dealer on the outskirts of Ann Arbor, where I spent 30 minutes looking at used (excuse me, previously owned) cars. I found one that seemed satisfactory, and I immediately wrote a check for the sticker price. Did I pay more than I might have? Yes. Did I get the best car in town? No. Am I satisfied with the car? Absolutely.

Let me contrast my experience with that of a friend elsewhere who took a prolonged—and I must say tortured—approach to replacing his car. He researched what *Consumer Reports* had to say, scoured the local newspapers, and searched the Internet. He spent a lot of time on the telephone and even more time driving to check out potential vehicles. He bargained with several sellers over a period of time. Finally, he made a decision, after spending several hours a day for several months. I suspect he found one of the better cars within 150 miles of where he lived, and I am sure he paid a reasonable price. Is he satisfied with the car? Not remotely. "The one that got away" still haunts him.

Despite his studies showing that satisficers are in general happier than maximizers, Schwartz did not advocate becoming a satisficer in all domains of life. Consider raising children. Do we ever hear a parent say, "I found a good-enough pediatrician for my child?" Rather, Schwartz suggested that people learn to choose when to satisfice and when to maximize, much as I suggested in chapter 5 that we should learn when to be optimistic and when to be more cautious.

In short, we need to choose when and how to choose. In the spirit of this suggestion, here is an exercise for you to try. Review some of the recent decisions you have made, from simple ones to more-complex ones. How much time, research, and worry went into each decision, and how satisfied are you at present with each decision?

If it turns out that choosing a birthday card for your second cousin was as involved a process as deciding to get married or which house you and your spouse should purchase, I dare say something is out of whack. If finding what you hoped was the "perfect" card did not result in an ecstatic reaction from your distant relative, then why did you agonize so? Or if you spent 20 hours making a purchase that perhaps saved you $3, and you are still fretting that you did not save $5, take a step back and reflect on the minimum wage rate. What does your decision process imply about how you value your own time?

Schwartz proposed that you identify the minor consumer domains where decision making proves to be an ordeal. Then impose an arbitrary restriction on how you make decisions in these domains. Visit no more than two stores. Devote no more than 15 minutes to making any purchase less than $10. Buy only items that are blue.

Make your decisions irreversible, which may cut down on the regret and the what-ifs that plague maximizers. Go to stores with a no-return policy. Throw out your receipts. Make purchases while far from home on vacation or business.

Finally, be grateful for what you have, not wistful about what you do not have. You may even want to write down three good things about each purchase that you have made (chapter 2).

Try these steps out with respect to your next several choices in some problematic decision domain. Then take stock of the aftermath. Were your decisions quicker and easier? Are you satisfied with what you decided? Most important, do you see that your decision style is something that you can choose? You may decide that being a maximizer is something that you want to be, but if so, you should choose this style forthrightly.

GLOSSARY

attitude: favorable or unfavorable evaluation of a specific object or issue

ceiling effect: bunching up of scores at the upper end of a rating scale

convenience sample: sample of research participants chosen for study because they are readily available

generational replacement: changes in a society over time as young people come of age under different circumstances than did their parents or grandparents

hierarchy of needs: arrangement of human motives into a hierarchy reflecting the order in which people typically attend to them.

instrumental value: belief about ideal modes of conduct that presumably aid and abet terminal values

ipsative scores: measurement in which comparisons are made only with respect to the same individual

maximizer: individual who typically chooses the "best" option in order to optimize an outcome

minimalist values: values minimally necessary for a viable society

modeling: emulation of what powerful or respected others say, do, and believe

need: biological motive that moves us to behave in ways to satisfy it, e.g., hunger, thirst
norm: shared belief that one should act in a certain way in a certain circumstance
representative sample: sample of research participants that resembles the larger population to which a researcher wishes to generalize
satisficer: individual who typically chooses a good-enough or merely satisfactory option
self-expressive values: values corresponding to one's need to express talents, capacities, and potentialities
survival values: values corresponding to one's pressing biological needs
terminal value: belief about an ideal state of existence
trait: disposition to think, feel, and act in a consistent way
value: goal about what is morally desirable
value self-confrontation: deliberate strategy of changing one's values by exposing them to contradiction among one's value priorities
values clarification: self-help techniques for helping people to identify values they hold
World Values Survey: ongoing research project that periodically ascertains the values of people in dozens of countries around the world

RESOURCES

Books and Journals

Bok, S. (1995). *Common values.* Columbia: University of Missouri Press.
Schwartz, B. (2004). *The paradox of choice: Why less is more.* New York: HarperCollins.
Burrell, B. (1997). *The words we live by.* New York: Free Press.
Shi, D. E. (1985). *The simple life: Plain living and high thinking in American culture.* New York: Oxford University Press.
Kasser, T. (2002). *The high price of materialism.* Cambridge, MA: Bradford.
de Graaf, J., Wann, D., & Naylor, T. H. (2001). *Affluenza: The all-consuming epidemic.* San Francisco: Berrett-Koehler.
Twitchell, J. B. (1999). *Lead us into temptation: The triumph of American materialism.* New York: Columbia University Press.
Gleick, J. (2000). *Faster: The acceleration of just about everything.* New York: Vintage.

Articles

Schwartz, S. H. (1994). Are there universal aspects in the structure and content of human values? *Journal of Social Issues, 50*(4), 19–45.
Rokeach, M. (1971). Long-range experimental modification of values, attitudes, and behavior. *American Psychologist, 26,* 453–459.

Web Sites

http://wvs.isr.umich.edu. This is the Web site for the World Values Survey, "a world-wide investigation . . . carried out [with] representative national surveys of the basic values and beliefs of publics in more than 65 societies on all six inhabited continents, containing almost 80 percent of the world's population."

http://www.hartmaninstitute.org. This is the Web site for the Robert S. Hartman Institute, devoted to the study of values. It contains examples of value measures.

Films

Citizen Kane (1941)
Cheaper by the Dozen (1950)
Guess Who's Coming to Dinner? (1967)
In the Heat of the Night (1967)
Patton (1970)
Sling Blade (1996)
American History X (1998)
ABC News's *20/20*: "Affluenza" (2000)

Songs

"Everyday People" (Sly and the Family Stone)
"My Favorite Things" (from *The Sound of Music*)
"My Way" (Frank Sinatra)
"Where Were You?" (Alan Jackson)

8 Interests, Abilities, and Accomplishments

Do you get to do what you do best every day?
—GALLUP ORGANIZATION, AS CITED IN BUCKINGHAM & CLIFTON, 2001

The Gallup Organization is famous for its public opinion polls, but most of what Gallup does is advise work organizations about how to improve their operations. Their clients include a who's who of the world's best-known companies—Disney, Wells Fargo, Toyota, Best Buy, and the U.S. Postal Service, among others.

Gallup has learned that posing the simple question to workers: "Do you get to do what you do best every day?" provides powerful information. Ask yourself this same question about your daily life at work or at school. If your answer is no, you are in the majority. No more than 20% of workers in the United States believe that their jobs allow them on a regular basis to do and be their best. My own questioning of college students over the past few years yields even fewer yes answers. Often what I hear is incredulity: "What's school got to do with me at my best?"

For the handful of you who can answer this question with a yes, you already know the conclusion reached by Gallup from studying many thousands of workers. A job where you can regularly do what you do best is a job that you love. A company filled with people allowed to do their best not only performs well in terms of its financial bottom line but also has low rates of absenteeism and turnover, along with high levels of morale and loyalty.

The practical implication is that all of us would be better off if companies matched people with jobs that they can do well, precisely the approach Gallup recommends. This strengths-based philosophy seems commonsensical, but it flies in the face of how most people and work organizations approach things, which is to focus on weaknesses and how to correct them.[1]

According to Gallup, we can most improve by strengthening what we already do well. Consider someone who writes beautifully but speaks poorly. Are she and her work organization better served by giving her increased opportunities to write memos, letters, and manuals or by having her take remedial classes in public speaking? The Gallup answer is that the former strategy would lead to an even more outstanding writer, and the latter strategy—at best—would produce a mediocre speaker.

This strengths-based philosophy of course needs to be implemented with common sense.[2] For any job, there are some skills that must be present above a minimal level (Warr, 1987). A worker who is thoroughly inarticulate when speaking is not going to be valued regardless of how well she can write. Anyone indifferent to punctuality will find it difficult to offset that weakness with strengths in other areas.

So far I have discussed happiness, hope, strengths of character, and values. If you have these in place, are you leading the good psychological life? Not exactly, because something critical is missing: what you *do* with these laudable characteristics. We all behave in the course of life, and we can do what we do well, or not. The Gallup Organization reminds us that we need to be in a position that allows us to excel. And we additionally have to know what our interests and talents might be so that we can capitalize on optimal situations and accomplish something important. These are the topics of concern in the present chapter: interests,

1. You may have heard of the whimsical Peter Principle, which holds that people who do well at a given job are promoted to a "better" job, and so on, until they have a position at which they do not do well, and that is where they stay (Peter & Hull, 1969). Over time, a work organization becomes staffed by people promoted to their level of incompetence. The Peter Principle is worth taking seriously because it contains a kernel of descriptive truth. For many workers, job performance declines after a promotion, if only because promotions often result from a singular achievement unlikely to be repeated on a regular basis (Lazear, 2004).

2. The Gallup Organization and especially its former chief executive officer, Donald Clifton, and its current CEO, James Clifton, have been great friends to positive psychology as this field has taken form. They have generously sponsored conferences and, more important, provided an example of the benefits of attending to the positive. When we began our project on character strengths (chapter 6), we found the Gallup philosophy so persuasive that we even speculated that people should not try to improve their character weaknesses (lesser strengths) but instead try to burnish their signature strengths (Seligman, 2002). I no longer agree with this extrapolation to good character, especially with respect to children and adolescents. What makes sense in a work setting makes less sense in the world as a whole, given that certain strengths of character are robustly associated with life satisfaction. If these happen to be among your lesser strengths, it is glib to advise you to forget about them. Similarly, the character strengths of youth are in the process of being formed, so it makes sense to focus most deliberately on the cultivation of those that pack the most life satisfaction bang, regardless of their initial levels (Park & Peterson, in press d).

abilities, and accomplishments. I will discuss what positive psychology has learned about these aspects of a life well lived.

Some psychologists shy away from these topics—or at least their manifestation in the form of intelligence, genius, giftedness, and the like—because they smack of elitism. Past studies of human excellence have indeed become mired in debates that are more political than scientific—e.g., are Whites and Blacks inherently different in their intelligence, do women have the "right stuff" to excel at mathematics and natural science, are genius and madness closely allied (Gould, 1981; Jamison, 1993; Lynn, 1994). However, there is more to the study of excellence than these worn arguments.[3]

There are two themes that run throughout this chapter. First is the importance of the context in determining who does or does not excel at some endeavor. Second is the plurality of talents. While we might on occasion identify someone who has no interests and is no damn good at anything (e.g., our brother-in-law), in point of fact it proves difficult to find someone devoid of all interests and skills (Travers, 1978). It is our task to identify these interests and skills, to nurture them, and following the Gallup Organization's lead, to place people in settings—occupational or otherwise—where they can shine.

Interests

I once had a friend named Jack, a 30-something high school teacher who was married with a small child. Invariably, when I introduced him to someone, the innocent question would arise, "So, Jack, what do you do?" I was always taken aback when he would say, "I play second base." He could have said he was a teacher. He could have said he was a husband. Or a father. For goodness' sake, he could have said he was my friend.

But his lifelong passion was the American pastime, and specifically playing second base. He was always a decent player in his circle of schoolmates and friends, but he was not that good. He had played Little League baseball as a child but was never an all-star, even in leagues where almost all players received some sort of award. He did not make his high school team. None of this he denied, and as he became older, he switched from baseball to softball and then to the slow-pitch variant played in Chicago with a 16-inch ball and no gloves.

At first I thought Jack was trying to be funny when he described himself as a second baseman, but I eventually decided that he was presenting himself truthfully. To his credit, if someone did not pick up the thread of conversation about

3. I like the point made by Murray (2003) that debates about the inherent brain differences of males versus females are a bit silly at present given all of the pending breakthroughs in neuroimaging technology that will allow brain structures and functions to be described more fully. If we are patient, answers to these contentious debates may be available soon.

softball, he would discuss other things like his work, his family, politics, or the weather.

Very familiar to all of us but sometimes overlooked by psychologists is that we all have **interests**—passions, if you will—that define who we are. For some, it is a recreational activity like Jack's softball. For others, it is something for which they are paid; they are said to have a professional calling (Wrzesniewski, McCauley, Rozin, & Schwartz, 1997). For others, it is their family. Or cats. Or dolphins. Or romance novels. Or National Public Radio. Or the *New York Times.* We are our passions, and part of the good life is understanding what these might be and then developing and indulging them. Hence their inclusion in this book on positive psychology.

Some passions are very private, but others are shared. "Common interests" seem to be a critical aspect of friendship (Rubin, 1973), and if the other person is the subject of your interest, then you probably have abiding friendship or true love.

We need to be careful not to privilege some passions over others, even though many can be classified as low culture versus high culture. Someone may have a passion for Milwaukee beer over French wine, for Sousa marches over Italian operas, for flapjacks over foie gras, for movies with Adam Sandler over those by Ingmar Bergman, or for novels by Sue Grafton over sonnets by William Shakespeare. In psychological terms, I think these diverse passions function much the same.[4] The bottom line is that we all have activities to which we are drawn.

Why are we drawn to such activities? The answer is deep within human nature. Almost 50 years ago, psychologist Robert White (1959) introduced the notion of **competence**, arguing that people are motivated to behave in a competent way, regardless of what they are doing. White wrote at the height of behaviorism, which held that we do what we do because of prevailing rewards and punishments that presumably satisfy our biological needs (chapter 7). But competence is a different sort of motive because it is never sated in the way that hunger or thirst can be. We experience pleasure in doing things well regardless of what else our behavior produces (Meier, 1993; Pittman & Heller, 1987). Remember the first time you figured out how to tie your shoelaces, drive a car, or send an e-mail message? All of these simply felt good. Or remember when your young children learned to crawl, walk, or speak? You did not need to reward them for their efforts. Their growing competence was enough to sustain their efforts, and they did these things over and over until they became second nature.

4. Our interests vary in terms of their inherent complexity, which may provide a more-objective basis for deeming some to be more fulfilling than others (Murray, 2003). Remember the notion of flow and how its preconditions—challenge and skill—need to be matched in an ever-evolving dance (chapter 4)? Chess is a much more complex game than checkers and more readily affords a lifelong interest for those who play. People can and do play checkers throughout their lives, but it might be the companionship afforded by the game that makes it appealing as opposed to the game itself.

Competence may be fulfilling because it produces the flow state (chapter 4), which provides insight into the sorts of activities that often attract us. They must afford *degrees* of skilled performance and thus allow improvement. Something we can do perfectly well the first time we try it is not likely to become a lifelong passion.

Philosopher John Rawls (1971, p. 414) elaborated this idea into what he called the **Aristotelian Principle**:[5]

> Other things being equal, human beings enjoy the exercise of their realized capacities . . . and thus enjoyment increases the more the capacity is realized, or the greater its complexity.

Think of your favorite activities, at work or at home. Do they fit this principle of greater enjoyment as your knowledge and ability increase?

Some interests entail physical activity—hiking, climbing, running—and other interests are more cerebral, like working crossword puzzles, reading poetry, surfing the Internet. The Aristotelian Principle applies in either case.

When psychologists have studied interests, they have focused on three topics: leisure interests, school interests, and work interests, and I focus on these in this section.

Leisure and Recreation

Much of the research investigating leisure and recreation is descriptive, cataloging what people do when they are not working, going to school, or keeping house (e.g., Scott & Willits, 1998). Several findings consistently emerge.

The first is that almost everyone reports doing something during their down time. Workaholic stereotypes notwithstanding, it is virtually impossible to find an actual person whose life entails nothing but working, eating, and sleeping.

Second is the incredible variety of activities that people most enjoy doing when they are not working. For example, a 2001 Harris poll of more than 1,000 adults in the United States found that the leisure activities most frequently mentioned were (H. Taylor, 2001):

- reading (28% of respondents)
- watching television (20%)
- spending time with the family (12%)
- fishing (12%)
- gardening (10%)
- swimming (8%)
- computer activities (7%)
- going to the movies (7%)

5. In *The Nicomachean Ethics*, Aristotle (2000, Book 10, 1175a, 12–14) proposed that "life is an activity, and each man actively exercises his favored faculties upon the objects he loves most."

- walking (6%)
- playing golf (6%)

Respondents in the telephone poll could mention up to three different activities, so it is striking that no single activity came close to being popular among the majority of adults. Even the most commonly pursued activities—reading and watching television—are broad categories within which people have specific preferences. It is doubtful that people like reading per se or watching television per se. Instead, they like to read novels but not short stories. They like soap operas but not crime dramas.

A third finding to note is that the amount of time people devote to their leisure activities varies greatly (Argyle, 1996). On average, women have less leisure time than do men, especially if they have full-time jobs or children, or both. As you well know, housekeeping and childrearing duties fall disproportionately to women.

Available leisure time does not differ on average between those in the lower class and those in the middle class, but lower-class individuals uniformly do fewer things—except for watching television—than do middle-class individuals. Those in the lower class have more physically demanding jobs, less money, and fewer opportunities to develop recreational interests. Argyle (2001) speculated that college, more likely to be attended by children of the middle class, if nothing else opens the door to diverse recreational activities that can be pursued for the rest of one's life. Tell that to your parents when they receive the $37,000 tuition bill.

Retired individuals obviously have more time for recreation than those still in the workforce, but few take up new interests after retirement. Here is a very practical lesson about your eventual retirement: Develop the interests *now* that you envision pursuing once you stop working.

Fourth, as mentioned in chapter 4, one of the strong predictors of life satisfaction is how much time someone devotes to leisure activities (Argyle, 2001). Keeping that in mind, think about the following. Pollsters have regularly asked U.S. respondents how much time they spend at work and how much time they have available for leisure. In recent decades, two trends are clearly apparent: more hours spent at work and fewer hours available for leisure[6] (Figure 8.1).

Why is leisure so strongly related to life satisfaction? Besides the intrinsic satisfaction produced by exercising one's skills[7] and the fact that many leisure activi-

6. Analogous polls in Europe find the opposite trends: increasingly less time at work and increasingly more time for leisure.

7. Television is a common leisure activity, whether or not people identify it as one of their favorite things to do. Research consistently shows that television has few if any psychological benefits, except for producing a state resembling relaxation (Kubey & Csikszentmihalyi, 1990). However, being relaxed like a potato does not translate into happier moods or increased life satisfaction. If anything, more television watching is usually associated with less happiness (Argyle, 2001). Watching television does not build or exercise any skill. At its best, a television show can demand our attention,

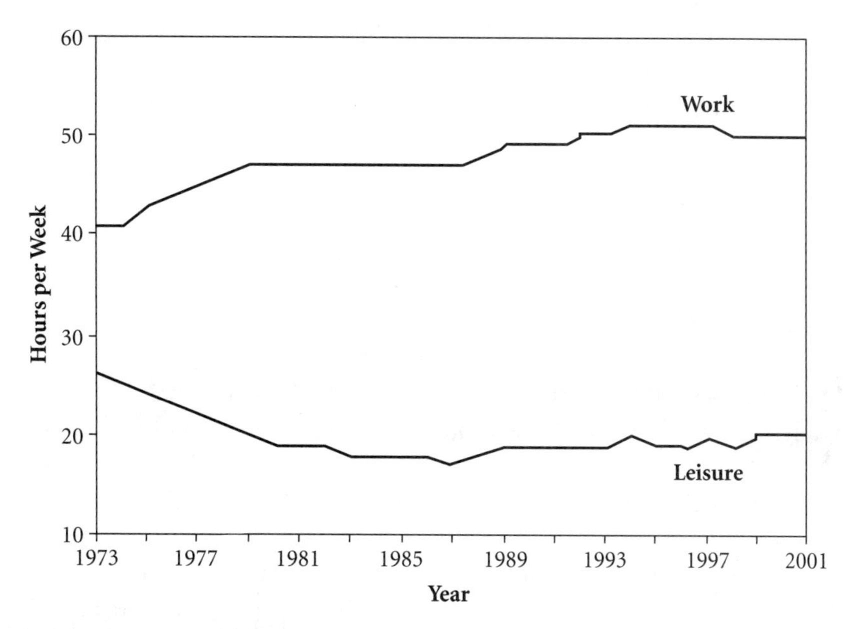

Figure 8.1. Work Hours and Available Leisure Hours Per Week of U.S. Adults (H. Taylor, 2001)

ties directly produce pleasure, we can point to additional pathways, depending on the activity in question.

Physical activities like swimming, walking, golfing, exercising, and playing team sports increase positive emotions and specifically feelings of vitality (Thayer, 1989). People who engage in regular aerobic exercise report better mental health and a reduced response to stressful life events (Crews & Landers, 1987; McCann & Holmes, 1984). This comes as no surprise. The benefits of exercise on physical health and longevity are well known (Paffenbarger, Hyde, & Dow, 1991).

Those who like to listen to music report more positive moods, both of the quiet kind (contentment) and the more-aroused kind (excitement; Hills & Argyle, 1998). Again, this is not surprising. Researchers regularly use music to "induce" different emotions in their laboratory experiments (chapter 4), and many of us at one time or another have deliberately used music to regulate how we are feeling. High-pitched sounds with regular rhythms and an upward trend are re-

---

but we would not want to go so far as to say that it produces flow. Also, those who watch a lot of television are necessarily *not* doing other things that might make them happy, like being physically active or socializing with others (Robinson, 1990). One exception may be soap operas, and by extension any television show with recurring characters and a developing plot. Watching shows like these turns out to be modestly linked to greater life satisfaction (Lu & Argyle, 1993), perhaps because viewers start to treat the characters as "real" and become concerned with their well-being (Livingstone, 1988). The problem, of course, is that Erica Kane does not care at all about me.

garded as happy, whereas slow, low, and falling sounds are experienced as sad (Scherer & Oshinsky, 1977).

Any recreational activity that brings us into contact with other people carries all the benefits associated with social communion and companionship (chapter 10). Indeed, one of the reasons for recreation is that it provides a reason and a means to interact with other people. Men's friendships often revolve around shared activities, whereas women's friendships are more likely to entail simply talking to one another (Elkins & Peterson, 1993). But in either case, social needs are served, and social benefits are accrued.

Argyle (2001) used the term **leisure world** to describe the culture that develops around shared leisure activities, from birdwatching to sailing. Those residing in a leisure world have their own values, traditions, history, and sometimes their own costumes—think Trekkies or Oakland Raiders fans. The group may meet regularly, publish a newsletter, and elect officers. This is just like real life, except more fun.

A recreational interest I developed only in the past few years is playing Scrabble. I am not that good, so motives for achievement or competence have not driven my interest. Instead, it is my opponents who keep me going back to Scrabble clubs, to tournaments, and to games on the Internet. In some cases, I simply like the other players; they are smart, funny, interesting, or otherwise attractive. In other cases, I think the other players are weird and therefore intriguing in a different—very different—way (Fatsis, 2001). Regardless, Scrabble has brought me into contact with all sorts of people outside my regular travels, and I am the happier for it.

Not to be overlooked is that recreational activities can provide someone a positive identity, as we saw for my friend Jack, and this identity is a way to belong and to matter. Recreational identities may be especially important during adolescence, a period in which identity formation is thought to be *the* critical developmental task (Erikson, 1963). Most adolescents are students, but not all of them are excellent or even good students. It is obviously beneficial when alternative identities are made available through extracurricular and after-school activities.[8] As it turns out, adolescents who participate in these sorts of activities usually perform better as students than those who do not, and they avoid teen pitfalls like pregnancy, dropping out, and drug use (Mahoney, 2000; Mahoney & Cairns, 1997; Mahoney & Stattin, 2000, 2002; Mahoney, Stattin, & Magnusson, 2001). But the benefits of these activities extends beyond what they preclude. Given that the

8. Following this logic, we would expect that the well-intended requirement in some school districts linking participation in extracurricular activities to academic performance—if you don't pass, you don't play—can backfire. Being a jock is an identity readily embraced by a fair number of high school students, but jocks who do not play sports are likely to drop out (Eccles & Barber, 1999). Sports may have been the main reason they continued to attend school.

typical job does not allow people to do what they do well, recreational activities can take on huge psychological significance (Eccles & Gootman, 2002).

Well-Developed Individual Interests

Whether or not you liked school in general, you still had a favorite subject.[9] A student's attraction to a given academic field—such as mathematics, literature, or physics—is called a **well-developed individual interest** when it is marked by a deep intellectual and emotional involvement (Renninger, 1990, 2000). Those with such an interest are incessantly curious about the subject and driven to learn ever more about it. Their learning is intrinsically motivated and marked by a dogged persistence, even in the face of setbacks and failures (Krapp & Fink, 1992; Prenzel, 1992; Renninger & Hidi, 2002; Renninger & Leckrone, 1991). Students with a well-developed individual interest may or may not show any immediate achievement, but in the long run, few excel in a field without passion for what they do. Well-developed individual interests set the stage for expertise in any venue and certainly sustain people—in and out of school—over the many years it takes to become an expert.[10]

If you have them, identifying your well-developed personal interests is no mystery, but think about your various school subjects and ask yourself how much you agree with the following statements (Peterson & Seligman, 2004):

- I can't do this _______________ task now but I think I will be able to do it in the future.
- I like to learn new things about _______________.
- I will do whatever it takes in order to do a _______________ task correctly.
- Learning about _______________ is a great experience.
- I care more about doing a thorough job at _______________ than whether I receive a good grade.

Because personal interests lead you to create articulate structures of knowledge, you would probably agree with these statements about your favorite school subject:

- Relative to the other things that I know, I know a lot about _______________.

9. The ideas in this section draw on a chapter drafted by K. Ann Renninger, Carol Sansone, and Jessi L. Smith for Peterson and Seligman's (2004) book on character strengths and virtues.

10. Those who study prodigious achievement talk about the **10-Year Rule**, referring to the fact that people who make important contributions to a particular field have usually devoted a full decade to the mastery of necessary knowledge and skills (Hayes, 1989). I have also heard of the **12-7 Rule**, meaning that this decade needs to be filled with 12-hour work days, 7 days a week. Sound daunting? Of course, but "American Idol" notwithstanding, there are no shortcuts to excellence.

- Relative to the other things that I like, I like ______________ a lot.
- I spend as much of my time doing ______________ as possible.
- Working on ______________ is hard work, but it never really feels like it.
- I know that if I put my mind to it, I can figure out how to do ______________ really well.

Consider Linnea, a 10th-grader in a blue-collar public school outside a large U.S. city (Peterson & Seligman, 2004, pp. 161–162):

> Linnea signed up to take Latin because she liked mythology. During Language Month at school, she showed up in class dressed as a goddess. Her teacher described her behavior as wonderful, in character, and eccentric. "Linnea likes the idea of doing Latin," her teacher reports. "She speaks Latin with me. Who does that?!"
>
> The other students took in stride the fact that she showed up dressed as a goddess. In fact, each day when students in the Latin class recount the "Latin moments" that they have had since the last class meeting—references to a Latin word, the history and/or mythology of Rome and Ancient Greece, and so on—Linnea typically recounts about 17 of them, almost always connected to movies she has just seen. The other students in the class roll their eyes as Linnea goes down her list, but because they like her, they listen with good humor.
>
> Linnea feels good about learning Latin and is confident that she can master its nuances. She feels supported in her efforts to learn, despite a school culture in which doing homework and pursuing the study of Latin are uncommon, to say the least. Interestingly, although she earns good grades in her other classes, she has not thrown herself into them, and she feels like she retains little of what she learns.
>
> What is special about Latin? Perhaps it is the encouragement that she has received from the teacher to engage fully the subject matter. Perhaps it is the way in which she has made Latin her "own" by creating or identifying out-of-class resources that further her learning. Perhaps it is the success she has had in learning a great deal about Latin, a base of information that fuels her further curiosity.

For teachers and parents, the vexing question is why some students develop an interest in Latin or mathematics, whereas others turn their backs on school and find their passions in video games or the shenanigans of teen idols. Rather than railing against popular culture, we should instead ask why business-as-usual school is so boring (Noddings, 2003).

What makes a pursuit interesting is *not* its tangible outcomes. Objectively, learning Latin is as useless for most teenagers as playing a Gameboy. One must look to the inherent properties of activities, and among those that make a pursuit interesting are its novelty, complexity, and uncertainty (Berlyne, 1960). There comes a point where an activity can be too confusing or ambiguous to be interesting, but good education includes finding the optimal levels with which to introduce a topic to a student. The *1812 Overture* is more "interesting" to musical neophytes than a Bach fugue (Murray, 2003). Dinosaurs are more "interesting" than pond scum. And bless my parents, who taught me how to read via comic books and how to do addition via blackjack. Once the basics are established, specific knowledge evokes further interest, and an upward spiral ensues (Loewenstein, 1994).

Also critical in sparking and sustaining academic interests are teachers or mentors, as we saw in the case of Linnea. Well-developed personal interests may be intrinsically rewarding, but they do not emerge in a vacuum. While a sophomore in college, I took an introduction to psychology course reputed to be easy while I was pursuing a demanding (and boring) major in aeronautical engineering. Not only did I find the subject of psychology fascinating, but the teaching assistant who led my discussion section was an engaging fellow with a genuine interest in my learning. I switched my major to psychology, and here I am today as a psychologist.

Well-developed personal interests, if they are to be sustained, must be nurtured (Fried, 1996, 2001). Teachers impart not just information and instruction but also challenge and support (Renninger, 2000). Peers must also be supportive, as we saw in the story of Linnea, and it is of course helpful when parents are on the same page as well. When I was growing up, there was not a lot of money available for a lot of things, but there was *always* enough money for books.

The kind of support that a student needs differs with age. Very young children need little encouragement to throw themselves into learning (Piaget, 1950). But as they get older, constraints emerge, and more-explicit support for learning becomes critical. In general, academic interest wanes as students enter middle school (P. Gardner, 1985; Wigfield, Eccles, MacIver, Reuman, & Midgley, 1991). The features of the school may be the culprit here, e.g., limited course options, competitive grades, and dysfunctional pedagogical practices (Fölling-Albers & Hartinger, 1998; Hoffmann, 2002). Once a student has a well-established interest, it needs less generic support, but specific instruction is still crucial.

Even though academic interests are intrinsically motivated, they can have distant payoffs. The obvious result is eventual accomplishment in the specific field of study. There are more generic benefits as well. Greater engagement in education early in life may protect against cognitive impairment later in life (Katzman, 1973). The ability to sustain interest and develop new interests is associated with healthy and productive aging (Krapp & Lewalter, 2001; Renninger & Shumar, 2002; Snowdon, 2001). Individuals in the workforce with a greater love of learning are better at meeting challenges (McCombs, 1991). More generally, the degree to which individuals experience interest and enjoyment as they learn translates into decreased stress (Sansone, Wiebe, & Morgan, 1999), which over the long haul should result in greater physical and emotional well-being (Elliot & McGregor, 2001; Helson & Srivastava, 2001).

Vocational Interests

"What do you want to be when you grow up?"

Children as young as 3 years old have a ready answer to this question, although their answers are usually drawn from their world of fantasy, e.g., they want to be a princess or a lion (Gottfredson, 1981). Occupational fantasies can persist into adolescence or beyond, with "professional athlete" cited as a career goal by a surprisingly large number of teenagers, especially males (Helwig, 1998).

Be that as it may, most of us eventually become more realistic. The problem is that we might still fail to grasp the range of possibilities—after all, there are more than 30,000 different jobs in the United States alone (U.S. Department of Labor Statistics, 2004)—and we can fumble about when we first enter the workforce. The jobs taken by adolescents are usually not good preparation for adult work. They are rigidly split into boy jobs and girl jobs: lawn mowing versus babysitting. Not only are these jobs boring, but they rarely bring young workers into contact with adults[11] (Steinberg, 1985).

In years of advising college students about jobs and careers, the most important thing I have learned is that they should try out as many jobs as possible during the summer, as interns, or as part-time volunteers. Along these lines, they should talk to adults about what jobs really entail and the positive roles they can play in one's life. The points made about leisure interests and school interests apply as well to vocational interests. Knowledge begets curiosity and interest, which lead to further knowledge, expertise, and accomplishment. Again, mentors matter mightily.

In the best of all worlds, we would have sampler plates for jobs at which our children could nibble and decide that they like some but not others. This is not possible, although psychology provides an approximation in the form of **interest inventories** (Hansen, 1990, 1994). These are questionnaires used by vocational counselors to "fit round pegs into round holes" by matching a person's expressed interests with those apt to be satisfied by a particular job (Zytowski, 1973).

The Strong Vocational Interest Blank (SVIB) is probably the best known of the interest inventories[12] (D. P. Campbell, 1971). You may have completed this

11. If you are a parent, I urge you to take your children to work as often as possible to demystify it. And be careful about what you say about work in the earshot of your kids. Many children follow the career paths of their parents, and I suspect that part of this process includes adopting the values and attitudes of their parents about these jobs (Mortimer, 1976).

12. "Strong" is not an adjective—although it does imply a certain soundness and solidity that cannot have hurt the popularity of the test. Rather, Edward Strong created the measure. After his death in 1963, David Campbell continued to develop the survey, and the SVIB is sometimes called the Strong-Campbell Inventory.

questionnaire at some point in your life; it has been around since 1927. The format and underlying logic of the SVIB are simple. Respondents are presented a list of hundreds of activities (e.g., visiting an art museum, collecting stamps, playing golf) and asked to indicate if they like it, dislike it, or are indifferent.

The individual's profile of responses is then compared to the average responses of other people who have worked successfully in different occupations. The greater the match—calculated by a variant of a correlation coefficient (chapter 4)—the more seriously the respondent might consider exploring that occupation.

The SVIB embodies what psychologists label a *cookbook procedure* or an *actuarial approach* because the development, scoring, and interpretation of the test follow simple and objective rules. One of the best-known tests in all of psychology—the MMPI (Minnesota Multiphasic Personality Inventory)—uses the same actuarial approach (Butcher, Dahlstrom, Graham, Tellegen, & Kaemmer, 1989; Hathaway & McKinley, 1943). The MMPI helps clinicians to diagnose individuals by matching their responses on the MMPI to those of other individuals known to meet the diagnostic criteria for a given psychological disorder. Items may or may not be transparent—i.e., interpretable—but the rationale underlying a cookbook approach does not require them to be. So, one of the MMPI items used to ask whether Washington or Lincoln was the greater U.S. president. A person's choice nudges him toward one diagnosis or another, but I defy anyone to infer what these might be.

The SVIB matches people to occupations in which they might be interested and steers them away from others. If one is interested in an occupation, one is more likely to stay in it and to perform well (Reeves & Booth, 1979). It is worth pointing out that the SVIB does not measure ability. I might be interested in dentistry, for example, but if I lack the physical dexterity to fill or extract teeth, then this is not a good field for me. Or consider something I see with frequency among my undergraduate psychology students: They are "interested" in psychological disorders and therefore want to be clinical psychologists, overlooking the requisite skills of patience, empathy, and appropriate detachment, not to mention the years of graduate training required to become a clinical psychologist and the fact that troubled people are of course troubling. Some of my students have a rude awakening when they follow their interest into a career.

Interest inventories like the SVIB nonetheless provide useful information. Scores are highly stable over time (Johansson & Campbell, 1971), and they predict the professions that people actually enter (Hansen, 1984). Furthermore, the interest profiles associated with many occupations have stayed the same over decades. Despite all of the changes in the world, chemists today express much the same likes and dislikes as did chemists in the 1930s.

The biggest problem with the SVIB and related inventories is that they use already-existing groups to provide the norms. They are necessarily tied to the status quo, and their reliance on a cookbook procedure means that they reflect inadvertent confounds. If most chemists are White males, how reasonable is it to use the SVIB to counsel a Black female if she is considering chemistry as a career? Traditionally, separate questionnaires for men and women have been used to solve this sort of problem, but this strategy falls short if an insufficient number of women (or men) work at a particular profession.[13]

The more-general shortcoming of interest inventories is that jobs themselves may change. Indeed, jobs emerge all the time that did not exist before. If the interests associated with future jobs overlap with those of past jobs, and if we understand the overlap, then interest inventories will help to steer people toward these new occupations. But if future jobs combine interests in novel ways, then these questionnaires will not help respondents to choose them.

Many interest inventories lack a theoretical basis—that is the cost of their cookbook approach—which means that it is difficult for them to be changed deliberately or to be generalized. A notable exception is the work by John Holland (1966, 1985), which is based on an explicit theory. Holland's work falls within the tradition of personality psychology (Peterson, 1992) but adds a creative twist. Usually, a personality psychologist interested in occupations will take a general measure of personality dispositions and then try to correlate scores on these with people's occupational choices or performances. Holland instead started with the jobs, under the assumption that what most people do more than 40 hours a week, 50 weeks a year, from ages 18 to 65+, *is* their personality.

From numerous studies of interest inventories and vocational preferences, Holland identified six basic types of people in terms of their work-relevant interests and the kinds of jobs at which they excel:[14]

- *realistic types*: people who prefer the manipulation of objects, tools, machines, and/or animals, e.g., mechanic, contractor
- *investigative types*: people who prefer to observe and investigate physical, biological, and/or cultural phenomena, e.g., scientist, journalist
- *artistic types*: people who prefer to create art forms, e.g., novelist, musician
- *social types*: people who prefer to work with other people, informing, training, developing, curing, or otherwise enlightening them, e.g., social worker, teacher

13. At one time, the SVIB was printed on blue paper for men and pink paper for women. David Campbell has himself labeled this a blunder. I only mention this to show that inadvertent bias can run deep. But the problem lies not in the tests themselves. Society encourages men and women—and even boys and girls as young as 6 years of age (Gottfredson, 1981)—to channel themselves into "appropriate" vocations, and most follow this advice. The SVIB is not to be faulted because it reflects our social reality.

14. Remember the point I made in chapter 7 that "types" of people should be regarded as prototypes or pure cases rather than as an exhaustive set of categories into which everyone can unambiguously fit.

- *enterprising types*: people who prefer to work toward organizational goals and/or economic gains, e.g., salesperson, stockbroker
- *conventional types*: people who prefer the systematic manipulation of data and the keeping of records, e.g., accountant, librarian

A worker's satisfaction is highest and his performance best when his type matches his job requirements (e.g., Smart, 1982), which you may recognize as the premise of the Gallup Organization with which this chapter began.

Abilities

As I have emphasized, interests are not the same thing as abilities, although an interest may lead us to spend the time and acquire the instruction needed to develop a talent. Psychologists have studied abilities in their own right, so let us turn now to this topic. An **ability** is shown when people differ in their performance of some behavior for which there is an objective standard. Sprinters can run fast or slowly, as measured by a stopwatch. Students can spell obscure words correctly or incorrectly, as judged against a dictionary. Composers can create music that moves listeners to tears or to yawns.

Psychologists have introduced all sorts of terms to describe the ability domain: *talent, skill, aptitude, capacity*, and—notably—*intelligence*. These terms do not have identical connotations, and one recurring contrast is whether the term in question refers to what people have actually done or to what they have the potential to do. So, when students apply to college, they forward to the admissions committee their high school transcripts and their SAT scores. Transcripts presumably measure their academic accomplishment, whereas the SATs presumably measure their potential for accomplishment. Sometimes this distinction is described as one between *achievement* and *ability*.

There is a long-standing and legitimate debate about how valid this distinction actually is, given that ability must be inferred from some sort of performance. I prefer to sidestep the debate by using all of these terms as rough synonyms and by privileging what people actually do. For example, one common use of the term *genius* is to describe a person with an extremely high IQ,[15] but I prefer to define a **genius** as someone whose actual accomplishments have exerted a profound influence on contemporary and subsequent generations (Simonton, 1984). Aristotle, Confucius, Leonardo da Vinci, Ludwig Beethoven, and Charles Darwin

15. *IQ* stands for "intelligence quotient," traditionally defined as the ratio of one's mental age to one's chronological age, multiplied by 100 (to avoid decimal places; Stern, 1914). Mental age is calculated by comparing your performance at some test to that of people of different ages. If you perform on the test like the typical 10-year-old performs, then your mental age is 10. There is no further meaning to IQ than this, and you can see that one's IQ is a function of the particular test administered as well as the groups providing the age norms.

are geniuses, whereas the genius jury is still out on Poindexter and his perfect score on the SAT.

You have likely figured out from previous chapters that psychologists enjoy making lists, although we give them high-sounding scientific names like classifications, nosologies, taxonomies, or typologies. The psychological study of abilities is no exception. Early efforts enumerated those things at which people are presumably skilled or not so skilled, relying on the "faculties" proposed centuries ago to underlie human rationality: attention, logic, memory, and the like (Nunnally, 1970). They are heavily tilted toward the abstract and the intellectual, a point to which I will shortly return.

If we take a step back, we see that there are hundreds or thousands or even millions of abilities that people have, with new ones emerging all the time as the world changes to afford new skills. For example, when I was growing up, I had never heard of *multitasking*, much less regarded it as an ability to cultivate and celebrate. Things of course are different today. For many of us, multitasking is a more-useful skill than the ability to add or subtract numbers in our head.

To say that there may be millions of abilities does not get us very far, so psychologists try to group them together into smaller sets of basic skills. An ongoing issue is how parsimonious this grouping can be while still doing justice to the diversity of abilities. Accordingly, a great deal of attention has been paid to whether intelligence (ability) is one thing, several, or many.

General and Specific Intelligence

One venerable point of view holds that intelligence is singular: a highly general characteristic widely exhibited across different areas (Galton, 1869). A century ago, psychologist Charles Spearman (1904), a pioneer investigator of skilled performance, was struck by the finding that when a group of people were given tests measuring different abilities (such as tests of knowledge of the classics, mathematics, and French), their test scores often correlated with each other. Those who scored high on one test tended to score high on the others, and those who scored low on one test scored low on the others as well. From findings like these, Spearman argued for the existence of **general intelligence**, abbreviated as **g**. For Spearman, g is whatever underlies the fact that tests tend to correlate with each other, and g is the factor common to all instances of skilled performance. By this view, people are generically skilled or not, and it is a matter of chance whether the talented make their mark as economists, cinematographers, or football coaches.

However, different tests do not show perfect consistency. Spearman therefore concluded that besides g, there are also **specific intelligences** that influence a person's performance on particular tests. A specific intelligence is abbreviated as **s**. So, someone's performance on any given test reflects a combination of her general intelligence and her specific intelligence for whatever that test measures.

Spearman proposed that if two different tests correlated, it was because they both reflect g. By definition, they cannot reflect the same s. But this is not the only way to make sense of these data, and indeed, many disagree with Spearman. Two tests might correlate because they both reflect the same s. It is a matter of judgment whether a test of French and a test of classics do or do not reflect anything in common except general intelligence. Spearman's tests were not an infinite sampling of areas in which people perform—there is no way that they could be—so we should not be surprised that he was unable to convince everyone that intelligence was singular.

In contrast to Spearman, other psychologists have emphasized s over g, suggesting that intelligence is composed of a set of abilities and capacities largely independent of one another. For instance, in 1938, L. L. Thurstone proposed that intelligence spanned a handful of distinct abilities, such as being able to perform arithmetic operations, to define words, to recognize objects rotated in space, and to recall information. Another vision of intelligence as plural was proposed by J. P. Guilford (1967). He argued that the number of separate abilities and skills typically subsumed under intelligence exceeds 100. By this view, people are best described as having *profiles of skills*, and one achieves best when one's skills are brought to bear in a domain where these fit. Accordingly, we would not know the names of John McEnroe, Keith Jennings, and Howard Stern were it not for tennis, "Jeopardy," and talk radio. Again, we see the premise of the Gallup Organization exemplified.

Multiple Intelligences

The best-known contemporary statement about the plurality of abilities is Howard Gardner's (1983) theory of **multiple intelligences**. He distinguished seven basic abilities:

- *linguistic*: sensitivity to the meanings and functions of language; exhibited by orators, poets, and lyricists
- *logical-mathematical*: competence at organizing ideas in abstract ways; evident in the work of mathematicians and theoretical physicists
- *spatial*: capacity for visual or spatial imagery, including the ability to transform images; shown by navigators, billiard players, and sculptors
- *musical*: ability to produce and organize sounds according to prescribed pitch and rhythm; displayed by musicians
- *bodily*: kinesthetic mastery over body movements; present in dancers, surgeons, and athletes
- *personal*: ability to access one's own feelings; shown by introspective novelists
- *social*: ability to understand other people and what motivates them; displayed by politicians, religious leaders, clinicians, and salespeople

The first three types of intelligence are the abstract and intellectual skills usually measured by intelligence and ability tests, but Gardner felt that the others are just as important, despite the historical fact that psychologists neglected them.

To Gardner, intelligence is a set of problem-solving skills that allows the individual to resolve difficulties that he encounters. He speculated that the abilities enumerated in his theory arose in the course of evolution. Hence, they are based in biology. These skills are presumably independent of each other. A person can be high or low on one type of intelligence yet low or high on another type.

It is important to consider someone's profile and how different intelligences are blended together. We can discuss the seven intelligences individually, but as Gardner (1993b, p. 9) himself observed, "[They] can be seen in pure form only in individuals who are, in the technical sense, freaks." Sigmund Freud well exemplified personal intelligence, for example, but he was also a brilliant writer (linguistic intelligence) and highly skilled at attracting followers and capturing the interest of the general public (social intelligence; Gardner, 1993a).

How did Gardner go about identifying these seven types of intelligence from the many possible candidates? He employed several criteria, including whether or not a particular set of skills is selectively isolated by brain damage. If damage to nervous tissue selectively attacks or spares a given competence, then one can argue that it has a biological basis. Gardner also looked for a distinctive developmental history for a set of skills, an associated set of symbols that people use in exercising these particular skills, and the existence of prodigies[16] who excel at them. When all of these criteria pointed to the same ability, he labeled it a basic intelligence.

Gardner (1993b) described the origin of his theory in a critique of theorizing by developmental psychologist Jean Piaget (1950), who proposed that abstract linguistic and logical skills are the ideal to which all human thought strives. Gardner proposed instead that there was a range of ideals. In his own words (pp. xi–xii):

16. A *prodigy* is a child who shows a special skill or talent advanced far beyond what is considered normal for her age (Barlow, 1952). Prodigies seem at odds with one of the principles of developmental psychology: that development proceeds in an orderly sequence. You have to crawl before you walk, and you have to walk before you run. Prodigies challenge this truism, seeming to run from the start. However, this is not what actually happens (Feldman, 1980, 1993). Prodigious achievements are not spontaneous. Rather, prodigies develop through stages, just more quickly than the rest of us (Goldsmith, 1992). Furthermore, they do not achieve their advanced levels without extensive instruction, usually of a formal nature. Without guidance through the stages involved in mastering a skill, their expert accomplishment does not occur (Korzenik, 1992). So, the majority of the top U.S. chess players under age 13 come from New York or California, where instructors abound. Aside from their particular skill, prodigies are otherwise normal children. The stereotype of a child prodigy as a miniature adult is simply incorrect. Finally, prodigies may or may not grow up to make noted contributions within their fields as adults. History shows that some prodigies—like Mozart—indeed become accomplished adults, but it is much more common for a child prodigy to return to the pack as an adult.

> Had I simply noted that human beings possess different talents, the claim would have been uncontroversial—and my book would have gone unnoticed. But I made a deliberate decision to write about "multiple intelligences": "multiple" to stress an unknown number of separate human capacities . . . "intelligences" to underscore that these capacities were as fundamental as those historically captured within the IQ test.

He further commented that he did not anticipate the excitement his theory would generate among the general public as well as among educators. Perhaps he tapped into widespread discontent with the tyranny of IQ tests and its vision that there is but one way to be talented.

I can still remember my 1955 first-grade class, where we were divided into two groups based on how well we could read. And I kid you not, the groups were named the Jets and the Gliders. Guess which group read at the higher level? Guess which group was privileged in every possible way throughout our elementary and secondary school years? The point, echoing Gardner, is not that we should do away with distinctions. We should make more distinctions. Of course students have different reading abilities, but this particular skill should not be automatically used to sort out students in art, music, and physical education.

Howard Gardner may or may not regard himself as a positive psychologist, but he certainly helped to set the stage for the field by his attention to excellence in a way that did not diminish anyone. For the past two decades, he has devoted much of his attention to the educational implications of his theory.

How can the different intelligences be assessed? Gardner (1991a) argued against what he called "formal assessment"—all of the students in a school taking the same written test of ability or achievement on the same day at the same time, which is then scored according to a simple rubric to yield a single quantitative score. These scores are then used to evaluate students and schools, to steer students into some courses and away from others, and—subtly but most important—to decide what should be emphasized by the school and larger society. Subject matters that lend themselves to efficient formal assessment, like mathematics and science, are valued more than other disciplines that resist formal assessment, like the arts.

Gardner's (1991a) alternative to formal assessment is **assessment in context**, which relies on information about individuals' abilities obtained in the course of their everyday activities. A student's artistic ability can be assessed by looking at the drawings and paintings he produces. Another student's athletic ability can be assessed by seeing how she performs in games. Gardner links assessment in context to strategies used over the millennia by master craftspeople to train and evaluate their apprentices. The young person would observe and help the master, slowly entering the practice of the trade. Assessment was ongoing, constant, individualized, and obviously based on the apprentice's demonstration of the precise skills of interest. Assessment in context has the methodological virtue of ecological validity, which means that inference is minimized.

Depending on the skill, different types of assessment are needed. Assessment in context is therefore as multiple as people's actual abilities. Gardner (1993b) suggested that students—and, by implication, those in the workforce—present not just SAT scores or GPAs to admissions or hiring committees but also portfolios of their actual projects and accomplishments. Artists and musicians already do so as a matter of course, and I can imagine the day when I am on a committee to hire a college teacher, and we review videotapes of actual classroom lectures.

The nurturance of talents needs to be as multiple as the talents. Not only do people start school with different skills and styles of learning, the day is long past when we can expect anyone to master most of the world's knowledge or even a representative sampling of it (Gardner, 1991b). A uniform curriculum serves an impossible goal. The school of the future should be student centered—not in the sense that students run the show but in the sense that what a given student learns is tailored to her proclivities and abilities. The fact that intelligences are to be *used* in everyday life should be kept in mind, especially as everyday life changes. If the only rationale for including a subject matter in a school's curriculum is historical, then that is pale justification.

Accomplishments

> A story is told about the medieval stone masons who carved the gargoyles that adorn the great Gothic cathedrals. Sometimes their creations were positioned high upon the cathedral, hidden behind cornices or otherwise blocked from view, invisible from any vantage point on the ground. They sculpted these gargoyles as carefully as any of the others, even knowing that once the cathedral was completed and the scaffolding was taken down, their work would remain forever unseen by human eye[s]. It was said that they carved for the eye of God. That, written in a thousand variations, is the story of human accomplishment.
>
> —CHARLES MURRAY (2003)

Interest and ability—with a large dose of perseverance—are the recipe for accomplishment, whether it occurs on a small scale or a large one (Murray, 2003). I conclude this chapter by discussing remarkable achievements. I have two reasons for this focus. First, accomplishments for the ages are interesting and—indeed—awe inspiring. And second, an important point about positive psychology is thereby illustrated. If our interest is in people at their best, we should study the most-talented people, and we should study them in settings and circumstances that have allowed them to do their best.

These settings can be described as the "natural homes" for positive psychology, and they include places in which virtuosity is recognized, celebrated, and encouraged (Peterson & Seligman, 2003b). Among the obvious examples that qualify as natural homes are the workplace, sports, the performing arts, friendships and romances, childrearing, and school—exactly the sorts of settings mentioned in this chapter and throughout the book.

Studies in such settings are often segregated as applied psychology, but in the present context, this is a curious label if it implies that basic psychology can stay away from these places. I find the applied-basic partition profoundly false. Positive psychology must seek its subject matter where it is most likely to be found.[17] These places may not always include the typical sources of research participants: psychology subject pools and psychiatric clinics. Along these lines, positive psychologists cannot rely simply on convenience samples of callow youth or troubled souls. Without putting too fine a point on it, studies of college students are somewhat suspect if our interest is with general psychology and downright bizarre if our interest lies in positive psychology.

To study the most-accomplished people, we can focus on exceptional individuals and conduct case studies, as Howard Gardner (1993a, 1997) has done in his extended examinations of the lives of luminaries like Albert Einstein, Martha Graham, Pablo Picasso, Igor Stravinsky, and Virginia Woolf. It is worth emphasizing that psychological case studies go beyond mere biographies to create and evaluate theories that can be applied to other people, including the rest of us leading our more-mundane lives.

Gardner proposed that there are four ways to be extraordinary: by being a *master* of some domain of accomplishment (e.g., Mozart and musical composition); by being a *maker* of an entirely new field (e.g., Freud and psychoanalysis); by being an *introspector* and exploring inner life (e.g., novelist James Joyce); and by being an *influencer* (e.g., Gandhi and politics). Again we see the theme of plurality of excellence. I hope you also see that this particular typology can be applied as readily to supervisors at our own places of work as to the world's most-esteemed geniuses.

Another research strategy is to look at larger numbers of eminent people. Here, studies have the look and feel of more-conventional psychological investigations that assess the characteristics of a large sample of folks and determine the

17. There is a familiar joke about the drunk in the middle of the night crawling around on his hands and knees under a street lamp. A police officer walks by. "What are you doing?" "I dropped my keys, and I am looking for them." The police officer starts to help, but neither man finds the keys. "Are you sure you dropped your keys here?" "Actually, I dropped them over there in the bushes." "Then why are we looking here under the street lamp?" "Because the light is so much better here." This reminds me of another story told about former bank robber Willie Sutton. "Why did you rob banks?" he was asked. "That's where the money was," he replied (Sutton & Linn, 1976). The positive psychology point is twofold. Avoid what is merely convenient, and find whatever banks have the currency most meaningful to you.

antecedents and consequences of these characteristics. The difference of course is that calling these people research "participants" is misleading because they did not agree to participate in a given study but instead participated in life, doing so in such a way that a public record was left behind. It is the public record that is studied (Smith, 1992).

The drawback of this approach is that the researcher is a victim of the historical record, what was entered into it in the first place, and what has survived. Some of the most-notable human accomplishments—written language, deliberate agriculture, animal domestication, and the wheel—were no doubt created by some individual, but we do not know who these geniuses happened to be. And there is always the legitimate worry that the historical record reflects a bias because it is usually written by those with power.

Be that as it may, what has been learned from these at-a-distance studies of eminent individuals provides ample food for thought. Psychologist Dean Simonton (1984, 1994, 1997, 2000) is the best-known practitioner of such investigations. He has devoted his career to ways of reliably coding variables of interest from historical material, starting of course with relative eminence.[18] He has studied several samples of historically intriguing individuals: political leaders, writers, artists, generals, composers, and even famous psychologists.

What does Simonton conclude? Accomplishment in any given field never has a single determinant but instead always reflects a complex of psychological, social, and historical factors. Some generalizations are possible. Being the firstborn in a family is modestly correlated with the degree of later attainment, as are intellectual flexibility and the personality traits of dominance and extraversion. Skill in the field, formal instruction, and the presence of a role model are usually the most-important determinants of accomplishment.

Furthermore, as I keep emphasizing, one must be in the right place at the right time for one's accomplishments to be influential. For instance, Simonton (1992) studied female writers in Japan over the last 1,500 years. Within any given era, the impact of these women depended on societal ideologies about male superiority. A similar point can be made about the achievements of women in the United States (Mowrer-Popiel, Pollard, & Pollard, 1993).

A recently published book by Charles Murray[19] (2003) extends the kinds of

18. There is the argument that "eminence" is socially constructed and ultimately arbitrary. That Plato, Shakespeare, Newton, and Mozart still receive ample mention and attention in contemporary books does not mean that they were more accomplished than their peers, just that they won the Dead White Guy Lottery. While acknowledging bias in the historical record—all data sources are fallible—I take issue with the implied argument that there is no such thing as excellence. I believe that there really are good things in the world (chapter 1) and that prodigious human accomplishments are among them. We can debate what these accomplishments might be but not the fact of their existence.

19. You may recognize Murray as the coauthor of *The Bell Curve* (Herrnstein & Murray, 1994), which ignited controversy in the 1990s because of some of its speculation about Black-White differ-

studies that Simonton has done to the largest possible landscape: the greatest human accomplishments of the ages and the people who made them. Murray focused on a number of fields of endeavor[20]—art, astronomy, biology, chemistry, geology, literature, mathematics, medicine, music, philosophy, physics, and technology—and, within each, quantified eminence by counting the amount of space devoted to individuals in different encyclopedias and handbooks prepared by contemporary scholars from around the world. In each case, the agreement across sources about the eminence of an individual was as substantial as the reliability of any psychological measure (chapter 4). Bias of course exists in the historical record, but it is widely shared.

Although Murray discussed accomplishments in each of the fields on which he focused, here are some of the conclusions he advanced about accomplishment in general, based on comparisons among the "top" several hundred individuals in each field:

- **Polymaths.** Those eminent in more than one field requiring arguably different skills are exceedingly rare, with Aristotle and Leonardo da Vinci as the best and perhaps only examples.
- Hard work is critical; the most eminent put in much longer hours and produced much more than the merely eminent.
- Mentors are critical.[21]

ences in IQ (Fraser, 1995). This was in my opinion an unfortunate detour because it obscured what was more interesting about the book: a sustained argument for the validity of general intelligence tests based on evidence that these tests predict not only academic performance but also occupational attainment, socioeconomic status, marital stability, parenting, citizenship, and law abidingness. Notice that this argument favors g over s and that this book therefore takes issue with Gardner's notion that each of his multiple intelligences is equally important. According to the authors of *The Bell Curve*, the linguistic, logical, and mathematical skills measured by conventional IQ tests are precisely the skills that matter most in our modern society. Consider the demands made in almost all quarters for acquiring and using complex information, skills made possible by these forms of intelligence as opposed to others (Hunt, 1995). Herrnstein and Murray (1994) proposed that an ever-smaller number of people can truly succeed in the modern world. They labeled this group a "cognitive elite": individuals—of all ethnic groups—who by virtue of their intelligence win admission to the best schools and thus receive the best jobs, make the most money, have the best marriages, and assert the most societal influence.

20. Why are these fields considered to be so important? Why do we celebrate eminent composers and mathematicians but not—for example—the world's best players at tiddly winks? Perhaps the fields that are widely regarded as meaningful are those that take specific advantage of the multiple intelligences distinguished by Howard Gardner (1983).

21. The Pinnacle Project began in 2001 to match highly talented teenagers with world-class experts in their respective fields of interest, endeavors like writing, biology, music, and mathematics (Pinnacle Project, 2001–2002). The youths and the experts met for a week in a retreat in the Berkshires to talk about ideas and to plan the activities of the young people during the coming year. The hope embodied in the Pinnacle Project is that mentoring relationships will be forged, which will encourage the careers of the young people beyond what they might otherwise be.

- It is helpful to be in the right place at the right time; societies that are prosperous (but not necessarily those at peace) have more eminent citizens, as do cities that are political or financial centers and home to an elite university.
- Eminence is most likely to occur in a culture that believes life to have a transcendent purpose (chapter 4) and where individuals believe in their own efficacy (chapter 5).

These conclusions seem to apply to the rest of us and indeed have been suggested throughout the chapter. To do your best, you need to identify your interests and skills, choose an endeavor where these fit, find a mentor, put in lots of time, and believe in the significance of what you are doing and in your own autonomy.

EXERCISE *Recrafting Your Work to Capitalize on Your Interests and Abilities*

The exercise in chapter 6 asked you to recraft your everyday life at school or at work by identifying your signature strengths of character and using them in new ways. The exercise here is similar in spirit and asks you to identify your interests and abilities and use them in new ways at school or at work.

This exercise will fail if you are too literal or too concrete in identifying your interests or abilities. If your only avowed interest is topiary gardening, and you work as an investment banker in a downtown office building, then I am not sure how you can bring this specific interest to bear on your work unless you commandeer the lobby of the building and start planting trees. But if you can recast your interest in broader terms, e.g., as symmetry, and likewise your ability—e.g., the talent to see long-term potential—then maybe you can be a topiary investor specializing in diversified and conservative retirement accounts.

To identify your interests, I suggest you keep track for a week of how you spend your leisure time. Then try to identify themes that underlie your leisure activities that can be brought to bear on your job.

To identify your abilities, I suggest you first take honest stock of yourself and what you do well in terms of Gardner's (1983) seven multiple intelligences (p. 211). Remember his emphasis on actual accomplishments, so pay attention to what you have achieved so far in your life. If an answer is not immediately evident, follow through on an idea that Gardner suggested: People with a given intelligence are attuned to its display in others. So, think of movies you have seen, television shows you have watched, or books you have read in which a given character has struck you as memorable or admirable. Look beyond their good looks and intriguing lives to see if there is a common intelligence. For me, this exercise leads quickly to the identification of linguistic intelligence[22] as the one to which I am most attuned and—by implication—what may be my most-developed ability. Or you might go through the yearly issue of *Time* magazine that lists the 100 most influential people on the planet. Which of these people most intrigue you, and do they have a common intelligence?

Once you have identified an interest or an ability, ask yourself how you can use it at work or at school in a novel way. Follow through every day for at least 1 week—and, I hope, longer. Do you do better at work or school by capitalizing on your strengths? Are you happier than you were before starting the exercise?

GLOSSARY

ability: skill underlying differential performance of some task for which there is an objective standard
Aristotelian Principle: proposition that people enjoy doing what they do well
assessment in context: evaluation of an individual's abilities obtained in the course of his or her everyday activities
competence: motive to do things well
general intelligence (g): presumably, general factor common to all instances of skilled performance
genius: person whose actual accomplishments exert a profound influence on contemporary and subsequent generations
interest: topic or activity pursued with passion
interest inventory: questionnaires that attempt to match people to appropriate occupations by comparing their interests to those apt to be satisfied by a particular job
leisure world: culture that develops around a shared leisure activity
multiple intelligences: theory that there are a number of basic and distinct forms of intelligence
polymath: individual eminent in more than one field, which require arguably

22. One of my favorite movie scenes is when Michael Douglas in *An American President* gives an extemporaneous speech at a press conference defending his girlfriend against the attacks of a political opponent: "My name is Andrew Shepherd, and I *am* the president." My favorite comedian is Robin Williams, at least when he is ad-libbing. My favorite sports commentators are Chris Berman and Charles Barkley. On the political front, I like to listen to James Carville *and* to Rush Limbaugh. The common thread is that all of these folks are wonderful wordsmiths. They—or the parts they play—embody linguistic genius.

different skills

specific intelligence (s): presumably, specific factor that influences skilled performance at one task but not necessarily others

10-Year Rule: idea that people who make important contributions to a particular field have usually devoted a full decade to the mastery of necessary knowledge and skills

12-7 Rule: idea that people who make important contributions to a particular field have usually put in 12-hour days, 7 days a week, for years

well-developed individual interest: attraction to a field marked by a deep intellectual and emotional involvement

RESOURCES

Books and Journals

Gardner, H. (1983). *Frames of mind: The theory of multiple intelligences.* New York: Basic.

Simonton, D. K. (1984). *Genius, creativity, and leadership: Historiometric methods.* Cambridge, MA: Harvard University Press.

Murray, C. (2003). *Human accomplishment: The pursuit of excellence in the arts and sciences, 800 BC to 1950.* New York: HarperCollins.

Gladwell, M. (2005). *Blink: The power of thinking without thinking.* New York: Little, Brown.

Huntford, R. (1998). *Nansen: The explorer as hero.* New York: Barnes & Noble.

Creativity Research Journal

Journal of Creative Behavior

Articles

Silvia, P. J. (2001). Interest and interests: The psychology of constructive capriciousness. *Review of General Psychology, 5,* 270–290.

Simonton, D. K. (2000). Creativity: Cognitive, developmental, personal, and social aspects. *American Psychologist, 55,* 151–158.

Winner, E. (2000). The origins and ends of giftedness. *American Psychologist, 55,* 159–169.

Ripley, A. (2005, March 7). Who says a woman can't be Einstein? *Time,* pp. 51–60.

Kluger, J. (2005, November 14). Ambition: Why some people are most likely to succeed. *Time,* pp. 48–58.

Web Sites

http://www2.fmg.uva.nl/sociosite/topics/leisure.html. This is a Web site with lots of information and resources on leisure, recreation, and sports.

http://www.pz.harvard.edu. This is the Web site of Howard Gardner's Project Zero at

Harvard University. Its "mission is to understand and enhance learning, thinking, and creativity in the arts, as well as humanistic and scientific disciplines, at the individual and institutional levels."

http://www.jvis.com. For a fee, you can take on-line the "Jackson Vocational Interest Survey (JVIS) . . . [which] . . . was developed to assist high school students, college students, and adults with education and career planning."

http://quintcareers.testingroom.com. This Web site "includes access to numerous on-line tests and assessments for self-discovery (including career assessment, values competencies, and work personality). Membership, assessments, and abbreviated results are free, but you must pay for detailed test results."

http://psychology.ucdavis.edu/Simonton/homepage.html. This is the Web site of Dean Keith Simonton at the University of California at Davis. He is the world's leading investigator of achievement and creativity in the historical record.

Films

The Miracle Worker (1962)
To Sir, With Love (1967)
Chariots of Fire (1981)
Flashdance (1983)
Amadeus (1984)
Shaka Zulu (1987)
Rain Man (1988)
My Left Foot (1989)
Little Man Tate (1991)
ABC News's *Nightline*: "The Streak" (1995)
Best in Show (2000)
Edison: The Wizard of Light (2000)
Steeplechase Entertainment: "Leonardo: A Dream of Flight" (2000)
Steeplechase Entertainment: "Marie Curie: More Than Meets the Eye" (2000)
A Beautiful Mind (2001)
A&E's *Biography*: "Albert Einstein" (2005)
ABC News's *Primetime*: "Invention Ideas" (2005)

Songs

"To Sir, With Love" (LuLu)
"Centerfield" (John Fogerty)

9 Wellness

Psychiatry is always talking about mental health, but no one ever does anything about it. —GEORGE E. VAILLANT (2003)

On November 7, 1991, basketball player Earvin "Magic" Johnson announced that he was retiring from his professional career because he had tested positive for HIV, the virus that causes AIDS. AIDS had already claimed tens of thousands of lives by the time that he made his announcement, but many people had been able to distance themselves from the disease. Johnson's celebrity and candor helped to bring the message to the general public that AIDS was everyone's problem.

Magic Johnson retired because it was believed that the physical demands made on a professional athlete would weaken his body and hasten the appearance of full-blown AIDS. Also figuring into his retirement was the fear on the part of other players that they might contract the virus through physical contact with him. The immediate reaction of many people was that Johnson had received a death sentence. Magic seemed upbeat about his condition, but many of us at the time thought that he was fooling himself. Stories written about him read like obituaries.

More than 4 years later, on January 30, 1996, Magic Johnson was not only alive and well, but returning to play in the National Basketball Association. He was bigger and stronger and as skilled as ever. Again, he attracted a great deal of attention, but this time around the sports media focused not on how long he would live but on how much his presence would improve the record of his team, the Lakers.

There was grumbling by a few players about his HIV-positive status, but most players hailed his return. As Charles Barkley remarked, "It's not like we're going to have . . . sex. . . . We're just going to play basketball." Speaking louder than any sound bite was the way Dennis Rodman of the Chicago Bulls guarded Magic in the second game of his resumed career. Rodman bumped, shoved, and fouled him with as much vigor as Rodman bumped, shoved, and fouled any player, which is to say with considerable vigor.

It is now some 15 years later, and Magic Johnson remains alive and well. He has had numerous accomplishments, as a businessman, a philanthropic fund-raiser, and a sports commentator. He is involved with the front office of the Lakers and even had a brief stint as the team's coach. He is married and has children. And just to show that not everything works out well for Magic Johnson, he was an abysmal failure as the host of a television talk show.

We have no way of knowing the rest of his story, although it continues to be of interest. The important point here is that we need to think about illness and health in ways that go beyond the presence or absence of a virus.

There are many ways to be ill. Consider the factors that count toward our judgment that an individual is ill (Peterson, 1996):

- general complaints about feeling ill
- specific symptoms, such as shortness of breath
- identifiable damage to the body
- presence of germs
- diagnosis of specific illnesses
- impairment of daily activities
- a short life as opposed to a long one

These criteria sometimes disagree with one another. Someone might feel fine but harbor all sorts of germs. Someone else might be free of germs but feel poorly. Or someone might live a long but impaired life, or a short but vigorous one. One of the intriguing puzzles of modern epidemiology is why women have more illnesses than men but also live longer (Verbrugge, 1989).

There are also many ways to be healthy, and I will discuss these later in this chapter, which concerns itself with good health and the interplay between psychological well-being and physical well-being. The theme of plurality emphasized throughout the book is played out here as well.

Some call the broad state of health **wellness** (Ralph & Corrigan, 2005). Wellness embodies a widely quoted formulation advanced decades ago by the World Health Organization (1946, p. 100): "Health is a state of complete physical, mental, and social well-being and not merely the absence of disease or infirmity." The meaning of wellness is sometimes expanded to include spiritual well-being, occupational satisfaction, and environmental safety (Owen, 1999) as well as balance and integration of these various components (Adams, Bezner, & Steinhart, 1997).

You are by now familiar with the premise of positive psychology that there is more to the good life than problems minimized or negated (chapter 1), and you should note that what is a radical notion within psychology has long been recognized with respect to physical health. How did those interested in physical health arrive at this insight, and what can positive psychologists learn from their journey?

Health and Illness Throughout History

Let us take a brief look at how health and illness have been regarded in the Western world (Taylor, Denham, & Ureda, 1982). We can distinguish three major eras. In the first era, starting at the dawn of time and continuing to the mid-19th century, when germ theory[1] won acceptance, the focus was solely on disease treatment. People went about their lives until they fell ill; then physicians and other healers attempted to combat their illnesses.

In the second era, ushered in by germ theory, the focus expanded to disease prevention. Public health workers tried to prevent germs from entering the body. Swamps that hosted malaria-carrying mosquitoes were drained. Surgeons began to wash their hands before and after they operated. Food was inspected and dated for freshness. Disease treatment of course continued, and germ theory provided a powerful rationale for the effectiveness of certain drugs for certain diseases: They eradicated the culprit germ.

These two eras share something in common: the assumed passivity of the individual. He or she needed to do nothing except to follow the advice of the physician or the public health expert. But in the third era, which took form only in the last few decades, the individual is called upon to behave in ways that encourage good health. This is the era of health promotion.

Once good health is regarded as something that can be deliberately promoted, our conception of what good health means necessarily changes. There is no upper limit, or at least not one defined as the absence of a germ.

Decades ago, internists began to study the physiology of those who lived at high altitudes, finding that they had higher aerobic capacity, lower blood pressure, and greater cold tolerance than people who lived at sea level. In at least these ways, high-altitude dwellers were supernormal (e.g., Schull & Rothhammer, 1981). These sorts of studies were extended to other special populations like athletes, pilots, and eventually astronauts (e.g., Klein, Wegmann, Bruner, & Vogt,

1. *Germ theory* holds that the necessary and sufficient condition for illness is the presence of a microscopic organism. The generalization of germ theory to include any and all biological causes of pathology is sometimes labeled the *medical model*, which has been as popular in psychology as in medicine (Bursten, 1979), once we recognize that notions like Freud's conflicts and Aaron Beck's automatic thoughts function like metaphorical germs (Peterson, 1996).

1969). What became clear was that the opposite of illness was not freedom from disease but rather fitness and resilience (Vaillant, 2003). There is a story told about Mercury astronaut Scott Carpenter whose 1962 reentry to the atmosphere after an orbital flight was threatened by a dangerously low fuel level. His heart rate hardly increased during the ordeal, and he piloted the Aurora 7 capsule safely back to earth.

Good health sets the stage for later longevity and resilience, but its bottom line may well be in the here and now. The person in good health feels alive, exuberant, and vital and reaps all of the psychological and social benefits of feeling good (chapter 4).

The third era shifts our attention to lifestyle, and the door is opened wide for psychology to contribute to our understanding of good health. Given how we are nowadays bombarded by messages in the popular media about healthy habits and practices, it is remarkable that the idea that our behavior has something to do with our health is a relatively new one. But past conceptions of illness left no room for behavioral factors. To be sure, people could make injuries more or less likely, depending on how they behaved, but illnesses were brought about by invading germs that overwhelmed the immune system. These are microscopic events that presumably take place in isolation from our behavior.

However, as epidemiological data became increasingly available in recent decades, researchers were struck by the nonrandom distribution of particular illnesses across the population as a whole. Some groups of people were more likely to develop certain illnesses than others. Part of this variation could of course be explained by differential exposure to germs or toxins. Syphilis was long recognized as a disease more likely to be experienced by sailors than other people, and so was scurvy. Theorists eventually realized that both illnesses had something to do with the lifestyle of many sailors: sexual activity with those carrying the syphilis germ and a diet deficient in vitamin C, respectively.

Throughout the 20th century, as researchers took an ever-closer look at who fell ill and who did not, they discovered a set of behaviors that was related to people's general health or illness. Belloc and Breslow (1972), for example, studied such behaviors as

- not eating between meals
- sleeping 8 hours a night
- exercising
- not smoking
- not drinking alcohol to excess

Those who engaged in such habits were on average healthier than those who did not. They also lived longer (Belloc, 1973). All of these enabling factors are behavioral in nature, which suggests that if people can be encouraged to change their behaviors, then they should live longer and better.

Minds and Bodies: The Legacy of Descartes

A sound mind in a sound body is a short but full description of a happy state in this world. He that has these two has little more to wish for; and he that wants either of them will be little the better for anything else.
—JOHN LOCKE, *Some Thoughts Concerning Education* (1693)

Early Western thinkers such as Aristotle made no firm distinction between minds and bodies. They expected that minds and bodies would show continuity, with the health of one reflecting the health of the other. Greek standards of beauty referred not merely to good looks but also to an inner beauty that was necessarily shown in a person's physical appearance. And the earliest physicians, individuals like Hippocrates and Galen, routinely ministered to the whole person, treating a patient's physical symptoms as well as his psyche.

If I were writing this book in Athenian Greece, there would be no need for a chapter discussing how psychological factors influence physical well-being because the mutual influences of minds and bodies would need no particular explanation. Between the there and then and the here and now, a great deal has happened, and I want to highlight an intellectual event that has profoundly changed how we in the Western world think about minds and bodies and, by implication, wellness.[2]

Among the most far-reaching contributions of French philosopher René Descartes (1596–1650) was a strong stance concerning the separateness of mind and body, a position that has come to be known as **mind-body dualism**. Contrast this notion with the view of the Greek thinkers who preceded him. Do you see how mind-body dualism poses a considerable problem in explaining (or even allowing for) the existence of psychological influences on physical health and illness?

How did Descartes arrive at mind-body dualism? He was one of the first theorists to propose an account of how the body moved (Peterson, 1996). As a young man in Paris, he would stroll through the parks to see the popular mechanized statues that were connected to plates in the walkways. When passersby stepped on a plate, a hydraulic mechanism forced water through pipes into the limbs of the statue, causing the statue to move, to the apparent delight of onlookers.

2. I have been careful to describe this history as a Western one, because other intellectual traditions understand health and illness in radically different ways. Traditional Chinese medicine, for example, assumes that a person's vital energy (*qi*) needs to be in balance for good health, psychological and physical. The three arms of Chinese medicine—herbs, acupuncture, and *qi gong*—are viewed within this system as ways to achieve optimal energy balance. Although these healing strategies have been imported to Western medicine, often with practical success, their underlying rationale remains difficult for at least this particular Westerner to grasp (Ai et al., 2001).

Descartes's thinking was stimulated by these statues. If mechanical beings moved about in this way, perhaps people did too. After all, the parts of the body are connected by tubes (nerves). Muscles appear to swell when they are used. And the brain contains hollow spaces (cerebral ventricles) filled with fluid. Putting this all together, Descartes hypothesized that our bodies moved when fluid traveled from the brain through the nerves to swell the muscles and make such movement possible.

This theory is more than quaint. Descartes correctly anticipated the role of the brain in initiating movement and the importance of the nerves in making it possible. He was wrong about the mechanism of this effect—we now know that nerves work via electrical and chemical processes as opposed to hydraulic ones—but his theory is still impressive. It provided a thoroughly scientific (mechanistic) view of people and their overt behavior.

But in saying that our behavior has causes, Descartes was implying that people did not have free will. This implication was a direct assault on Christian doctrine and its assumption of free will. The Catholic Church saw the views of Descartes as heresy and punishable by death. To solve this dilemma, he proposed that the body works in the mechanical fashion he had described; it is subject to causes and effects. But the soul (mind) is free.

By the 1800s, theorists found that scientific concepts—including causality—could be applied to the mind, and psychology took form (chapter 1). This development in effect dismissed the basis of Descartes's distinction. But altogether different disciplines had by then sprung up to explain bodies on the one hand (neurology, biology) and minds on the other (psychology, psychiatry). The mind-body dualism originally proposed by Descartes had become the mind-body problem: a puzzle to be explained.

What we have seen since is the development of various scientific fields that try to explain mutual mind-body influence, especially with respect to health and illness. In a sense, these fields are all the legacy of Descartes and the conceptual problems he created by splitting minds and bodies.

No matter how difficult it is to explain mind-body interactions, they certainly exist. For example, Donald Redelmeier and Sheldon Singh (2001) looked at the longevity of actors and actresses who had won Academy Awards. Celebrities are fascinating in their own right, but these researchers had a theoretical motive behind their investigation. A link between high social status and good health is well established, but its meaning is difficult to unpack (e.g., Marmor, Shipley, & Rose, 1984). Social status brings with it not only psychological states of satisfaction and accomplishment but also confounds like income, education, and access to health care. What is responsible for the correlation between status and health?

Academy Award winners have high status and ample material assets. But so too do other notable actors and actresses, which means that a comparison between Oscar winners and their peers with respect to longevity starts to pull apart status as a purely psychological characteristic from other factors with which sta-

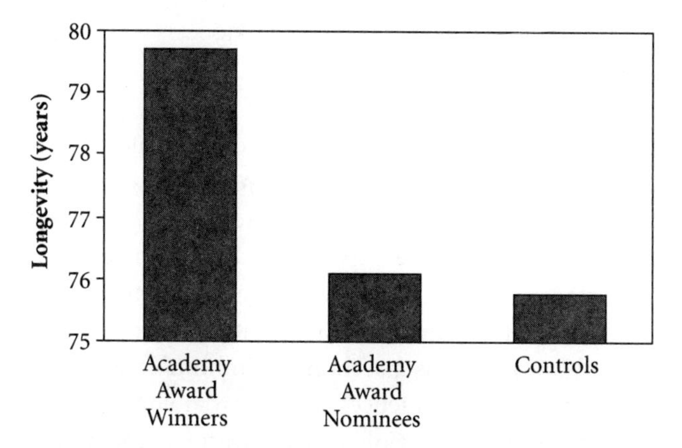

Figure 9.1. Longevity of Academy Award Winners, Nominees, and Other Actors. From Redelmeier & Singh, 2001

tus is usually associated. Looking at the past 7 decades, Redelmeier and Singh (2001) identified 235 Academy Award winners, 527 actors and actresses who had been nominated for Oscars but never won, and another 887 control subjects—actors and actresses who had appeared in the same films as the winners and had been born in approximately the same year. All sorts of statistical controls were applied to the survival data for individuals in these groups,[3] but the bottom line is simple: Winners on average lived almost 4 years longer than nominees or controls (see Figure 9.1). There was even a modest tendency for multiple-Oscar winners (e.g., Katharine Hepburn) to live longer than single-Oscar winners, which would seem to bode well for Tom Hanks, Jack Nicholson, Meryl Streep, and Hillary Swank.

It is said that being nominated for an Academy Award is a testament to one's acting ability, whereas actually winning one is a matter of luck (Redelmeier & Singh, 2001). If there is any truth at all to this quip, it means that this particular study has some of the methodological virtues of a true experiment in which research participants are randomly assigned to different conditions, allowing definitive conclusions about causality to be advanced. The psychological experience of success and victory may actually add years to someone's life.[4]

3. For example, the researchers controlled for the number of films in which each actor and actress had appeared, their age when they first appeared in a film, gender, and ethnicity. Other analyses were limited just to actors and actresses who had lived to at least age 65. The results were the same.

4. In 1996, to celebrate its 50th anniversary, the National Basketball Association named the 50 greatest players in its history and gathered them together for a televised ceremony. I remember being struck that 49 of the 50 players named were still alive at the time. Only Pete Maravich had died. Magic Johnson of course is among this elite group of the NBA's greatest players, and who would want to say that the acclaim he has received throughout his life has nothing to do with his evident well-being?

Mind-Body Fields

Let us turn from these intriguing examples of mind-body interactions to the scientific fields that try to make sense of them. **Health psychology** applies psychological theories and research to the topic of physical well-being (Krantz, Grunberg, & Baum, 1985). **Behavioral medicine** expands traditional medical approaches to include the psychological context of health and illness (Gentry, 1984). They meet in the middle to give us a richer conception of what it means to be healthy or ill.

Another mind-body field is **psychoneuroimmunology** (PNI), which explicitly recognizes the mutual influences among psychological, neurological, and immunological factors[5] (Ader & Cohen, 1993; Daruna, 2004; Fleshner & Laudenslager, 2004; Maier, Watkins, & Fleshner, 1994). Only in the past few decades has this field emerged, and it was sparked by the discovery that the body's immune response could be conditioned. In a classic experiment with rats as research subjects, Robert Ader and Nicholas Cohen (1975) paired a saccharine taste with a drug that suppressed their immune functioning. This pairing was done several times. Then the taste was presented alone, and antigens were introduced into their bodies. The immune systems of the rats responded sluggishly to the invasion. Immunosuppression did not occur when the taste was not presented.

Assuming we can generalize from the immune functioning of a rat to that of a person, do you see the importance of this demonstration? On a theoretical level, it shows that psychological factors—learning, in this particular case—directly influence the operation of the immune system. On a practical level, it means that certain environmental stimuli can become associated with poor immune func-

5. Until the last century, the body's **immune system** was hardly described, much less understood (Silverstein, 1989). It was recognized much later than the other major systems of the body because it is not a single entity, but rather a host of cells present throughout the body.

The immune system fights off infection by recognizing foreign material and combating it. The foreign material that invades the body is called an *antigen.* Antigens include germs, of course, but also cells from other individuals or species, drugs, and cancer cells that form within our own bodies. And in autoimmunological diseases, such as rheumatoid arthritis, the immune system mistakenly treats its own cells as antigens.

Antigens stimulate various immunological responses. One is the production of B cell lymphocytes, which originate in bone marrow (hence the B) and are carried to the lymph nodes, spleen, and tonsils. Another mode of fighting off an invasion is by T cell lymphocytes, produced in the thymus (hence the T). These fight antigens in several ways, including killing foreign cells and stimulating the activity of phagocytes, cells which literally "eat" (or engulf) foreign material. T cells also interact with B cells, activating or deactivating them as needed. In a healthy person, antigens stimulate these various and appropriate immunological responses. When the response is sluggish or nonexistent, we call it *immunosuppression.* AIDS illustrates this point. HIV attacks the cells that alert the immune system about the initial antigen invasion. Illnesses which are rare in the general population become much more likely among those with AIDS because their bodies never start to defend against them in the first place.

tioning. If and when these stimuli are encountered, the individual is at increased risk for poor health.

The other side of the coin, by implication, is that optimal functioning of the immune system can be maintained by avoiding "negative" stimuli and perhaps by seeking out "positive" stimuli. Although people's immune systems vary in their robustness, it is not clear in theory or in practice whether superimmunity can be conditioned. Immunosuppression can be quickly brought about by the administration of a drug, whereas immunocompetence cannot.

Consider the account by Norman Cousins (1976) of how he mustered his body's psychological resources to combat a potentially fatal disease. He checked out of his hospital room and into a plush hotel, where he watched funny movies. After his recovery, Cousins argued that he "elicited" good health from his body, although perhaps it is more accurate (and more modest) to conclude that he avoided a stimulus (the hospital) associated with immunosuppression.

Regardless, his story has become a well-known parable in PNI circles. Whether it is a scientifically accurate one does not detract from the more-rigorous demonstrations that psychological factors like stress and depression indeed compromise immune functioning (e.g., Cohen, Tyrell, & Smith, 1991; Schleifer, Keller, Siris, Davis, & Stein, 1985; Segerstrom & Miller, 2004), whereas factors like social support, relaxation training, and confiding in others can boost it (e.g., Kiecolt-Glaser & Glaser, 1992; Pennebaker, Kiecolt-Glaser, & Glaser, 1988; Spiegel, Bloom, Kraemer, & Gottheil, 1989).

Wellness Promotion

Several hundred years ago, physicians in the West did not believe that the body could heal itself because to assume so—despite ample evidence that this did happen—seemed mystical and at odds with prevailing materialism (Weil, 1988). Because diseases were not seen as self-limiting, the physician was expected to intervene aggressively, and extreme measures like blood letting were common. These "treatments" look bizarre in retrospect, but they were motivated by the assumption that in their absence, the patient would die as his illness inevitably progressed to death. The discovery of the immune system made it possible for physicians of a materialistic bent to explain how people could recover from illness without positing a mystical will to live.

We know now that people can and do heal themselves from many infectious illnesses. We also know that germ theory is not strictly true. People's bodies all of the time harbor certain germs, which may or may not create an illness, depending on a host of other factors, including the robustness of the immune system. Finally, we know that people's habits contribute importantly to the functioning of their immune systems and thereby to overall well-being.

An irony of our increased understanding of the immune system is that infectious diseases, at least in the Western world, are no longer the scourge that they once were (Purtilo & Purtilo, 1989). AIDS is notable in part because it is an exception to this generalization. Advances in immunization and antibiotic treatment means that most people in the United States and Europe die not from infectious diseases but from heart disease or cancer, afflictions of the body to be sure but not caused by a germ in any obvious way.

Accordingly, contemporary attempts to combat illness and promote health look beyond the physical body and certainly the immune system to target behavioral, psychological, and social factors. We know that behavioral risk factors for poor health, such as smoking or not exercising, can be changed, and that doing so has beneficial effects. Emotional styles and ways of relating to others, when changed by therapy, may also provide health benefits. Health psychologists are interested in how to encourage people to behave in healthy ways. They have adapted a variety of therapy techniques, particularly from the cognitive-behavioral arena, to promote health. Strategies involving relaxation, stress management, and biofeedback have been especially popular (Goleman & Gurin, 1993).

Sometimes these techniques are merged with mass communication strategies to give us broad, media-based programs to promote health (Winett, King, & Altman, 1989). For example, in one project, health psychologists undertook a community-based health promotion program that targeted more than 100,000 California residents (Farquhar, Maccoby, & Solomon, 1984). The goal of the program was to increase knowledge about health and illness, encourage healthier habits, and decrease mortality rates. A variety of strategies was employed, including informational messages about healthy behaviors delivered through television, radio, and newspapers; classes and lectures concerning psychological influences on health; and environmental changes such as identifying calories, fat, and cholesterol in food served in restaurants. These interventions continued for 6 years and were successful in meeting their goals. When the residents in these communities were compared to those of otherwise comparable towns, they showed increased knowledge of the risk factors for disease, decreased blood pressure and heart rates, decreased smoking, and reduced risk for cardiovascular disease.

Health promotion campaigns are not always successful. People might believe that there is a link between behavior and health, but then think that they are immune to these principles. For instance, Weinstein (1989) documented a widespread tendency on the part of most people to see themselves as below average in risk for different illnesses; this unrealistic optimism undercuts efforts at health promotion (chapter 5). Even if people believe they are at risk, they may regard themselves as incapable of a lifestyle change or unwilling to make the necessary sacrifices. Further, people often desire unrealistically immediate results from their efforts.

If it is to be useful, health-promoting programs must do more than provide simple information and occasional encouragement (Peterson & Stunkard, 1989). Health promotion campaigns that are successful—like the California project I just described—are deliberately broad-based, changing people's abstract knowledge as well as their personal beliefs and attitudes, their habits, and their social environments.

Collectively, such health-promoting endeavors are called **wellness promotion**, and they are proliferating in the form of wellness centers established in schools, the community, and the workplace (e.g., Guerra & Williams, 2003; Watson & Gauthier, 2003). Like programs of any ilk, some of these are successful—promoting the psychological and physical health of participants—and others less so.

Some wellness programs do justice to the notion of wellness by providing a broad spectrum of services, from fitness activities to nutritional advice to stress management to couples counseling. Others are much more narrow, despite a name that promises more. Sometimes a wellness center is just a gym that sells bottled water.

It is also fair to say that even broad-service wellness centers may be geared more toward preventing problems than toward promoting well-being (Garofalo, 1994), in part because those who pay for them—communities or employers—have an understandable goal of reducing pressing problems like alcoholism, obesity, absenteeism, and attrition. Although the boosting of good health pays similar dividends as the reduction of poor health, these benefits are necessarily further down the road and harder to justify in an era of scarce resources.

Not everyone eligible to participate in an available wellness program actually does so (Spillman, 1988), and the irony is that those most in need—the least healthy—are often unlikely to enroll in the first place or to stay involved (Bungam, Osark, & Chang, 1997). The good news is that regular participation leads to less illness and better health (e.g., Gebhardt & Crump, 1990; Goetzel, Kahr, Aldana, & Kenny, 1996), but the bad news is that these individual benefits might not translate themselves into organizational-level improvement because of the small number of participants. In other words, although participating individuals benefit from wellness programs, the group per se may not benefit in a measurable way, which can only be disappointing to the sponsors.

In terms of health-promoting activities, there are neither quick fixes nor magic bullets. Promoting wellness takes time and effort. Antibiotics start to eradicate a germ within hours, but there is no equivalent with respect to wellness. Late-night television infomercials promise us effortless fitness and rapid weight loss, but this is absolute nonsense.

Years ago, when my research showing that optimists were healthier than their pessimistic counterparts was first published (chapter 5), I received many phone calls from the popular media, from *Star Magazine* to the *New York Times* and most stops in between. The interviewers were clearly interested in the research and especially its implications. But even though I could not see them on the other end of the phone line, I could tell that their eyes glazed over when I would say that optimists are healthier than pessimists because they *behave* differently and do the sorts of things that make health more likely. No shortcuts. No miracles. No smiley-faced phagocytes engulfing germs. If you want to be healthy, it is not enough to be cheerful and wish others a good day. I think the writers who interviewed me wanted to hear a quick-fix message, or at least they acted as if their readers wanted one. I never entered into the implied conspiracy, and so my career as a media darling was nipped in the bud.

And here I go again: Wellness results from a healthy lifestyle—sustained habits—as opposed to singular events. Consider that weight loss books are among the most popular in the self-help genre in the United States. They have been for years, and they probably will be for years, which suggests the obvious: There are no shortcuts to weight loss.

Let me offer some further generalizations about achieving a healthy weight (Peterson, 1996):

- Prevention is much more effective than treatment; in other words, the most effective way not to be overweight as an adult is to have avoided being overweight at earlier points in life.
- Most forms of weight loss, from diets and fasts to individual psychotherapy to behavior therapy to family therapy to exercise programs, work in the short run in the sense that people lose weight.
- Most forms of weight loss fail in the long run in the sense that people tend to gain back the weight that they have lost.

People cannot maintain weight loss if they go back to the style of life that led them to gain weight in the first place. This sounds terribly commonsensical, but it is a message that the general public does not want to hear. Extreme diets are popular because they promise that a few weeks of deprivation will permanently solve weight problems. But weight loss does not work this way. The only way to keep weight off is to change one's life (Wing, 1992). Studies show that the interventions which do work in the long run are those that lead people to approach eating in a self-consciously moderate way (e.g., Epstein, Wing, Koeske, & Valoski, 1987).

Also worth mentioning are the topics of aging and physical decline. Are these inevitable? Evolutionary theorists have argued that organisms can sometimes further the survival of their own genes if they sacrifice themselves, so long as their deaths enhance the survival of their close relatives (Hamilton, 1964). Perhaps it is adaptive for the elderly, who have already passed on their genes, to move out of the way and not use up resources that their offspring need. A maximum life expectancy might therefore be inherited, with the physical declines of aging the mechanism that sets the limit.

Each species appears to have a characteristic maximum life expectancy. Even under the best of conditions, dogs do not live much longer than 20 years of age, and people do not live much longer than 110 years of age. Claims of extreme longevity among groups of people, like yogurt eaters living in the Caucasus Mountains of the former Soviet Union, always prove to be exaggerated. Such claims persist, but 120 years is the oldest well-documented age of any male who has ever lived, achieved for example by a Japanese man, Shigechiyo Izumi (Woodruff-Pak, 1988), and 122 years is the oldest well-documented age of any female, achieved by a French woman, Jeanne Calment (Thomas, 1995). Some theorists believe that people's maximum life expectancy has not appreciably changed for centuries (Fries & Crapo, 1981). Our average life expectancy has increased, but it has an upper limit. The point, of course, is to live well while we are alive (Barsky, 1988).

One more caveat. Much of what passes as wellness promotion smacks of the New Age—aromatherapy, aura enhancement, crystal healing, and the like. I mean no disrespect, but I suggest that there are excellent lessons to be learned from the Old Age about how to promote well-being. Your grandmother might know as much as your guru. If you want to be healthier, you should eat a balanced diet, exercise regularly, and not smoke. You should have good relationships with other people and pursue activities that are fulfilling. These generalizations need not be accepted on faith; the data are unequivocal.

You can certainly explore what the New Age offers, and perhaps there are some benefits waiting to be found. But you should not take an either-or approach to what might promote your health. There are biological realities of health and illness that cannot be overridden by your beliefs and wishes.

Vaillant (2003) observed that people in colonial America did not recognize the health hazards of excess alcohol consumption. The colonists often drank to great excess, and it was even a common practice to quiet a crying baby with whiskey. No one thought that any of this was harmful, but liver and brain damage occurred regardless. Stated another way, it is one thing to say that our thoughts, moods, and behaviors influence well-being but quite another to believe that only these things do. Sometimes biology trumps psychology.

Mental Health

At the beginning of this chapter, I pointed out that there are different ways to be ill. Since then, I have made the complementary point that there are different ways to be healthy, including resistance to disease, resilience in the wake of stress, physical fitness, and having a zest for life. As with illness, these criteria for well-being often line up with one another, but there are cases where they do not. Our task is to take an appropriately broad view of well-being and not to privilege a single criterion above all others. Does anyone other than me remember with irony that two of the icons of physical fitness during the 1980s—Arnold Schwarzenegger and Jane Fonda—were, respectively, a man who used steroids and a woman with an eating disorder? From the outside, they looked fabulous, but wellness means more than muscles and muscle tone.

There is a tendency, perhaps, to regard hard measures of health and illness—

those based on physical or biological tests—as more valid, but from a broad perspective, this bias is not warranted (chapter 4). Biological criteria, such as aerobic capacity or immunocompetence, are no more basic than psychological criteria, such as a person's general sense of well-being or the degree to which one leads an active life.

In this section, I would like to focus specifically on mental health—psychological well-being—and what it means. The theme of plurality remains front and center, and in previous chapters, I have touched upon many of the relevant psychological components of well-being, from positive affect (chapter 3) to happiness (chapter 4) to hope and optimism (chapter 5) to good character (chapter 6) to values (chapter 7) to interests and abilities (chapter 8). Here, I try to weave these together, coupling them with an additional component of wellness: good social relationships (chapter 10). I rely on a recent essay by psychiatrist George Vaillant (2003) on the multiple meanings of mental health.[6]

As emphasized, discussions of mental health have lagged behind discussions of physical health, for all of the reasons that positive psychology and its focus on doing well have been neglected by business-as-usual social sciences (chapter 1). As partly responsible for this neglect, Vaillant (2003) noted Sigmund Freud's dismissal of mental health as a fiction. Also hampering our understanding of mental health are more practical issues in measuring and thereby documenting it. But Freud's influence in the mental "health" professions has waned, and we have taken great strides in measurement. The time is right to claim mental health as an important topic of concern, not just by positive psychologists but by people in general.

Mental Health as Above Normal

What is typical—normal—should not be confused with what is healthy, given that any population includes a fair number of people with demonstrable psychological problems, necessarily bringing down the average of whatever indicators of psychological well-being we choose to assess (Kessler et al., 1994). However, it is still sensible to suggest that mental health entails being above average—supernormal—with respect to criteria reflecting good psychological functioning. We can quibble over where the line between normal and healthy should be drawn, but most theorists agree that it is found in the important domains of work, love, and play.

6. Influenced by positive psychology, Vaillant (2003) also discussed how mental health entails the character strengths and virtues, social and emotional intelligence, and subjective well-being. Because these have been the subjects of previous chapters, I simply refer you to these discussions as additional perspectives on mental health. Remember as well that all implicate interpersonal relationships as crucial for psychological well-being. Earlier, I said that there may be no happy hermits (p. 93). Just as scarce may be healthy hermits.

We can identify people who are doing well in one or more of these domains and ask what else is true about them. Earlier in this chapter, I mentioned the physical health of the original astronauts. They were also studied with respect to their mental health, and all were exceptional (Ruff & Korchin, 1964). All came from intact, happy, small-town families. All were married with children. They trusted others. They could tolerate both close interdependence and extreme isolation. They experienced emotions—positive and negative—strongly, but they did not dwell on them. They were not particularly introspective, but each was socially intelligent and rarely squabbled with others. Although the original astronauts were chosen from the ranks of test pilots, none was considered to be rash. They had experienced remarkably few accidents in their prior careers.[7]

What is responsible for supernormal psychological functioning like that evident in the Mercury astronauts? In 1958, Marie Jahoda wrote a prescient book—*Current Concepts of Positive Mental Health*—which made the case for understanding psychological well-being in its own right, not simply as the absence of disorder or distress. Jahoda surveyed what previous thinkers—mainly clinicians—had to say about mental health and integrated their views. She proposed a half dozen underlying processes that produce the states and traits we usually identify as psychologically healthy:

- acceptance of oneself
- accurate perception of reality
- autonomy (freedom from social pressures)
- environmental mastery
- growth, development, becoming
- integration of personality

At the same time that Jahoda (1958) published her book, William Scott (1958a, 1958b) surveyed the existing research literature on mental health, focusing on research definitions (measures) of well-being and empirically established correlates of these measures. Then as now, the majority of studies ostensibly looking at health were really studies of disorder. He could draw firm conclusions only about the factors that characterized lack of pathology; good social relationships were the most common correlate. Scott cited a personal communication from Jahoda in which she described her attempts to develop measures of several of her

7. This is an important fact, because investigators of traumatic injuries have concluded that there are very few "accidents" if we mean literally random catastrophes. Rather, those who experience mishaps often do so because of a reckless lifestyle coupled with psychological factors, such as depression, pessimism, and sensation seeking (e.g., Dahlback, 1991; McKenna, 1983; Peterson et al., 2001). A trauma surgeon once told me that accident victims so frequently explain their injuries with the same expression that it has earned its own acronym in hospital notes: STMOB—"I was just sitting there minding my own business." Upon further inquiry, one discovers the rest of the story: "I was just sitting there minding my own business when this guy came up to me. I had wrecked his car, I had stolen his drugs, and I had insulted his sister."

criteria for mental health (i.e., accurate perception of reality and environmental mastery) as less than satisfactory, which is probably why her ideas did not stimulate further work for decades.

More recently, Carol Ryff and her colleagues (1989, 1995; Ryff & Keyes, 1995; Ryff & Singer, 1996, 1998) extended Jahoda's analysis by surveying and integrating what different theorists, again mostly clinicians, said about the psychological components of being and doing well—striving and thriving, as it were. They identified what she called six points of convergence across discussions of psychological well-being, which agree substantially with those specified decades earlier by Jahoda:

- autonomy
- environmental mastery
- personal growth
- positive relations with others
- purpose in life
- self-acceptance

Notable about Ryff's work is that she and her colleagues have solved the measurement problem and have created reliable and valid self-report surveys of these components of psychological well-being. Using these measures, they are currently exploring the links between psychological well-being and physical health (e.g., Ryff & Singer, 2001; Singer & Ryff, 2001). Echoing the conclusions I offered in chapter 4, mental health as measured by Ryff's scales shows a stronger association with physical health than does a hedonistic orientation (Ryff, Singer, & Love, 2004). Furthermore, the role of the left prefrontal cortex—believed to aid in the organization of goal-directed activity—has been implicated in this association (Urry et al., 2004).

Mental Health as Resilience

If isolated in a sterile bubble, we would never encounter germs, and it would not matter whether our immune systems worked well, poorly, or not at all. Although such bubbles exist and are used medically, there is no equivalent in the psychological realm.[8] As we lead our lives, we take missteps, encounter failures, and experience losses. How we respond to the bumps in the road provides another perspective on what mental health means.

8. In his book *Victims of Groupthink*, Yale University psychologist Irving Janis (1982) analyzed colossal blunders in U.S. history, like the failure to prepare for Japan's attack on Pearl Harbor in 1941, the decision to mount the Bay of Pigs invasion of Cuba in 1961, and the escalation of the Vietnam War from 1964 to 1967. Noteworthy about these blunders is that they were all products of supposedly careful group consideration by the brightest political and military leaders of the times. To account for such disastrous group decisions, Janis proposed that in certain groups, processes are set into mo-

Because this perspective on mental health focuses on difficult situations, we know a fair amount about how people respond. Typically, psychologists are interested in the damage done by these difficult situations, but if we look at the results from the positive psychology point of view, we see that some people do well in the wake of trauma and stress (Bonnano, 2004; Linley & Joseph, 2004a; Masten, 2001; Rutter, 1985).

For example, children can overcome adversity and thrive (Damon, 2004). Although children are often regarded as psychologically vulnerable, even fragile, this characterization does not apply to all youngsters. The first direct challenges to the fragile-child assumption were longitudinal studies conducted in the 1980s. In one line of research, Norman Garmezy (1983) introduced the notion of the *invulnerable child.* Some—not all, but some—of Garmezy's young research participants showed resistance to life's most severe stressors, flourishing in spite of every prediction to the contrary. In a cross-cultural study conducted in Hawaii and the mainland United States, Emmy Werner (1982) found the same result. Werner adopted the term **resiliency** to describe the quality that enables many young people to thrive in the face of adversity. And in a monograph that became enormously influential in the youth development field, Bonnie Benard (1991) extended Werner's findings to virtually all young people, claiming that every child possesses the potential to develop resiliency. Benard proposed that resilience entails a cluster of adaptive response patterns that can be learned by anyone during childhood. The components of resilience, according to Benard, are

- persistence
- hardiness
- goal-directedness
- healthy success orientation
- achievement motivation

---

tion that suppress criticism and preclude the consideration of alternatives. Collectively, he termed these processes *groupthink.* Groupthink has several components, and for our purposes, consider what Janis called *mindguards,* individuals who protect group leaders from criticism and worry, just as bodyguards protect them from physical assault. The problem, of course, is that mindguards can make matters worse, because criticism is indispensable for a leader as he or she makes difficult decisions. In any event, mindguards try to create a psychological bubble for those they guard.

Along these lines, I am reminded of a talk I once heard in which a sociologist described separate interviews with husbands and wives about stressful events in their families. The original intent of the research was to check the reports of one spouse against the reports of the other, but an interesting pattern emerged. Wives usually reported a greater number of stressful events than did their husbands. Was this an exaggeration on the part of the women and/or an understatement on the part of the men? In most cases, it was neither. Both wives and husbands were accurately describing events as they knew them, but part of the marital "work" of the wives was to protect their husbands from knowing certain things. So, if their son was flunking high school chemistry, he told his mother, who shouldered not only that burden but also the burden of *not* telling her husband. Again, we see the attempt to create a psychological bubble, and in this case, the bubble maker experiences stress as a result.

- educational aspirations
- a belief in the future
- a sense of anticipation
- a sense of purpose
- a sense of coherence

Those with resilience adapt to stressful events in healthy and flexible ways (Luthar, Cicchetti, & Becker, 2000). Resilient people are clearly among those we should regard as mentally healthy. When life gives them lemons, they make lemonade.

Another perspective on resilience starts with Freud's **defense mechanisms**, familiar to anyone who has studied psychology or—indeed—lived in the modern world, where Freud's terms for the unconscious strategies people use to protect themselves against threats have become part of our everyday vocabulary. In *projection*, for example, people attribute their own unacceptable characteristics to other individuals. Some types of prejudice involve projection, as when sexually preoccupied individuals criticize the sexual behavior of other groups—"those" kinds of people. In *repression*, we actively keep an upsetting memory out of our conscious minds. Repression is responsible for cases of amnesia that have psychological bases. In *rationalization*, we rewrite personal history after a disappointment, like the fox in Aesop's fables who decided that the grapes he could not have were probably sour anyway.

Taken as a whole, defense mechanisms seem bizarre and far from healthy, but George Vaillant (1977, 1992, 1995, 2000, 2002) had the insight that they could be arranged in a hierarchy from the relatively immature to the relatively mature, depending on the degree to which the defense is at odds with reality. *Denial*, for example, grossly distorts what actually happened by saying that it flat out did not occur. *Humor*, in contrast, reframes reality without denying it. And in *sublimation*, we channel our conflicts and impulses into socially valued activities. People with severe psychological problems tend to favor immature defense mechanisms, and—more to the point—those who live long and prosper tend to use mature defenses.

Moving from this psychodynamic emphasis on the unconscious, we can find another perspective on resilience and mental health in a line of research that looks at stressful life events and their consequences. Initial studies of stressful life events were done in the early 1960s by epidemiologists like Thomas Holmes and Richard Rahe (1967). Their research procedure was simple: Determine the number of stressful events that people have experienced in the recent or distant past, measure their health status, and then calculate the correlation between the two. In general, the correlation is negative. When psychologists became interested in this type of research, they looked not just at the occurrence or nonoccurrence of stressful events but also how people thought about them. This inquiry began in earnest in the late 1960s, as cognitive theorizing swept through psychology as a whole (chapter 1).

As research progressed, it became clear that taking into account particular ways of thinking about stressful events improved the ability to predict which events would or would not take a toll on well-being. Exits, such as divorce, bring more problems in their wake than do entrances, such as beginning college. Events seen as unpredictable, uncontrollable, and/or meaningless are more likely to lead to illness and even death (Mineka & Henderson, 1985). Furthermore, events associated with emotional conflict are particularly harmful.

The best-known cognitive treatment of stress was introduced by psychologist Richard Lazarus (1966, 1982, 1991; Lazarus & Folkman, 1984). He argued that stressful events and their impact must be understood in terms of how the individual perceives them. In *primary appraisal*, the individual asks what is at stake in the event. Events take on altogether different significance depending on their implications for the individual. A speeding ticket, for example, means one thing if a person is driving on a suspended driver's license, and something else if she is not. In *secondary appraisal*, the individual takes stock of the resources at her disposal for meeting the demands of the event. Again, events differ drastically depending on whether the person believes she can handle it, and how. So, the impact of a speeding ticket varies depending on whether a person has enough money to pay for it and the increased cost of car insurance that will follow.

Problem-focused coping refers to attempts to meet the stressful event head on and remove its effects. **Emotion-focused coping** is more indirect, referring to attempts to moderate one's own emotional response to an event that itself cannot be altered. Lazarus pointed out that no strategy of coping is always preferred. Different events demand different coping styles. Broken radiators require problem-focused coping, whereas broken hearts respond best to emotion-focused coping. But the point is that the impact of a stressful event depends on how the individual appraises it. The mentally healthy person appraises events in ways that allow appropriate strategies of coping. As Reinhold Niebuhr's Serenity Prayer requests: "God give me the serenity to accept things which cannot be changed; give me courage to change things which must be changed; and the wisdom to distinguish one from the other" (Sifton, 2003).

Some researchers interested in stress and coping from a cognitive perspective have investigated the role of habitual ways of thinking about stressful events and have discovered links between certain styles of thinking and subsequent well-being. Suzanne Kobasa (1979), for instance, studied a personality dimension labeled **hardiness**: the ability to find meaning and challenge in the demands of life. In a series of studies, she found that hardy individuals were less likely than others to be overwhelmed when confronted with stressful events (Kobasa, 1982; Kobasa, Maddi, & Courington, 1981; Kobasa, Maddi, & Kahn, 1982).

Mental Health as Maturity

Decline over time is the rule for the body but not necessarily for the mind.[9] Most psychological disorders wane with age, and the elderly are certainly better able to moderate their emotions than are the young (Jones & Meredith, 2000). Accordingly, yet another perspective on mental health views it in terms of greater psychological maturity. The relevance to the present discussion is that maturity is not the sole province of the elderly. And conversely, advancing age need not bring psychological maturity, as one of my favorite bumper stickers reminds us: "You are only young once, but you can be immature forever."

Much of what psychology has to say about maturity has been shaped by the theorizing of Erik Erikson (1963, 1968, 1982). He built upon and modified Freud's stage theory of psychological development. Erikson proposed that throughout their lives, people pass through a series of stages in which a particular challenge is central. In each case, satisfactory resolution must be achieved if the individual is to progress through subsequent stages. Erikson called his approach a theory of **psychosocial stages** because each challenge revolves around a specific social milestone with far-reaching psychological implications:

- *Trust versus mistrust.* The newborn infant must first achieve a sense of safety, trusting that his environment (in the form of caretakers) will provide for his well-being. If a child's needs for food, warmth, and physical contacts are met, then the child develops trust. If not, the child develops mistrust, which is shown as anxiety and insecurity.
- *Autonomy versus self-doubt.* At about 18 months, when the child's physical development allows movement and exploration, she begins to confront the notion of her own self. She is somebody who can make things happen or prevent them from happening. Central to this task is the control of her own body, and here is the social significance of toilet training. Toilet training can be an area of conflict between children and their parents. Who will prevail? If the child successfully resolves this stage, she achieves a sense of autonomy. Otherwise, children doubt their own ability to make things happen.
- *Initiative versus guilt.* The next stage takes place from about ages 3 to 6, when the child starts to initiate his own activities, intellectual and physical. Erikson regarded this stage as critical in allowing the child to gain self-confidence. If thwarted by parents in these self-initiated activities, the child is likely to experience guilt and a lack of self-worth.

9. To be sure, the brain as the organ of the mind is hardly immune to the effects of aging or the damage due to illness, injury, or insult like alcohol abuse. But the brain is designed to be plastic in a way that kidneys, hearts, and skin are not, and barring injury or disease, the central nervous system can function extremely well across the entire lifespan (Vaillant, 2003).

- *Competence versus inferiority.* From age 6 to the onset of puberty, the child begins to explore systematically her skills and abilities. School begins, and she starts to interact with peers. A number of possible skills can be developed: physical, intellectual, and social. Children take lessons in ballet or gymnastics, or throw themselves into art classes or swimming pools or the intense study of dinosaurs. Successful resolution of this stage produces feelings of competence. Children who experience failure in mastering skills during this stage may suffer feelings of inferiority.
- *Identity versus role confusion.* For Erikson, the central issue of adolescence is the creation of an ideology: a set of personal values and goals by which to live. An ideology translates itself into an occupational identity, a gender identity, a sexual identity, a political identity, a religious identity, a social identity, and so on. These identities orient adolescents to the future, determining not just who they are but who they will be. An identity can only be chosen after one has the cognitive skills to do so, in particular, the ability to think in hypothetical terms.
- *Intimacy versus isolation.* For those who leave adolescence with an identity, the next task is to merge this identity with that of another individual to achieve intimacy. By Erikson's view, people cannot find out who they are in a relationship. Just the contrary: Identity is a prerequisite for a relationship that is characterized by shared feelings and closeness. Those who fail to achieve an intimate relationship with another person feel isolated.
- *Generativity versus stagnation.* When identity and intimacy are achieved, men and women enter Erikson's next psychosocial stage. Here the concern is with matters outside oneself, with the world and the next generation. Erikson termed this concern *generativity*. An obvious way to resolve this issue is by raising one's own children. There are other ways as well, through an occupation such as teaching, or through one's support for causes like environmentalism or the elimination of nuclear weapons. According to Erikson, those who do not achieve generativity will feel stagnant and self-absorbed.
- *Ego integrity versus despair.* The final Eriksonian stage comes at the end of life, as a person looks back over the issues he faced. If they have been resolved successfully, the person feels content, having achieved the state of *ego integrity*. One leads but a single life, and integrity results from the conviction that one has led it well (Wong, 1989). If not, the person feels despair. Life has been too short, too unfair, too filled with failure. But if the person has achieved integrity, he has achieved mental health in the form of maturity.

More generally, maturity means doing the psychosocial tasks well that are appropriate to one's stage in life. We can speak of a mature 10-year-old, as well as a mature 50-year-old, but they are of course mature in different ways. Butterflies are not healthier than caterpillars (Vaillant, 2003), but a healthy caterpillar is much more likely to become a healthy butterfly.

We can regard Erikson's theory with varying degrees of skepticism. There is little evidence to support a strict stage approach to social development, and people may deal with psychosocial challenges in a somewhat different order than he proposed (B. E. Peterson & Stewart, 1993). Nonetheless, the general trend of development is in the direction Erikson proposed, toward expanding social connectedness, based on the earlier establishment of an authentic identity.

In several longitudinal studies, George Vaillant (2004) studied the predictors of what he called *positive aging*—being physically healthy *and* satisfied with life at age 75. What he discovered supports the notion that maturity is closely aligned with well-being.

First, let me mention some surprising findings about factors that were *not* strongly associated with successful aging: longevity of one's ancestors, cholesterol levels at age 50, social class of one's parents, and stressful life events before age 65. I hasten to say that such factors prove to be important earlier in life, even to the point of determining who made it into Vaillant's final sample of research participants, but among those still alive at age 75, these factors did not predict how well they were doing. Instead, successful aging was foreshadowed by

- *not* being a smoker (or having quit before age 45)
- *not* having a history of alcohol abuse
- normal weight
- regular exercise
- years of education
- stable marriage
- use of mature defense mechanisms

Let me elaborate on the education finding. Wellness was predicted by years of education, not because more education meant higher IQ scores or greater income, but rather because education was associated with greater future orientation and perseverance.

EXERCISE *Changing a Habit*

As a long-time member of the American Psychological Association's Media Referral Service, I speak to a number of writers from magazines and newspapers about psychological topics. In late December of every year, I can always count on at least one call from a writer doing a story on New Year's resolutions, and I try to convey what psychologists have learned about eradicating bad habits or establishing good ones. That these calls keep coming underscores the difficulty in changing our habits and the unpleasant truism that good intentions and nebulous "will power" are not enough. Mark Twain once observed that it was so easy to quit smoking that he had done it dozens of times.

That said, psychologists do know something about how to change habits, but like so much practical advice, the devil is in the details. For starters, one needs to be ready to change. In an important theory, University of Rhode Island psychologist James Prochaska and his colleagues (Prochaska, DiClemente, & Norcross, 1992; Prochaska, Redding, & Evers, 1997) formalized the notion that change of any sort takes place through a series of steps or stages, beginning with *contemplation* (when one thinks about the benefits of change) and progressing through *preparation* (when one thinks about the difficulties of change and sets a goal) to *action* (when one actually starts to change by arranging appropriate rewards or punishments) and finally to *maintenance* (when one takes steps to prevent relapse).

So, the purpose of the present exercise is for you to change some health-relevant habit, but only try it if you are beyond the precontemplation stage. That is, if you have not already thought about change, this exercise is not the right trigger for the subsequent steps.

You may want to reduce or eliminate some habitual behavior or add a new one to your repertoire. Sometimes you can do both at the same time, and you may actually want to do so, under the assumption that the bad habit may serve some purpose for you. Merely eliminating it can leave that purpose hanging and result in backsliding. If you want to quit drinking at the neighborhood bar, perhaps you need to join a chess club that meets every afternoon and fulfills whatever social needs the local tavern has been satisfying.

It is important to define the habit for yourself in concrete ways that allow you to monitor changes. "Becoming a better person" is a wonderful goal, but it is a lot easier to know that you have succeeded at "greeting the doorman of your apartment building every morning." Along these lines, it is easier to change a habit that allows you to do so in small steps, so that you can note and relish your progress. So, Weight Watchers provides participants with a target weight goal, but it is the individual pounds that they shed in a given week that are tracked and celebrated at meetings.

You probably want to get into the practice of keeping a journal with respect to whatever habit you want to change. If you want to cut back on smoking or drinking, write down at the end of every day how many cigarettes or drinks you have had. If you want to increase exercising, write down the number of blocks you walked, the distance you covered, or the amount of time during which you experienced an accelerated heart rate. It is a good idea to keep the journal for a week or two before you try to change the habit. This will give you a handle on exactly what the habit entails.

Researchers who study goals and their attainment agree that hard and specific goals are more motivating than easy or nebulous ones, what are derisively termed *DYB* (do-your-best) *goals* (Locke, Shaw, Saari, & Latham, 1981). However, you need to break hard goals into more-manageable components. And when you do start to change the habit, focus not just on what you still need to accomplish but also on what you have already done. "I have 50 pounds to lose" is daunting, whereas "I already lost 10 pounds" is affirming.

Expect occasional backsliding. If you are on a diet, do not interpret one cookie as a sign that you are an utter failure. Weight loss specialists have documented the *abstinence violation effect*, which refers to a common but thoroughly irrational response to breaking one's diet (Marlatt & Gordon, 1980). Many people conceptualize dieting only in terms of good days and bad days. A good day is when you stay on the diet. A bad day is when you violate the diet, which I have just emphasized will happen on occasion. Craziness enters the picture when one makes no distinctions among degrees of bad days. One cookie at lunch leads a person to give up dieting for the entire day, finishing the bag of cookies in the afternoon and topping it off with a quart of ice cream in the evening or a pizza at midnight.

If you can enlist a friend or family member in your efforts, that might help so long as you each can provide support and encouragement to one another. I know a happily married couple who embarked on a diet and exercise program together. At first, things worked very well. But then one of them began to make much more rapid progress than the other, and the program turned into a competition that tarnished what had always been a wonderfully cooperative relationship. When they saw the damage being done to their marriage, they were smart enough to go their own ways with respect to diet and exercise.

Making a change is never as difficult as maintaining the change, whenever the steps taken to change a habit prove impossible to incorporate into one's ongoing lifestyle. This is why extreme diets have only short-term success, or why an exercise program begun on your vacation falls by the wayside when you return to work. So, while you think of how to change a habit, also keep in mind what you will do to keep the change permanent. Do *not* celebrate the loss of 50 pounds by ordering the entire right side of the menu at the International House of Pancakes.

I do not urge you to do your best. I urge you to succeed.

GLOSSARY

behavioral medicine: field that expands traditional medical approaches to include the psychological context of health and illness

defense mechanism: unconscious strategy that people use to protect themselves against threat

emotion-focused coping: reaction to stress that entails changing one's emotional reaction

hardiness: ability to find meaning and challenge in the demands of life

health psychology: field that applies psychological theories and research to physical well-being
immune system: cells throughout the body that fight off infection by recognizing foreign material and combating it.
mind-body dualism: philosophical stance that minds and bodies are altogether separate
problem-focused coping: reaction to stress that entails meeting the stressful event head on and removing its effects
psychoneuroimmunology (PNI): field that studies the relationships among psychological, neurological, and immunological factors
psychosocial stages: periods of life characterized by specific social milestones to be achieved
resiliency: quality that enables people to thrive in the face of adversity
wellness: broad state of health, including physical, mental, and social well-being and not merely the absence of disease or infirmity
wellness promotion: deliberate interventions to promote health

RESOURCES

Books and Journals

Jahoda, M. (1958). *Current concepts of positive mental health.* New York: Basic.
Vaillant, G. E. (2002). *Aging well.* New York: Little, Brown.
Ryff, C. D., & Singer, B. H. (2001). *Emotion, social relationships, and health.* New York: Oxford University Press.
Weil, A. (1988). *Health and healing* (Rev. ed.). Boston: Houghton Mifflin.
Cousins, N. (1981). *The anatomy of an illness.* New York: Norton.
Pennebaker, J. W. (1997). *Opening up: The healing power of expressing emotion.* New York: Guilford.
Wolfe, T. (1979). *The right stuff.* New York: Farrar, Straus, & Giroux.
Health Psychology

Articles

Vaillant, G. E. (2003). Mental health. *American Journal of Psychiatry, 160,* 1373–1384.
Seeman, J. (1989). Toward a model of positive health. *American Psychologist, 44,* 1099–1109.
Ryff, C. D., & Singer, B. H. (1998). The contours of positive mental health. *Psychological Inquiry, 9,* 1–28.
Maier, S. F., Watkins, L. R., & Fleshner, M. (1994). Psychoneuroimmunology: The interface between behavior, brain, and immunity. *American Psychologist, 49,* 1004–1017.
Stokols, D. (1992). Establishing and maintaining healthy environments: Toward a social ecology of health promotion. *American Psychologist, 47,* 6–22.

Web Sites

http://www.healthsurvey.org/cgi-bin/WebObjects/Project. This is the Web site of the National Health Survey, which "provides a free, on-the-spot analysis of your diet, physical activities, and lifestyle choices."

Films

On Golden Pond (1981)
Terms of Endearment (1983)
Regarding Henry (1991)
The Doctor (1991)
Philadelphia (1993)
ABC News's *Primetime*: "Are Health Foods Really Healthier?" (1995)
ABC News's *Turning Point*: "Alternative Medicine: Hope or Hype" (1996)
As Good as It Gets (1997)
One True Thing (1998)
Montana PBS: "Introducing Positive Psychology: Personal Well-Being, Social Support, Health and Aging Well" (2004)
ABC News's *20/20*: "Myths and Lies: Health and Beauty" (2005)

Songs

"A Touch of Gray" (Grateful Dead)
"It Was a Very Good Year" (Frank Sinatra)
"As Good as I Once Was" (Toby Keith)

10 Positive Interpersonal Relationships

Immature love says: "I love you because I need you." Mature love says: "I need you because I love you." —ERICH FROMM (1956)

If you have read this far in the book, you will not be surprised by my three-word summary of positive psychology: *Other people matter.*

Despite relative neglect by psychologists over the years, the topic of love now resides front and center in any discussion of human nature, especially from a positive perspective (Reis & Gable, 2003). The capacity to love and to be loved is viewed by contemporary theorists as an inherently human tendency with powerful effects on well-being from infancy through old age.

Researchers have even started to investigate the biochemical basis of love, with special attention to the hormone-like substance **oxytocin**, which is released in the brain in response to social contact, especially skin-to-skin touch (Insel, 1997). Oxytocin increases during pregnancy and surges during the process of childbirth. Its presence facilitates the production of milk and more-general "maternal" behavior. Please note that fathers are not left out of the oxytocin picture. The oxytocin levels of a father-to-be rise as well during the pregnancy of his spouse, and to the degree that he spends time with his infant, his oxytocin levels continue to increase. So too does his interest in his child. And finally, there need not be an infant present for oxytocin to have an effect on adults. It has been called the *cuddle hormone*, and it has been linked to the creation of a loving bond between two individuals and perhaps even to monogamy (Carter, 1998; Porges, 1998; Young, Wang, & Insel, 1998).

Some of the ideas in this chapter, especially about attachment, draw on a chapter drafted by Cindy Hazan for Peterson and Seligman's (2004) book on character strengths and virtues.

Oxytocin is associated with the neurotransmitter dopamine (chapter 3), which is broadly responsible for reinforcement, pleasure, and—indeed—addiction, which means that being "addicted to love" is a metaphor with a biochemical underpinning. Neuroimaging studies of individuals who describe themselves as madly in love show that their brains work differently when they are looking at pictures of their true loves versus pictures of good friends of the same age and gender (Bartels & Zeki, 2000). The neural circuitry implicated is the same that is active when individuals are high on cocaine. Further research finds that when mothers look at pictures of their own children, brain regions responsible for negative emotions and social comparison are *deactivated* (Bartels & Zeki, 2004). We thus have scientific support for what most us already know in the core of our being: Mom's love has the potential to be unconditional.

The point is not that love is *just* biology. The point is that love is *also* biology, and the fact that our biological bodies are designed to draw us to one another is a strong argument that social relationships are neither arbitrary nor merely convenient ways to obtain other things that matter—food, sex, power, whatever. Our biology teaches us that relationships in and of themselves matter.

How could this not be? The prolonged helplessness of infants requires love to be built deep within them and us to ensure survival (Mellen, 1981). Our ancestors needed not only the means to attract a mate for the purposes of procreation but also to create the bond between mates to guarantee that the child would be protected and raised. The child in turn needed to be appealing enough to the parents to elicit their care and concern, even to the point of personal sacrifice.[1]

I once attended a lecture in which George Vaillant (2005) contrasted reptiles and mammals, and he focused not on the differences that meet the eye, striking though they may be. Rather, he pointed out that baby reptiles, newly emerged from their eggs, are thoroughly silent, whereas newborn mammals are remarkably noisy. The evolutionary interpretation is that a noisy reptile would signal itself to its parents as a meal, and the whole species would end rather quickly. A noisy mammal—a kitten, a puppy, or a human infant—signals to its parents that it needs care, and the species continues, generation after generation. What's love got to do with it? Everything.

1. We are attracted to creatures with a youthful appearance and those with large eyes and heads, from kittens and puppies to Mickey Mouse and Penelope Cruz. "Cuteness" so characterized may be what ethologists call a *releasing stimulus* for nurturing behavior (Lorenz, 1966). Other mammals, like cats and dogs, show the same response, implying that such tendencies evolved because they contribute to the survival of the young and helpless. Very few parents physically attack their own children, in part because the appearance of a young child inhibits attack (Southwick, Pal, & Siddiqui, 1972). Those parents who do abuse their children tend to have poor impulse control, suggesting that they are oblivious to the inhibiting effects of an infant's appearance (Parke & Collmer, 1975). Furthermore, premature children are particularly apt to be abused, perhaps because they neither look nor sound like normal infants (Gill, 1970).

The L Word in Psychology

In 1975, two young social scientists—Ellen Berscheid and Elaine Hatfield—received an $84,000 grant from the National Science Foundation to study romantic love. The grant attracted the attention of Wisconsin senator William Proxmire, who strenuously objected on the floor of the U.S. Senate and awarded them his first Golden Fleece Award for cheating the American taxpayers. Proxmire issued a press release stating:

> I object to this not only because no one—not even the National Science Foundation—can argue that falling in love is a science; not only because I'm sure that even if they spend $84 million or $84 billion they wouldn't get an answer that anyone would believe. I'm also against it because I don't want the answer.
>
> I believe that 200 million other Americans want to leave some things in life a mystery, and right on top of the things we don't want to know is why a man falls in love with a woman and vice versa. . . .
>
> So National Science Foundation—get out of the love racket. Leave that to Elizabeth Barrett Browning and Irving Berlin. Here if anywhere Alexander Pope was right when he observed, "If ignorance is bliss, tis folly to be wise." (Hatfield & Walster, 1978, p. viii)

The *Chicago Tribune* ran a reader poll pitting the research plan of Berscheid and Hatfield against the criticism of Senator Proxmire, and the senator won by an overwhelming 88% of the votes cast. Berscheid and Hatfield did garner some support, though, from several Nobel Prize laureates and Arizona senator Barry Goldwater. *New York Times* columnist James Reston offered the opinion that love may forever remain a mystery, but if "sociologists and psychologists can get even a suggestion of the answer to our pattern of romantic love, marriage, disillusions, divorce—and the children left behind—it would be the best investment of federal money since Jefferson made the Louisiana purchase" (Hatfield, 2001, p. 141).

Although public opinion of course matters in determining what sort of science a society supports, we ultimately judge science in terms of the specific theory and research to which it leads. The devil is in the nitty-gritty details, even with respect to love, and by this test, the science of love that Berscheid and Hatfield helped to create has been thoroughly successful.

Why did a modest proposal to study the L word arouse such strong negative feelings? The common criticisms seem to stumble over one another. Love is too important to study—and too trivial. Love is commonsensical—and a deep mystery. Love is sacred—and, at least in the form of sexual intimacy, crass. Perhaps the pervasive bias within the social sciences to focus on the negative led an unalloyed good to be overlooked (chapter 1).

But, as James Reston observed, there are casualties of love in the form of heartbreak and divorce, in the abuse of spouses and the neglect of children. Loneliness has not earned its own diagnostic label from psychiatrists but certainly lies near the center of such bona fide disorders as anxiety, depression, schizophrenia, and substance abuse (Booth, 1983; McWhirter, 1990). One of the ways that researchers legitimized the study of love was to highlight the problems ensuing from its absence. Other researchers studied love under the radar, giving their lines of work neutral labels like *interdependence, equity, social exchange, social support, interpersonal relations*, and the like (Cobb, 1976; S. Cohen, 1988; Foa & Foa, 1975; Homans, 1958; Kelley et al., 1983; Kelley & Thibaut, 1978; Thibaut & Kelley, 1959).

Social psychologist Zick Rubin (1970) deserves credit for focusing explicit attention on love by showing that this apparently fuzzy topic could be approached with as much rigor as any other topic within psychology. He developed self-report scales that distinguished liking from loving.[2] The scales are filled out by an individual with respect to some other individual. For example, the liking items include:

- I think that __________ is unusually well adjusted.
- Most people would react favorably to __________ after a brief acquaintance.
- __________ is one of the most likable people I know.
- __________ is the sort of person whom I myself would most like to be.

The loving items include:

- I feel I can confide in __________ about virtually everything.
- I would do almost anything for __________.
- If I could never be with __________, I would feel miserable.
- I would forgive __________ for practically anything.

A respondent indicates his agreement on a scale ranging from "not at all true" through "definitely true." As is obvious, the liking items reflect one's positive evaluation of another person, whereas the loving items reflect one's emotional attachment.

These scales look valid—that is, they have face validity—but more important, each is reliable and has distinct patterns of correlations with other variables. In his research, Rubin studied college students in Ann Arbor who were dating one another. The Love Scale, which by the way does not use the word *love* in any item, was

2. Rubin (1973) wrote a popular book describing his research titled *Liking and Loving*. I was taken with the title of the book and used it on my course syllabus to describe a topic midway through the semester in the first social psychology class I ever taught, at Kirkland College back in 1977. The day of that class arrived, and I was pleasantly surprised that every single student was in attendance and indeed most seemed to have brought others with them to class. As I looked at the crowded room, I thought to myself that I must be getting the hang of teaching. My smugness quickly evaporated when one of the students remarked, "Wow, we can't wait to hear what you have to say about 'licking and loving' in your lecture today." I have since learned to proofread a course syllabus carefully and to regard Freudian slips as embarrassingly real.

substantially associated with reports of being in love with the target person and with expectations of eventual marriage to him or her. In a laboratory study, in which couples were observed through a one-way mirror by a researcher, the Love Scale predicted how much simultaneous eye-to-eye contact the two people made.

Additionally, in a longitudinal study of dating couples, scores on the Love Scale predicted continuation of a romantic relationship months later and even its intensifying, but only if *both* partners scored high in the first place. Couples mismatched on the Love Scale were less likely to stay together. Liking played less of a role in these findings, although it is important to note that the Liking Scale also predicted the continuation of loving, soap opera plots notwithstanding.

None of these findings is surprising, but the real importance of this research was demonstrating that romantic love could be studied with the sorts of methods used by psychologists to investigate other topics. Arguments about what is or is not possible in science have a way of being resolved rather quickly when a researcher actually does what a theorist, politician, or pundit says cannot be done.

Another love pioneer made his mark by studying baby monkeys—inoffensive and heart-warming. Make no mistake, though. Iconoclast Harry Harlow (1958) was really interested in love. If you have studied psychology, I am sure you remember Harlow's famous studies.

He wanted to know if the attachment of infants to their mothers was due just to the fact that infants need to be fed. Or is social attachment significant in its own right? Remember my brief digressions into the history of psychology elsewhere in this book. The 1950s were the height of behaviorism and its attempt to "reduce" what looked like complex behaviors to simple processes of reward and punishment (chapter 8). One prevailing view at the time was that the mother-infant bond was another reducible phenomenon. The infant was attached to his mother because she fed him.

Harlow separated monkeys at birth from their mothers and raised them individually in cages with two stationary models. One figure was made of wire and the other of terry cloth (see Figure 10.1). The wire mother had a nipple that provided milk, whereas the cloth mother provided no food but had a pleasing texture. If attachment is the result of being fed, then the infant monkeys should have formed attachments to the model associated with food.

However, the infant monkeys preferred the cloth model. They sought out the wire model when hungry but otherwise stayed closer to the cloth one. When the infants were frightened, by an unfamiliar sight or sound, they ran to the cloth mothers and clung to them. Harlow concluded that infants are predisposed to form attachments with objects that are easy to cuddle, like the terry cloth models. Blankets and teddy bears may be popular among human children for exactly the same reason. Harlow's (1974) research is important for showing that even among animals, social bonds reflect more than the satisfaction of physiological needs.

In a related line of research, Harlow (1965) raised rhesus monkeys in complete isolation. After a year without contact with other monkeys, these animals were

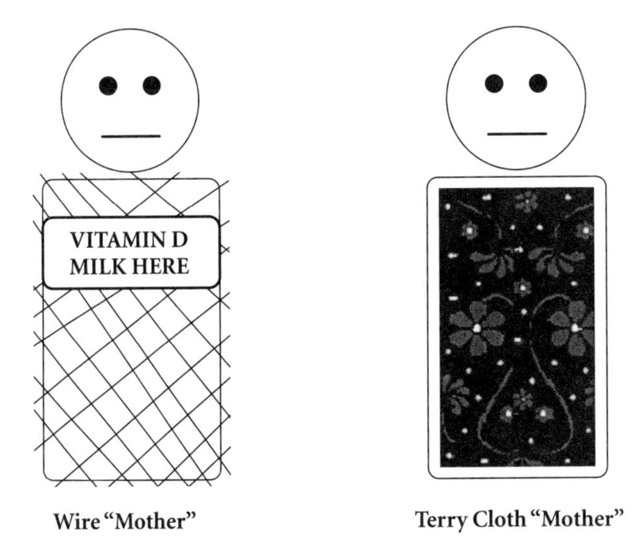

Figure 10.1. Harry Harlow's Surrogate Mothers
One "mother" is made of wire and provides milk, and the other is made of terry cloth and has a pleasing texture.

fearful and withdrawn. Some of their common behaviors—like biting themselves—can only be described as bizarre. The isolated monkeys did not interact normally with other monkeys, and they could not interact with infants. They were not malnourished or physically traumatized, but because they did not have contact with their own kind, their social development was profoundly impaired.

Other studies show that such problems can be corrected if deprived monkeys are placed together with normally raised monkeys (Novak & Harlow, 1975). Eventually, the isolated monkeys learn to interact normally and display few effects of their earlier isolation. Similarly, studies with human children also find that many of the effects of early deprivation can be reversed if the child subsequently finds herself in a supportive environment (White, 1967). But if the deprivation takes place for too long a time, it cannot be easily reversed, suggesting that there is some merit to the idea of critical periods for social development.[3]

3. Shortly after hatching, baby ducklings follow whatever moving object they first encounter, in a process called **imprinting** (Lorenz, 1937). Usually, this object is their mother, but ducklings can also imprint on other animals or even people if they encounter them during the critical period. In most cases, imprinting keeps the vulnerable ducklings out of danger. The process can be disrupted, though, if there is no moving object for them to follow. Human infants do not start out life by following their mothers around. But some theorists suggest that a newborn must form an attachment with a caretaker during a critical period within the first few years of life. If an attachment is not formed, or is formed poorly, then later social development is, by this view, thwarted (e.g., Curtiss, 1977).

As research on love took form, two perspectives emerged, one emphasizing the head and the other the heart—thoughts versus feelings, as it were—which still serve as a useful way to describe psychology's approaches to love. Let me sketch each.

Equity Theory

Equity theory suggests that close relationships—friendships or romances—persist to the degree that both people involved believe that what they are getting out of the relationship is proportional to what they are putting into it (Walster, Walster, & Berscheid, 1978). Equitable relationships last, and inequitable ones break up (Winn, Crawford, & Fischer, 1991). Surely, we have all been friends with people who cannot remember our birthday, neglect to return our phone calls, or fail to defend us against gossip, although we do all of these things for them. This is an unstable relationship, and something has to change. Our friends need to do more, or we need to do less, or there is no future.

Equity theory assumes that people calculate the costs and benefits involved in interacting with others. It is an economic theory and draws our attention to the kinds of things that people give to and receive from another. One representative list of **interpersonal resources**, as they are called, includes the following (Foa & Foa, 1975):

- goods
- information
- love
- money
- services
- status

If you stop and think about it, you will see that some of these resources can be exchanged for one another without arousing any special attention, e.g., goods for money, whereas other exchanges, e.g., love for money, seem less legitimate, although they of course take place.

A similar list comes from studies of **social support**, which refers to how others help us to cope with stressful events (House, 1981):

- appraisal support: constructive feedback, affirmation, and social comparison
- emotional support: empathy, trust, caring, and nurturance
- informational support: advice, suggestions, and solutions
- instrumental support: tangible aid and service

Social support has been linked to good health because it buffers against the effects of stress (Cassel, 1976). In the present context, it is worth emphasizing that not any old support will do. Rather, social support is protective when it occurs in the context of a naturally occurring social network into which the individual is well integrated. Although strangers on the bus, television characters, and pets can provide what looks like social support, real social support is provided in a mutually caring relationship (Berkman, Glass, Brisette, & Seeman, 2000).

Numerous studies support the general predictions of equity theory. For instance, people in a romance bring with them comparable degrees of physical attractiveness.[4] Good looks in a romantic partner are desirable and thus constitute a benefit in a relationship. One of the simplest ways of achieving equity with a person who is good-looking is to be good-looking yourself. This is exactly what happens: Lovers often pair up according to looks, which is why couples like Julia Roberts and Lyle Lovett attract our confused attention and why the reality television show "Beauty and the Geek" is so jarring (McKillip & Riedel, 1983; Murstein, 1976). And interestingly, same-sex friends also pair up according to their physical attractiveness, although this trend is more apparent among males than females (Feingold, 1988).

Equity theory also predicts that when people in a relationship are mismatched on one dimension, like physical attractiveness, then there needs to be a compensating mismatch on another dimension, like occupational success. For example, highly attractive women are more likely to marry rich men, whose wealth can compensate for other shortcomings (Elder, 1969). We can lament that physical attractiveness is a commodity in our social world, but it is a fact that psychologists repeatedly discover.

According to evolutionary psychologists, males and females differ in how they evaluate the desirability of a potential opposite-sex mate (Buss & Schmitt, 1993). Studies in a variety of cultures show that men place more emphasis on youth and physical attractiveness, whereas women tend to value industriousness and the accumulation of resources (Buss et al., 1990). These preferences may be

4. Is someone's physical attractiveness an objective characteristic? Yes and no. On the one hand, there is a great deal of agreement—even across ethnic groups and disparate cultures—that the same sorts of faces and figures are attractive. For example, an "attractive" female's eyes tend to be about 30% of the width of her face, and her nose tends to occupy about 5% of the area of her face (M. R. Cunningham, 1986). Facial symmetry is critical as well, as shown by studies that superimpose facial photographs of many individuals. The resulting composite, an average face if ever there were one, is usually rated as more attractive than the component faces, which belong to actual people (Langlois & Roggman, 1990; Perrett, May, & Yoshikawa, 1994). Mothers of attractive babies interact more with their infants than do the mothers of unattractive babies (Langlois, Ritter, Casey, & Sawin, 1995), and young infants in turn are more attentive to attractive adult faces than to less-attractive ones (Langlois et al., 1987; Rubenstein, Kalakanis, & Langlois, 1999). On the other hand, those of us who are not so attractive can take comfort in the finding that these results—intriguing though they may be—largely go away when the research participants actually know the people whose attractiveness they are rating (Kniffin & Wilson, 2004). In this case, *physical* attractiveness becomes largely a function of *nonphysical* characteristics, such as how much we like the people and how we evaluate their characters. Years ago, Dion, Berscheid, and Walster (1972) wrote an article on stereotypes based on physical attractiveness, "What Is Beautiful Is Good," but the flipside is also true—what is good is beautiful.

the result of evolved psychological mechanisms solving the different survival problems faced by our male and female ancestors in choosing the best mates.

This evolutionary interpretation is compatible with equity theory, although it proposes that men and women calculate the perceived benefits of a romantic partner differently. Consider that young men and women in the United States experience romantic jealousy for different reasons (Buss, Larsen, Westen, & Semmelroth, 1992). Men become more jealous at the prospect of their (female) partner's sexual infidelity. Women become more jealous at the prospect of their (male) partner's emotional infidelity. Buss et al. (1992) advanced an evolutionary interpretation of these results, suggesting that men value sexual fidelity because they want to be certain they have fathered their partners' children, whereas women value emotional fidelity because they want to be certain of the continued presence and support of their partners once a child has been born to them.

Equity in the here and now is not the only influence on whether long-term relationships continue. Psychologists have documented other factors that determine who stays together and who parts company. For example, a couple is less likely to break up if they are satisfied with their relationship, if no suitable alternatives are present, and if each has invested a great deal of time and effort in their relationship (Rusbult, 1980; Rusbult, Zembrodt, & Gunn, 1982).

However, equity theory has limits in its ability to explain love in all of its forms. It cannot account for selfless love or acts of altruism because—after all—these are not done with any quid pro quo expectation. Consider organ donors (e.g., Batten & Prottas, 1987). Consider the Christians in Nazi Germany who sheltered Jews at the risk of their own deaths (Oliner & Oliner, 1988). Consider the Japanese concept of *amae*, which is roughly translated as "indulgent interdependence" and experienced by the child who knows that he is dependent on his mother but at the same time is completely assured that she will take care of him and his needs (Doi, 1973). *Amae* pervades other sorts of relationships and defies interpretation in equity terms (Berger, Ono, Kumano, & Suematsu, 1994).

And consider studies showing that volunteer work is associated with high life satisfaction and good health (e.g., Dulin & Hill, 2003; Hunter & Linn, 1981; Krause, Ingersoll-Dayton, Liang, & Sugisawa, 1999; Morrow-Howell, Hinterloth, Rozario, & Tang, 2003; C. Schwartz, Meisenhelder, Ma, & Reed, 2003). These findings challenge equity theory when coupled with other studies suggesting that giving social support is more beneficial than receiving it (S. L. Brown, Nesse, Vinokur, & Smith, 2003; Liang, Krause, & Bennett, 2001). In other words, it is not an equitable relationship that is rewarding but rather one in which a person can provide love and support, whether or not the score card comes out even.

Another challenge to equity theory comes from the insight that interpersonal relationships exist on two levels (Kelley & Thibaut, 1978). First, there are the specific actions and characteristics of the people involved. These more or less line up in terms of equity, as in "you wash, and I'll dry." But second, there are the various ways in which people interpret their relationships. Their interpretations cannot be greatly at odds with their specific behaviors. However, a relationship that is strictly a mutual exchange can only be thought of as a business deal. To prevent this cynical construal, individuals in a friendship or romance must sacrifice some of their own rewards for the good of their partners. Then the relationship can be interpreted as a genuine one. What is the point? Outside of commerce, a purely equitable relationship cannot work, because no one wants to think of a friendship or romance in these terms.

Finally, equity theory fails most profoundly because it ignores the feelings that people bring to their relationships. You have seen throughout this book how Western thinkers have frequently placed thoughts over feelings, but you have also seen how the actual data of positive psychology imply just the opposite. Again and again, the heart trumps the head.[5] We do not have friends and spouses because we "think" they will benefit us. We have friends and spouses because we love them.

Attachment Theory

Accordingly, the second important perspective on relationships is **attachment theory**, which emphasizes the feelings that bind us together. The giant figure here is British psychiatrist John Bowlby, who in 1950 was asked by the World Health Organization (WHO) to report on the mental health of children who had been orphaned by World War II. The important conclusion of his report was that normal development requires a "warm and continuous relationship" with at least one adult caregiver. Children reared in orphanages, even where their basic needs for food and safety were adequately met, nevertheless suffered if they lacked the opportunity to form an enduring emotional bond. Most of the benignly neglected orphans displayed pathological behaviors, like head banging or depression. Many failed to thrive physically. Indeed, some died simply from the lack of love.

Bowlby's (1951) WHO report stressing the importance of emotional bonds resulted in major changes in the way children in orphanages and residential nurseries were treated, but it left unanswered several important questions. Why should the absence of an emotional attachment have such profound effects on well-being? And how did the effects occur? Bowlby devoted the next 20 years of his life to searching for the answers.

His quest led him into literatures far removed from his psychoanalytic training. It was in the field of ethology, and specifically in the work of Konrad Lorenz (1937) on imprinting among goslings and Harry Harlow (1958) on bonding in rhesus monkeys, that he eventually found the explanation he had been seeking. The young of many species, who are too immature at birth to care for themselves,

5. Remember the saying about children: They are economically worthless but emotionally priceless.

have an evolved predisposition to become attached to an adult caregiver. Bowlby reasoned that the human infants and children who were not faring well despite adequate physical care were suffering the consequences of a thwarted need for attachment.

This new theory ultimately filled three volumes (Bowlby, 1969, 1973, 1980). The core of attachment theory is the proposition that attachment enhances survival by regulating an infant's relationship and proximity to his caregiver. He continuously monitors her whereabouts and plays contentedly as long as she is nearby. If the distance between them becomes too great, he will be upset and redirect his attention and effort toward reestablishing proximity. Bowlby (1979) proposed that this attachment system operates throughout the lifespan, from the cradle to the grave.

Inspired by Bowlby's theory, other researchers started to take a close look at infants and their social behavior. Here is a consensus summary. Very early in life, human infants are socially responsive but make few if any distinctions among people (Goldberg, 1991; Schneider, 1991). They look at everyone, especially at their faces. In an important study, Johnson, Dziurawiec, Ellis, and Morton (1991) showed that within the *first hour* following birth, infants are more likely to track with their eyes a moving stimulus that looks like a face than they are to track similar but nonface-like stimuli (see Figure 10.2). This tendency cannot have been learned. The newborn is predisposed by evolution to attend to the most-important aspect of the environment—the parent—and the parent's attention in turn is drawn to the responsiveness of the infant.

Within a few months of birth, the human infant starts to discriminate her primary caretakers from others. She responds differently to familiar people, smiling and vocalizing in their presence, and being more easily comforted by them.

After about 6 or 7 months, a third period is entered, where the child shows a strong attachment to a single individual, usually the mother but not inevitably. This stage is marked by the infant actively seeking contact with the person to

Figure 10.2. What Catches the Eye of an Infant?
Newborn infants are more likely to track with their eyes a moving stimulus that looks like a face (a) than they are to track similar but nonface-like stimuli (b).

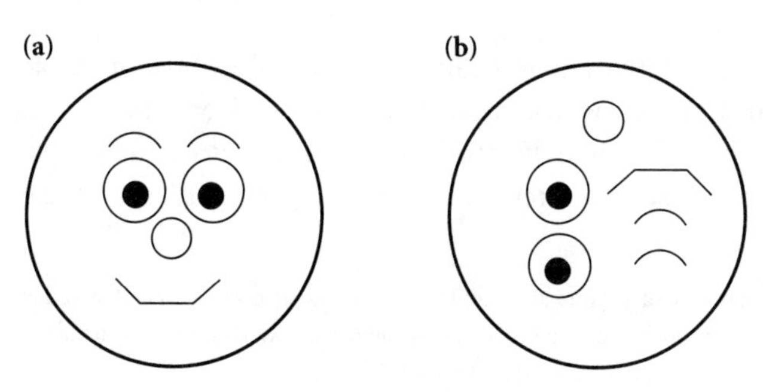

whom she is attached. She crawls after the person and calls out to her. Strangers bring about fear. This pattern continues for the next several years of the child's life.

This third stage of attachment has been studied by observing how one-year-old infants react when separated from their mothers, a strategy called the **Strange Situation Test** (Ainsworth, Blehar, Waters, & Wall, 1978; Ainsworth & Wittig, 1969). The young child, accompanied by his mother (or other caretaker), comes to an infant research laboratory, which is equipped with its own playroom filled with toys. A carefully scripted series of encounters take place, observed by researchers behind a one-way mirror:

- The mother puts the baby on the floor, some distance from the toys, and then takes a seat.
- A stranger enters the playroom and also sits down.
- The stranger talks to the mother, and then the stranger attempts to play with the baby.
- Next, the mother leaves her baby alone with the stranger for a few minutes.
- She returns shortly to be reunited with her infant.
- Then both the mother and stranger leave, again for a few minutes.
- The stranger returns first and attempts to play with the baby.
- Finally, the mother returns and picks up her baby.

This procedure provides rich information about how the child reacts to separation. When the mother first leaves the room, about half of the children cry before she comes back. More than three quarters respond to her return by reaching out to her in some way: smiling, touching, or speaking. When the mother leaves the room again, the typical child becomes upset again. The stranger is unsuccessful in soothing the child. When the mother returns, half of the children keep on crying, and three quarters of them climb into her arms.

Children respond to the Strange Situation Test in various ways.[6] Ainsworth (1973) described three different patterns of behavior in these circumstances. *Avoidant* children (about 20% of those tested) do not cry when their mother leaves and either ignore her or turn away upon her return. *Securely attached* children (about 70%) show the pattern of seeking and maintaining contact with their mother. The third pattern, shown by only about 10% of children, is termed *ambivalent.* These kids cry when their mother leaves but are not comforted when she returns.

The Strange Situation Test can be used to assess how other factors influence attachment. Children whose mothers are supportive and affectionate in dealing with them show the securely attached pattern: They are sad to see their mothers leave and glad to see them return. Mothers who are critical and rejecting produce

6. The majority of infants are readily classified as securely attached, avoidant, or ambivalent, but a very small minority show a mix of ambivalence and avoidance; they are sometimes placed in a fourth attachment category called *disorganized* (Main & Solomon, 1990).

avoidant or ambivalent infants. If a mother is depressed, she may be emotionally unavailable to her child, and what can result is an avoidant child (Lowenstein & Field, 1993). Whatever pattern is established has lasting effects on how the child relates to others. For instance, insecurely attached children are less sociable with peers at age 2, less flexible and persistent at age 4, and more likely to be depressed and withdrawn at age 6 (Clarke-Stewart, Friedman, & Koch, 1985).

Children who were securely attached in infancy are appropriately assertive with their parents (Lyons-Ruth, 1991). They explore the world with more enthusiasm, and they are more persistent at solving problems; at the same time, they are more willing to ask for help and to seek comfort when frustrated (e.g., Londerville & Main, 1981; Matas, Arend, & Sroufe, 1978; Waters, Wippman, & Sroufe, 1979). In short, securely attached children strike a balance between dependency and autonomy.

When they enter school, securely attached children require less contact, guidance, and discipline from their teachers, and they are less likely to seek attention, to act impulsively, to express frustration, or to display helplessness (Sroufe, Fox, & Pancake, 1983). Their teachers like them more and expect more of them. In relation to their peers, children with secure attachment histories are more socially skilled and elicit more positive responses from others (Pierrehumbert, Iannotti, & Cummings, 1985; Pierrehumbert, Iannotti, Cummings, & Zahn-Waxler, 1989; Vandell, Owen, Wilson, & Henderson, 1988). Not surprisingly, they have more friends and are more popular (Sroufe, 1983). They are also unlikely to be bullies or victims (Troy & Sroufe, 1987).

Secure attachment in infancy does not guarantee all of these desirable outcomes, but the consistency of the research is striking (Colin, 1996). Secure attachment leads to good relationships with others, and we know that good relationships with others are in turn associated with all of the manifestations of the good life discussed so far in this book. Other people figure in our pleasures and how we savor them (chapter 3). Social predictors of life satisfaction are especially robust (chapter 4). Character strengths of the heart are more satisfying than those of the head (chapter 6). Teachers and mentors make our accomplishments possible (chapter 8). And good relationships with others underlie wellness and longevity (chapter 9).

Two of today's leading love researchers, Harry Reis and Shelly Gable (2003), went so far as to conclude that good relationships with others may be the *single most important* source of life satisfaction and emotional well-being, across different ages and cultures (Berscheid & Reis, 1998; Klinger, 1977; Sears, 1977). And conversely, when asked to describe bad events or things that have gone wrong in their lives, the majority of people recount relationship conflicts or losses (Veroff, Douvan, & Kukla, 1981). The typical person enters psychotherapy because of a troubled relationship (Pinsker, Nepps, Redfield, & Winston, 1985).

Secure attachment in infancy has a lifelong impact because it does not stay in infancy. Children, adolescents, and adults bring their prior attachment history with them, which means that we can be described as secure or not at any age. The Strange Situation Test has been used by researchers long enough that the infants initially studied with it have grown up and are now able to speak to researchers about their childhood recollections. So, George, Kaplan, and Main (1985) created the Adult Attachment Interview, which asks a series of questions regarding childhood relationships with parents. There is a high correspondence between what adults have to say and their attachment classification years earlier (Van Ijzendoorn, 1992).

Even more interesting is the finding that attachment styles established in infancy show up in how adults conduct themselves in romantic relationships. In 1987, psychologists Cindy Hazan and Phillip Shaver had the insight that adults could be described as secure, avoidant, or ambivalent in how they approached their intimate relationships. Here is a very simple quiz devised by these researchers. Read the following blurbs, and choose the one that best describes how you relate to the people in your life:

- ☐ I find it relatively easy to get close to other people. I am comfortable depending on other people and having them depend on me. I don't usually worry about being abandoned or about having someone get too close to me.
- ☐ I find it difficult to trust people completely. I am somewhat uncomfortable being close to others. I feel nervous when people start to get too close. Often, I feel like people want me to be more intimate than I feel comfortable being. I find it difficult to allow myself to depend on other people.
- ☐ I find that other people are reluctant to get as close as I would like. I often worry that someone I am close to doesn't really love me or won't want to stay with me. I want to merge completely with another person, and this sometimes scares people away.

Some of us enjoy closeness and find intimacy easy to establish; we expect partners to be trustworthy and reliable; and we readily turn to them for comfort and support, and they to us. These are secure relationships[7] (the first option on the test). Others of us are uncomfortable with closeness; we find it difficult to trust our partners; and we maintain emotional distance from them, valuing independence over closeness and withdrawing when distressed rather than seeking comfort (the second option: avoidant relationships). And still others among us worry constantly about being abandoned; we may want more closeness than our partners are able or willing to give (the third option: ambivalent relationships).

7. Subsequent research has refined the measurement by asking more questions about attachment styles and allowing respondents to indicate degrees of endorsement. This research suggests that people do *not* fall into discrete clumps (Fraley & Waller, 1998). I will continue to use the shorthand way of describing people as secure, avoidant, or ambivalent, but you will need to remember that I am describing only generalizations (chapters 7 and 8).

Here is a potpourri of research findings about securely attached adults (Feeney, 1999; Hazan & Shaver, 1994; Peterson & Seligman, 2004; Shaver & Hazan, 1993). They are

- more supportive of their partners in joint problem-solving tasks (Kobak & Hazan, 1991)
- more likely to practice safer sex (Brennan & Shaver, 1995)
- less upset in the wake of stress (Mikulincer, Florian, & Weller, 1993)
- more likely to seek support from others when it is needed (Simpson, Rholes, & Nelligan, 1992)
- more likely to compromise in conflicts (Pistole, 1989)
- less likely to be depressed (Carnelley, Pietromonaco, & Jaffe, 1994)
- more likely to have good self-esteem (Brennan & Bosson, 1998)
- less likely to abuse their spouse (Dutton, Saunders, Starzomski, & Bartholomew, 1994)
- less likely to divorce (Hazan & Shaver, 1987)

I assume those of you who do not experience securely attached relationships are feeling uncomfortable in light of all these findings. Rest assured, psychologists have learned something about the cultivation and recultivation of love among adults. **Emotionally focused couples therapy** is a well-validated approach for troubled couples, which is based on attachment theory and teaches a more-flexible approach to the expression and satisfaction of needs (S. M. Johnson, 1996; S. M. Johnson, Hunsley, Greenberg, & Schlinder, 1999). Partners learn to comfort, to reassure, and to support one another—in short, to open the door to new emotional experiences, those that bind people together in a secure relationship.

In closing this section, I want to underscore the contrast between equity theory and attachment theory, while also observing that they need not be incompatible. In equity theory, we see an emphasis on the calculation of perceived costs and benefits. It is a thoroughly cognitive approach to relationships. In contrast, attachment theory emphasizes feelings and emotions. As you know, the tension between thoughts and feelings is an enduring issue in psychology, but it does not have to be inherent. I believe that we can integrate these perspectives to view relationships in terms of how we think about one another as well as how we feel. The relative emphasis might depend on the type of relationship, but thoughts *and* feelings matter in all of them (M. S. Clark & Mills, 1979).

Typologies of Love

A relationship between two people can obviously take many different forms (Berscheid, 1994). Norms prescribe relationships, both formal and informal, and relationships in different historical eras and cultures vary according to the society's dominant values (Lee, 1988; Murstein, Merighi, & Vyse, 1991). Hatfield and

Rapson (1993) made the provocative observation that personal relationships around the world are becoming more similar as Western culture is spread through the global media. For example, the pursuit of pleasure and the avoidance of pain, traditionally goals in Western relationships, are becoming increasingly relevant to Asian relationships (chapter 3).

Affiliation

Let us consider some of the relationships that individuals may have with others. In **affiliation**, the people involved simply want to be associated with some other person—his or her specific identity is not all that important. Leon Festinger's (1954) notion of *social comparison* provides a motive for affiliation. In order to evaluate our skills, aptitudes, attitudes, and values, we compare them to those of others. We cannot do this without associating with other people. In short, affiliation helps us to evaluate ourselves (Buunk, Van Yperen, Taylor, & Collins, 1991; Kulik & Mahler, 1989).

Psychologist Stanley Schachter's (1959) interest in affiliation led him to investigate the maxim that "misery loves company." He recruited psychology students to participate in an experiment and told them that they were to receive a series of painful electric shocks. Other research participants in a comparison group were not told this. For students in both groups, there was a 10-minute delay while the researcher supposedly set up the experimental equipment. The participants could wait alone or with others. Which did they choose? Compared with those not expecting to be shocked, those in the experimental group preferred to pass the 10 minutes in the company of others. We thus seek out others when we are anxious, presumably because other people decrease our worries. Again, social comparison processes may be at work here. Other people provide clues about how we should act and feel in an ambiguous situation.

Further research by Schachter clarified this phenomenon. When given a further choice, anxious people prefer to associate with other anxious individuals: Misery loves miserable company. The positive psychology perspective suggests further that it is not the misery per se that is attractive but rather what miserable people might be able to teach us.[8]

Liking

In **liking**, the people involved have a positive attitude toward each other, and psychologists know a fair amount about the factors that predispose these positive attitudes (Byrne, 1971):

8. A recent study with rats as research subjects showed that the mere physical presence of another rat reduced the physiological effects of stress, although in this case, it was a nonstressed rat that was most beneficial (Kiyokawa, Kikusui, Takeuchi, & Mori, 2004).

- *proximity*: other things being equal, we like those who live close to us
- *similarity*: other things being equal, we like those whose personality traits, values, and beliefs are similar to our own
- *complementarity of needs*: other things being equal, we like those who satisfy our needs
- *high ability*: other things being equal, we like those who are competent
- *attractiveness*: other things being equal, we like those who are physically attractive or otherwise pleasing[9]
- *reciprocity*: other things being equal, we like those who like us

Think about how these findings might be used by enlightened social engineers. Suppose you were put in charge of creating an apartment building, a college dormitory, a neighborhood, or a workplace where people would actually like one another. What would you do?

Friendship

When liking is coupled with a mutual perception of similarity and expectations of reciprocity and parity, we call it **friendship**. Again, psychologists know a fair amount about friendship. Here is some of what they have learned (Hartup & Stevens, 1997).

The word *friend* enters the vocabulary of children as early as 3 or 4 years of age, shortly after they start to interact preferentially with their peers (Howes, 1983). As many as 75% of nursery school students have reciprocated friendships, at least as judged by time freely spent in each other's company. To be sure, the friendships of young children are concrete and center on common activities: "We play together."

By adolescence, 80–90% of teenagers report having mutual friends, and they usually distinguish between "best" friends and "good" friends. In either case, these sorts of friendships are marked not only by shared activities but also by emotional support and self-disclosure: "We tell each other everything."

For adults, friends are often found among one's fellow workers, and adult friendships often center on shared work activities to such a degree that theorists describe adult friendship as "fused" with work (Winstead, Derlega, & Montgomery, 1995). Similar fusions occur when friends are found among neighbors with children of the same age. More than 90% of adults have friends, although

9. This stereotype has widespread consequences (Cialdini, 1985). Consider that attractive individuals are more likely to win elections, to be offered help when in distress, and to receive favorable treatment from the judicial system. In an intriguing experiment, prisoners were given plastic surgery to correct their facial disfigurements (Kurtzburg, Safar, & Cavior, 1968). When compared to a group of prisoners whose appearance had not been changed, they were less likely to return to jail following their release. Do these findings mean that they had been rehabilitated by their surgery and thus were less likely to commit crimes, or do they merely show that good-looking criminals avoid punishment?

the proportion declines a bit among the elderly. In old age, friendships often involve support and companionship: "We do each other favors."

The number of close friends that someone has is always rather small, no more than one or two for toddlers and three to five for schoolchildren. Newlyweds seem to have the most friends—seven to nine—which apparently reflects the coming together of their social circles. But by middle age, the typical person again has about five close friends, a number which slowly decreases throughout life. People who have friends at one age are likely to have friends at other ages, and the same close friends are often kept throughout one's entire life (Elicker, Englund, & Sroufe, 1992). Old friends are deliberately kept later in life in preference to making new ones, with shared histories and experiences being the commonly cited reason (Lang & Carstensen, 1994). What does change across the lifespan is the amount of time one spends with friends. Teenagers spend almost a third of their waking hours in the company of friends, whereas adults spend less than 10% of their time with friends.

Although the surface features of friendship obviously change, having friends[10] is a consistently robust correlate of life satisfaction and well-being (B. B. Brown, 1981; Gupta & Korte, 1994; Larson, 1978; Newcomb & Bagwell, 1995; Rutter & Garmezy, 1983). However, the conclusions about the benefits of friendship must be qualified by whether the friends in question are supportive or not (e.g., Weiss, 1986). Bad friends do exist—those who drain us and undercut us—and research suggests that they subtract more from our well-being than good friends add (Hartup & Stevens, 1997).

Bad friends are those who violate the reciprocity that characterizes most friendships. Earlier in the chapter, I pointed out the shortcomings of equity theory as an account of relationships, but this perspective can shed light on bad friendships. These may be relationships in which we have emotional attachment but little equity. Said another way, perhaps bad friends are not friends at all.

In any event, what is a good friend? Let me describe the results of a very simple study I did several years ago with Tracy Steen, using an Internet sample of adults. Positive psychology was just taking form, and so we decided to explore relationships from this new perspective. We wanted to know about the best friend whom someone had ever had. Researchers interested in friendship and love typically ask respondents about their current relationships, some of which are good and others not so good. But are any of these described relationships the *best* that one has ever had?

Our respondents logged onto a Web site and answered a series of questions about a person they designated as the best friend they had ever had. Of the 289

10. The research jury is still out on whether the sheer number of friends is the important determinant of well-being or whether we need to take into account as well the *quality* of these friendships as measured by features like closeness, commitment, intimacy, and affective tone. Conclusions are hampered because people with more friends also tend to have higher-quality friendships.

respondents—mostly middle-aged, college-educated Americans—fully 97% could think of one such person. Only 15% said that this person was their first best friend, although 76% said that they were still friends with the person. Indeed, on average, the respondents had been friends with the person they described for more than half of their lives. Male respondents tended to have male best friends, and female respondents tended to have female best friends, but this was not a strong finding. In other words, best friends could be same sex or opposite sex. However, these special best friends were usually quite close in age to those describing them (Matthews, 1986).

We asked respondents to describe the features of their friend and their relationship on a five-point scale reflecting how important they regarded the feature in explaining their friendship. We presented dozens of features, drawn from different theories and our own brainstorming. Those that consistently emerged as most important (> 4.0 on our scales) converged on a view of a best friend as someone with whom one has a reciprocated and sustained relationship marked by positive emotions. Best friends support the premises of equity theory *and* attachment theory. Our respondents described their best friends as dependable, honest, loyal, and committed. They described them as kind and loving and also as playful and fun. My friend "brings out the best in me" was also frequently endorsed as a description. Rated as rather unimportant (< 2.5 on our scales) were features like a friend's status, attractiveness, physical health, skills, ambitions, and accomplishments. These sorts of features might open the door for a potential friendship, but they do not transform the relationship into the best one that a person has ever had.

Love

When a relationship is characterized by reciprocated exclusiveness, absorption, predispositions to help one another, and interdependence, we call it—at least in Western culture—**love.** Love in turn can be subdivided (Hendrick & Hendrick, 1992, 2002; Lee, 1973).

One common distinction is between passionate love and companionate love (Berscheid & Walster, 1978; Walster, Walster, & Berscheid, 1978). **Passionate love** occurs at the beginning of an affair and is marked by extreme absorption and dramatic mood swings, from ecstasy to anguish. **Companionate love** is the unshakable affection shared by two people whose lives have become intertwined. It is common to observe that passionate love gives rise to companionate love as sexual desires cool, but the relationship between these two types of love is more complex. They may coexist rather than be sequential (Hatfield, 1988), or we may experience one type of love without the other ever occurring before or after. Indeed, the research I described in the previous section on best friends seems to be research as well about companionate love, so we should beware of drawing a firm line between friendship and love—I suspect only teenagers do that. In any event, the important point is that love can be marked by passion *and* companionship and that both are desired in a romantic relationship (Noller, 1996; Sprecher & Regan, 1998).

The Nature of Love is a three-volume philosophical history of love from antiquity until the modern era, and its author, Irving Singer (1984a, 1984b, 1987), distinguished four traditions in thinking about love. *Eros* approaches love in terms of desire. *Phila* refers to love as friendship.[11] *Nomos* is submission to God's will or obedience to the desires of a loved one. And *agape* is selfless love that approaches the divine.

An ongoing historical debate is whether romantic love as we think about it today even existed prior to the last few centuries. Certainly, marriage based on romantic love is a relatively modern invention, dating only to the 18th century in the Western world, and it is still not common in many other parts of the world (e.g., Gadlin, 1977; Murstein, 1974). But these facts do not mean that there was no passion prior to the cultural invention of courtly love during the European Middle Ages, a stylized ritual that eventually morphed into the modern Western marriage. Others have argued that passionate love—defined simply as an intense attraction between two people—is a human universal that eventually joined company with sexuality and marriage.

In the United States, about 95% of the population marries at some point. This overall figure has stayed much the same over recent decades, although the average age of first marriage has increased, particularly among women with professional careers. How does the transition into marriage take place? Speaking about the Western marriage for love,[12] developmental psychologists describe the process as a series of steps (Karney & Bradbury, 1995). The most superficial step involves judging a prospective mate on such characteristics as appearance, social class, and behavior. The next involves looking deeper at her beliefs and attitudes. It is important that these agree. Finally, prospective mates choose each other on the basis of how well their needs mesh. Two individuals with a need to dominate an interaction do not get along as well as a leader and a follower (Winch, 1958).

Researchers have extensively studied marital satisfaction[13] and find, not sur-

11. I am writing this section while visiting Philadelphia, the City of Brotherly Love.

12. In much of the world, especially those with collectivist cultures, arranged marriages are the norm. Although these may seem strange to those of us from more-individualistic cultures, where we apparently marry for love, the evidence shows that arranged marriages can be quite satisfying for the partners (e.g., Myers, Madathil, & Tingle, 2005). If we stop and think about it, we see why arranged marriages should be successful. After all, they are created by family members who know the principals well and have their best interests at heart. Families work with an expert—a marriage planner as opposed to a wedding planner—who actually knows something about match making. So, arranged marriages may also be "love" marriages, although the love is between parents and their children.

13. In years past, you were either married or single. But more recently, living together, or cohabitation, has become common in the United States. More than 2 million couples live together without being married, highlighting cohabitation as a significant social phenomenon. There is some

prisingly, that satisfaction is high early in the marriage (O'Leary & Smith, 1991). It reaches a low point when a couple has adolescent children. Among those who stay married for decades, marital satisfaction starts to rise again once the children have left home.

These are descriptive trends, and we should not assume that time is the critical factor. Many other factors are linked with marital satisfaction—for example, emotional security, respect, communication, sexual intimacy, and loyalty—and the way in which these factors combine to influence satisfaction depends on how long a couple has been together (Levenson, Carstensen, & Gottman, 1993; Swensen, Eskew, & Kohlhepp, 1981). On the whole, men report greater satisfaction with marriage than do women. Women tend to value their marriage more if they have children or if they work outside the home (Baruch, Barnett, & Rivers, 1983; Russell & Wells, 1994).

Many women today have both a family and a career, but those committed to both their children and their work tend to experience decreased satisfaction with their marriage (Philliber & Hiller, 1983). The likely explanation is that their husbands more often than not fail to share equally in raising the children or doing household chores, and the women become overextended.

An interesting fact is that married adults are physically and emotionally healthier than their single counterparts (chapter 9). There are various explanations for this phenomenon. Perhaps the less healthy do not get married in the first place. Perhaps the companionship that marriage provides protects a person against poor health (Cobb, 1976). Perhaps a good marriage even has direct effects on the competence of the immune system (Kiecolt-Glaser, 2005). Whatever the reasons, the health benefits of marriage on health are greater for men than for women (Kiecolt-Glaser & Newton, 2001).

Some words about divorce. In the mid-1800s, only about 4% of U.S. marriages ended in divorce. By the 1970s and thereafter, this figure had grown to more than 40% (Castro-Martin & Bumpass, 1989). At first glance, we seem to have an incredible crisis for the American family. But if we place these figures in a historical context, we find another perspective (Peterson, 1997). There is the same proportion of intact marriages today as there was more than a century ago because

---

debate as to whether it represents a true alternative to marriage, or a step in the process of courtship (Bower & Christopherson, 1977). Among those couples living together who eventually get married, marital satisfaction is lower than among couples who did not live together prior to marriage (Nock, 1995). Divorce may be more likely (Browder, 1988). In thinking about these results, keep in mind the possibility of confounds. People who live together before marrying are different in the first place than those who do not (Axinn & Thornton, 1993; J. D. Cunningham & Antill, 1994; Huffman, Chang, Rausch, & Schaffer, 1994). For instance, men and women who live together before marriage tend to have slightly less education and are somewhat more likely to be employed than those who marry without first living together (R. E. L. Watson, 1983). Perhaps these differences and not cohabitation produce the differences in later marital satisfaction and stability (Teachman, Polonko, & Scanzoni, 1987).

people on the average live much longer today. Once upon a time, marriages ended with the untimely death of one partner or the other. Today, the same proportion of marriages end with divorce. Of course, the end of a marriage by death is different than the end of a marriage by divorce, but the fact remains that the proportion of intact American families changed not at all throughout the 20th century.

The average divorce, if there is such a thing, occurs after 6 or 7 years of marriage (Norton, 1983). But divorce can occur at any point during marriage. Surprisingly, marital dissatisfaction is not a strong predictor of divorce. Considerations like alternative mates, career decisions, and financial crises combine to create a divorce. The degree to which divorce is regarded as legitimate within a person's cultural group is another crucial factor. For an obvious example, among those whose religion prohibits divorce, it is less likely than among the general population.

Regardless of what causes divorce, it is a painful experience. During the immediate aftermath of a divorce, depression or alcohol abuse may occur. There is also an increased risk of physical illness (chapter 9). These problems are increased when the couple has children. In the majority of cases, mothers receive custody following a divorce, causing single mothers to be especially burdened (Pledge, 1992). None of these findings suggests that divorce is always harmful for individuals (Masheter, 1990). Most people make a satisfactory adjustment within 2 years following a divorce (Hetherington, Cox, & Cox, 1979). The majority of those who divorce remarry, particularly if they have divorced early in adulthood. A second marriage is necessarily different than a first marriage, but on the average, it is as satisfying (Huyck, 1982). Whether second marriages are more or less likely to end in divorce is not clear, because the comparison is confounded by age and hence the increased possibility of the death of one partner.

But what about marriages that work? Psychologist John Gottman and his colleagues studied marriages longitudinally—as opposed to retrospectively, as is usually the case—and found that disagreement and anger are not necessarily harmful (e.g., Gottman & Krokoff, 1989; Gottman & Levenson, 1992). All couples have disagreements. What makes a marriage a good one is that the couple has learned a productive way of responding to disputes. In fact, couples that avoid disputes, despite a short-term gain in satisfaction, pay a long-term price in terms of the success of their marriage. The couple must confront conflicts and express dissatisfaction in such a way that underscores what can be called *relational efficacy*, the shared belief that the couple can weather conflict together (Notarius & Vanzetti, 1983).

Whining, defensiveness, and stubbornness during disagreements foreshadow divorce, whereas humor, affection, and more generally positive interpretations mark successful marriages. Gottman went so far as to suggest that the ratio of the explicitly positive to the explicitly negative during actual interactions must exceed 5:1. Said another way, for every complaint or criticism that one spouse voices, there need to be at least five compliments! These cannot be muted, muttered, or otherwise implied because no one's spouse is a mind reader.

Gable, Reis, Impett, and Asher (2004) elaborated this insight by describing four ways that we can respond to our partners when something happens to them, including good events, like a raise at work:

- *active-constructive responding* (an enthusiastic response): "That's great! I bet you'll receive many more raises."
- *active-destructive responding* (a response that points out the potential downside): "Are they going to expect more of you now?"
- *passive-constructive responding* (a muted response): "That's nice, dear."
- *passive-destructive responding* (a response that conveys disinterest): "It rained all day here."

Couples who use active-constructive responding have great marriages. The other responses, if they dominate, are associated with marital dissatisfaction.

We need not be Pollyannas to live happily ever after. Some events indeed require criticism or caution. The point, again, is that the ratio of the positive to the negative matters, and Gable et al. suggested that it needs to exceed 3:1.

The exact number is not critical and no doubt varies as a function of the couple and the other details of their relationship. However, all researchers who calculate these sorts of ratios agree that the ratio of the positive to the negative must exceed 1:1 for a relationship to survive and flourish (Diener, 2005). This may mean that the negative is more powerful than the positive, if only because we are more likely to attend to it (chapter 5). This may mean that most of the time we experience more good events than bad events in our relationships, which means that the satisfaction oomph provided by one more good thing does not compensate for what one bad thing can take away. Regardless, these results encourage us to accentuate the positive if we want a good thing to last.

EXERCISE *Active-Constructive Responding*

As I have described in this chapter, good marriages are characterized by active-constructive responding between partners. Implied in these findings is an exercise you can try that might make any relationship—with a spouse, a friend, a child, or a fellow worker—a better one (Seligman, 2003).

Choose a person with whom you are close, and then start keeping track of how you respond whenever she relays some good news: "I just got an A on my term paper!" "My softball team won the tournament!" "My diet is working!" Do this long enough to discern a stable pattern.

Do you respond enthusiastically, asking questions and sharing in the glory of the other person? Do you do this much more frequently than any other sort of response? If so, you are displaying active-constructive responding, and you probably already have an excellent relationship with this person. If that is the case, choose another target for this exercise. Keep at it until you find someone to whom you do not typically respond in this way.

You may care deeply about the person, and your critical reaction may stem sincerely from your love. You may not want your child to get a big head. You may not want your spouse to be disappointed if the good news heads south. But a steady stream of "constructive" criticism or tempered enthusiasm will take a toll because that is all that the person hears from you. Accordingly, resolve to respond to every piece of good news in an active and constructive way. Keep track of what you do, and make sure the number of active-constructive responses outweighs other responses by at least three to one.

As I always say about these exercises, use some common sense. Your spouse announcing that he has found someone else to marry or your child saying that she has dropped out of middle school to join the circus need not be responded to in a positive way. And you certainly should not tell the person that you are responding positively because this book told you to do so.

But most of the good news you hear from someone you love warrants enthusiasm, so let it show, and see what happens to your relationship.

GLOSSARY

affiliation: relationship resulting from desire to be associated with some other person whose specific identity is unimportant

attachment theory: theory proposing that close relationships persist because of the feelings that both people have for one another

companionate love: relationship marked by unshakable affection shared by those whose lives have become intertwined

emotionally focused couples therapy: approach for troubled couples based on attachment theory that directly teaches a more-flexible approach to the expression and satisfaction of needs

equity theory: theory proposing that close relationships persist to the degree that both people involved believe that what they are getting out of the relationship is proportional to what they are putting into it

friendship: relationship marked by liking, a mutual perception of similarity, and expectations of reciprocity and parity

imprinting: tendency of the young of some species, like ducklings, to follow and become attached to the first moving object they see

interpersonal resources: things that people give to and receive from another

liking: relationship in which people have positive attitudes toward one another

love: relationship marked by reciprocated exclusiveness, absorption, predisposition to help, and interdependence

oxytocin: hormone-like substance released in the brain in response to social contact, especially skin-to-skin touch

passionate love: relationship marked by extreme absorption and dramatic mood swings, from ecstasy to anguish

social support: how others help us to cope with stressful events

Strange Situation Test: laboratory procedure for assessing the attachment style of a child by briefly separating the child from the mother

RESOURCES

Books and Journals

Blum, D. (2002). *Love at Goon Park: Harry Harlow and the science of affection.* Cambridge, MA: Perseus.

Bowlby, J. (1979). *The making and breaking of affectional bonds.* London: Tavistock.

Rubin, Z. (1973). *Liking and loving: An invitation to social psychology.* New York: Holt, Rinehart, & Winston.

Buss, D. M. (1994). *The evolution of desire: Strategies of human mating.* New York: Basic.

Gottman, J. W. (1994). *What predicts divorce?* Hillsdale, NJ: Erlbaum.

Journal of Social and Personal Relationships

Articles

Harlow, H. F. (1958). The nature of love. *American Psychologist, 13,* 673–685.

Hazan, C., & Shaver, P. R. (1987). Romantic love conceptualized as an attachment process. *Journal of Personality and Social Psychology, 52,* 511–524.

Web Sites

http://www.unlimitedloveinstitute.org. This the Web site of the Institute for Research on Unlimited Love at Case Western Reserve University. Its mission is "to significantly increase our knowledge of unselfish love through scientific research, education, and publication."

http://www2.hawaii.edu/~elaineh. This is the Web site of pioneering love researcher Elaine Hatfield at the University of Hawaii.

Films

Casablanca (1942)
The Sound of Music (1965)
The Graduate (1967)
Butch Cassidy and the Sundance Kid (1969)
Brian's Song (1971)
Charlotte's Web (1973)

The Sting (1973)
The Big Chill (1983)
Hannah and Her Sisters (1986)
Stand by Me (1986)
84 Charing Cross Road (1987)
Driving Miss Daisy (1989)
Field of Dreams (1989)
Steel Magnolias (1989)
When Harry Met Sally (1989)
Nell (1994)
Toy Story 2 (1999)
ABC News's *20/20*: "Fair Fighting" (2000)
My Big Fat Greek Wedding (2002)

Songs

"Addicted to Love" (Robert Palmer)
"Always on My Mind" (Willie Nelson)
"Back in His Arms Again" (Supremes)
"Call Out My Name" (James Taylor)
"Crazy in Love" (Beyonce Knowles)
"Danny's Song" (Kenny Loggins)
"Help" (Beatles)
"I Got You Babe" (Sonny & Cher)
"I Walk the Line" (Johnny Cash)
"I Was Made to Love Her" (Stevie Wonder)
"It Takes Two" (Marvin Gaye & Tammy Terrell)
"Lean on Me" (Al Green)
"My Girl" (Temptations)
"On the Street Where You Live" (from *My Fair Lady*)
"Second That Emotion" (Miracles)
"Something to Talk About" (Bonnie Raitt)
"Stand by Me" (Ben E. King)
"The First Time Ever I Saw Your Face" (Roberta Flack)
"Time After Time" (Cyndi Lauper)
"Your Song" (Elton John)

11 Enabling Institutions

Institutions—government, churches, industries, and the like—have properly no other function than to contribute to human freedom; and in so far as they fail, on the whole, to perform this function, they are wrong and need reconstruction. —C. H. COOLEY (1902)

In 2003, I team-taught with Marty Seligman a course in positive psychology to 120 undergraduate students. At that time, it was the largest positive psychology course ever conducted. We realized that we could not teach the course like our previous small seminars, each of which had evolved in response to the emerging interests of the students and the teachers (chapter 2). So, part of the course entailed weekly lectures that we planned in advance. We structured them according to the positive psychology framework originally articulated by Seligman and Csikszentmihalyi (2000): positive experiences, positive traits, and positive institutions (chapter 1). Seligman and I had no difficulty putting together lectures on positive experiences and positive traits. There were all sorts of theories, findings, and applications we could incorporate into our lectures, and many of these ideas have been discussed in previous chapters of this book. To teach our students about positive institutions, we invited speakers who knew a great deal about education, government, social service, business, and religion. We asked the guests to speak about the "good" institution in the context of their particular areas of expertise.

My favorite speaker was a woman from Pennsylvania who worked for the Federal Emergency Management Agency (FEMA) as a rescue dog handler. She brought her dog with her, and she spoke to the class for 90 minutes about their work at the World Trade Center looking for survivors following the September 11, 2001, attacks. She told us how the feet of her dog and the other dogs blistered and bled and how they kept on working. The dogs only became frustrated when they did not find survivors, just bodies, because the dogs are—above all—trained to locate the living. The only way to deal with this situation was for the handlers to ask other workers on the scene to hide themselves in the rubble to be "discovered" by the dogs and thereby sustain their motivation. Her story was heartbreaking and heart warming at the same time.

The FEMA presentation was fascinating and even inspiring, but when we and our students reflected on it, we realized that a characterization of the positive institution remained elusive. Rescue dog handlers are of course doing good work when they make it into the field, but whether this happens in the first place is subject to all kinds of economic and even political considerations, as we all learned in the wake of Hurricane Katrina in 2005.

Another speaker was Judith Rodin, who at the time was president of the University of Pennsylvania, and she reflected on her 10 years at the helm of the school. Again, what she said was fascinating and inspiring. When she became president, a plan was being tossed about to build a wall between the university and the extremely rough West Philadelphia neighborhood in which the school was located. (If you think that sounds strange, then you have never been to the University of Chicago, which for years has had just such a wall in place.) Rodin disagreed strongly with this plan, and she set about to make West Philadelphia a better place in which to live, to work, and of course to study. As I see it, she and her administrative colleagues succeeded in spectacular fashion. West Philadelphia now has grocery stores, restaurants, and shops that were not in business before her tenure as president. The university helped to create an excellent neighborhood elementary school. Furthermore, the university made available to staff and faculty low-rate mortgages for those who wanted to buy a home in West Philadelphia, and many people took advantage of the opportunity. The houses and yards began to look better and to be better.

They also began to cost more, and here is the downside. Some lamented that West Philadelphia was becoming gentrified and thus too expensive for some of its long-time residents. They were forced to move to other parts of the city, and the West Philadelphia renaissance was accordingly offset by poor conditions elsewhere in the city. Whether this is an accurate criticism, I do not know, and I am tempted to dismiss it as carping. Philadelphia after all is the city where fans at an Eagles football game once booed Santa Claus.

But there is a more-substantive lesson to be gleaned from this story and indeed from all of the other accounts we heard of organizations and institutions trying to do the right thing. Because institutions are necessarily complex, it is all but impossible to characterize them as across-the-board positive, or for that matter as across-the-board negative. Growing up in the 1950s and 1960s in the United States, I repeatedly heard about "evil" communist dictators like Marshal Tito of Yugoslavia. With the demise of Tito in 1980 and the ensuing events, Yugoslavia dramatically fell apart, and all sorts of horrific things happened from which Eastern Europe is still recovering. So was Tito as bad as he was made out to be? Perhaps, but the alternative proved to be worse, at least in the short run.[1]

Institutions are invariably a mix of the good and the bad. Consider McDonald's, which is problematic when it encourages its customers to supersize themselves and damage their health, but laudable when it provides jobs for seniors and when it sponsors Ronald McDonald Houses around the country. Consider Microsoft, rightly criticized for its aggressive tack toward competition and just as rightly praised for the charitable contributions that its near-monopoly has made possible. Consider the Roman Catholic Church, under whose auspices very good things have been done as well as very bad things.

In short, *positive* is not an adjective sensibly applied to an institution as a whole. My own take on the matter is that we have to ask *positive for what purpose?* in discussing the roles that institutions play in producing and encouraging the psychological good life. In my own thinking, I have therefore replaced the term *positive institution* with the notion of an *enabling institution.* My point is simply that some institutions can enable certain outcomes better than other institutions can. Whether one thinks a given outcome is desirable is of course informed by one's own values (chapter 7).

Enable is light-handed, because it implies that pronouncements about what enables what should not be thought of as relentless laws of the universe (p. 112). So, it is a perfectly sound generalization to say that children from intact families are on average physically and psychologically healthier than children growing up without a father or without a mother. The institution of the nuclear family therefore *enables* the well-being of children, but of course there are exceptions: children from single-parent homes who thrive and those from the most-intact families who do not.

At the same time, a given institution can do a better or a worse job at its acknowledged purpose, and here comparisons across institutions and across time are informative. Harris polls (2005), for example, have for years surveyed the confidence of U.S. citizens in the leaders of their major societal institutions, finding that over the decades, confidence has in general decreased for virtually all institutions. Figure 11.1 shows representative results from a telephone survey done in early 2005. Whether this decrease constitutes an institutional crisis I do not know, but certainly leaders of Congress, large businesses, newspapers, and law firms cannot take pride in the current results. Expressed confidence is not a perfect measure of how well an institution is doing its job, but it certainly flavors how people interact with the institution in question. How can the public's confidence be restored? This is a question to which I return at the end of this chapter.

1. I am reminded of the comment by Winston Churchill in a November 11, 1947, speech to the House of Commons that democracy is "the worst form of government—except for all [the] others."

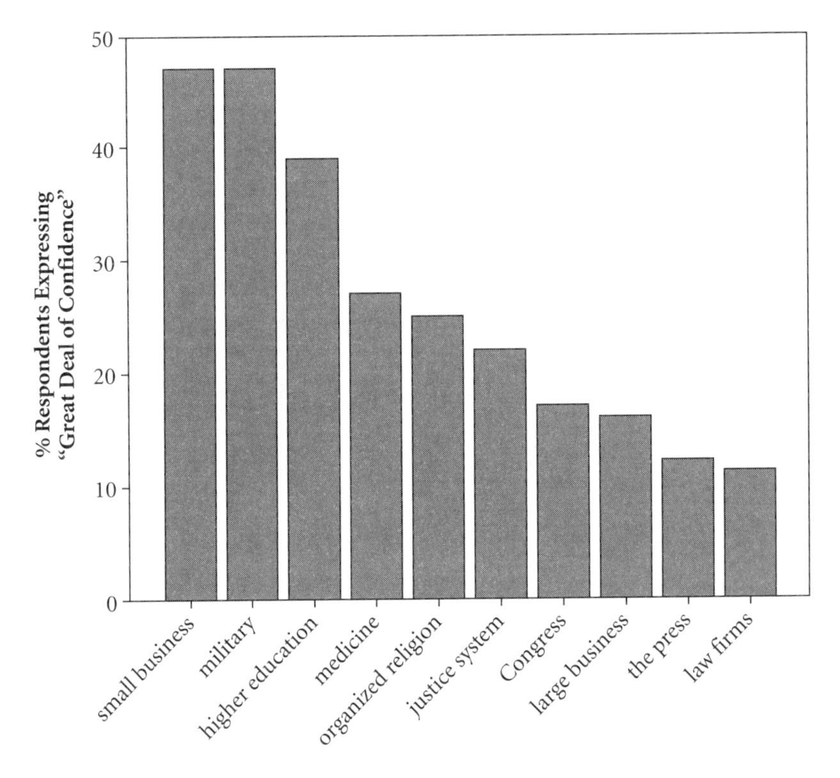

Figure 11.1. Confidence in Societal Institutions
Harris poll (2005) of 1,012 U.S. adults contacted by telephone and asked about their confidence in the leaders of major societal institutions. Results reflect the proportion of respondents expressing a "great deal of confidence."

A Catalog of Social Groupings

Obviously, social interactions take place between and among specific people. But can we explain the characteristics of social interaction simply in terms of the characteristics of the individual participants? When is the whole equal to the sum of its parts and when is it different? Almost all social scientists acknowledge that social interactions have features not readily derived from the characteristics of individual participants, and it is valuable to have a vocabulary for describing different sorts of social groupings.

Social scientists use the term **aggregation** to describe an assembly of individuals physically in the same place. They may have nothing more to do with each other than the fact that they are in that place at that time, like Christmas shoppers in a Wal-Mart, pedestrians hurrying along Walnut Street at lunchtime, or joggers on a high school track.

What is psychologically interesting about aggregations is that the mere presence of others—whether or not we know them—influences how we act, in part because even a disinterested "audience" makes us self-conscious and in part because the presence of others increases our autonomic arousal. When aroused, we perform well-learned behaviors with proficiency and poorly learned behaviors ineptly (Zajonc, 1965). So, as a beginning lecturer, I tried to relax before I spoke. As an experienced lecturer, I now try to be as stirred up as possible.

A **collectivity** is simply a social category: two or more individuals who can be discussed as a whole (R. Brown, 1954). All aggregations are collectivities, by definition, but not all collectivities are aggregates, because people in a collectivity do not have to be gathered in the same place at the same time: e.g., voters over 65 years of age, Elvis impersonators, people with unlisted telephone numbers, basketball players with green eyes, jugglers, and employees of the U.S. Postal Service.

Social categories provide the way we think about ourselves and others, and some of these categories are deeply part of our psychological makeup. For example, consider that conversational errors like calling a person by the wrong name are similar across cultures, implying regularity to what at first seem to be random acts (Fiske, 1993). These slips are most common when the misidentified person is of the same gender as the intended individual and when the basic social relationship (such as friend, child, or employer) is the same. Slips tend not to occur along lines of age, race, or—interestingly—name similarity. These findings suggest that gender and social role are highly general categories that we use in thinking about other people.

A **group** is a set of interacting individuals who mutually influence each other (Shaw, 1981). The group in group therapy is a good example, as are families, athletic teams, dance bands, and juries. Groups are incredibly important. Evolutionary theorists believe that we as a species evolved in groups consisting of about 30 interacting individuals (Glantz & Pearce, 1989). And even today, we live in small groups, we learn in small groups, we work in small groups, we play in small groups, and we worship in small groups. Even when these groups are embedded in much larger institutions, it is in the small group where the day-to-day psychological action takes place. Here is a more-benign way to think about the results of the Harris poll I just described. Americans may have little confidence in Congress, but their own representative is probably judged differently. The U.S. Postal Service may be the subject of jokes, but our own letter carrier is a good and dependable person.

An **organization** is an enduring and structured group. Usually an organization has a body of traditions and customs. Its members think of the organization as a whole, and their roles are differentiated and specialized. By this definition, many work groups qualify as organizations. Consider IBM or the lunch shift at the local Burger King. Youth groups like the Boy Scouts, political groups like the Democratic National Committee, and special interest groups like the National Rifle Association are also examples of organizations. One way to distinguish organizations from other groups is to ask whether particular members are dispensable. Regardless of who is coaching, playing, or ailing, National Football League teams go on. Thus, they are organizations. In contrast, particular families would not have much of an existence without Mom and Dad and the kids. They are not organizations.

Finally, an **institution** is a set of like organizations with especially sustained and pervasive influences within a society or even the world as a whole. Most societies have some form of religion, some form of marriage, and some form of education; we therefore speak of these as institutions. Those of us in the Western world usually include democracy, a free press, and an independent judiciary as important institutions.

It is impossible to survey all possible groups, organizations, and institutions and their roles in facilitating positive experiences and positive traits, so what I will do in this chapter is offer some general comments about enabling institutions and then focus on what positive psychology has learned about particular institutions, like the family and the workplace. If and when a book on positive sociology or positive anthropology is written, I direct you to it for a fuller discussion.[2]

Common Features of Enabling Institutions

Although positive traits are by definition characteristics of the individual, I believe that counterparts exist at the institutional level (Park & Peterson, 2003). There is a flourishing genre of popular books that discusses "good" organizations, and a common strategy within these books is to articulate the relevant characteristics. Many of these characteristics resemble the individual-level positive traits described in chapter 6, and some even carry the same names. Not only do these characteristics contribute to the stated goals of the institution, they also—certainly not by chance—contribute to the fulfillment of the individuals within it. What are the most important of these institutional-level virtues? Are they general across different types of institutions or thoroughly specific?

By **institutional-level virtues**, I mean the moral characteristics of the group as a whole, not simply summaries or composites of the characteristics of its individual members. As such, institutional-level virtues need to be an enduring part of the institutional culture. A school might happen to employ a number of teachers dedicated to the intellectual growth of students, but if the school does not

2. Promising starts to macroscopic versions of positive social science can be found in recent work in positive organizational scholarship (aka positive organizational behavior), where the focus is on work groups that thrive (Cameron, Dutton, & Quinn, 2003; Luthans, 2003; Wright, 2003); in positive youth development, where the concern is with after-school programs like 4-H or the Girl Scouts and how they encourage optimal development among their young participants (Larson, 2000; Lerner, Jacobs, & Wertlieb, 2003); and in discussions of happiness in schools (Noddings, 2003).

have practices in place that allow such dedication to survive personnel turnover, there is no institutional-level virtue.

Institutional-level virtues serve the moral goals of an organization and not simply its bottom line, whether this be profit, power, or persistence. The fact that any institution has multiple goals, all deemed good ones from that institution's perspective, challenges us as we attempt to separate institutional-level virtues from characteristics that contribute to other desired goals.

I have read a number of popular books that attempt to describe what makes some work organizations better than others (e.g., Buckingham & Coffman, 1999; Collins, 2001; Collins & Porras, 1997; Levering & Moskowitz, 1993; Peters & Waterman, 1982; Shaw, 1997). These endeavors are in effect multiple case studies, comparing and contrasting a handful of consensually good businesses with a handful of those that are presumably not so good, with the goal of discerning critical features (Rosenwald, 1988). The problem with these otherwise provocative comparisons is that the criteria used for deciding goodness conflate profitability, longevity, customer satisfaction, and notoriety with moral goodness, and debate ensues about the moral desirability of some of the critical features thereby identified.

One solution to this dilemma is to return to my characterization of individual-level virtues as "contributing to fulfillment" and to propose that an analogous rule be used to identify institutional-level virtues (chapter 6). That is, institutional-level virtues are characteristics of the organization that contribute to the fulfillment of its members. Fulfillment should not be confused with momentary pleasure or happiness per se, if happiness is construed only as the presence of positive affect and the absence of negative affect (chapter 3). Rather, fulfillment must reflect effort, the willful choice and pursuit over time of morally praiseworthy activities (chapter 4). This is why I choose my language carefully here: Virtues contribute to fulfillments rather than cause them in the automatic way that Jägermeister causes intoxication. There are no shortcuts to a fulfillment.

I hope this analysis does not smack too strongly of Puritanism. I am not opposed to pleasure or happiness, and I am certainly not opposed to shortcuts. Self-adhering postage stamps, cruise control, and automatic redial are among the most noteworthy inventions of the modern world precisely because they are shortcuts with little downside. But the value of these and other shortcuts is that they save time and effort that would otherwise be spent on unfulfilling pursuits. The moral significance of a shortcut is only indirect, judged by what one does with the time and effort that have been saved.

What then is the contributory relationship of virtues to fulfillments? I turn again to the Aristotelian notion of *eudaimonia*, which holds that well-being is not a consequence of virtuous action but rather an inherent aspect of such action (chapter 4). Fulfillment is part and parcel of the actions which manifest virtue. For instance, when a work supervisor fairly adjudicates a dispute between two workers, her act does not cause her (or the workers) to feel satisfied at some later point in time; being satisfied is an inherent aspect of justice in action.

It should go without saying that institutional-level virtues need to influence actual conduct within the group in ways that people can recognize. No less than do individuals, institutions may pay lip service to values that are ignored or even contradicted by their everyday practices.

The institutional-level virtues of most interest in the present context are those that are cultivated and celebrated and that serve as a source of identity and pride for the organization's members. To the degree that membership in an organization is fluid, members point to the institutional-level virtues as reasons to remain a member. When people say that this block is a *good* neighborhood in which to reside, that this company is a *good* place to work; or that this college is a *good* school to attend, they mean that they are fulfilled—satisfied and gratified—by so doing. In the language of positive psychology, a good organization is one that enables the good life for its members, and we know that the good life is not simply code for money, status, or pleasure (Myers & Diener, 1995).

I have so far sidestepped any definition of what is moral because of the hoary issues raised by the notion of cultural relativism. The clichéd examples of Nazi Germany or the ferocious Yanomamo of South America make it seem impossible to talk about the moral goals of an organization from the outside. But another point of view holds out the possibility of identifying across groups agreement about the features of good (i.e., moral) organizations. Indeed, I think the ubiquity of given institutional-level virtues is settled by looking at what different organizations actually value. Let me begin this examination.

The Good Family

The family is an important institution in all societies, although its form varies greatly, even within a given society. Consider these recent changes just within the United States. First, except for the post–World War II burst between 1947 and 1957, which gave us the baby boom generation, the birth rate in the United States has steadily decreased throughout the 20th century. Families are therefore becoming smaller. Second, because of effective birth control, most U.S. adults become parents later in life than they did generations ago. Families are therefore becoming older. Third, with the increase in divorce and subsequent remarriage, there is a growing number of families that includes stepparents. When we consider the additional trend of parents never being married to one another, families are certainly becoming more complex.

We hear a lot in the popular media about the crisis in the American family and the need to preserve family values. Often this discussion takes place at a very superficial level that ignores the heterogeneity of actual families and the realities that shape this heterogeneity. Given the current variety, is it possible to talk about a "good" family without resorting to a stereotype based on television shows from the 1950s like *Leave It to Beaver*?

Psychologists attempting to answer this question have often been interested less in the demographics of families and more in the styles of parenting—how parents encourage behaviors they like in their children and discourage others. At least in the United States, three major styles of parenting have been identified (Baumrind, 1971, 1978).

Authoritarian parenting is firm, punitive, and emotionally cold. Such parents value obedience from their children and do not encourage their independence or involve them in decision making: "Why? Because I said so." **Permissive parenting** is loving but lax. Such parents exert little control over their children. Indeed, these children are given freedom and are allowed to make decisions, but they have little guidance: "Oh sure, honey, whatever you want." **Authoritative parenting** involves negotiating with children. Such parents set limits for a child, but explain why, and they encourage independence. As the child demonstrates responsibility, the parents allow more freedom. Decisions are arrived at through give and take: "Let's talk this through."

These different styles of parenting affect the subsequent social development of children (Becker, 1964; Durbin, Darling, Steinberg, & Brown, 1993; Parish & McCluskey, 1994). Authoritarian parents tend to produce children who are unhappy, dependent, and submissive. Permissive parents raise children who are likely to be outgoing and sociable, but also immature, impatient, and aggressive. The best approach appears to be that of authoritative parents, whose children tend to be friendly, cooperative, socially responsible, and self-reliant. Regardless of the style of parenting that children experience, they tend to raise their own children in much the same way (Van Ijzendoorn, 1992).

Mothers and fathers sometimes differ in their parenting styles, which introduces further complexities into any description of how their children are affected (Bentley & Fox, 1991; Forehand & Nousiainen, 1993; Fox, Kimmerly, & Schafer, 1991). Even so, parenting style is only one influence on the social development of children. Just as important as the type of discipline is the love shown by parents (chapter 10). It is also important to consider a two-way influence between parent and child. Because children differ with respect to their temperaments, parents may use the method of discipline that their children "allow" them to.

Researchers find that being a parent is both a rewarding and a stressful aspect of adult life (Mowbray, Oyserman, & Ross, 1995). The vast majority of parents report that if given the chance to start their lives over, they would choose again to have babies (Yankelovich, 1981). Nonetheless, the presence of children in a household profoundly changes the relationship between husbands and wives. Childrearing responsibilities often fall to mothers, perhaps contributing to the increased depression found among them (Brown & Harris, 1978). Following the birth of a child, the typical mother takes on more household chores, regardless of how she and her mate divided the tasks before (Cowan, Cowan, Coie, & Coie, 1978).

When children grow up and leave home, the roles of parents change. At one time, psychologists thought that parents, particularly mothers, were vulnerable to the so-called empty nest syndrome—a loss of purpose experienced when all of the children have left home. But research fails to bear out this notion. If anything, just the opposite occurs: Mothers report the most satisfaction and the highest morale once their children leave home (Neugarten, 1970). Why not? On the one hand, life becomes less demanding. And on the other hand, the successful development of offspring from dependent children to autonomous adults means that a parent has done well.

The Good School

As institutions, schools have unique characteristics. Students are crucial members of schools, the equivalent of customers or clients, and they are the ultimate goal or product. School is sometimes called a *life industry*, which means that educational practices affect students not just in the here and now but also across the lifespan in settings far removed from the classroom. The pervasive influence of schools is not an interesting by-product of education but an integral part of a school's explicit purpose. Schools of course intend to impart knowledge and to encourage intellectual excellence, but the intent of a school includes much more than teaching multiplication or verb conjugation.

Discussions of excellent schools often focus just on achievement and not on the people who achieve, but we should not confuse graduation rates and test scores with the moral goals of education. Likewise, excellent schools may play a role in reducing such negative outcomes as violence, substance abuse, and other unhealthy behaviors (Elias & Weissberg, 2000), but the avoidance of problems cannot be the whole picture. Otherwise, schools would be indistinguishable from police departments.

Here I am interested in the features of schools that contribute to the moral fulfillment of students and the adults they become. In doing background research for this section, I had to look hard for such discussions by educational theorists. The thriving industry of *character education* was less useful for my purpose than I had hoped. Many character education statements dwell at length on the aspects of individual-level character to be cultivated as opposed to the characteristics of schools that actually enable these aspects. When practices are recommended by character education advocates, they often seem psychologically naïve. Reciting the Pledge of Allegiance every morning is not an automatic route to good citizenship, and viewing the Ten Commandments on the wall of a classroom is no guarantee that the exposed students will become moral adults. After all, I stared for years at the periodic table of elements at the front of a classroom, and I certainly did not become a chemist.

Much more useful for my present purpose were the psychologically focused studies by Martin Maehr and his colleagues at the University of Michigan on the sorts of schools that encourage students to be engaged and enthusiastic about learning (e.g., Maehr & Braskamp, 1986; Maehr & Midgley, 1996; Maehr, Midgley & Urdan, 1992). Positive attitudes and motives about school translate themselves into good academic performance but, more important, make students lifelong learners who reap psychological benefits long after graduation (Cowen, 1997; Schneider, 2000).

The features of good schools so defined include an articulated and shared vision of the school's purpose: For what does it stand, and for what does it strive (Maehr, 1991)? Only when a school provides explicit goals can students adopt them. Goals increase the motivation to learn, investment in the process, and commitment to the hard work that achievement requires (Maehr & Midgley, 1996). Good schools emphasize the individual student and reward his or her effort and improvement (Anderman & Maehr, 1994; Maehr, Ames, & Braskamp, 1988; Midgley, Anderman, & Hicks, 1995). In contrast, schools that emphasize ability might actually undercut performance and certainly work against positive attitudes. There is much to commend in the recent movement within the United States to hold students to high standards, but if this entails teaching to the test, the movement is self-defeating. There is little reason to believe that drilling youngsters on how to take multiple-choice exams will change their intellectual values or sense of self (Roeser & Eccles, 1998).

As I have noted, a good school is one that prepares students to be effective learners throughout life. Accordingly, such a school starts by providing an environment where students feel safe and proceeds by explicitly guiding them to be caring, responsible, and ultimately productive members of society (Elias et al., 1997; Pepler & Slaby, 1994; Weissberg, Barton, & Shriver, 1997). Social competence and emotional competence can be encouraged by appropriate exercises and activities, which need not be expensive and in any event are not incompatible with traditional academic pursuits.

Consider the ongoing intervention by Kathleen Hall Jamieson (2000) to encourage civic engagement among U.S. high school students by teaching what she calls "civic literacy" through a combination of student-led classroom discussions and community activities. As a local election approaches, high school students survey the electorate about the issues that matter most to them. They determine the positions on these issues of the respective candidates and evaluate the viability of these positions. The students sponsor public discussions and debates. They help to turn out the vote, and those of legal age of course vote themselves.

Rigorous evaluation of educational programs that build character are just beginning in earnest (Collaborative for Academic, Social, and Emotional Learning, 2002), but in the meantime, we can look at the more-extensive studies of programs that reduce problems such as school violence. Here are some conclusions about good schools judged in these terms (Felner, 2000; Felner, Felner, & Silverman, 2000; Hawkins & Lam 1987; Hunter & Elias, 1998):

- Students perceive courses to be relevant.
- Students perceive that they have control over what happens to them at school.
- Students perceive school discipline policies to be firm, fair, clear, and consistently enforced, with a focus on correction and skills building rather than on punishment.
- Students see the school reward system as rational: The school recognizes students for their achievement and rewards their positive behavior.
- There exists a strong and effective school governance.
- The school principal displays strong leadership.
- Practices are in place which decrease the impersonality of the school and increase contact between students and teachers, which in turn increase students' feeling of belonging and connectedness.[3]

The Good Workplace

The psychological significance of the work we do cannot be overestimated. Brief and Nord (1990, p. 1) introduced their book on the psychology of work with the following observation:

> We did not set out to examine the meaning of life, but found it difficult to keep our study of the meaning of work from growing to include such an examination. In fact, given the American preoccupation with work . . . if we had assumed work and life are one, the assumption might not even have been challenged by many readers.

Work is conventionally defined in economic terms—what people do for financial compensation in order to earn a living—but this definition obscures its richer psychological meaning.

The work we do often defines who we are. An occupation does more than pay the bills; it consumes one third to one half of the average adult's waking hours. It provides one of our most-important identities by directing our lives in certain directions rather than others. "What do you do?" is a conversational gambit that could be answered in any number of ways, but most of us hear it as a question about our occupation (chapter 7).

The U.S. Department of Labor Statistics (2004) lists more than 30,000 types of jobs in this country alone. In trying to understand the meaning of jobs to

3. While writing this chapter, I watched a brief report on television about a school that had dramatically turned around decades-long trends of high absenteeism and dropping out. One of the students was interviewed and asked why he comes to school. His reply was simple: "If I am not there, someone will miss me." To be sure, there is more to excellent education than students feeling that they matter, but it is difficult to imagine a good school in which this is not the case.

workers, psychologists have proposed dimensions with which to classify these various ways of earning a living. For example, jobs differ in terms of physical requirements, intellectual demands, and interpersonal characteristics: whether they involve goods (producing things) or services (assisting people).

Work in its broadest sense must also be placed in its historical and cultural context. The meaning of work to an individual varies according to societal conditions. During a recession or depression, workers are simply grateful to be employed. During prosperous times, workers are less satisfied and more willing—because they are more able—to explore alternatives to their current jobs.[4] If the country is at war, those who work for defense contractors are more fulfilled by their jobs than when the country is at peace (Turner & Miclette, 1962).

England and Whitely (1990) studied workers in six different nations with respect to

- the centrality of work to an individual's life;
- the goals and values preferred by a worker, ranging broadly from economic motives (good pay and job security) to expressive motives (opportunity to learn new things, harmonious relationships with other people at work, autonomy); and
- whether work was regarded as a societal right or a societal obligation.

From responses to questionnaires about work, the researchers discerned several common patterns, and they proposed a typology of workers in terms of work's meaning:

- *alienated* worker: For this individual, work is not central to his or her life; it is pursued for neither economic nor expressive reasons; and it is not seen as fulfilling any obligation to the larger society.
- *economic* worker: The meaning of work for this individual revolves solely around good pay and high security.
- *duty-oriented* worker: This individual regards work as highly central to his or her life, undertakes it for expressive reasons, and regards it as a societal obligation.
- *balanced* worker: Here, work is highly central to the individual's life; and it allows both economic and expressive goals to be satisfied

Across all of the nations studied, alienated workers in general tended to be younger and female, and they performed low-paying jobs with little variety or responsibility. As you would imagine, they rated their satisfaction with work as low. Economic workers in general had less education than other types of workers and were somewhat more likely to be males. Their jobs had little variety or responsi-

4. Years ago, I remember talking with my father on the phone. I complained that I did not have a good job. My father, who had grown up in the Great Depression, asked me if I were being paid. When I said that of course I was being paid, he remarked, "Then you have a good job."

bility. Despite the importance of pay to these workers, they tended not to earn much money. Their satisfaction with work was also low. Duty-oriented workers in general were older and somewhat more likely to be females; they often worked as managers or in sales, in jobs with high variety and responsibility, and usually earned good salaries. Their work satisfaction was high. Balanced workers were usually older males with more education than other types of workers. They worked at a variety of jobs, typically those high in autonomy. They put in the longest hours; and they earned the highest salaries. They rated their work satisfaction as quite high.

These results are not surprising, but note that the meaning of work to an individual—as captured by her classification—is associated with a range of personal and occupational characteristics, from motives to educational level to salaries. No single characteristic proves to be of overriding importance in terms of its association with the meaning of work. The significance of work is complexly determined (Kelly & Kelly, 1994; Lundberg & Peterson, 1994).

What did England and Whitely (1990) learn about work in different nations? Let us consider just the contrasts between workers in the United States and in Japan. These differences shed some light on the often-heard charge (in both countries) that Japanese workers are "better" than those in the United States.

On average, workers in Japan put in more hours per week than do U.S. workers. They are less likely to describe their work as possessing variety and as utilizing a considerable amount of their skills. However, Japanese workers report much more satisfaction with their work than do U.S. workers. They are more likely to say that they would choose the same job again if given the opportunity, and they are more likely to say that they would keep working even if they had no financial reason to do so.

These findings seem contradictory. Why are Japanese workers more satisfied with work that takes more time, has less variety, and uses fewer of their skills? Perhaps the answer lies in the psychological meaning of work. Workers in Japan are more likely to be classified as duty-oriented or balanced, whereas those in the United States are more likely to be classified as economic or alienated.

There are innumerable reasons for these national differences in the meaning of work and its translation into satisfaction or dissatisfaction. It is unlikely that they can be reduced to a handful of simple practices and procedures. Rather, we need to consider the larger cultural context from which the significance of work emerges if we wish to understand these differences between Japanese and U.S. workers.

A generation ago, there was a great deal of discussion in the United States about the feasibility of borrowing Japanese work and management techniques (Kono, 1982; Smith, Reinow, & Reid, 1984; Viau, 1990). In retrospect, this seems silly. For instance, Japanese companies encourage their workers to participate in group calisthenics. But calisthenics, in and of themselves, will not make American workers feel less alienated or more balanced in their motivation to work. The meaning of work needs to be changed in a more positive direction by undertaking innovations that make sense in terms of U.S. culture. So, given the importance of the individual "self" in the United States, jobs allowing workers to put their own identifiable spin on what they do should be more satisfying than jobs that demand uniform and anonymous performance.

Besides being culturally congruent with their workers, good workplaces are characterized by certain institutional-level virtues. Excellent work organizations have an articulated moral goal or vision that can be embraced by workers and customers alike. This vision must guide the actual conduct within the organization. Slogans and logos provide clues about the vision of a work organization, but it is our observation of day-to-day practices that provides the real proof of their existence.

Workers are treated fairly in moral work organizations, which have reward structures both explicit and equitable. The parallel with good parenting as just discussed is interesting. In contrast to authoritarian or permissive styles of raising children, an authoritative style entails limits with explanations and ongoing negotiations. Authoritative parenting leads to children who—simply put—have good character. An authoritative managerial style similarly leads to employees who are independent yet responsible—workers with good character (Peters & Waterman, 1982). The trend in the United States toward employee-owned businesses, like Avis, facilitates authoritative management (Levering & Moskowitz, 1993).

The organization must additionally treat people as individuals and not just as a pair of hands. In the case of employees, this means giving them the autonomy to be innovative. It means humane concern not only for workers but also for their families. There are U.S. companies, for example, that provide health insurance not only for employees and their families but also for their pets (Levering & Moskowitz, 1993). It means placing people in jobs that allow them to do what they do best. It means promoting from within. In the case of customers, treating them as individuals entails being honest about the goods or services that can be delivered; it means listening to what customers have to say about the work organization and then following their suggestions. Finally, excellent work organizations follow through on commitments—to workers and to customers. Promises and contracts, even implied ones, are honored. Said another way, in a good workplace, the spirit of the law trumps the letter of the law.

The Good Society

What characterizes the good society? This question has been posed—and answered—for as long as people have lived together. Consider the vision of the good society articulated in ancient Rome (Starr, 1985). The Roman ideal of the good society has pervaded Western organizations and institutions for the past two millennia. In fact, the Latin words used to describe institutional-level virtues have become familiar in the Western world.

The Romans recognized personal virtues—what I call character strengths (chapter 6)—like *gravitas* (a sense of the importance of the matter at hand) and *veritas* (honesty) but also municipal virtues—that is, institutional-level virtues—that characterize an entire society (Forbis, 1996). So, abundance means that there must be enough food for all members of society. Only a society per se can be characterized by *concordia* (harmony) and *pax* (peace). Here are some of the other Roman municipal virtues, many of which recur in contemporary characterizations of good institutions:

- *equity*: fair dealing within the society
- *good fortune*: remembrance of important positive events
- *justice*: sensible laws and governance
- *patience*: the ability to weather crises
- *providence*: the sense that the society has a destiny
- *safety*: public health and welfare

It is interesting to compare and contrast this vision with an equally influential one—the societal vision articulated by Confucius (1992)—which has pervaded Asian institutions for millennia. In his writings, Confucius extensively addressed the good society, although he did not enumerate its institutional-level virtues as explicitly as did the Romans. Nonetheless, we can discern his emphases. Basically, he valued social order and thus stressed explicit role expectations. He discussed at length these expectations in terms of relationships between and among people, so an inherent aspect of the Confucian vision of the good society is interpersonal—institutional, as it were. Confucius identified six relationships as crucial, those between

1. ruler and subjects
2. parents and children
3. husband and wife
4. older sibling and younger sibling
5. teacher and student
6. friend and friend

Confucius believed that in each of these relationships, there was a superior and a subordinate member, except for friend and friend, although even here, if one individual is older than the other, it may become an older-younger sibling relationship. In each relationship, the subordinate individual has the responsibility of obedience to the superior, but only when the superior in turn displays benevolence and care. Remember the notion of *amae* mentioned in chapter 10 (p. 257).

At least in principle, the Confucian ideal of duty does not prescribe humble acquiescence of the powerless to the powerful but rather calls for mutual respect, which persons should have in relation to one another, beginning with the familial relationship and extending outward to the state and citizen (Haberman, 1998). Put another way, duty is not permission for tyranny but rather the obligation to act honorably and with self-control in all personal affairs, rather than with a motive for personal gain. Likewise, the Confucian precept of good etiquette is best understood as a directive to respect others. The cultivation of courteousness and deference in one's everyday behavior is more about consideration for another's feelings than about strict adherence to rules and empty customs.

The Confucian vision of the good society can therefore be captured by a small number of institutional-level virtues embodied in the edicts to honor one's parents, to love others, to do what is right instead of what is advantageous, to practice reciprocity (i.e., the Golden Rule as articulated in the Western world), and to have rulers who lead by moral example instead of by force.

In the last few years, the United Kingdom and the European Union have discussed how to track the psychological well-being of citizens, just as economic indicators of well-being have been tracked for decades.[5] As you know, research in positive psychology has shown repeatedly that material affluence is at best a small ingredient of the good life, yet policy decisions are based on economic considerations to the explicit exclusion of psychological ones (Diener & Seligman, 2004). If successful, the assessment of national well-being will allow comparisons across time and political entities. We will have the information we need to offer conclusions about good societies, at least insofar as the goodness of a society is defined in terms of the greatest (psychological) good for the greatest number of people. The impact of societal reforms can thus be ascertained.

National indicators of psychological well-being will rely largely or exclusively on the self-report of citizens, which raises a caution about the likely success of these intriguing endeavors. Remember the discussion in chapter 5 about what self-report measures really ascertain. If they end up reflecting relative judgments, they are not apt to change much over time, even if a nation objectively improves in all possible ways, because people will constantly adjust their bases of comparison. What will result is a consistently flat line that cannot inform policy. Stay tuned.

The Good Religion?

Is it possible to talk about a "good" religion? To do so is to imply that there must be "bad" religions, dangerous territory into which I care not to enter. I repeat my earlier point that any conclusions about good or bad institutions must be carefully specified with respect to particular outcomes. So, to use what I hope is a

5. You may have heard about the small Himalayan nation of Bhutan, whose king has called for explicit attention to the country's "gross national happiness," which is akin to the economic gross national product (Thinley, 1998).

noncontroversial example, religion in general confers health benefits, although Christian Scientists—who eschew conventional medical care as an article of their faith—on average do not live as long as U.S. followers of other religions (W. F. Simpson, 1989). Being a Christian Scientist does not enable longevity, although I am sure this faith has other desirable consequences. For the most part, I cannot offer even qualified pronouncements about good and bad religions,[6] so I will simply describe what psychologists have learned about religion over the past century (Peterson & Park, in press).

The first great psychologist in the United States was William James, and he was deeply concerned with religious phenomena. His 1902 book, *The Varieties of Religious Experience*, remains in print (reprinted in 1985) more than a century later and is notable for its focus on the subjective experience of religion. James was especially interested in topics like conversion, mysticism, trance states, saintliness, and repentance.

Another early U.S. psychologist, G. Stanley Hall, established a journal devoted to the psychology of religion that was published between 1904 and 1915. Hall was a developmental psychologist who is often credited with "inventing" the concept of adolescence, and he also pioneered the use of the questionnaire as a research tool. He was most interested in the moral and religious training of youth (Hall, 1882).

Religion all but fell off psychology's radar screen from 1930 to 1960 (Beit-Hallahmi, 1974). We can cite various reasons. Behaviorism held sway, and researchers and theorists tended to focus on what people and animals had in common, which obviously did not include religion. The associated philosophical stance of logical positivism created a strict fact-value distinction,[7] and religion was seen by many psychologists as too value-laden to be a suitable subject for a scientifically objective psychology. Some have speculated that 20th-century psychologists themselves were not an especially devout group, which means that religion did not strike many of them as interesting or important. Finally, large state universities, where many of the leading figures in psychology have worked, usually do not have separate departments of religion or religious studies, the presence of which might have spurred interest in the psychology of religion.

There were, however, sporadic forays into the psychology of religion. For example, in well-known works like *Totem and Taboo* (1913/1953b), *The Future of*

6. George Vaillant (2005) has opined that all of the world's major religions—meaning those with many followers which have lasted for many centuries—like Judaism, Christianity, Hinduism, Islam, Buddhism, and (if we regard it as a religion) Confucianism—are based on love (chapter 6). At least in principle, if not always in fact, each of these religions endorses a broad moral circle and preaches the essential humanity of all people. Perhaps it would be interesting to compare and contrast sects and denominations within each of these religions and see if their viability is a function of their inclusiveness. Maybe then we would know something about especially good religions.

7. Logical positivists believe that the subject matter of science consists only of those "facts" that can be proven to be true or false with unambiguously specified procedures.

an Illusion (1927/1953c), and *Moses and Monotheism* (1939/1964), Sigmund Freud proposed that religion emerged as a consequence of the human need to defend against infantile impulses and fears (chapter 5). God and other divine figures are inventions (illusions) that fulfill the human wish for an omnipotent father whose love and protection have the kind of enduring power that can never be achieved by actual fathers.

Here, we see the beginning of an issue that still characterizes the psychological study of religion. Can (or should) religion be reduced to the merely psychological? To do so makes religion no different in principle from any other activity or experience that galvanizes people. Not to do so moves religion outside the realm of a deterministic science. Said another way, the issue for psychologists is whether their attempts to link religion to psychological phenomena "explain" religion or "explain it away." The distinction may be largely in the eye of the beholder. Regardless, religion is an extremely important factor in the lives of many people, as shown by its link with all manner of thoughts, feelings, and actions.

In 1950, Harvard psychologist Gordon Allport made an important distinction between **extrinsic religiosity** (religion as a means to other ends) and **intrinsic religiosity** (religion as an end in itself), one that still undergirds a great deal of theory and research in the psychology of religion. The extrinsically religious participate in institutionalized religion because it provides security, satisfies social needs, or confers status. The intrinsically religious in contrast internalize religious beliefs and bring their other needs into harmony with them.

To measure these two orientations, Allport and his colleagues developed a brief self-report questionnaire that is still widely used (Allport & Ross, 1967). One of the often-cited findings was that extrinsically religious people were the most likely to be prejudiced. Largely overlooked was the additional finding that intrinsically religious people were the least likely to be prejudiced. Indeed, if we limit our attention to church attendees, the most actively and intrinsically involved among them are still among the least prejudiced in the contemporary United States. If we are looking for a feature of a good religion, I suspect that the degree to which its followers have internalized its teachings would be one place to start.

When researchers did include religion in their studies, it was rarely a main focus, which means that they did little more than ascertain a handful of simple indices, like church attendance, which fail to make important distinctions like the one between extrinsic and intrinsic motivation. What resulted was an amorphous depiction of religion that did little to inspire further research.

Matters started to change around 1960 (Emmons & Paloutzian, 2003; Gorsuch, 1988; Hood, 1998). Journals like the *Review of Religious Research* and the *Journal for the Scientific Study of Religion* were founded and served as outlets for empirical research articles. Textbooks on the psychology of religion were written (e.g., Spilka, Hood, & Gorsuch, 1985; Wulff, 1991), and courses began to be offered. In 1975, an American Psychological Association division devoted to the psychology of religion was created.

As clinical and counseling psychologists began to take seriously the diversity of their clients, explicit interest in therapy with religious individuals began to emerge, and today, many of the books and articles written about the psychology of religion are framed within the context of therapy. Private foundations like the Fetzer Institute and the John Templeton Foundation began to support research into the psychology of religion. Measures were devised and disseminated. Apropos to the new millennium, there is even a psychology of religion Web page, which contains a variety of useful resources for psychology researchers and instructors.

Research findings began to accumulate that showed that religion had certain benefits in a variety of psychological domains (Pargament, 1997). Everyone's imagination was captured by the possibility that religious beliefs could help a person to cope with problems and even to avoid physical illnesses in the first place (e.g., Kalb, 2003; McCullough, Hoyt, Larson, Koenig, & Thoresen, 2000; Miller & Thoresen, 2003). Faith-based organizations were found to be effective in providing social and community services. Whether or not one agrees that the U.S. government should formally support such organizations, their success remains clear.

Following the lead of the larger U.S. culture, psychologists also began to distinguish between **religiosity** and **spirituality**. The former term subsumes traditional (religion-based) ways of experiencing the sacred and transcendent, whereas the latter term is an ever-expanding one that may include religious experience but also one's compassionate experience of nature or humanity. Thus, people may describe themselves as spiritual because they feel elevated in a beautiful setting or because they have "moral" values, but they may not believe in God or congregate with like-minded individuals in worship. This is an important distinction, but too much emphasis on it overlooks the fact that, however they are defined, religiousness and spirituality overlap substantially in their features and usually co-occur in the same person.

Concerns about the definitions of spirituality and religiousness highlight long-standing questions about how we can know that a phenomenon is religious (or spiritual) or not. One tradition, which can be traced to William James, suggests that religious events are extraordinary happenings characterized by mystical experiences. Another view is that religious events are not in themselves extraordinary or transcendent but are simply those attributed by the individual to divine forces.

Contemporary approaches to the psychological study of the religious and spiritual life tend to fall into several general domains. One important body of work is largely theoretical in nature. Here, several influential schools of thought exist. The *psychoanalytic school* draws upon the work of Freud and emphasizes the role of unconscious motives for religious beliefs. Contemporary psychoanalytic theorists are not necessarily as hostile toward religion as was Freud. The *analytic school* is based upon the ideas of Freud's one-time follower Carl Jung. Well known is Jung's theorizing about universal archetypes (symbols), many of which have religious significance. The *object relations school* draws on more-contemporary psychodynamic theorizing and often emphasizes maternal influences. The *transpersonal school* assumes that religious phenomena—although immaterial—are nonetheless real and can be studied directly. Finally, the *phenomenological school* attempts to describe religion as it is experienced by the individual.

Another approach to the psychology of religion is a body of work that attends to quantitative measurement (e.g., Fetzer Institute, 1999; Hill & Hood, 1999). What are the important domains of religious and spiritual experience? How can they be measured? What are the psychometric properties (reliability and validity) of these empirical measures?

It is unfortunate that the measurement tradition is often separate from the rich theoretical traditions represented by the influential schools of thought, which tend to rely on single case studies. One would think that theory and quantitative research could mutually inform one another. Regardless, the measurement tradition has yielded a variety of intriguing findings about the psychology of religion.

For example, professed religiousness among young people in the United States is associated with a tendency to avoid all manner of antisocial activities (Johnson, Jang, Larson, & Li, 2001). Children and adolescents who score higher on indices of religiousness (i.e., church attendance) show greater emotional self-regulation, engage in fewer acts of aggression, have better records of academic performance, are less likely to use drugs and alcohol, and tend to delay their sexual involvement. They see the world as more coherent. Much the same results are found for adults (Koenig, McCullough, & Larson, 2001). Furthermore, religious involvement among adults predicts individual happiness and family well-being.

Another line of work is more sociologically oriented, and it maps patterns of involvement in institutionalized religion and delineates the impact of that involvement on social cohesion (Maton & Pargament, 1987; Maton & Wells, 1995). Churches, particularly those with strong social justice and service orientations, play demonstrably important roles in providing a range of resources that benefit their respective communities. These churches are able to instill in their congregations a sense of civic responsibility, which is shown in volunteerism and other forms of civic involvement. African American churches play particularly important roles in promoting the well-being of their communities by providing a range of services, including education, psychological counseling, financial support, housing, clothing, and food to those who are in need (Billingsley, 1999; Billingsley & Caldwell, 1991; Lincoln & Mamiya, 1990).

Following the early example of Hall, researchers have again turned their attention to religious socialization (Stolzenberg, Blair-Loy, & Waite, 1995). For example, what role do parents play in the religious beliefs and practices of their children? There is some evidence that fathers and mothers play distinct roles (Clark, Worthington, & Danser, 1988). Fathers appear to structure the formal religious involvement of their children, whereas mothers play a more-central role in the ways that their children apply the principles of religion in everyday life (Taylor & Chatters, 1991). At least within the United States, children raised in nuclear families, children whose mothers are not employed full time, and children whose parents share similar religious beliefs are more likely themselves to be religiously involved (S. Myers, 1996).

Under the influence of positive psychology, there has been increased interest in character strengths and virtues (chapter 6), including the explicitly theological (faith, hope, and charity) and the more-secular but still religiously linked (gratitude and forgiveness). What are their causes and consequences? How can they be encouraged among youth?

Finally, there is a body of work that examines the neurophysiology of religious and spiritual experiences, attempting to identify the brain structures and mechanisms involved in religious experiences (Ashbrook & Albright, 1997; Newberg & d'Aquili, 2001). These investigations spill into a related line of theoretical work that addresses religion and spirituality in broadly biological—usually evolutionary—terms. The argument is that people are hard-wired (biologically predisposed) to seek the sacred. For instance, anthropologist Lionel Tiger (1979) proposed that hope, typically embedded in religious beliefs, arose in the human species to counteract the despair that resulted from people's growing capacity to contemplate their own demise (chapter 5).

The psychology of religion has clearly been reborn, but the field has yet to arrive fully within mainstream psychology (Peterson & Park, in press). It still tends to be marginalized in specialty journals, books, and courses. Researchers often seem apologetic for their interest in religion and are occasionally suspected by their colleagues of having a hidden agenda. The trajectory is nonetheless upward.

One can offer more-substantive criticism of the contemporary psychology of religion. Most of the research under the psychology of religion umbrella is done in the United States and is most accurately described as the psychology of mainstream Protestantism, reflecting the makeup of the typical sample of research participants. For the most part, researchers have been reluctant to compare people who follow different religions, which means that the resulting data are not at all fine-grained.[8]

The United States has been characterized as a particularly religious nation. More than 40% of Americans attend weekly religious services, in contrast to only

8. Interesting exceptions do exist, which underscore the potential utility of comparative studies. So, one study has shown that religious fundamentalists—whether Christian, Jewish, or Muslim—are more optimistic than their liberal counterparts (Sethi & Seligman, 1993). Another study has shown that Jews are more likely than Christians to judge morality in terms of people's overt actions as opposed to their thoughts and intentions (Cohen & Rozin, 2001).

4% of adults in Japan (Inglehart & Norris, 2004). If we take these data at face value, they reflect the historical fact that the United States was largely settled by religious refugees from Europe seeking freedom to worship as they wished (chapter 7). But another interpretation is that these data are an artifact of researchers using Western (Christian) conceptions of religion and what it means to be devout. Because Japanese are mostly Shintoists or Buddhists, not Christians, they are more likely to seek the sacred in the mundane. Church attendance is a category mistake when used to judge how religious the Japanese are. Regardless, the psychology of religion needs to be extended to all forms of religion. Whether findings established among U.S. Protestants generalize to Jews, Muslims, Hindus, Buddhists, and others—inside and outside the United States—is a critically important question that deserves much more attention than it has so far received.

Additionally, the psychology of religion often follows the lead of psychology per se by studying unselected samples of college students enrolled in introductory psychology courses. They are given batteries of questionnaires to complete, including measures of religiosity and spirituality, and the correlations among these measures are explored. Although the religious experience of young adults can be interesting in its own right, given that late adolescence is a time of intellectual exploration and identity consolidation, this is far from an ideal research strategy if one's interest is in the psychology of religion more broadly construed and especially if we are interested in the long-term consequences of religion.

Many researchers to date have also been content to use very simple research designs, which hamper interpretation. For example, a study may show that people who frequently attend church have better physical health than those who do not. We might be tempted to conclude that church attendance is good for one's health, but such data might show instead that health is good for one's church attendance or that some unmeasured third variable (e.g., affluence) is responsible for both. In fairness, researchers are recognizing the need for more-sophisticated research designs that follow individuals over time and that control for confounding variables (Flannelly, Ellison, & Strock, 2004). The unsurprising but meatier conclusion from more-sophisticated studies is that religion confers physical health benefits when it has been well integrated into the individual's life (McCullough, Hoyt, Larson, Koenig, & Thoresen, 2000).

Still not established to any certainty is the means by which religion confers benefits (George, Ellison, & Larson, 2002). Are the relevant processes intrapsychic (emotional or cognitive) or interpersonal? Do these mechanisms differ in accord with the consequence of interest? Do they differ from person to person even for the same consequence? Again, more-sophisticated research designs are needed.

A final point is that those who study the psychology of religion at times seem almost too respectful of their subject matter. After decades of neglect if not outright antipathy toward religion, psychology today appears to be uncritically enthusiastic about the benefits of religion. Surely there are both psychologically healthy and psychologically unhealthy aspects of religion, both of which should be acknowledged and studied.

Kenneth Pargament (2002), one of today's leading psychologists of religion, has phrased well the need for more-articulate research questions:

> Religion is a richer, more complex process than psychologists have imagined, one that has the potential both to help and to harm. Questions about the general efficacy of religion should give way to the more difficult but appropriate question, How helpful or harmful are particular forms of religious expression for particular people dealing with particular situations in particular social contexts according to particular criteria of helpfulness or harmfulness? (p. 168)

In sum, the psychology of religion today is a moving target, and as analytic questions like those posed by Pargament begin to be answered, the field may be increasingly embraced by the larger discipline.

Conclusions

I trust that you have seen agreement across the previous sections about widely valued institutional-level virtues:

- *purpose*: a shared vision of the moral goals of the organization, which are reinforced by remembrances and celebrations
- *safety*: protection against threat, danger, and exploitation
- *fairness*: equitable rules governing reward and punishment and the means for consistently enforcing them
- *humanity*: mutual care and concern
- *dignity*: the treatment of all people in the organization as individuals regardless of their position

A sweatshop or forced-labor camp fails to be "good" by any of these criteria. But a family, a school, a workplace, a society, and—perhaps—a religion are likely to contribute to fulfillment to the degree that more of these virtues are present.

I believe that other institutions, like sports teams, nonprofit organizations, and government agencies, can also be described in terms of these virtues. I am further encouraged that this suggested scheme converges with the one offered by philosopher Sissela Bok (1995) in her attempt to articulate universal societal values (chapter 7). As you recall, Bok proposed that people in all times and places endorse the values identified here as safety, fairness, and humanity. Missing from her scheme are the values that I have identified as purpose and dignity, but I believe that they belong as well.

I speculate that a good organization can inspire its members to be more than they are—to reveal strengths of character that are dormant or to create new ones that allow them to rise to the occasions deemed to be important by the organization. A worthy future goal of positive psychology is to turn its attention to how institutional practices can be engineered so that moral excellence and personal fulfillment on the part of all institutional members are enabled.

In the meantime, we have the insights from *Good Work*, an important book by psychologists Howard Gardner, Mihaly Csikszentmihalyi, and William Damon (2001). Their names should be familiar to you because of their contributions to the topics of multiple intelligences (Gardner, 1983), flow (Csikszentmihalyi, 1990), and moral development (Damon, 1988). In this book, they have blended their considerable skills to function as a positive psychology dream team to address a topic of mutual interest discovered while all three were in residence in the mid-1990s at the Center for Advanced Study in the Behavioral Sciences in Palo Alto: what it means to do "good work" in a profession, work that is excellent as well as ethical.

Good Work examined in detail two different professions—genetics and journalism—in terms of good work. Approximately 100 accomplished geneticists and 100 accomplished journalists were interviewed by the authors and their colleagues. The bulk of the book presented what was learned from these interviews, mainly in narrative form in which major conclusions were supported by extensive quotes from representative research participants.

The original impetus for choosing these two fields was the a priori contrast between a discipline that tries to change the body (genetics) and one that tries to change the mind (journalism). But in the course of the research, another contrast emerged that struck the authors as even more important: whether the profession is in alignment versus misalignment. That is, do the abstract values of the field agree with what people actually do at work? "When these conditions exist, individual practitioners are free to operate at their best, morale is high, and the professional realm flourishes. We term this a situation of authentic alignment" (Gardner, Csikszentmihalyi, & Damon, 2001, p. 27).

According to the authors, alignment is rare and easily threatened. Different domains in a field compete with each other for cultural hegemony and societal resources, e.g., religion versus science; clinical psychology versus psychiatry; positive psychology versus business-as-usual psychology.

In these terms, genetics today is an aligned field, and most contemporary geneticists are excited by what they do. Good work ensues. Witness the Human Genome Project, a scientific tour de force that has vast promise for improving the well-being of us all. In contrast, journalism today is misaligned, and many contemporary journalists are demoralized and on the verge of leaving the field. It is difficult to do good work in journalism. Consider the relaxation of standards for accuracy, fairness, and objectivity; the blurring of journalism and entertainment; and the desire by some ostensible journalists to make news rather than to report it. And yes, Geraldo, you're so vain, you probably think this sentence is about you.

These characterizations are not fixed, and the future could see a misaligned genetics and an aligned journalism. The utility of this contrast lies in its ability to clarify good work under circumstances in which it is easy versus those in which it is much more difficult.

There are three threats to alignment detailed by Gardner, Csikszentmihalyi, and Damon (2001), who described how each has misaligned journalism and may someday misalign genetics. First is what they term *Promethean technology* and the unanticipated problems it can bring in its wake. So, 24-hour television news shows, talk radio, and the proliferation of e-zines and blogs on the Internet have eroded journalistic standards. And when human genetic engineering becomes more than a theoretical possibility, all kinds of troubling issues will come to the fore. We have already seen heated debates about genetically altered fruits and vegetables. Imagine the furor that would erupt over genetically altered friends, family members, or local sports heroes.

Second is the intrusion of the profit motive into these professions. Journalists have always competed to break stories, but now the competition is ruthless, and values may go by the wayside. For-profit-only media conglomerates are but one familiar symptom of the problem. In genetics, researchers not only aim to discover the function of particular genes but also to patent them. Secrecy is therefore paramount, and a rush to premature conclusions is all but inevitable.

A third threat to alignment is dumbing down what the profession does in order to appeal to the lowest common denominator among its various stakeholders. Dumbing down is obvious in journalism today. A generation ago, the phrase *sound bite* had no meaning except to acoustical engineers, and the on-again-off-again courtships of movie stars did not crowd stories about war and peace from the headlines. In genetics, what dumbing down means is more subtle, but according to Gardner, Csikszentmihalyi, and Damon (2001), it may someday show itself as a press to investigate only the diseases of the wealthy or to engineer only cosmetic changes in physical appearance.

The authors described what can be done to facilitate good work not just in these fields but in others, and here lies the major aspect of their contribution. New institutions can be created, and in this case, technology can be the friend of alignment rather than the foe. The functions of existing professions can be expanded, their memberships can be reconfigured, and their traditional values can be reaffirmed. Finally, prominent practitioners can take personal stands in favor of excellence, which will have institutional consequences.

"Excellence is generally transmitted from one individual to another through lineages of mentors and their apprentices" (Gardner, Csikszentmihalyi, & Damon, 2001, p. 216). As I have repeatedly noted, one of the emerging truisms of positive psychology is that other people matter. *Good Work* cites many examples of actual geneticists and journalists who have inspired others to do their best.

My initial reaction to these ideas about creating or restoring the conditions for good work was shameful. I dismissed them as difficult if not impossible to implement. On second thought, I realized that of course it is difficult to facilitate good work. To expect anything else is to dumb down what it means to live the good life.

EXERCISE *Working for an Institution*

Think of a group or an organization that is part of an institution in which you believe. It could be your own school, workplace, political party, church, or local Little League baseball team. It could be the neighborhood fire station or Big Brothers/Big Sisters. Perhaps there is a volunteer program near and dear to your values, like Meals on Wheels or Toys for Tots.

Are you doing what you can do to make this group a better one, thereby strengthening the institution and the goals that it endorses? If not, then consider this exercise, which asks you to spend 3 hours a week over the next few months working for the institution in ways that you are not already doing. You will probably need to speak to the powers-that-be to learn what you might be able to do that is most helpful. In other cases, you might be able to take some initiative, like organizing birthday lunches for your coworkers. Regardless, do what you can do, do it well, and keep track of how it makes you feel, about yourself as well as about the institution. This exercise may overlap with the fun-versus-philanthropy exercise I described in chapter 2, but the difference is that the present exercise takes place in an explicit institutional context and requires that you work in concert with other members of the institution. It certainly will overlap with the being-a-good-teammate exercise, also described in chapter 2.

Some social critics charge that the American "community" has collapsed and that individual pursuits have swamped collective pursuits. In an aptly named book—*Bowling Alone*—Robert Putnam (2000) cited the demise of bowling leagues in the United States as an instance of this collapse. Bowling is as popular as ever, but people today are more apt to bowl alone. We also play video games alone, and we surf the Internet alone. Even long-time favorite leisure activities like reading and watching television are usually pursued alone (chapter 8). Couple all of this with the growing trends toward long-distance education on the one hand and working from home on the other, and what we see is a replacement of groups, organizations, and institutions with what are at best aggregations and collectivities—and virtual ones at that. Is it surprising that Americans have little confidence in their major societal institutions? At least in a psychological sense, many Americans do not feel part of these institutions.

This exercise encourages you to reflect on whether institutional membership and participation are good things. I believe that they are, not just because they make society possible but also because they contribute to fulfillment in ways that individual pursuits cannot. This exercise also gives you the opportunity to be analytic. Remember the institutional-level virtues identified in this chapter: purpose, safety, fairness, humanity, and dignity. Once you become more familiar with your group, ask yourself whether these five virtues characterize its actual conduct. If not, is there a way that you can encourage them?

GLOSSARY

aggregation: assembly of individuals physically in the same place
authoritarian parenting: childrearing style that is firm, punitive, and emotionally cold, giving children little independence or voice
authoritative parenting: childrearing style that involves negotiating with children, setting limits but explaining why
collectivity: any social category of two or more individuals who can be discussed as a whole
extrinsic religiosity: religion as a means to other ends
group: set of interacting individuals who mutually influence each other
institution: set of like organizations with especially sustained and pervasive influences within a society
institutional-level virtues: moral characteristics of the group as a whole
intrinsic religiosity: religion as an end in itself
organization: enduring and structured group
permissive parenting: childrearing style that is loving but lax, giving children freedom but little guidance
religiosity: traditional (religion-based) ways of experiencing the sacred and transcendent
spirituality: ever-expanding term that includes religious experience but also one's compassionate experience of nature or humanity

RESOURCES

Books and Journals

Cameron, K. S., Dutton, J. E., & Quinn, R. E. (Eds.). (2003). *Positive organizational scholarship: Foundations of a new discipline.* San Francisco: Berrett-Koehler.
Brokaw, T. (1998). *The greatest generation.* New York: Random House.
Giacalone, R. A., Jurkiewicz, C. L., & Dunn, C. (Eds.). (2005). *Positive psychology in business ethics and corporate responsibility.* Greenwich, CT: Information Age.
Levering, R., & Moskowitz, M. (1993). *The 100 best companies to work for in America.* Garden City, NY: Doubleday.
McGregor, D. (1960). *The human side of enterprise.* New York: McGraw-Hill.
Noddings, N. (2003). *Happiness and education.* New York: Cambridge University Press.

Peters, T. J., & Waterman, R. H. (1982). *In search of excellence: Lessons from America's best-run companies.* New York: Warner.

Putnam, R. D. (2000). *Bowling alone: The collapse and revival of American community.* New York: Simon & Schuster.

Terkel, S. (1974). *Working: People talk about what they do all day and how they feel about what they do.* New York: Pantheon.

School Psychology Quarterly. Special issue (Summer 2003).

Psychology in the Schools. Special issue (January 2004).

American Behavioral Scientist. Special issue (February 2004).

Articles

Diener, E., & Seligman, M. E. P. (2004). Beyond money: Toward an economy of well-being. *Psychological Science in the Public Interest, 5,* 1–31.

Wrzesniewski, A., McCauley, C. R., Rozin, P., & Schwartz, B. (1997). Jobs, careers, and callings: People's relations to their work. *Journal of Research in Personality, 31,* 21–33.

McCullough, M. E., Hoyt, W. T., Larson, D. B., Koenig, H. G., & Thoresen, C. (2000). Religious involvement and mortality: A meta-analytic review. *Health Psychology, 19,* 211–222.

Web Sites

http://www.bus.umich.edu/Positive. This is the Positive Organizational Scholarship Web site at the University of Michigan. "It focuses on the dynamics that lead to developing human strength, producing resilience and restoration, fostering vitality, and cultivating extraordinary individuals, units and organizations."

http://appreciativeinquiry.cwru.edu. This is the Web site of the Appreciative Inquiry Commons at Case Western Reserve University. "Appreciative Inquiry is about the . . . search for the best in people, their organizations, and the relevant world around them. In its broadest focus, it involves systematic discovery of what gives 'life' to a living system when it is most alive, most effective, and most constructively capable in economic, ecological, and human terms."

http://www.fortune.com/fortune/bestcompanies. This Web site describes *Fortune* magazine's top companies for which to work.

http://www.psywww.com/psyrelig. This is the psychology of religion Web site of Michael Nielsen at Georgia Southern University, and it contains a variety of useful resources and links.

http://www.bbbsa.org. This is the Web site of Big Brothers/Big Sisters of America, the largest mentoring organization in the United States, where volunteers provide support and advice to youth.

Films

Miracle on 34th Street (1947)

The Ten Commandments (1956)

Kramer vs. Kramer (1979)
Norma Rae (1979)
Nine to Five (1980)
Absence of Malice (1981)
Silkwood (1983)
Working Girl (1988)
ABC News's *20/20*: "Sharing Sweet Success" (1992)
Bhutan: Gross National Happiness (Modernization) (1997)
City of Angels (1998)
CBS News's *60 Minutes*: "Working the Good Life" (2003)
America's Heart and Soul (2004)

Songs

"Be True to Your School" (Beach Boys)
"Blowing in the Wind" (Peter, Paul, & Mary)
"My Sweet Lord" (George Harrison)
"Get Up, Stand Up" (Bob Marley & the Wailers)
"Take This Job and Shove It" (Johnny Paycheck)
"Teach Your Children" (Crosby, Stills, Nash, & Young)
"We Are Family" (Sister Sledge)

12 The Future of Positive Psychology

Dreams come true; without that possibility, nature would not incite us to have them. —JOHN UPDIKE (1989)

What is the future of positive psychology? The details are impossible to predict, although the endeavor will swim or sink in accordance with the science it produces over the next decade. Will new findings, theories, and applications emerge about what makes life most worth living? Will these be interesting and meaningful? Accurate and generalizable? Time—and of course the efforts of positive psychologists—will tell us if this new perspective is a fad or a fixture in the making, a hula hoop or a Frisbee,[1] Duran Duran or the Beatles (Peterson & Seligman, 2003b).

One point of view is that a thoroughly successful positive psychology will result in the fading away of this perspective, leaving us with a balanced psychology, one that recognizes the positive and the negative and of course their interplay (Lazarus, 2003). As I have said, positive psychology does not deny the negative, and it may well be that what is most troubling in life can set the stage for what is most fulfilling. So, I have discussed how our complex emotional experiences sometimes blend the positive and negative, how optimism is most meaningfully apparent when we think about setbacks and failures, how crises can reveal our

1. I find it interesting that the same company (Wham-O) manufactured the short-lived hula hoop and the venerable Frisbee (named after a pie company and its plates, which were the inspiration for the original flying disk). Wham-O was also responsible for the Slip 'n Slide, Silly String, the Hacky Sack, and the Superball. Creativity certainly takes different forms (chapter 8).

strengths of character, how ongoing challenges are a prerequisite for us to experience flow in the moment and to achieve something important in a lifetime, and how relationship success is foreshadowed not by the absence of problems but by how we resolve those that arise.

One of the thorny matters with which positive psychology needs to grapple is why the negative is so appealing, not just as a topic of social science research but also in other domains of life. We do not gossip about what other people do well. We are more interested in trains that crash than those that run on time. We think that Sylvia Plath is an exceptional poet but that e. e. cummings and Ogden Nash are playful ones at best. Why is the tragic view of life so compelling, and how can it be supplemented with one that allows for triumph and fulfillment?

Let us take stock. This book has covered the current concerns of positive psychology, from pleasure and happiness to optimism, character, and values, to interests, abilities, and accomplishments, to health, to love, and finally to institutions that enable all of these desirable states and traits. A great deal of work needs to be done, and I conclude here with some of the questions that I would like to see answered sooner as opposed to later.[2]

What Is the Neurobiology of Pleasure?

As I noted in chapter 1, positive psychology has attracted more researchers from the social science end of psychology than from the natural science end, which means that we know much less about the biological bases of the psychological good life than we would like. We do know that some brain regions are more involved in positive experience than are others, and the evidence keeps bringing us back to some involvement of the neurotransmitter dopamine (Ashby, Isen, & Turken, 1999). What is interesting—and perhaps worrisome—is that the neurobiology of the good life seems to mirror that of addiction.

Perhaps researchers have not looked closely enough to distinguish "good" pleasure and its more-dangerous relative. Or perhaps biologically oriented researchers have focused on intense feelings, like passionate love, but not on more-serene ones, like contentment, which might have an altogether different neurobiological underpinning. But what if we discover that there really is no difference? We would expect that the pursuit of pleasure, like the use of drugs to get high, would be ultimately futile. We would habituate to pleasure and find its aftermath increasingly marked by negative feelings (Solomon & Corbit, 1974).

It seems only a matter of time before a pharmaceutical company markets a drug to make people happy. Indeed, the antidepressant Prozac, at least for some users, has been called "personality in a pill" and viewed by them as much more

2. Many of these questions emerged from discussions with Mike Csikszentmihalyi, Ed Diener, Marty Seligman, and George Vaillant during May and June 2005.

than a way to combat symptoms of depression (Kramer, 1993). And we certainly know that cocaine and the various opiates produce intense pleasure. So, what will be the fate of a happiness drug and those who use it?

Is There Really a Hedonic Set-Point?

In chapters 3 and 4, I reviewed the evidence for and against the notion that our typical level of subjective well-being is set by genetics. That we adapt to hedonic experiences is not at issue. The issue is how much room there is to change over the lifespan. Is happiness more like our height and therefore essentially fixed (Lykken & Tellegen, 1996), or is it more like a skill that is malleable if we work at it (chapter 8)?

To take an extreme example, people who are severely depressed or anxious can and do recover (Seligman, 1994), and their life satisfaction is then no different than that of people who were never so unhappy (Peterson, Park, & Seligman, 2006). Perhaps they learned something along the way that changed their world view and restored their well-being.

We can gain insight into the hedonic set-point by looking outside people to where and how they live. Years ago, psychologist Walter Mischel (1968) argued that the apparent stability of "personality" traits could be explained by the typical constancy of a person's environment. Perhaps subjective well-being stays much the same for most people because their settings—which enable happiness, or not—also stay much the same.

Whatever the reasons for the inertia of our well-being, what is clear is that if we are to change our typical level of happiness, it will not be through quick fixes or one-shot interventions. We will need to change permanently our lives and our lifestyles, just as if we were trying to change our weight or level of aerobic fitness (chapter 9).

What Is the Natural History of the Good Life?

Positive psychology provides a vision of the psychological good life. We need to allow for cultural variations as well as nuances introduced by where people happen to be in the course of their lives. But there is little disagreement that the good life includes

- more positive affect than negative affect
- satisfaction with life as it is lived
- hope for the future
- gratitude about the past
- the identification of what one does well

- the use of these talents and strengths in engaging and fulfilling pursuits
- close relationships with other people
- meaningful participation in groups and organizations

And, of course, safety and health provide the context for the good life.

It is unlikely that one person can have it all, at least at the same time, and the components of the good life seem to exist in degrees. But the more components that are present and to a greater degree, the more confident I am in concluding that a person is living well.

That said, we do not know much about how these components come about, the concrete mix of nature and nurture (and perhaps luck) that makes it all happen. Psychologists for decades have tracked the natural history of what goes wrong, and we can specify well the conditions that produce disease, defect, and despair. Missing to date—with a few exceptions like the Harvard Study of Adult Development (Vaillant, 1977, 1983, 2002)—are analogous longitudinal studies of the good life.

Positive psychology tells us that we need to do more than flip over the determinants of problems if we want to understand the determinants of what goes right in life. Important questions need to be addressed. For example, are some or all of the components of the good life defaults, simply happening in the absence of detrimental events (Peterson, 2000)? Or do they only come about because something special takes place? If I had to speculate, I would say that general life satisfaction (chapter 4) and secure attachment (chapter 10) are defaults for most people but that special talents (chapter 8) and strengths of temperance (chapter 6) need to be carefully nurtured.

To use once again my geographical metaphor, if positive psychology is the study of topics somewhere north of neutral, which are indigenous, and which are imported? Which are hardy, and which are fragile?

Can Nice Guys Finish First?

I have described many studies showing that positive characteristics usually have desirable consequences. The suspicion may still linger that "niceness" can get in the way of accomplishing certain things in life, and I admit that I share this skepticism. Do the more ruthless among us sometimes win at work and love? Of course, but to move beyond the striking examples highlighted on reality television shows, what is generally the case? Do the Donald Trumps of the world succeed because of their single-mindedness or in spite of it? If they had stopped more frequently to smell the roses, especially in the company of others, would their lives have unfolded differently? Would they be happier but also less rich?

The only way to answer these kinds of questions is with longitudinal studies of large numbers of people, the natural history investigations I just recommended. Such studies would need to go beyond existing ones to examine simultaneously all of the components of the good life, to see if there are tradeoffs among them and to see if more is always better. Aristotle's (2000) *doctrine of the mean* proposes that all virtues lie between the extremes of deficiency and excess. So, bravery is good, and cowardice is bad, but so too is foolhardiness. Is this doctrine applicable to the other components of the good life? Perhaps there are optimal levels for some of these components, and if we exceed them by too much, we may hamper the development and display of the others.

Why Don't People Seek Out What Will Make Them Happy?

In chapter 3, I called your attention to an important question unanswered to date. Flow is an invigorating state with desirable long-term consequences. So why don't we more frequently pursue activities that put us in flow? More generally, why don't we do more of the things that have the potential to make us happy? Having close friends is more fulfilling than surfing the Internet. Doing volunteer work pays more dividends than repeatedly catching the scores on ESPN. Living in accord with explicit values is more satisfying than constant compromising. So why do we live as we do? It may just be that those who fail to pursue the good life are hampered by anxiety or depression—distressingly common in the modern world—which implies that positive psychology needs to partner with business-as-usual psychology to understand and improve the human condition.

Absent the relevant research, I cannot answer definitively for all people. I do know that for me, part of the explanation of this paradox is my frustration with other people. So many of the activities that make life most worth living involve others, and they do not always cooperate. Just the other day, I was shopping and tried to chat with the cashier at the store, making a comment about the weather or something equally innocuous. I was being pleasant, but she did not smile, say anything, or even look me in the face. She simply slapped the change on the counter for me to pick up. Wow. I did not take this personally, but at the same time, it did not encourage me to be friendly to the next cashier I encountered.

In any event, the point is not about strangers working cash registers, but about the people who really do matter in our lives: family members, friends, neighbors, fellow workers. They too do not always cooperate with us, which makes solitary activities on our part more likely because they are easier to control and certainly not as risky.

The moral insight is that I probably make my loved ones as crazy as they sometimes make me, and I should "do unto others" to facilitate their good life and hope that the favor is somehow and someday reciprocated. But the psychological insight remains elusive. We know the dance is wonderful when all participate, so how do we get everyone onto the floor? Who makes the first move, and how does this intrepid soul sustain his or her good intentions in the absence of supportive responses? Perhaps we are unwilling or unable to look beyond short-term annoyance to see long-term benefit, an insidious example of the duration neglect I discussed in chapter 3.

Can the Psychological Good Life Be Deliberately Created?

Psychologists, at least in the United States, are a pragmatic bunch. John Watson, B. F. Skinner, Martin Seligman, and the rest of us are experimentalists at heart, and we do our experiments not just in the laboratory but in the real world. It is an article of faith among many psychologists—and certainly among most positive psychologists—that the human condition can be improved by the intelligent application of what we have learned.

One of the most famous quotes by a psychologist is John Watson's (1925, p. 65) declaration:

> Give me a dozen healthy infants, well-formed, and my own specified world to bring them up in, and I'll guarantee to take any one at random and train him to become any type of specialist I might select—doctor, lawyer, artist, merchant-chief, and yes even beggar-man and thief, regardless of his talents, penchants, activities, vocations and race of his ancestors.

Psychologists today do not believe that people are quite the blank states that Watson assumed them to be (Pinker, 2002), but it is not a stretch to imagine positive psychologists expanding this assertion and saying that they could take people at random and make them more happy, hopeful, virtuous, accomplished, and socially involved. The exercises I have suggested in each chapter embody this conviction, and in some cases, rigorous research supports it (e.g., Gillham, Reivich, Jaycox, & Seligman, 1995; Seligman, Steen, Park, & Peterson, 2005).

But even the most-compelling research is not based on follow-up that extends beyond a few years, and the research participants are usually motivated and willing volunteers. Over the years, hundreds if not thousands of potentially "positive" interventions have been proposed,[3] and we have just begun to operationalize and test them. How well these interventions will generalize—across diverse people and over time—is a research topic of high priority. Some will work as intended, and some will not, and the only way to know is to look at the evidence (Patrick & Olson, 2000). The good news, if we can extrapolate from research on therapy for psychological problems, is that a variety of interventions are effective

3. The world's religious traditions have supplied a huge number of practices that can be construed as positive psychology interventions, from meditation to repentance to charitable works. I think it would be interesting and important to evaluate the effects of these in their own right among the faithful as well as to explore the possibility that there are secular equivalents suitable for all.

and usually equally so (Smith & Glass, 1977). However, we need to consider the possibility that the most-useful positive psychology interventions are those that match the specific task to characteristics of the individual person (Peterson, 1996). The parameters of this match are completely unknown at present.

We have been experimenting with positive psychology interventions delivered over the Internet because they are highly cost effective and in principle available to much of the world's population, including those who do not have a positive psychologist living down the block. Skeptics worry—and so do we—that Internet interventions lack the human touch, and they cite the argument from the psychotherapy realm that a close relationship between a therapist and a client, the so-called therapeutic alliance, is a prerequisite for any treatment to work (Bordin, 1979). Perhaps positive interventions are different because they have less resistance to overcome. Perhaps not. In any event, the next generation of our Internet interventions will be interactive and feature a virtual counselor.

Is a Psychological Utopia Possible?

Never doubt that a small group of thoughtful, committed people can change the world. Indeed, it is the only thing that ever has.
—MARGARET MEAD (N.D.)

I have been discussing positive psychology interventions that focus on the individual, which follows from my stance as a psychologist. The problem is that there are lots of people who might benefit from deliberate attempts to make them happier, and changing the world one person at a time is daunting. Maybe this patient approach will suffice to create a psychological utopia. Once a sufficient number of people have been changed, perhaps a critical mass will be reached that will drag the rest of us along to a better world (Gladwell, 2000).

We can imagine more-efficient strategies. One of the things we are doing at the University of Pennsylvania Positive Psychology Center is teaching positive psychology to coaches, counselors, and clinicians—training the trainers, as it were, and presumably mushrooming the consequences. It is also possible to mount interventions at the level of the group or the community, creating the social settings that enable the psychological good life. To do so will require concerted effort and societal conviction that this is worth doing. Everything has a price, including utopia. The research surveyed in this book shows that the sorts of topics of concern to positive psychology matter not just for making people feel better but also for making them more productive and more healthy. Maybe these findings, if sufficiently disseminated, will convince policy makers in the private and public sectors that positive psychology is worth taking very seriously.

Indeed, it would be risky to treat avowed happiness as the only criterion by which to judge improvement of the human condition. Remember the possibility that people's statements about their life satisfaction are ultimately relative ones, which means that people's subjective standards are a moving target. We probably need to take into account more-objective bases for judging the attainment of the good life (Nussbaum, 1992; Sen, 1985).

Is Peace a Pipe Dream?

The richer we have become materially, the poorer we have become morally and spiritually. We have learned to fly the air like birds and swim the sea like fish, but we have not learned the simple art of living together as brothers.
—MARTIN LUTHER KING, JR. (1964)

Let me for the time being forget utopia, and ask why we can't all just get along. It has been said that the primary lesson of the 20th century is that there is no them, just us. The challenge of the 21st century is therefore to ask *how* we can all be us.

Conflicts between people and groups of people are sometimes about things—resources and access to resources (Wright, 1999). However regrettable these zero-sum conflicts may be, they are readily understandable. When they play themselves out, they at least result in one satisfied party. But what about conflicts that leave only losers in their wake? The world seems to have too many of these, and you can provide your own examples, at the personal or global level. What does positive psychology have to offer?

If business-as-usual psychology has shied away from what is good in life, it has also been squeamish about evil, at least in the sense of acknowledging it and grappling with it head on. Instead, psychologists try to explain away the bad things that people do by attributing them to ignorance, cognitive errors, and the like. They offer simplistic recommendations that seem more inspired by the Disney channel than by hard-headed science. Psychologists need to acknowledge evil as a real phenomenon urgently in need of investigation.

Philosopher Peter Singer (1981, 1993) has argued that moral progress over the millennia is one of expanding the circle of individuals treated as if their interests are equivalent to one's own, from the family, to the clan, village, state, nation, continent, and eventually all of the world. Most members of democracies today grant the humanity—if not the attractiveness—of every human group on the planet, a fact that may explain why *none* of the more than 200 armed conflicts between nations in the 20th century pitted one democracy against another.

Consider South Africa's Nelson Mandela, who included not only fellow members of the African National Congress in his relevant moral circle but also the White Afrikaners responsible for apartheid and his decades of imprisonment. What is remarkable—and I think extremely encouraging—about the demise of apartheid is that it has ended.

Or consider Abraham Lincoln's second inaugural address, delivered March 4, 1865, in which he called for mercy on the part of those in the North to their brethren in the South:

> With malice toward none, with charity for all, with firmness in the right as God gives us to see the right, let us strive on to finish the work we are in, to bind up the nation's wounds, to care for him who shall have borne the battle and for his widow and his orphan, to do all which may achieve and cherish a just and lasting peace among ourselves and with all nations.

Lincoln could have called for massive retribution and retaliation against the Confederacy, but he did not. And without putting too fine an interpretation on Lincoln's Gettysburg Address, it seems important that he tersely honored all of the men who had died in the battle, not just the fallen Union soldiers.

All of the compassion and information in the world may be less relevant to eventual peace than the simple conviction that "they" are all "us" and that killing them is therefore not an option. As psychologists and as citizens of the world, we all need to embrace this belief and foster it, in ourselves and in others.

RESOURCES

Books and Journals

Frisch, M. (2006). *Quality of life therapy: Applying a life satisfaction approach to positive psychology and cognitive therapy.* Hoboken, NJ: Wiley.
Wright, R. (1999). *Nonzero: The logic of human destiny.* New York: Pantheon.
Bellamy, E. (1888/1960). *Looking backward: 2000–1887.* New York: Signet.
Thoreau, H. D. (1854). *Walden; or, Life in the woods.* Boston: Ticknor & Fields.
Skinner, B. F. (1948). *Walden two.* New York: Macmillan.
Huxley, A. (1932). *Brave new world.* London: Chatto & Windus.
Journal of Peace Psychology

Articles

Seligman, M. E. P. (2003). Foreword: The past and future of positive psychology. In C. L. M. Keyes & J. Haidt (Eds.), *Flourishing: Positive psychology and the life well-lived* (pp. xi–xx). Washington, DC: American Psychological Association.
Linley, P. A., Joseph, S., Harrington, S., & Wood, A. M. (2006). Positive psychology: Past, present, and (possible) future. *Journal of Positive Psychology, 1,* 3–16.

Web Sites

http://www.utoronto.ca/utopia/index.html. This is the Web site for the Society of Utopian Studies, which was "founded in 1975 . . . an international, interdisciplinary association devoted to the study of utopianism in all its forms, with a particular emphasis on literary and experimental utopias."

Films

Mr. Smith Goes to Washington (1939)
The Day the Earth Stood Still (1951)
One Flew Over the Cuckoo's Nest (1975)
Koyaanisqatsi (1983)
ABC News's *Nightline*: "Tipping Point" (2005)

Songs

"I Wonder What Would Happen to This World" (Harry Chapin)
"Imagine" (John Lennon)
"Wouldn't It Be Nice" (Beach Boys)

References

Abelson, R. P., Aronson, E., McGuire, W. J., Newcomb, T. M., Rosenberg, M. J., & Tannenbaum, P. H. (Eds.). (1968). *Theories of cognitive consistency: A sourcebook.* Chicago: Rand McNally.

Abramson, L. Y., Metalsky, G. I., & Alloy, L. B. (1989). Hopelessness depression: A theory-based subtype of depression. *Psychological Review, 96,* 358–372.

Abramson, L. Y., Seligman, M. E. P., & Teasdale, J. D. (1978). Learned helplessness in humans: Critique and reformulation. *Journal of Abnormal Psychology, 87,* 49–74.

Ackermann, R., & DeRubeis, R. J. (1991). Is depressive realism real? *Clinical Psychology Review, 11,* 565–584.

Adams, T., Bezner, J., & Steinhart, M. (1997). The conceptualization and measurement of perceived wellness: Integrating balance across and within dimensions. *American Journal of Health Promotion, 11,* 208–281.

Ader, R., & Cohen, N. (1975). Behaviorally conditioned immunosuppression. *Psychosomatic Medicine, 37,* 333–340.

Ader, R., & Cohen, N. (1993). Psychoneuroimmunology: Conditioning and stress. *Annual Review of Psychology, 44,* 53–85.

Adler, A. (1927). *The theory and practice of individual psychology.* New York: Harcourt, Brace.

Adler, A. (1964). Inferiority feelings and defiance and obedience. In H. L. Ansbacher & R. R. Ansbacher (Eds.), *The individual psychology of Alfred Adler* (pp. 52–55). New York: Harper. (Original work published 1910)

Adler, F. (1956). The value concept in sociology. *American Sociological Review, 62,* 272–279.

Ahadi, S., & Diener, E. (1989). Multiple determinants and effect size. *Journal of Personality and Social Psychology, 56,* 398–406.

Ai, A. L., Bolling, S. F., Peterson, C., Gillespie, B., Jessup, M. G., Behling, B. A., & Pierce, F. (2001). Designing clinical trials on energy healing: Ancient art encounters medical science. *Alternative Therapies and Medicine, 7,* 93–99.

Ainsworth, M. D. S. (1973). The development of infant-mother attachment. In B. M. Caldwell & H. N. Ricciuti (Eds.), *Review of child development research* (Vol. 3, pp. 1–94). Chicago: University of Chicago Press.

Ainsworth, M. D. S., Blehar, M. C., Waters, E., & Wall, S. (1978). *Patterns of attachment: Assessed in the strange situation and at home.* Hillsdale, NJ: Erlbaum.

Ainsworth, M. D. S., & Wittig, B. A. (1969). Attachment and exploratory behavior of one-year-olds in a strange situation. In B. M. Foss (Ed.), *Determinants of infant behavior* (Vol. 4, pp. 111–136). London: Methuen.

Akhtar, S. (1996). "Someday . . . " and "if only . . . " fantasies: Pathological optimism and inordinate nostalgia as related forms of idealization. *Journal of the American Psychoanalytic Association, 44,* 723–753.

Albee, G. W. (1982). Preventing psychopathology and promoting human potential. *American Psychologist, 37,* 1043–1050.

Alessandri, S. M., & Wozniak, R. H. (1989). Continuity and change in intrafamilial agreement in beliefs concerning the adolescent: A follow-up study. *Child Development, 60,* 335–339.

Allison, M., & Duncan, M. (1988). Women, work, and flow. In M. Csikszentmihalyi & I. Csikszentmihalyi (Eds.), *Optimal experience: Psychological studies of flow in consciousness* (pp. 118–137). New York: Cambridge University Press.

Alloy, L. B., & Abramson, L. Y. (1979). Judgment of contingency in depressed and nondepressed college students: Sadder but wiser? *Journal of Experimental Psychology: General, 108,* 441–487.

Allport, G. W. (1921). Personality and character. *Psychological Bulletin, 18,* 441–455.

Allport, G. W. (1927). Concepts of trait and personality. *Psychological Bulletin, 24,* 284–293.

Allport, G. W. (1937). *Personality: A psychological interpretation.* New York: Holt.

Allport, G. W. (1950). *The individual and his religion.* New York: Macmillan.

Allport, G. W. (1961). *Pattern and growth in personality.* New York: Holt, Rinehart, & Winston.

Allport, G. W., & Ross, J. M. (1967). Personal religious orientation and prejudice. *Journal of Personality and Social Psychology, 5,* 432–433.

Allport, G. W., & Vernon, P. (1930). The field of personality. *Psychological Bulletin, 27,* 677–730.

Allport, G. W., Vernon, P., & Lindzey, G. (1960). *A study of values* (Rev. ed.). Boston: Houghton Mifflin.

American Psychiatric Association. (1994). *Diagnostic and statistical manual of mental disorders* (4th ed.). Washington, DC: Author.

Anderman, E., & Maehr, M. L. (1994). Motivation and schooling in the middle grades. *Review of Educational Research, 64,* 287–309.

Angner, E. (2005). *The evolution of eupathics: The historical roots of subjective measures of well-being.* Unpublished manuscript. University of Alabama, Birmingham.

Anthony, E. J., & Cohler, B. J. (Eds.). (1987). *The invulnerable child.* New York: Guilford.

Aquinas, T. (1966). *Treatise on the virtues* (J. A. Oesterle, Trans.). Englewood Cliffs, NJ: Prentice-Hall.

Argyle, M. (1996). *The social psychology of leisure.* London: Routledge.

Argyle, M. (1999). Causes and correlates of happiness. In D. Kahneman, E. Diener, & N. Schwarz (Eds.), *Well-being: The foundations of hedonic psychology* (pp. 353–373). New York: Russell Sage.

Argyle, M. (2001). *The psychology of happiness* (2nd ed.). East Sussex, England: Routledge.

Aristotle. (2000). *The Nicomachean ethics* (R. Crisp, Trans.). Cambridge: Cambridge University Press.

Arnett, J. J. (1999). Adolescent storm and stress, reconsidered. *American Psychologist, 54,* 317–326.

Asch, S. E. (1956). Studies of independence and conformity: A minority of one against a unanimous majority. *Psychological Monographs, 70*(9).

Ashbrook, J. B., & Albright, C. A. (1997). *The humanizing brain: Where religion and neuroscience meet.* Cleveland, OH: Pilgrim.

Ashby, F. G., Isen, A. M., & Turken, A. U. (1999). A neuropsychological theory of positive affect and its influence on cognition. *Psychological Review, 106,* 529–550.

Aspinwall, L. G., & Brunhart, S. M. (1996). Distinguishing optimism from denial: Optimistic beliefs predict attention to health threats. *Personality and Social Psychology Bulletin, 22,* 993–1003.

Aspinwall, L. G., & Richter, L. (1999). Optimism and self-mastery predict more rapid disengagement from unsolvable tasks in the presence of alternatives. *Motivation and Emotion, 23,* 221–245.

Averill, J. R., Catlin, G., & Chon, K. K. (1990). *Rules of hope.* New York: Springer-Verlag.

Axinn, W. G., & Thornton, A. (1993). Mothers, children, and cohabitation: The intergenerational effects of attitudes and behavior. *American Sociological Review, 58,* 233–246.

Bailey, K. D. (1994). *Typologies and taxonomies: An introduction to classification techniques.* Thousand Oaks, CA: Sage.

Baker, D., & Stauth, C. (2003). *What happy people know: How the new science of happiness can change your life for the better.* New York: St. Martin's.

Baker, W. (2005). *America's crisis of values: Reality and perception.* Princeton, NJ: Princeton University Press.

Ball, S. (1976). Methodological problems in assessing the impact of television programs. *Journal of Social Issues, 32*(4), 8–17.

Ball-Rokeach, S. J., Rokeach, M., & Grube, J. W. (1984). *The great American values test: Influencing behavior and belief through television.* New York: Free Press.

Baltes, P. B., & Staudinger, U. M. (2000). Wisdom: A metaheuristic (pragmatic) to orchestrate mind and virtue toward excellence. *American Psychologist, 55,* 122–136.

Bandura, A. (1969). *Principles of behavior modification.* New York: Holt, Rinehart, & Winston.

Bandura, A. (1989). Human agency in social cognitive theory. *American Psychologist, 14,* 175–184.

Barkow, J. H. (1997). Happiness in evolutionary perspective. In N. L. Segal, G. E. Weisfeld, & C. C. Weisfeld (Eds.), *Uniting psychology and biology: Integrating perspectives on human development* (pp. 397–418). Washington, DC: American Psychological Association.

Barlow, F. (1952). *Mental prodigies.* New York: Philosophical Library.

Barrett, P. M., & Ollendick, T. H. (Eds.). (2004). *Handbook of interventions that work with children and adolescents: Prevention and treatment.* West Sussex, England: Wiley.

Barsky, A. J. (1988). *Worried sick: Our troubled quest for wellness.* Boston: Little, Brown.

Bartels, A., & Zeki, S. (2000). The neural basis of romantic love. *NeuroReport, 11,* 3829–3834.

Bartels, A., & Zeki, S. (2004). The neural correlates of maternal and romantic love. *NeuroImage, 21,* 1155–1166.

Barth, F. (1993). Are values real? The enigma of naturalism in the anthropological imputation of values. In M. Hechter, L. Nadel, & R. E. Michod (Eds.), *The origin of values* (pp. 31–46). New York: de Gruyter.

Baruch, G., Barnett, R., & Rivers, C. (1983). *Life prints: New patterns of love and work for today's woman.* New York: McGraw-Hill.

Batten, H. L., & Prottas, J. M. (1987). Kind strangers: The families of organ donors. *Health Affairs, 6,* 325–347.

Baumrind, D. (1971). Current patterns of parental authority. *Developmental Psychology Monographs, 4*(1), Part 2.

Baumrind, D. (1978). Parental disciplinary patterns and social comparison in children. *Youth and Society, 9,* 239–276.

Baylis, N. (2004). Teaching positive psychology. In P. A. Linley & S. Joseph (Eds.), *Positive psychology in practice* (pp. 210–217). New York: Wiley.

Beck, A. T. (1967). *Depression: Clinical, experimental, and theoretical aspects.* New York: Hoeber.

Beck, A. T. (1991). Cognitive therapy: A 30-year retrospective. *American Psychologist, 46,* 368–375.

Beck, A. T., Rush, A. J., Shaw, B. F., & Emery, G. (1979). *Cognitive therapy of depression.* New York: Guilford.

Becker, S. W., & Eagly, A. H. (2004). The heroism of women and men. *American Psychologist,* 59, *163–178.*

Becker, W. C. (1964). Consequences of different types of parental discipline. In M. L. Hoffman & L. W. Hoffman (Eds.), *Review of child development research* (Vol. 1, pp. 509–535). New York: Russell Sage.

Beit-Hallahmi, B. (1974). Psychology of religion 1880–1930: The rise and fall of a psychological movement. *Journal of the History of the Behavioral Sciences, 10,* 84–90.

Bell, R. M. (1985). *Holy anorexia.* Chicago: University of Chicago Press.

Belloc, N. B. (1973). Relationship of health practices and mortality. *Preventive Medicine, 2,* 67–81.

Belloc, N. B., & Breslow, L. (1972). Relationship of physical health status and family practices. *Preventive Medicine, 1,* 409–421.

Benard, B. (1991). *Fostering resiliency in kids: Protective factors in the family, school and community.* San Francisco, CA: Western Regional Center for Drug Free Schools and Communities, Far West Laboratory.

Bentley, K. S., & Fox, R. A. (1991). Mothers and fathers of young children: Comparison of parenting styles. *Psychological Reports, 69,* 320–322.

Berenbaum, H., Raghavan, C., Le, H.-N., Vernon, L., & Gomez, J. (1999). Disturbances in emotion. In D. Kahneman, E. Diener, & N. Schwarz (Eds.), *Well-being: The foundations of hedonic psychology* (pp. 267–287). New York: Russell Sage.

Berger, D., Ono, Y., Kumano, H., & Suematsu, H. (1994). The Japanese concept of interdependency. *American Journal of Psychiatry, 151,* 628–629.

Berkman, L. F., Glass, T., Brisette, I., & Seeman, T. E. (2000). From social integration to health: Durkheim in the new millennium. *Social Science and Medicine, 51,* 843–857.

Berkowitz, M. W., & Bier, M. C. (2004). Research-based character education. *Annals of the American Academy of Political and Social Science, 591,* 72–85.

Berlyne, D. E. (1960). *Conflict, arousal, and curiosity.* New York: McGraw-Hill.

Berscheid, E. (1994). Interpersonal relationships. *Annual Review of Psychology, 45,* 79–129.

Berscheid, E., & Reis, H. T. (1998). Attraction and close relationships. In D. T. Gilbert, S. T. Fiske, & G. Lindzey (Eds.), *The handbook of social psychology* (4th ed., Vol. 2, pp. 193–281). New York: McGraw-Hill.

Berscheid, E., & Walster, E. (1978). *Interpersonal attraction* (2nd ed.). Reading, MA: Addison-Wesley.

Bierce, A. (1999). *The devil's dictionary.* New York: Oxford University Press. (Original work published 1911)

Billingsley, A. (1999). *Mighty like a river: The Black church and social reform.* New York: Oxford University Press.

Billingsley, A., & Caldwell, C. (1991). The church, the family and the school in the African American community. *Journal of Negro Education, 60,* 427–440.

Biswas-Diener, R. (in press). From the equator to the north pole: A study of character strengths. *Journal of Happiness Studies.*

Biswas-Diener, R., & Diener, E. (2001). Making the best of a bad situation: Satisfaction in the slums of Calcutta. *Social Indicators Research, 55,* 329–352.

Bok, S. (1995). *Common values.* Columbia: University of Missouri Press.

Bonnano, G. A. (2004). Loss, trauma, and human resilience: Have we underestimated the human capacity to thrive after extremely aversive events? *American Psychologist, 59,* 20–28.

Booth, R. (1983). Toward an understanding of loneliness. *Social Work, 28,* 116–119.

Bordin, E. S. (1979). The generalizability of the psychoanalytic concept of the working alliance. *Psychotherapy: Theory, Research, and Practice, 16,* 252–260.

Boring, E. G. (1950). *A history of experimental psychology* (2nd ed.). New York: Appleton-Century-Crofts.

Bouchard, T. J., Jr. (2004). Genetic influence on human psychological traits: A survey. *Current Directions in Psychological Science, 13,* 148–151.

Boucher, J., & Osgood, C. E. (1969). The Pollyanna hypothesis. *Journal of Verbal Learning and Verbal Behavior, 8,* 1–8.

Bower, D. W., & Christopherson, V. A. (1977). University student cohabitation: A regional comparison of selected attitudes and behavior. *Journal of Marriage and the Family, 39,* 447–453.

Bowlby, J. (1951). *Maternal care and mental health.* Geneva, Switzerland: World Health Organization.

Bowlby, J. (1969). *Attachment and loss: Vol. 1. Attachment.* New York: Basic.

Bowlby, J. (1973). *Attachment and loss: Vol. 2. Separation: Anxiety and anger.* New York: Basic.

Bowlby, J. (1979). *The making and breaking of affectional bonds.* London: Tavistock.

Bowlby, J. (1980). *Attachment and loss: Vol. 3. Loss, sadness, and depression.* New York: Basic.

Bradburn, N. M. (1969). *The structure of psychological well-being.* Chicago: Aldine.

Braithwaite, V. A., & Law, H. G. (1985). Structure of human values: Testing the adequacy of the Rokeach Value Survey. *Journal of Personality and Social Psychology, 49,* 250–263.

Braithwaite, V. A., & Scott, W. A. (1991). Values. In J. P. Robinson, P. Shaver, & L. Wrightsman (Eds.), *Measures of personality and social psychology attitudes* (pp. 661–753). New York: Academic.

Brennan, K. A., & Bosson, J. K. (1998). Attachment-style differences in attitudes toward and reactions to feedback from romantic partners: An exploration of the relational bases of self-esteem. *Personality and Social Psychology Bulletin, 24,* 699–714.

Brennan, K. A., & Shaver, P. R. (1995). Dimensions of adult attachment, affect regulation, and romantic relationship functioning. *Personality and Social Psychology Bulletin, 23,* 23–31.

Brickman, P., & Campbell, D. T. (1971). Hedonic relativism and planning the good society. In M. H. Appley (Ed.), *Adaptation-level theory* (pp. 287–305). New York: Academic.

Brickman, P., Coates, D., & Janoff-Bulman, R. (1978). Lottery winners and accident victims: Is happiness relative? *Journal of Personality and Social Psychology, 36,* 917–927.

Brief, A. P., & Nord, W. R. (Eds.). (1990). *Meanings of occupational work: A collection of essays.* Lexington, MA: Lexington.

Brokaw, T. (1998). *The greatest generation.* New York: Random House.

Brothers, L. (1990). The neural basis of primate social communication. *Motivation and Emotion, 14,* 81–91.

Browder, S. (1988, June). Is living together such a good idea? *New Woman,* pp. 120–124.

Brown, B. B. (1981). A life-span approach to friendship: Age-related dimensions of an ageless relationship. In H. Lopata & D. Maines (Eds.), *Research in the interweave of social roles* (Vol. 2, pp. 23–50). Greenwich, CT: JAI.

Brown, G. W., & Harris, T. O. (1978). *Social origins of depression.* New York: Free Press.

Brown, R. (1954). Mass phenomena. In G. Lindzey (Ed.), *Handbook of social psychology* (Vol. 2, pp. 833–877). Cambridge, MA: Addison-Wesley.

Brown, R., & Kulik, J. (1977). Flashbulb memories. *Cognition, 5,* 73–99.

Brown, S. L., Nesse, R. M., Vinokur, A. D., & Smith, D. M. (2003). Providing social support may be more beneficial than receiving it: Results from a prospective study of mortality. *Psychological Science, 14,* 320–327.

Bruyer, R. (1981). L'asymetrie du visage humain: Etat de la question. *Psychologica Belgica, 21,* 7–15.

Bryant, F. B. (2001, October 6). *Capturing the joy of the moment: Savoring as a process in positive psychology.* Paper presented at the 3rd Annual Positive Psychology Summit, Washington, DC.

Bryant, F. B. (2003). Savoring Beliefs Inventory (SBI): A scale for measuring beliefs about savoring. *Journal of Mental Health, 12,* 175–196.

Bryant, F. B. (in press). *The process of savoring: A new model of positive experience.* Mahwah, NJ: Erlbaum.
Buchanan, G. M., & Seligman, M. E. P. (Eds.). (1995). *Explanatory style.* Hillsdale, NJ: Erlbaum.
Buckingham, M., & Clifton, D. O. (2001). *Now, discover your strengths.* New York: Free Press.
Buckingham, M., & Coffman, C. (1999). *First, break all the rules.* New York: Simon & Schuster.
Bungam, T. J., Osark, K. C., & Chang, C. L. (1997). Factors affecting exercise adherence at a worksite wellness program. *American Journal of Health Behavior, 21,* 60–66.
Burrell, B. (1997). *The words we live by.* New York: Free Press.
Bursten, B. (1979). Psychiatry and the rhetoric of models. *American Journal of Psychiatry, 136,* 661–666.
Buss, D. M. (1987). Selection, evocation, and manipulation. *Journal of Personality and Social Psychology, 53,* 1214–1221.
Buss, D. M. (1991). Evolutionary personality psychology. *Annual Review of Psychology, 42,* 459–491.
Buss, D. M. (1995). Evolutionary psychology: A new paradigm for psychological science. *Psychological Inquiry, 6,* 1–30.
Buss, D. M. (2000). The evolution of happiness. *American Psychologist, 55,* 15–23.
Buss, D. M., et al. (1990). International preferences in selecting mates: A study of 37 cultures. *Journal of Cross-Cultural Psychology, 21,* 5–47.
Buss, D. M., Larsen, R. J., Westen, D., & Semmelroth, J. (1992). Sex differences in jealousy: Evolution, physiology, and psychology. *Psychological Science, 3,* 251–255.
Buss, D., & Schmitt, D. P. (1993). Sexual strategies theory: An evolutionary perspective on human mating. *Psychological Review, 100,* 204–232.
Butcher, J. N., Dahlstrom, W. G., Graham, J. R., Tellegen, A., & Kaemmer, B. (1989). *Manual for the restandardized Minnesota Multiphasic Personality Inventory: MMPI-2. An interpretative and administrative guide.* Minneapolis: University of Minnesota Press.
Buunk, B. P., Van Yperen, N. W., Taylor, S. E., & Collins, R. L. (1991). Social comparison and the drive upward revisited: Affiliation as a response to marital stress. *European Journal of Social Psychology, 21,* 529–546.
Byrne, D. (1971). *The attraction paradigm.* New York: Academic.
Cameron, K. S., Dutton, J. E., & Quinn, R. E. (Eds.). (2003). *Positive organizational scholarship: Foundations of a new discipline.* San Francisco: Berrett-Koehler.
Campbell, A. (1981). *The sense of well-being in America: Recent patterns and trends.* New York: McGraw-Hill.
Campbell, A., Converse, P. E., & Rodgers, W. L. (1976). *The quality of American life.* New York: Sage.
Campbell, D. P. (1971). *Manual for the Strong Vocational Interest Blank.* Stanford, CA: Stanford University Press.
Campbell, D. T., & Fiske, D. W. (1959). Convergent and discriminant validation by the multitrait-multimethod matrix. *Psychological Bulletin, 56,* 81–105.
Cantril, H. (1965). *The pattern of human concerns.* New Brunswick, NJ: Rutgers University Press.

Cappella, J. N. (1993). The facial feedback hypothesis in human interaction: Review and speculation. *Journal of Language and Social Psychology, 12,* 13–29.

Carnelley, K. B., Pietromonaco, P. R., & Jaffe, K. (1994). Depression, working models of others, and relationship functioning. *Journal of Personality and Social Psychology, 66,* 127–140.

Carson, R. C. (2001). *Depressive realism: Continuous monitoring of contingency judgments among depressed outpatients and non-depressed controls.* Unpublished doctoral dissertation, Vanderbilt University.

Carter, C. S. (1998). Neuroendocrine perspectives on social attachment and love. *Psychoneuroendocrinology, 23,* 779–818.

Carver, C. S., Pozo, C., Harris, S. D., Noriega, V., Scheier, M. F., Robinson, D. S., Ketcham, A. S., Moffat, F. L., & Clark, K. C. (1993). How coping mediates the effect of optimism on distress: A study of women with early stage breast cancer. *Journal of Personality and Social Psychology, 65,* 375–390.

Carver, C. S., & Scheier, M. F. (1981). *Attention and self-regulation: A control-theory approach to human behavior.* New York: Springer-Verlag.

Carver, C. S., & Scheier, M. F. (1990). Origins and functions of positive and negative affect: A control-process view. *Psychological Review, 97,* 19–35.

Carver, C. S., & Scheier, M. F. (2003). Optimism. In S. J. Lopez & C. R. Snyder (Eds.), *Positive psychological assessment: A handbook of models and measures* (pp. 75–89). Washington, DC: American Psychological Association.

Cassel, J. (1976). The contribution of the social environment to host resistance. *American Journal of Epidemiology, 104,* 107–123.

Castro-Martin, T., & Bumpass, L. (1989). Recent trends in marital disruption. *Demography,* 26, 37–51.

Cattell, R. B. (1944). Psychological measurement: Normative, ipsative, interactive. *Psychological Review, 51,* 292–303.

Cawley, M. J., Martin, J. E., & Johnson, J. A. (2000). A virtues approach to personality. *Personality and Individual Differences, 28,* 997–1013.

Chang, E. C. (1996). Evidence for the cultural specificity of pessimism in Asians versus Caucasians: A test of a general negativity hypothesis. *Personality and Individual Differences, 21,* 819–822.

Chapin, M. H., & Kewman, D. G. (2001). Factors affecting employment following spinal cord injury: A qualitative study. *Rehabilitation Psychology, 46,* 400–416.

Chapman, L. J., Chapman, J. P., & Miller, E. N. (1982). Reliabilities and intercorrelations of eight measures of proneness to psychosis. *Journal of Consulting and Clinical Psychology, 50,* 187–195.

Cialdini, R. B. (1985). *Influence: Science and practice.* Glenview, IL: Scott, Foresman.

Clark, C., Worthington, E., & Danser, D. (1988). The transmission of religious beliefs and practices from parents to firstborn early adolescent sons. *Journal of Marriage and the Family, 50,* 463–472.

Clark, D., & Watson, D. (1999). Temperament: A new paradigm for trait psychology. In L. A. Pervin & O. P. John (Eds.), *Handbook of personality* (2nd ed., pp. 399–423). New York: Guilford.

Clark, M. S., & Mills, J. (1979). Interpersonal attraction in exchange and communal relationships. *Journal of Personality and Social Psychology, 37,* 12–24.

Clarke-Stewart, K. A., Friedman, S., & Koch, J. (1985). *Child development: A topical approach.* New York: Wiley.

Cobb, S. (1976). Social support as a moderator of life stress. *Psychosomatic Medicine, 38,* 300–314.

Cohen, A. B., & Rozin, P. (2001). Religion and the morality of mentality. *Journal of Personality and Social Psychology, 81,* 697–710.

Cohen, S. (1988). Psychosocial models of the role of social support in the etiology of physical disease. *Health Psychology, 7,* 269–297.

Cohen, S., Tyrell, D. A. J., & Smith, A. P. (1991). Psychological stress and susceptibility to the common cold. *New England Journal of Medicine, 325,* 606–612.

Cohn, M. A. (2004). Rescuing our heroes: Positive perspectives on upward comparisons in relationships, education, and work. In P. A. Linley & S. Joseph (Eds.), *Positive psychology in practice* (pp. 218–237). New York: Wiley.

Colin, V. L. (1996). *Human attachment.* New York: McGraw-Hill.

Collaborative for Academic, Social, and Emotional Learning (CASEL). (2002). *Safe and sound: An education leader's guide to evidence-based social and emotional learning programs.* Chicago: Author.

Collier, P. (2003). *Medal of Honor: Portraits of valor beyond the call of duty.* New York: Workman.

Collins, J. C. (2001). *Good to great.* New York: HarperCollins.

Collins, J. C., & Porras, J. I. (1997). *Built to last.* New York: HarperCollins.

Comfort, A. (1972). *The joy of sex: A gourmet's guide to lovemaking.* London: Mitchell Beazley.

Compton, W. C., Smith, M. L., Cornish, K. A., & Qualls, D. L. (1996). Factor structure of mental health measures. *Journal of Personality and Social Psychology, 71,* 406–413.

Comte-Sponville, A. (2001). *A small treatise on the great virtues* (C. Temerson, Trans.). New York: Metropolitan.

Confucius. (1992). *Analects* (D. Hinton, Trans.). Washington, DC: Counterpoint.

Costa, P. T., Jr., & McCrae, R. R. (1992). Trait psychology comes of age. In T. B. Sonderegger (Ed.), *Nebraska symposium on motivation: Psychology and aging* (pp. 169–204). Lincoln: University of Nebraska Press.

Cousins, N. (1976). Anatomy of an illness (as perceived by the patient). *New England Journal of Medicine, 295,* 1458–1463.

Cowan, P., Cowan, C., Coie, J., & Coie, L. (1978). Becoming a family: The impact of a first child's birth on the couple's relationship. In L. Newman & W. Miller (Eds.), *The first child and family formation* (pp. 296–324). Chapel Hill, NC: University of North Carolina Press.

Cowen, E. L. (1994). The enhancement of psychological wellness: Challenges and opportunities. *American Journal of Community Psychology, 22,* 149–179.

Cowen, E. L. (1997). Schools and the enhancement of children's wellness: Some opportunities and some limiting factors. In T. P. Gullota, R. P. Weissberg, R. L. Hampton, B. A. Ryan, & G. R. Adams (Eds.), *Healthy children 2010: Establishing preventive services* (pp. 87–123). Thousand Oaks, CA: Sage.

Cowen, E. L., & Kilmer, R. P. (2002). "Positive psychology": Some plusses and some open issues. *Journal of Community Psychology, 30,* 440–460.

Crews, D. J., & Landers, D. M. (1987). A meta-analytic review of aerobic fitness and reactivity to psychosocial stressors. *Medicine and Science in Sports and Exercise, 19*(Suppl. 5), S114–S120.

Cronbach, L. J. (1951). Coefficient alpha and the internal structure of tests. *Psychometrika, 16*, 297–334.

Crowne, D. P., & Marlowe, D. (1964). *The approval motive: Studies in evaluative dependence.* New York: Wiley.

Csikszentmihalyi, I. (1988). Flow in a historical context: The case of the Jesuits. In M. Csikszentmihalyi & I. Csikszentmihalyi (Eds.), *Optimal experience: Psychological studies of flow in consciousness* (pp. 232–248). New York: Cambridge University Press.

Csikszentmihalyi, M. (1990). *Flow: The psychology of optimal experience.* New York: Harper & Row.

Csikszentmihalyi, M. (1999). If we are so rich, why aren't we happy? *American Psychologist, 54*, 821–827.

Csikszentmihalyi, M. (2000). *Beyond boredom and anxiety.* San Francisco: Jossey-Bass. (Original work published 1975)

Cunningham, J. D., & Antill, J. K. (1994). Cohabitation and marriage: Retrospective and predictive comparisons. *Journal of Social and Personal Relationships, 11*, 77–93.

Cunningham, M. R. (1979). Weather, mood, and helping behavior: Quasi experiments with the sunshine Samaritan. *Journal of Personality and Social Psychology, 37*, 1947–1956.

Cunningham, M. R. (1986). Measuring the physical in physical attractiveness: Quasi-experiments on the sociobiology of female facial beauty. *Journal of Personality and Social Psychology, 50*, 925–935.

Curtiss, S. (1977). *Genie: A psycholinguistic study of a modern-day wild child.* New York: Academic.

Cushman, L. A., & Hassett, J. (1992). Spinal cord injury: 10 and 15 years after. *Paraplegia, 30*, 690–696.

Dahlback, O. (1991). Accident-proneness and risk-taking. *Personality and Individual Differences, 12*, 79–85.

Dahlsgaard, K., Peterson, C., & Seligman, M. E. P. (2005). Shared virtue: The convergence of valued human strengths across culture and history. *Review of General Psychology, 9*, 203–213.

Damon, W. (1988). *The moral child: Nurturing children's natural moral growth.* New York: Free Press.

Damon, W. (2004). What is positive youth development? *Annals of the American Academy of Political and Social Science, 591*, 13–24.

Danner, D. D., Snowdon, D., & Friesen, W. V. (2001). Positive emotions in early life and longevity: Findings from the nun study. *Journal of Personality and Social Psychology, 80*, 804–813.

Darling, C. A., Davidson, J. K., & Jennings, D. A. (1991). The female sexual response revisited: Understanding the multiorgasmic experience in women. *Archives of Sexual Behavior, 20*, 527–540.

Daruna, J. H. (2004). *Introduction to psychoneuroimmunology.* San Diego, CA: Elsevier Academic.

Darwall, S. L., Gibbard, A., & Railton, P. (1992). Toward fin de siècle ethics: Some trends. *Philosophical Review, 101*, 115–189.

Darwin, C. (1859). *The origin of species.* London: Murray.

Darwin, C. (1872). *The expression of the emotions in man and animals.* London: Murray.

Davidson, R. J. (1984). Hemispheric asymmetry and emotion. In K. R. Scherer & P. Ekman (Eds.), *Approaches to emotion* (pp. 39–57). Hillsdale, NJ: Erlbaum.

Davidson, R. J. (1992). Emotion and affective style: Hemispheric substrates. *Psychological Science, 3,* 39–43.

Davidson, R. J. (1993). The neuropsychology of emotions and affective style. In M. Lewis & J. M. Haviland (Eds.), *Handbook of emotions* (pp. 143–154). New York: Guilford.

Davidson, R. J. (1999). Neuropsychological perspectives on affective styles and their cognitive consequences. In T. Dalgleish & M. Power (Eds.), *The handbook of cognition and emotion* (pp. 103–123). Sussex, England: Wiley.

Deci, E. L. (1975). *Intrinsic motivation.* New York: Plenum.

Deci, E. L., & Ryan, R. M. (2000). The "what" and "why" of goal pursuits: Human needs and the self-determination of behavior. *Psychological Inquiry, 11,* 227–268.

Delle Fave, A., & Massimini, F. (1992). The ESM and the measurement of clinical change: A case of anxiety disorder. In M. deVries (Ed.), *The experience of psychopathology* (pp. 280–289). Cambridge: Cambridge University Press.

DeMartini, J. R. (1983). Social movement participation: Political socialization, generational consciousness, and lasting effects. *Social Forces, 64,* 1–16.

Dennett, D. C. (1991). *Consciousness explained.* Boston: Little, Brown.

Derryberry, D., & Tucker, D. M. (1992). Neural mechanisms of emotion. *Journal of Consulting and Clinical Psychology, 60,* 329–338.

Dewey, J. (1998). *Human nature and conduct.* Carbondale and Edwardsville: Southern Illinois University Press. (Original work published 1922)

Diener, E. (1984). Subjective well-being. *Psychological Bulletin, 95,* 542–575.

Diener, E. (1994). Assessing subjective well-being: Progress and opportunities. *Social Indicators Research, 31,* 103–157.

Diener, E. (2000). Subjective well-being: The science of happiness and a proposal for a national index. *American Psychologist, 55,* 34–43.

Diener, E. (2005, June 28). *Subjective well-being and marginal utility.* Lecture given at the Positive Psychology Center, University of Pennsylvania, Philadelphia.

Diener, E., & Diener, C. (1996). Most people are happy. *Psychological Science, 7,* 181–185.

Diener, E., Diener, M., & Diener, C. (1995). Factors predicting the subjective well-being of nations. *Journal of Personality and Social Psychology, 49,* 851–864.

Diener, E., Emmons, R. A., Larsen, R. J., & Griffin, S. (1985). The Satisfaction with Life Scale. *Journal of Personality Assessment, 49,* 71–75.

Diener, E., Horwitz, J., & Emmons, R. A. (1985). Happiness of the very wealthy. *Social Indicators Research, 16,* 229–259.

Diener, E., & Larsen, R. J. (1984). Temporal stability and cross-situational consistency of affective, behavioral, and cognitive responses. *Journal of Personality and Social Psychology, 47,* 871–883.

Diener, E., & Lucas, R. E. (2000). Explaining differences in societal levels of happiness: Relative standards, need fulfillment, culture, and evaluation theory. *Journal of Happiness Studies, 1,* 41–78.

Diener, E., & Seligman, M. E. P. (2002). Very happy people. *Psychological Science, 13,* 80–83.

Diener, E., & Seligman, M. E. P. (2004). Beyond money: Toward an economy of well-being. *Psychological Science in the Public Interest, 5,* 1–31.

Diener, E., & Suh, E. M. (2000). Measuring subjective well-being to compare the quality of life of cultures. In E. Diener & E. M. Suh (Eds.), *Culture and subjective well-being* (pp. 3–12). Cambridge, MA: MIT Press.

Diener, E., Suh, E. M., Lucas, R. E., & Smith, H. (1999). Subjective well-being: Three decades of progress. *Psychological Bulletin, 125,* 276–302.

Diener, E., Suh, E. M., Smith, H., & Shao, L. (1995). National differences in reported subjective well-being: Why do they occur? *Social Indicators Research, 34,* 7–12.

Dion, K., Berscheid, E., & Walster, E. (1972). What is beautiful is good. *Journal of Personality and Social Psychology, 24,* 285–290.

Dobson, K. S., & Pusch, D. (1995). A test of the depressive realism hypothesis in clinically depressed subjects. *Cognitive Therapy and Research, 19,* 170–194.

Doi, T. (1973). *The anatomy of dependence.* Tokyo: Kodansha International.

Doris, J. M. (2002). *Lack of character: Personality and moral behavior.* Cambridge: Cambridge University Press.

Duchenne, G.-B. (1990). *The mechanism of human facial expression* (R. A. Cuthbertson, Ed. & Trans.). Cambridge: Cambridge University Press. (Original work published 1862)

Dukes, W. F. (1955). Psychological studies of values. *Psychological Bulletin, 52,* 24–50.

Dulin, P., & Hill, R. (2003). Relationships between altruistic activity and positive and negative affect among lower-income older adult service providers. *Aging and Mental Health, 7,* 294–299.

Dunker, K. (1941). On pleasure, emotion, and striving. *Philosophy and Phenomenological Research, 1,* 391–430.

Durbin, D. L., Darling, N., Steinberg, L., & Brown, B. B. (1993). Parenting style and peer group membership among European-American adolescents. *Journal of Research on Adolescence, 3,* 87–100.

Dutton, D. G., Saunders, K., Starzomski, A., & Bartholomew, K. (1994). Intimacy-anger and insecure attachment as precursors of abuse in intimate relationships. *Journal of Applied Social Psychology, 24,* 1367–1386.

Dykema, K., Bergbower, K., & Peterson, C. (1995). Pessimistic explanatory style, stress, and illness. *Journal of Social and Clinical Psychology, 14,* 357–371.

Easterbrook, G. (2001, March 5). I'm OK, you're OK. *New Republic,* pp. 20–23.

Easterbrook, G. (2003). *The progress paradox: How life gets better while people feel worse.* New York: Random House.

Eccles, J. S., & Barber, B. L. (1999). Student council, volunteering, basketball, or marching band: What kind of extracurricular involvement matters? *Journal of Adolescent Research, 14,* 10–43.

Eccles, J. S., & Gootman, J. A. (Eds.). (2002). *Community programs to promote youth development.* Washington, DC: National Academy Press.

Egloff, B., Tausch, A., Kohlmann, C.-W., & Krohne, H. W. (1995). Relationships between time of day, day of the week, and positive mood: Exploring the role of the mood measure. *Motivation and Emotion, 19,* 99–110.

Eid, M., & Diener, E. (2004). Global judgments of subjective well-being: Situational variability and long-term stability. *Social Indicators Research, 65,* 245–277.

Eisenberger, R. (1992). Learned industriousness. *Psychological Review, 99,* 248–267.
Ekman, P. (1993). Facial expression and emotion. *American Psychologist, 48,* 384–392.
Elder, G. H. (1969). Appearance and education in marriage mobility. *American Sociological Review, 34,* 519–533.
Elias, M. J., & Weissberg, R. P. (2000). Wellness in the schools: The grandfather of primary prevention tells a story. In D. Cicchetti, J. R. Rappaport, I. Sandler, & R. P. Weissberg (Eds.), *The promotion of wellness in children and adolescents* (pp. 243–269). Washington, DC: CWLA.
Elias, M. J., Zins, J., Weissberg, R. P., Frey, K., Greenberg, M., Haynes, N., Kessler, R., Schwab-Stone, M., & Shriver, T. (1997). *Promoting social and emotional learning: Guidelines for educators.* Alexandria, VA: Association for Supervision and Curriculum Development.
Elicker, J., Englund, M., & Sroufe, L. A. (1992). Predicting peer competence and peer relationships in childhood from early parent-child relationships. In R. D. Parke & G. W. Ladd (Eds.), *Family-peer relationships: Models of linkage* (pp. 77–106). Hillsdale, NJ: Erlbaum.
Elkins, L. E., & Peterson, C. (1993). Gender differences in best friendships. *Sex Roles, 29,* 497–508.
Elliot, A. J., & McGregor, H. M. (2001). A 2 x 2 achievement goal framework. *Journal of Personality and Social Psychology, 80,* 501–519.
Elliot, T. R., & Frank, R. G. (1996). Depression following spinal cord injury. *Archives of Physical Medicine and Rehabilitation, 77,* 816–823.
Emmons, R. A., & Crumpler, C. A. (2000). Gratitude as a human strength: Appraising the evidence. *Journal of Social and Clinical Psychology, 19,* 56–69.
Emmons, R. A., & McCullough, M. E. (2003). Counting blessings versus burdens: Experimental studies of gratitude and subjective well-being in daily life. *Journal of Personality and Social Psychology, 84,* 377–389.
Emmons, R. A., & Paloutzian, R. F. (2003). The psychology of religion. *Annual Review of Psychology, 54,* 377–402.
England, G. W., & Whitely, W. T. (1990). Cross-national meanings of working. In A. P. Brief & W. R. Nord (Eds.), *Meanings of occupational work: A collection of essays* (pp. 65–106). Lexington, MA: Lexington.
Epstein, L. H., Wing, R. R., Koeske, R., & Valoski, A. (1987). Long-term effects of family-based treatment of childhood obesity. *Journal of Consulting and Clinical Psychology, 55,* 91–95.
Epstein, S. (1989). Values from the perspective of cognitive-experiential self-theory. In N. Eisenberg, J. Reykowski, & E. Staub (Eds.), *Social and moral values: Individual and social perspectives* (pp. 3–22). Hillsdale, NJ: Erlbaum.
Erikson, E. (1963). *Childhood and society* (2nd ed.). New York: Norton.
Erikson, E. (1968). *Identity: Youth and crisis.* New York: Norton.
Erikson, E. (1982). *The life cycle completed.* New York: Norton.
Eron, L. D., Huesmann, L. R., Lefkowitz, M. M., & Walder, L. O. (1972). Does television violence cause aggression? *American Psychologist, 27,* 253–263.
Estepa, A., & Sánchez Cobo, F. T. (2001). Empirical research on the understanding of association and implications for the training of researchers. In C. Batanero (Ed.), *Training researchers in the use of statistics* (pp. 37–51). Granada, Spain:

International Association for Statistical Education and International Statistical Institute.

Evans, D. L., Foa, E. B., Gur, R., Hendrin, H., O'Brien, C., Seligman, M. E. P., & Walsh, B. T. (Eds.). (2005). *Treating and preventing adolescent mental health disorders: What we know and what we don't know.* New York: Oxford University Press, Annenberg Foundation Trust at Sunnylands, and Annenberg Public Policy Center of the University of Pennsylvania.

Eysenck, H. J. (1952). The effects of psychotherapy: An evaluation. *Journal of Consulting Psychology, 16,* 319–324.

Farquhar, J. W., Maccoby, N., & Solomon, D. (1984). Community applications of behavioral medicine. In W. D. Gentry (Ed.), *Handbook of behavioral medicine* (pp. 437–478). New York: Guilford.

Fatsis, S. (2001). *Word freak: Heartbreak, triumph, genius, and obsession in the world of competitive Scrabble players.* New York: Houghton Mifflin.

Feeney, J. A. (1999). Adult romantic attachment and couple relationships. In J. Cassidy & P. R. Shaver (Eds.), *Handbook of attachment: Theory, research, and clinical applications* (pp. 355–377). New York: Guilford.

Feingold, A. (1988). Matching for attractiveness in romantic partners and same-sex friends. *Psychological Bulletin, 104,* 226–235.

Feldman, D. H. (1980). *Beyond universals in cognitive development.* Norwood, NJ: Ablex.

Feldman, D. H. (1993). Child prodigies: A distinctive form of giftedness. *Gifted Child Quarterly, 37,* 188–193.

Felner, R. D. (2000). Educational reform as ecologically-based prevention and promotion: The project on high performance learning communities. In D. Cicchetti, J. R. Rappaport, I. Sandler, & R. P. Weissberg (Eds.), *The promotion of wellness in children and adolescents* (pp. 271–308). Washington, DC: CWLA.

Felner, R. D., Felner, T. Y., & Silverman, M. M. (2000). Prevention in mental health and social intervention: Conceptual and methodological issues in the evolution of the science and practice of prevention. In J. Rappaport & E. Seidman (Eds.), *Handbook of community psychology* (pp. 9–42). New York: Kluwer Academic/Plenum.

Festinger, L. (1954). A theory of social comparison processes. *Human Relations, 7,* 117–140.

Festinger, L. (1957). *A theory of cognitive dissonance.* Evanston, IL: Row, Peterson.

Fetzer Institute. (1999). *Multidimensional measurement of religiousness/spirituality for use in health research.* Kalamazoo, MI: Author.

Fineburg, A. C. (2004). Introducing positive psychology to the introductory psychology student. In P. A. Linley & S. Joseph (Eds.), *Positive psychology in practice* (pp. 197–209). New York: Wiley.

Finkel, D., & McGue, M. (1997). Sex differences in nonadditivity of the Multidimensional Personality Questionnaire scales. *Journal of Personality and Social Psychology, 72,* 929–938.

Fiorina, M. P., Abrams, S. J., & Pope, J. C. (2005). *Culture war? The myth of a polarized America.* New York: Pearson Longman.

Fiske, A. P. (1993). Social errors in four cultures: Evidence about universal forms of social relations. *Journal of Cross-Cultural Psychology, 24,* 463–494.

Fiske, S. T., & Taylor, S. E. (1984). *Social cognition.* Reading, MA: Addison-Wesley.

Flanagan, C. A., Jonsson, B., Botcheva, L., Csapo, B., Bowes, J., Macek, P., Averina, I., &

Sheblanova, E. (1998). Adolescents and the "social contract": Developmental roots of citizenship in seven countries. In M. Yates & J. Youniss (Eds.), *Community service and civic engagement in youth: International perspectives* (pp. 135–155). New York: Cambridge University Press.

Flannelly, K. J., Ellison, C. G., & Strock, A. L. (2004). Methodologic issues in research on religion and health. *Southern Medical Journal, 97*, 1231–1241.

Fleeson, W., Malanos, A. B., & Achille, N. M. (2002). An intraindividual process approach to the relationship between extraversion and positive affect: Is acting extraverted as "good" as being extraverted? *Journal of Personality and Social Psychology, 83*, 1409–1422.

Fleshner, M., & Laudenslager, M. L. (2004). Psychoneuroimmunology: Then and now. *Behavioral and Cognitive Neuroscience Reviews, 3*, 114–130.

Foa, U. G., & Foa, E. B. (1975). *Resource theory of social exchange.* Morristown, NJ: General Learning Press.

Fölling-Albers, M., & Hartinger, A. (1998). Interest of girls and boys in elementary school. In L. Hoffmann, A. Krapp, K. A. Renninger, & J. Baumert (Eds.), *Interest and learning: Proceedings of the Seeon Conference on interest and gender* (pp. 175–183). Kiel, Germany: IPN.

Folkman, S. (1997). Positive psychological states and coping with severe stress. *Social Science and Medicine, 45*, 1207–1221.

Folkman, S., & Moskowitz, J. T. (2000). Positive affect and the other side of coping. *American Psychologist, 55*, 647–654.

Forbis, E. (1996). *Municipal virtues in the Roman empire: The evidence of Italian honorary inscriptions.* Stuttgart, Germany: Teubner.

Fordyce, M. W. (1977). Development of a program to increase personal happiness. *Journal of Counseling Psychology, 24*, 511–520.

Forehand, R., & Nousiainen, S. (1993). Maternal and paternal parenting: Critical dimensions in adolescent functioning. *Journal of Family Psychology, 7*, 213–221.

Fox, R. A., Kimmerly, N. L., & Schafer, W. D. (1991). Attachment to mother/attachment to father: A meta-analysis. *Child Development, 62*, 210–225.

Fraley, R. C., & Waller, N. G. (1998). Adult attachment patterns: A test of the typological model. In J. A. Simpson & W. S. Rholes (Eds.), *Attachment theory and close relationships* (pp. 77–114). New York: Guilford.

Franken, A. (2003). *Lies and the lying liars who tell them: A fair and balanced look at the right.* New York: Dutton.

Fraser, S. (Ed.). (1995). *The bell curve wars: Race, intelligence, and the future of America.* New York: Basic.

Frederick, S., & Loewenstein, G. (1999). Hedonic adaptation. In D. Kahneman, E. Diener, & N. Schwarz (Eds.), *Well-being: The foundations of hedonic psychology* (pp. 302–329). New York: Russell Sage.

Fredrickson, B. L. (1998). What good are positive emotions? *Review of General Psychology, 2*, 300–319.

Fredrickson, B. L. (2000). Cultivating positive emotions to optimize health and well-being. *Prevention and Treatment, 3*. Document available at http://journals.apa.org/prevention. Accessed February 8, 2005.

Fredrickson, B. L. (2001). The role of positive emotions in positive psychology: The broaden-and-build theory of positive emotions. *American Psychologist, 56,* 218–226.

Fredrickson, B. L. (2004). The broaden-and-build theory of positive emotions. *Philosophical Transactions of the Royal Society of London (Biological Sciences), 359,* 1367–1377.

Fredrickson, B. L., & Branigan, C. (2005). Positive emotions broaden the scope of attention and thought-action repertoires. *Cognition and Emotion, 19,* 313–332.

Fredrickson, B. L., & Joiner, T. (2002). Positive emotions trigger upward spirals toward emotional well-being. *Psychological Science, 13,* 172–175.

Fredrickson, B. L., & Kahneman, D. (1993). Duration neglect in retrospective evaluations of affective episodes. *Journal of Personality and Social Psychology, 65,* 45–55.

Fredrickson, B. L., & Levenson, R. W. (1998). Positive emotions speed recovery from the cardiovascular sequelae of negative emotions. *Cognition and Emotion, 12,* 191–220.

Fredrickson, B. L., Mancuso, R. A., Branigan, C., & Tugade, M. M. (2000). The undoing effects of positive emotions. *Motivation and Emotion, 24,* 237–258.

Fredrickson, B. L., Tugade, M. M., Waugh, C. E., & Larkin, G. (2003). What good are positive emotions in crises? A prospective study of resilience and emotions following the terrorist attacks on the United States on September 11, 2001. *Journal of Personality and Social Psychology, 84,* 365–376.

Freud, S. (1953a). Humor and its relation to the unconscious. In J. Strachey (Ed. & Trans.), *The standard edition of the complete psychological works of Sigmund Freud* (Vol. 8, pp. 9–236). London: Hogarth. (Original work published 1905)

Freud, S. (1953b). Totem and taboo: Resemblances between the psychic lives of savages and neurotics. In J. Strachey (Ed. & Trans.), *The standard edition of the complete psychological works of Sigmund Freud* (Vol. 13, pp. 1–162). London: Hogarth. (Original work published 1913)

Freud, S. (1953c). *The future of an illusion.* In J. Strachey (Ed. & Trans.), *The standard edition of the complete psychological works of Sigmund Freud* (Vol. 21, pp. 1–56). London: Hogarth. (Original work published 1927)

Freud, S. (1964). Moses and monotheism: Three essays. In J. Strachey (Ed. & Trans.), *The standard edition of the complete psychological works of Sigmund Freud* (Vol. 23, pp. 36–53). London: Hogarth. (Original work published 1939)

Fridlund, A. J. (1991). Evolution and facial action in reflex, social motive, and paralanguage. *Biological Psychology, 32,* 3–100.

Fried, R. L. (1996). *The passionate teacher.* Boston: Beacon.

Fried, R. L. (2001). *The passionate learner: How teachers and parents can help children reclaim the joy of discovery.* Boston: Beacon.

Fries, J. F., & Crapo, L. M. (1981). *Vitality and aging.* San Francisco: Freeman.

Fromm, E. (1956). *The art of loving.* New York: Harper & Row.

Fulghum, R. (1986). *All I really need to know I learned in kindergarten: Uncommon thoughts on common things.* New York: Ballantine.

Gable, S. L., Reis, H. T., Impett, E. A., & Asher, E. R. (2004). What do you do when things go right? The intrapersonal and interpersonal benefits of sharing good events. *Journal of Personality and Social Psychology, 87,* 228–245.

Gadlin, H. (1977). Private lives and public order: A critical review of the history of intimate relations in the United States. In G. Levinger & H. L. Raush (Eds.), *Close rela-*

tionships: Perspectives on the meaning of intimacy (pp. 33–72). Amherst: University of Massachusetts Press.

Galton, F. (1869). *Hereditary genius.* London: Macmillan.

Gardner, H. (1983). *Frames of mind: The theory of multiple intelligences.* New York: Basic.

Gardner, H. (1985). *The mind's new science: A history of the cognitive revolution.* New York: Basic.

Gardner, H. (1991a). Assessment in context: The alternative to standardized testing. In B. R. Gifford & M. C. O'Connor (Eds.), *Changing assessments: Alternative views of aptitude, achievement, and instruction* (pp. 77–120). Boston: Kluwer.

Gardner, H. (1991b). The school of the future. In J. Brockman (Ed.), *Ways of knowing* (pp. 199–218). Englewood Cliffs, NJ: Prentice-Hall.

Gardner, H. (1993a). *Creating minds.* New York: Basic.

Gardner, H. (1993b). *Multiple intelligences: The theory in practice.* New York: Basic.

Gardner, H. (1997). *Extraordinary minds.* New York: Basic.

Gardner, H., Csikszentmihalyi, M., & Damon, W. (2001). *Good work: When excellence and ethics meet.* New York: Basic.

Gardner, P. L. (1985). Students' interest in science and technology: An international overview. In M. Lehrke, L. Hoffmann, & P. L. Gardner (Eds.), *Interests in science and technology education* (pp. 15–34). Kiel, Germany: IPN.

Garmezy, N. (1983). Stressors of childhood. In N. Garmezy & M. Rutter (Eds.), *Stress, coping, and development in children* (pp. 43–84). Baltimore: Johns Hopkins University Press.

Garofalo, K. (1994). Worksite wellness: Rewarding healthy behaviors. *American Association of Occupational Health Nurses Journal, 42,* 236–240.

Gebhardt, D. L., & Crump, C. E. (1990). Employee fitness and wellness programs in the workplace. *American Psychologist, 45,* 262–272.

Gentry, W. D. (Ed.). (1984). *Handbook of behavioral medicine.* New York: Guilford.

George, C., Kaplan, N., & Main, M. (1985). *The Adult Attachment Interview.* Unpublished manuscript, Department of Psychology, University of California at Berkeley. Cited in F. G. Lopez (2003), The assessment of adult attachment security. In S. J. Lopez & C. R. Snyder (Eds.), *Positive psychological assessment: A handbook of models and measures* (pp. 285–299). Washington, DC: American Psychological Association.

George, L. K., Ellison, C. G., & Larson, D. B. (2002). Explaining the relationships between religious involvement and health. *Psychological Inquiry, 13,* 190–200.

Georgia Skeptic. (1993, Fall). Ovulation vs. cretinism. *Georgia Skeptic Electronic Newsletter.* Document available at http://www.lysator.liu.se/skeptical/ newsletters/ Georgia_Skeptic/GS07–01.txt. Accessed January 17, 2005.

Gilbert, D. T., Pinel, E. C., Wilson, T. D., Blumberg, S. J., & Wheatley, T. (1998). Immune neglect: A source of durability bias in affective forecasting. *Journal of Personality and Social Psychology, 75,* 617–638.

Gill, K. G. (1970). *Violence against children.* Cambridge, MA: Harvard University Press.

Gillham, J. E., Reivich, K. J., Jaycox, L. H., & Seligman, M. E. P. (1995). Prevention of depressive symptoms in schoolchildren: Two-year follow-up. *Psychological Science, 6,* 343–351.

Gladwell, M. (2000). *The tipping point.* Boston: Little, Brown.

Glantz, K., & Pearce, J. K. (1989). *Exiles from Eden: Psychotherapy from an evolutionary perspective.* New York: Norton.

Goetzel, R. Z., Kahr, T. Y., Aldana, S. G., & Kenny, G. M. (1996). An evaluation of Duke University's Live for Life health promotion program and its impact on employee health. *American Journal of Health Promotion, 10,* 340–342.

Goldberg, S. (1991). Recent developments in attachment theory and research. *Canadian Journal of Psychiatry, 36,* 393–400.

Goldsmith, L. T. (1992). Wang Yani: Stylistic development of a Chinese painting prodigy. *Creativity Research Journal, 5,* 281–293.

Goleman, D., & Gurin, J. (Eds.). (1993). *Mind/body medicine: How to use your mind for better health.* Yonkers, NY: Consumer Reports Books.

Gorsuch, R. L. (1988). Psychology of religion. *Annual Review of Psychology, 39,* 201–221.

Gosling, S. D., Vazire, S., Srivastava, S., & John, O. P. (2004). Should we trust Web-based studies? A comparative analysis of six preconceptions about Internet questionnaires. *American Psychologist, 59,* 93–104.

Gottfredson, L. S. (1981). Circumscription and compromise: A developmental theory of occupational aspirations. *Journal of Counseling Psychology, 28,* 545–579.

Gottman, J. M., & Krokoff, L. J. (1989). The relationship between marital interaction and marital satisfaction: A longitudinal view. *Journal of Consulting and Clinical Psychology, 57,* 47–52.

Gottman, J. M., & Levenson, R. W. (1992). Marital processes predictive of later dissolution: Behavior, physiology, and health. *Journal of Personality and Social Psychology, 63,* 221–233.

Gould, S. J. (1981). *The mismeasure of man.* New York: Norton.

Gould, S. J. (1991). Exaptation: A crucial tool for an evolutionary psychology. *Journal of Social Issues, 47*(3), 43–65.

Greenberg, J., Pyszczynski, T., & Solomon, S. (1986). The causes and consequences of the need for self-esteem: A terror management theory. In. R. F. Baumeister (Ed.), *Public self and private self* (pp. 189–212). New York: Springer-Verlag.

Greenberg, S. B. (2004). *The two Americas.* New York: St. Martin's.

Greenberger, E., Josselson, R., Knerr, C., & Knerr, B. (1975). The measurement and structure of psychosocial maturity. *Journal of Youth and Adolescence, 4,* 127–143.

Greenwald, A. G. (1980). The totalitarian ego: Fabrication and revision of personal history. *American Psychologist, 35,* 603–618.

Griffin, J. (1986). *Well-being: Its meaning, measurement, and moral importance.* Oxford: Clarendon.

Grube, J. W., Mayton, D. M., & Ball-Rokeach, S. J. (1994). Inducing change in values, attitudes, and behaviors: Belief system theory and the method of value self-confrontation. *Journal of Social Issues, 50*(4), 153–173.

Guerra, N. G., & Williams, K. R. (2003). *Implementing school-based wellness centers. Psychology in the Schools, 40,* 473–487.

Guignon, C. (Ed.). (1999). *The good life.* Indianapolis, IN: Hackett.

Guilford, J. P. (1967). *The nature of human intelligence.* New York: McGraw-Hill.

Gupta, V., & Korte, C. (1994). The effects of a confidant and a peer group on the well-being of single elders. *International Journal of Aging and Human Development, 39,* 293–302.

Haaga, D. F., & Beck, A. T. (1995). Perspectives on depressive realism: Implications for cognitive theory of depression. *Behaviour Research and Therapy, 33,* 41–48.

Haberman, D. L. (1998). Confucianism: The way of the sages. In L. Stevenson & D. L. Haberman (Eds.), *Ten theories of human nature* (3rd ed., pp. 25–44). New York: Oxford University Press.

Haidt, J. (2002). *Psychology 101 strengths/weaknesses project: Suggested daily activities.* Unpublished manuscript, University of Virginia.

Hall, G. S. (1882). The moral and religious training of children. *Princeton Review, 9,* 26–48.

Hamilton, W. D. (1964). The genetical evolution of social behaviour. *Journal of Theoretical Biology, 7,* 1–16.

Hannity, S. (2004). *Deliver us from evil: Defeating terrorism, despotism, and liberalism.* New York: Regan.

Hansen, J. C. (1984). The measurement of vocational interests: Issues and future directions. In S. D. Brown & R. L. Lent (Eds.), *Handbook of counseling psychology* (pp. 99–136). New York: Wiley.

Hansen, J. C . (1990). Interest inventories. In S. Goldstein & M. Hersen (Eds.), *Handbook of psychological assessment* (pp. 173–194). Elmsford, NY: Pergamon.

Hansen, J. C. (1994). The measurement of vocational interests. In M. G. Rumsey, C. B. Walker, & J. H. Harris (Eds.), *Personnel selection and classification* (pp. 293–316). Hillsdale, NJ: Erlbaum.

Hardin, G. (1968). The tragedy of the commons. *Science, 162,* 1243–1248.

Harker, L. A., & Keltner, D. (2001). Expressions of positive emotion in women's college yearbook pictures and their relationship to personality and life outcomes across adulthood. *Journal of Personality and Social Psychology, 80,* 112–124.

Harlow, H. F. (1958). The nature of love. *American Psychologist, 13,* 673–685.

Harlow, H. F. (1965). Sexual behavior in the rhesus monkey. In F. Beach (Ed.), *Sex and behavior* (pp. 234–265). New York: Wiley.

Harlow, H. F. (1974). *Learning to love.* New York: Aronson.

Harlow, R. E., & Cantor, N. (1994). Social pursuit of academics: Side effects and spillover of strategic reassurance seeking. *Journal of Personality and Social Psychology, 66,* 386–397.

Harris Poll. (2005, March 17). *Overall confidence in leaders of major institutions declines slightly.* Document available at http://www.harrisinteractive.com/harris_poll/index.asp?PID=550. Accessed July 18, 2005.

Hartup, W. W., & Stevens, N. (1997). Friendships and adaptation in the life course. *Psychological Bulletin, 121,* 355–370.

Haslam, N., & Kim, H. C. (2003). Categories and continua: A review of taxometric research. *Genetic, Social, and General Psychology Monographs, 128,* 271–320.

Hatfield, E. (1988). Passionate and companionate love. In R. J. Sternberg & M. L. Barnes (Eds.), *The psychology of love* (pp. 191–217). New Haven, CT: Yale University Press.

Hatfield, E. (2001). Elaine Hatfield. In A. N. O'Connell (Ed.), *Models of achievement: Reflections of eminent women in psychology* (Vol. 3, pp. 135–147). Mahwah, NJ: Erlbaum.

Hatfield, E., & Rapson, R. L. (1993). Historical and cross-cultural perspectives on passionate love and sexual desire. *Annual Review of Sex Research, 4,* 67–97.

Hatfield, E., & Walster, G. W. (l978). *A new look at love.* Lanham, MD: University Press of America.

Hathaway, S. R., & McKinley, J. C. (1943). *The Minnesota Multiphasic Personality Inventory.* Minneapolis: University of Minnesota Press.

Hatta, T., Nakaseko, M., & Yamamoto, M. (1992). Hand differences on a sensory test using tactual stimuli. *Perceptual and Motor Skills, 74,* 927–933.

Hawkins, J. D., & Lam. T. (1987). Teacher practices, social development, and delinquency. In J. D. Burchard & S. N. Burchard (Eds.), *Prevention of delinquent behavior* (pp. 241–274). Newbury Park, CA: Sage.

Hayes, J. R. (1989). *The complete problem solver* (2nd ed.). Hillsdale, NJ: Erlbaum.

Hazan, C., & Shaver, P. R. (1987). Romantic love conceptualized as an attachment process. *Journal of Personality and Social Psychology, 52,* 511–524.

Hazan, C., & Shaver, P. R. (1994). Attachment as an organizational framework for research on close relationships. *Psychological Inquiry, 5,* 1–22.

Heath, C. W. (1945). *What people are.* Cambridge, MA: Harvard University Press.

Hefner, H. (1956, April). What is a playboy? *Playboy,* subscription page.

Heider, F. (1946). Attitude and cognitive organization. *Journal of Psychology, 21,* 107–112.

Heine, S. J., & Lehman, D. R. (1995). Cultural variation in unrealistic optimism: Does the West feel more vulnerable than the East? *Journal of Personality and Social Psychology, 68,* 595–607.

Helgeson, V. S. (1994). Relation of agency and communion to well-being: Evidence and potential explanations. *Psychological Bulletin, 116,* 412–428.

Helson, R. (1967). Personality characteristics and developmental history of creative college women. *Genetic Psychology Monographs, 76,* 205–256.

Helson, R., & Srivastava, S. (2001). Three paths of adult development: Conservers, seekers, and achievers. *Journal of Personality and Social Psychology, 80,* 995–1010.

Helwig, A. A. (1998). Occupational aspirations of a longitudinal sample from second to sixth grade. *Journal of Career Development, 24,* 247–265.

Hendrick, S. S., & Hendrick, C. (1992). *Romantic love.* Thousand Oaks, CA: Sage.

Hendrick, S. S., & Hendrick, C. (2002). Love. In C. R. Snyder & S. J. Lopez (Eds.), *Handbook of positive psychology* (pp. 472–484). New York: Oxford University Press.

Henry, O. (1906). *The four million.* New York: McClure, Phillips.

Herrnstein, R. J., & Murray, C. (1994). *The bell curve: Intelligence and class structure in American life.* New York: Free Press.

Hess, U., Kappas, A., McHugo, G. J., Lanzetta, J. T., & Kleck, R. E. (1992). The facilitative effect of facial expression on the self-generation of emotion. *International Journal of Psychophysiology, 12,* 251–265.

Hetherington, E. M., Cox., M., & Cox, R. (1979). Stress and coping in divorce: A focus on women. In J. E. Gullahorn (Ed.), *Psychology and women: In transition* (pp. 95–128). New York: Wiley.

Hibbs, E. D., & Jensen, P. S. (Eds.). (1996). *Psychosocial treatments for child and adolescent disorders: Empirically based strategies for clinical practice.* Washington, DC: American Psychological Association.

Highland Publishers. (2002). *United States of America's Congressional Medal of Honor recipients and their official citations.* Columbia Heights, MN: Author.

Hilgard, E. R. (1987). *Psychology in America: A historical survey.* San Diego, CA: Harcourt Brace Jovanovich.
Hill, P. C., & Hood, R. W. (Eds.). (1999). *Measures of religiosity.* Birmingham, AL: Religious Education Press.
Hill, W. F. (1960). Learning theory and the acquisition of values. *Psychological Review, 67,* 317–331.
Hills, P., & Argyle, M. (1998). Positive moods derived from leisure and their relationship to happiness and personality. *Personality and Individual Differences, 25,* 523–535.
Hitlin, S. (2003). Values as the core of personal identity: Drawing links between two theories of the self. *Social Psychology Quarterly, 66,* 118–137.
Hitlin, S., & Piliavin, J. A. (2004). Values: Reviving a dormant concept. *Annual Review of Sociology, 30,* 359–393.
Hobbes, T. (1982). *Leviathan.* New York: Penguin Classic. (Original work published 1651)
Hoffmann, L. (2002). Promoting girls' learning and achievement in physics classes for beginners. *Learning and Instruction, 12,* 447–465.
Hofstede, G. (2001). *Culture's consequences: Comparing values, behaviors, institutions, and organizations across nations.* Thousand Oaks, CA: Sage.
Holland, J. L. (1966). *The psychology of vocational choice: A theory of personality types and model environments.* Waltham, MA: Blaisdell.
Holland, J. L. (1985). *Making vocational choices: A theory of vocational personalities and work environments* (2nd ed.). Englewood Cliffs, NJ: Prentice-Hall.
Holmes, R. L. (1998). *Basic moral philosophy* (2nd ed.). Belmont, CA: Wadsworth.
Holmes, T. H., & Rahe, R. H. (1967). The Social Readjustment Rating Scale. *Journal of Psychosomatic Research, 11,* 213–218.
Homans, G. C. (1958). Social behavior as exchange. *American Journal of Sociology, 63,* 597–606.
Hood, R. W. (1998). Psychology of religion. In W. H. Swatos & P. Kvisto (Eds.), *Encyclopedia of religion and society* (pp. 388–391). Walnut Creek, CA: Altamira.
Hormuth, S. E. (1986). The sampling of experiences in situ. *Journal of Personality, 54,* 262–293.
House, J. S. (1981). *Work stress and social support.* Reading, MA: Addison-Wesley.
Howes, C. (1983). Patterns of friendship. *Child Development, 54,* 1041–1053.
Hubbard, E. (1927). *Note book of Elbert Hubbard: Mottoes, epigrams, short essays passages, orphic sayings, and preachments.* New York: Wise.
Huesmann, L. R., Moise, J., Podolski, C. L., & Eron, L. D. (2003). Longitudinal relations between childhood exposure to media violence and adult aggression and violence: 1977–1992. *Developmental Psychology, 39,* 301–321.
Huffman, T., Chang, K., Rausch, P., & Schaffer, N. (1994). Gender differences and factors related to the disposition toward cohabitation. *Family Therapy, 21,* 171–184.
Hull, C. H. (1945). Moral values, behaviorism, and the world crisis. *Transactions of the New York Academy of Science, 7,* 80–84.
Hunt, E. (1995). The role of intelligence in modern society. *American Scientist, 83,* 356–368.
Hunter, J. D. (2000). *The death of character: Moral education in an age without good or evil.* New York: Basic.
Hunter, K. I., & Linn, M. W. (1981). Psychosocial differences between elderly volunteers

and non-volunteers. *International Journal of Aging and Human Development, 12*, 205–213.

Hunter, L., & Elias, M. J. (1998). Violence in the high schools: Issues, controversies, policies, and prevention programs. In A. Roberts (Ed.), *Juvenile justice: Policies, programs and services* (2nd ed., pp. 71–94). Chicago: Nelson-Hall.

Huta, V., Park, N., Peterson, C., & Seligman, M. E. P. (2005). *Pursuing pleasure versus eudaimonia: Links with different aspects of well-being.* Unpublished manuscript, McGill University, Montreal.

Huyck, M. H. (1982). From gregariousness to intimacy: Marriage and friendship over the adult years. In T. M. Field, A. Huston, H. C. Quay, L. Troll, & G. E. Finley (Eds.), *Review of human development* (pp. 471–484). New York: Wiley.

Inglehart, R. (1990). *Culture shift in advanced industrial society.* Princeton, NJ: Princeton University Press.

Inglehart, R. (1993). *Modernization and postmodernization: Cultural, economic, and political change in 43 societies.* Princeton, NJ: Princeton University Press.

Inglehart, R., Basanez, M., & Moreno, A. (1998). *Human values and beliefs: A cross-cultural sourcebook.* Ann Arbor: University of Michigan Press.

Inglehart, R., & Klingemann, H.-D. (2000). Genes, culture, democracy, and happiness. In E. Diener & E. M. Suh (Eds.), *Culture and subjective well-being* (pp. 165–183). Cambridge, MA: MIT Press.

Inglehart, R., & Norris, P. (2004). *Sacred and secular: Religion and politics worldwide.* New York: Cambridge University Press.

Insel, T. R. (1997). A neurobiological basis of social attachment. *American Journal of Psychiatry, 154*, 726–735.

Izard, C. E. (1994). Innate and universal facial expressions: Evidence from developmental and cross-cultural research. *Psychological Bulletin, 115*, 288–299.

Jackson, S. W. (1986). *Melancholia and depression from Hippocratic times to modern times.* New Haven, CT: Yale University Press.

Jahoda, M. (1958). *Current concepts of positive mental health.* New York: Basic.

James, S. A., Hartnett, S. A., & Kalsbeek, W. D. (1983). John Henryism and blood pressure differences among Black men. *Journal of Behavioral Medicine, 6*, 259–278.

James, S. A., LaCroix, A. Z., Kleinbaum, D. G., & Strogatz, D. S. (1984). John Henryism and blood pressure differences among Black men: II. The role of occupational stressors. *Journal of Behavioral Medicine, 7*, 259–275.

James, S. A., Strogatz, D. S., Wing, S. B., & Ramsey, D. L. (1987). Socioeconomic status, John Henryism, and hypertension in Blacks and Whites. *American Journal of Epidemiology, 126*, 664–673.

James, W. (1985). *The varieties of religious experience.* Cambridge, MA: Harvard University Press. (Original work published 1902)

Jamieson, K. H. (2000). *Civic engagement conference.* Document available at http://www.positivepsychology.org/ppcivicengage.htm. Accessed July 20, 2005.

Jamison, K. R. (1993). *Touched with fire: Manic-depressive illness and the artistic temperament.* New York: Free Press.

Jang, K. L., McCrae, R. R., Angleitner, A., Riemann, R., & Livesley, W. J. (1998). Heritability of facet-level traits in a cross-cultural twin sample: Support for a hierarchical model of personality. *Journal of Personality and Social Psychology, 74*, 1556–1565.

Janis, I. L. (1982). *Victims of groupthink.* Boston: Houghton Mifflin.

Johansson, C. B., & Campbell, D. P. (1971). Stability of the Strong Vocational Interest Blank for men. *Journal of Applied Psychology, 55,* 24–26.

Johnson, B. R., Jang, S. J., Larson, D. B., & Li, S. D. (2001). Does adolescent religious commitment matter? A reexamination of the effects of religiosity on delinquency. *Journal of Research in Crime and Delinquency, 38,* 22–44.

Johnson, M. A., Dziurawiec, S., Ellis, H., & Morton, J. (1991). Newborns' preferential tracking of face-like stimuli and its subsequent decline. *Cognition, 4,* 1–19.

Johnson, S. M. (1996). *The practice of emotionally focused couples therapy.* New York: Brunner/Mazel.

Johnson, S. M., Hunsley, J., Greenberg, L., & Schlinder, D. (1999). Emotionally focused couples therapy: Status and challenges. *Journal of Clinical Psychology: Science and Practice, 6,* 67–79.

Johnston, W. A., & Dark, V. J. (1986). Selective attention. *Annual Review of Psychology, 37,* 43–75.

Jones, C. J., & Meredith W. (2000). Developmental paths of psychological health from early adolescence to later adulthood. *Psychology of Aging, 15,* 351–360.

Jung, C. G. (1933). *Modern man in search of a soul.* London: Kegan, Paul, Trench, Trubner.

Kahneman, D. (1999). Objective happiness. In D. Kahneman, E. Diener, & N. Schwarz (Eds.), *Well-being: The foundations of hedonic psychology* (pp. 3–25). New York: Russell Sage.

Kahneman, D., Diener, E., & Schwarz, N. (Eds.). (1999). *Well-being: The foundations of hedonic psychology.* New York: Russell Sage.

Kahneman, D., Fredrickson, B. L., Schreiber, C. A., & Redelmeier, D. A. (1993). When more pain is preferred to less: Adding a better end. *Psychological Science, 4,* 401–405.

Kahneman, D., Knetsch, J. L., & Thaler, R. H. (1991). The endowment effect, loss aversion, and status quo bias. *Journal of Economic Perspectives, 5,* 193–206.

Kahneman, D., Krueger, A. B., Schkade, D., Schwarz, N., & Stone, A. A. (2004). A survey method for characterizing daily life experience: The Day Reconstruction Method (DRM). *Science, 306,* 1776–1780.

Kahneman, D., & Tversky, A. (1973). On the psychology of prediction. *Psychological Review, 80,* 237–251.

Kalb, C. (2003, November 10). Faith and healing. *Newsweek,* pp. 44–56.

Kamen-Siegel, L., Rodin, J., Seligman, M. E. P., & Dwyer, J. (1991). Explanatory style and cell-mediated immunity. *Health Psychology, 10,* 229–235.

Kaplan, S., & Kaplan, R. (1982). *Cognition and environment: Functioning in an uncertain world.* New York: Praeger.

Karney, B. R., & Bradbury, T. N. (1995). The longitudinal course of marital quality and stability: A review of theory, method, and research. *Psychological Bulletin, 118,* 3–34.

Kasser, T. (2002). *The high price of materialism.* Cambridge, MA: Bradford.

Kasser, T. (2005, March 21). *Materialism: Consequences and alternatives.* Lecture delivered at the University of Michigan, Ann Arbor.

Katzman, R. (1973). Education and the prevalence of dementia and Alzheimer's disease. *Neurology, 43,* 13–20.

Kazdin, A. E., & Weisz, J. R. (Eds.). (2003). *Evidence-based psychotherapies for children and adolescents.* New York: Guilford.

Kelley, H. H., Berscheid, E., Christensen, A., Harvey, J. H., Huston, T. L., Levinger, G., McClintock, E., Peplau, L. A., & Peterson, D. R. (Eds.). (1983). *Close relationships.* New York: Freeman.

Kelley, H. H., & Thibaut, J. W. (1978). *Interpersonal relations: A theory of interdependence.* New York: Wiley.

Kelly, G. A. (1955). *The psychology of personal constructs.* New York: Norton.

Kelly, J. R., & Kelly, J. R. (1994). Multiple dimensions of meaning in the domains of work, family, and leisure. *Journal of Leisure Research, 26,* 250–274.

Keltner, D., & Haidt, J. (2003). Approaching awe, a moral, spiritual, and aesthetic emotion. *Cognition and Emotion, 17,* 297–314.

Kemp, B., Krause, J. S., & Adkins, R. (1999). Depression among African Americans, Latinos, and Caucasians with spinal cord injury: An exploratory study. *Rehabilitation Psychology, 44,* 235–247.

Kennedy, K. (Ed.). (2005, February 21). Players. *Sports Illustrated,* pp. 29–35.

Kessler, R. C., McGonagle, K. A., Zhao, S., Nelson, C. B., Hughes, M., Eshleman, S., Wittchen, H.-U., & Kendler, K. S. (1994). Lifetime and 12-month prevalence of DSM-III-R psychiatric diagnoses in the United States. *Archives of General Psychiatry, 51,* 8–19.

Kiecolt-Glaser, J. (2005, Match 3). *Marriage, stress, immunity, and wound healing: How relationships influence health.* Lecture at the 63rd Annual Scientific Meeting of the American Psychosomatic Society, Vancouver, BC, Canada.

Kiecolt-Glaser, J. & Glaser, R. (1992). Psychoneuroimmunology: Can psychological interventions modulate immunity? *Journal of Consulting and Clinical Psychology, 60,* 569–575.

Kiecolt-Glaser, J. & Newton, T. L. (2001). Marriage and health: His and hers. *Psychological Bulletin, 127,* 472–503.

King, L. A., & Napa, C. N. (1998). What makes a life good? *Journal of Personality and Social Psychology, 75,* 156–165.

Kiyokawa, Y., Kikusui, T., Takeuchi, Y., & Mori, Y. (2004). Partner's stress status influences social buffering effects in rats. *Behavioral Neuroscience, 118,* 798–804.

Kleiber, D., Larson, R., & Csikszentmihalyi, M. (1996). The experience of leisure in adolescence. *Journal of Leisure Research, 18,* 169–176.

Klein, K. E., Wegmann, H. M., Bruner, H., & Vogt, L. (1969). Physical fitness and tolerances to environmental extremes. *Aerospace Medicine, 40,* 998–1001.

Klinger, E. (1977). *Meaning and void: Inner experience and the incentives in people's lives.* Minneapolis: University of Minnesota Press.

Kluckhohn, C. (1951). Values and value orientations in the theory of action. In T. Parsons & E. A. Shils (Eds.), *Towards a general theory of action* (pp. 388–433). Cambridge, MA: Harvard University Press.

Kniffin, K. M., & Wilson, D. S. (2004). The effect of nonphysical traits on the perception of physical attractiveness: Three naturalistic studies. *Evolution and Human Behavior, 25,* 88–101.

Kobak, R. R., & Hazan, C. (1991). Attachment in marriage: The effects of security and accuracy of working models. *Journal of Personality and Social Psychology, 60,* 861–869.

Kobasa, S. C. (1979). Stressful life events, personality, and health: An inquiry into hardiness. *Journal of Personality and Social Psychology, 37,* 1–11.

Kobasa, S. C. (1982). Commitment and coping in stress resistance among lawyers. *Journal of Personality and Social Psychology, 42*, 707–717.

Kobasa, S. C., Maddi, S. R., & Courington, S. (1981). Personality and constitution as mediators in the stress-illness relationship. *Journal of Health and Social Behavior, 22*, 368–378.

Kobasa, S. C., Maddi, S. R., & Kahn, S. (1982). Hardiness and health: A prospective study. *Journal of Personality and Social Psychology, 42*, 168–177.

Koenig, H. G., McCullough, M. E., & Larson, D. B. (Eds.). (2001). *Handbook of religion and health.* New York: Oxford University Press.

Kohn, M. L. (1983). On the transmission of values in the family: A preliminary reformulation. *Research in Sociology of Education and Socialization, 4*, 1–12.

Kono, T. (1982). Japanese management philosophy: Can it be exported? *Long Range Planning, 15*(3), 90–102.

Konty, M. A., & Dunham, C. C. (1997). Differences in value and attitude change over the life course. *Sociological Spectrum, 17*, 177–197.

Korzenik, D. (1992). Gifted child artists. *Creativity Research Journal, 5*, 313–319.

Kramer, P. D. (1993). *Listening to Prozac.* New York: Penguin.

Krantz, D. S., Grunberg, N. E., & Baum, A. (1985). Health psychology. *Annual Review of Psychology, 36*, 349–383.

Krapp, A., & Fink, B. (1992). The development and function of interests during the critical transition from home to preschool. In K. A Renninger, S. Hidi, & A. Krapp (Eds.), *The role of interest in learning and development* (pp. 397–429). Hillsdale, NJ: Erlbaum.

Krapp, A., & Lewalter, D. (2001). Development of interests and interest-based motivational orientations: A longitudinal study in vocational school and work settings. In S. Volet & S. Järvela (Eds.), *Motivation in learning contexts: Theoretical and methodological implications* (pp. 201–232). London: Elsevier.

Krause, N. M., Ingersoll-Dayton, B., Liang, J., & Sugisawa, H. (1999). Religion, social support, and health among Japanese elderly. *Journal of Health and Social Behavior, 40*, 405–421.

Kristiansen, C. M., & Zanna, M. P. (1994). The rhetorical use of values to justify social and intergroup attitudes. *Journal of Social Issues, 30*(4), 47–65.

Kubey, R., & Csikszentmihalyi, M. (1990). *Television and the quality of life.* Hillsdale, NJ: Erlbaum.

Kubovy, M. (1999). On the pleasures of the mind. In D. Kahneman, E. Diener, & N. Schwarz (Eds.), *Well-being: The foundations of hedonic psychology* (pp. 134–154). New York: Russell Sage.

Kuczynski, L., Marshall, S., & Schell, K. (1997). Value socialization in a bidirectional context. In J. E. Grusec & L. Kuczynski (Eds.), *Parenting and children's internalization of values* (pp. 23–50). New York: Wiley.

Kuhn, T. S. (1970). *The structure of scientific revolutions* (2nd ed.). Chicago: University of Chicago Press.

Kulik, J., & Mahler, H. I. (1989). Stress and affiliation in a hospital setting: Preoperative roommate preferences. *Personality and Social Psychology Bulletin, 15*, 183–193.

Kurtzburg, R. L., Safar, H., & Cavior, N. (1968). Surgical and social rehabilitation of adult offenders. *Proceedings of the 76th Annual Convention of the American Psychological Association, 3*, 649–650.

Lang, F. F., & Carstensen, L. L. (1994). Close emotional relationships in late life: Further support for proactive aging in the social domain. *Child Development, 67,* 1103–1118.

Langlois, J. H., Ritter, J. M., Casey, R. J., & Sawin, D. B. (1995). Infant attractiveness predicts maternal behaviors and attitudes. *Developmental Psychology, 31,* 464–473.

Langlois, J. H., & Roggman, L. A. (1990). Attractive faces are only average. *Psychological Science, 1,* 115–121.

Langlois, J. H., Roggman, L. A., Casey, R. J., Ritter, J. M., Rieser-Danner, L. A., & Jenkins, V. Y. (1987). Infant preferences for attractive faces: Rudiments of a stereotype? *Developmental Psychology, 23,* 363–369.

Larsen, R. J. (1987). The stability of mood variability: A spectral analytic approach to daily mood assessments. *Journal of Personality and Social Psychology, 52,* 1195–1204.

Larsen, R. J., & Fredrickson, B. L. (1999). Measurement issues in emotion research. In D. Kahneman, E. Diener, & N. Schwarz (Eds.), *Well-being: The foundations of hedonic psychology* (pp. 40–60). New York: Russell Sage.

Larsen, R. J., & Kasimatis, M. (1990). Individual differences in entrainment of mood to the weekly calendar. *Journal of Personality and Social Psychology, 58,* 164–171.

Larsen, R. J., Kasimatis, M., & Frey, K. (1992). Facilitating the furrowed brow: An unobtrusive test of the facial feedback hypothesis applied to unpleasant affect. *Cognition and Emotion, 6,* 321–338.

Larson, R. (1978). Thirty years of research on the subjective well-being of older Americans. *Journal of Gerontology, 33,* 109–125.

Larson, R. (2000). Toward a psychology of positive youth development. *American Psychologist, 55,* 150–183.

Larson, R., & Csikszentmihalyi, M. (1978). Experiential correlates of time alone in adolescence. *Journal of Personality, 46,* 677–693.

Larson, R., & Csikszentmihalyi, M. (1983). The experience sampling method. *New Directions for Methodology of Social and Behavioral Science, 15,* 41–56.

Lazare, A. (2004). *On apology.* New York: Oxford University Press.

Lazarus, R. S. (1966). *Psychological stress and the coping process.* New York: McGraw-Hill.

Lazarus, R. S. (1982). Thoughts on the relations between emotion and cognition. *American Psychologist, 37,* 1019–1024.

Lazarus, R. S. (1983). The costs and benefits of denial. In S. Benitz (Ed.), *Denial of stress* (pp. 1–30). New York: International Universities Press.

Lazarus, R. S. (1991). *Emotion and adaptation.* New York: Oxford University Press.

Lazarus, R. S. (2003). Does the positive psychology movement have legs? *Psychological Inquiry, 14,* 93–109.

Lazarus, R. S., & Folkman, S. (1984). *Stress, appraisal, and coping.* New York: Springer.

Lazear, E. P. (2004). The Peter Principle: A theory of decline. *Journal of Political Economy, 112,* S141–S163.

Leary, M. R., & Forsyth, D. R. (1987). Attributions of responsibility for collective endeavors. In C. Hendrick (Ed.), *Review of personality and social psychology* (Vol. 8, pp. 167–188). Newbury Park, CA: Sage.

Lee, J. A. (1973). *The colors of love: An exploration of ways of loving.* Don Mills, Ontario: New Press.

Lee, J. A. (1988). Love-styles. In R. J. Sternberg & M. L. Barnes (Eds.), *Psychology of love* (pp. 38–67). New Haven, CT: Yale University Press.

Lee, Y.-T., & Seligman, M. E. P. (1997). Are Americans more optimistic than the Chinese? *Personality and Social Psychology Bulletin, 23,* 32–40.

Lehman, D. R., & Nisbett, R. E. (1990). A longitudinal study of the effects of undergraduate training on reasoning. *Developmental Psychology, 26,* 952–960.

Lerner, R. M., Jacobs, F., & Wertlieb, D. (Eds.). (2003). *Promoting positive child, adolescent, and family development: A handbook of program and policy innovations* (Vol. 4). Thousand Oaks, CA: Sage.

Levenson, R. W., Carstensen, L. L., & Gottman, J. M. (1993). Long-term marriage: Age, gender, and satisfaction. *Psychology and Aging, 8,* 301–313.

Levering, R., & Moskowitz, M. (1993). *The 100 best companies to work for in America.* Garden City, NY: Doubleday.

Levine, G. F. (1977). "Learned helplessness" and the evening news. *Journal of Communication, 27,* 100–105.

Levitt, A. J., Hogan, T. P., & Bucosky, C. M. (1990). Quality of life in chronically mentally ill patients in day treatment. *Psychological Medicine, 20,* 703–710.

Lewin, K. (1935). *A dynamic theory of personality.* New York: McGraw-Hill.

Lewin, K. (1947). Frontiers in group dynamics: I. Concept, method, and reality in social sciences; social equilibria; and social change. *Human Relations, 1,* 5–41.

Lewin, K. (1951). *Field theory in social science: Selected theoretical papers.* New York: Harper.

Liang, J., Krause, N. M., & Bennett, J. M. (2001). Social exchange and well-being: Is giving better than receiving? *Psychology and Aging, 16,* 511–523.

Lincoln, C., & Mamiya, L. (1990). *The Black church in the African-American experience.* Durham, NC: Duke University Press.

Linley, P. A., & Joseph, S. (2004a). Positive change following trauma and adversity: A review. *Journal of Traumatic Stress, 17,* 11–21.

Linley, P. A., & Joseph, S. (Eds.). (2004b). *Positive psychology in practice.* New York: Wiley.

Livingstone, S. M. (1988). Why people watch soap opera: Analysis of the explanations of British viewers. *European Journal of Communication, 3,* 55–80.

Locke, E. A., Shaw, K. N., Saari, L. M., & Latham, G. (1981). Goal setting and task performance: 1969–1980. *Psychological Bulletin, 90,* 124–152.

Loewenstein, G. (1994). The psychology of curiosity: A review and reinterpretation. *Psychological Bulletin, 116,* 75–98.

Loewenstein, G., & Schkade, D. (1999). Wouldn't it be nice? Predicting future feelings. In D. Kahneman, E. Diener, & N. Schwarz (Eds.), *Well-being: The foundations of hedonic psychology* (pp. 85–105). New York: Russell Sage.

Londerville, S., & Main, M. (1981). Security of attachment, compliance, and maternal training methods in the second year of life. *Developmental Psychology, 17,* 289–299.

Lorenz, K. (1937). The companion in the bird's world. *Auk, 54,* 245–273.

Lorenz, K. (1966). *On aggression.* New York: Harcourt Brace Jovanovich.

Lowenstein, M. K., & Field, T. (1993). Maternal depression effects on infants. *Analise Psicologica, 10,* 63–69.

Lu, L., & Argyle, M. (1993). TV watching, soap opera and happiness. *Kaohsiung Journal of Medical Sciences, 9,* 501–507.

Lucas, R. E., Clark, A. E., Georgellis, Y., & Diener, E. (2003). Reexamining adaptation and the set point model of happiness: Reactions to changes in marital status. *Journal of Personality and Social Psychology, 84,* 527–539.

Lucas, R. E., Clark, A. E., Georgellis, Y., & Diener, E. (2004). Unemployment alters the set-point for life satisfaction. *Psychological Science, 15,* 8–13.

Lundberg, C. D., & Peterson, M. F. (1994). The meaning of working in U.S. and Japanese local governments at three hierarchical levels. *Human Relations, 47,* 1459–1487.

Luthans, F. (2003). Positive organizational behavior (POB): Implications for leadership and HR development and motivation. In R. M. Steers, L. W. Porter, & G. A. Bigley (Eds.), *Motivation and leadership at work* (pp. 178–195). New York: McGraw-Hill/Irwin.

Luthar, S. S., Cicchetti, D., & Becker, B. (2000). The construct of resilience: A critical evaluation and guidelines for future work. *Child Development, 71,* 543–562.

Lykken, D. (2000). *Happiness: The nature and nurture of joy and contentment.* New York: St. Martin's.

Lykken, D., & Tellegen, A. (1996). Happiness is a stochastic phenomenon. *Psychological Science, 7,* 186–189.

Lynn, R. (1994). Sex differences in intelligence and brain size: A paradox resolved. *Personality and Individual Differences, 17,* 257–271.

Lyons-Ruth, K. (1991). Rapprochement or approchement: Mahler's theory reconsidered from the vantage point of recent research on early attachment relationships. *Psychoanalytic Psychology, 8,* 1–23.

Lyubomirsky, S., King, L. A., & Diener, E. (2005). The benefits of frequent positive affect: Does happiness lead to success? *Psychological Bulletin, 131,* 803–855.

Lyubomirsky, S., & Lepper, H. S. (1999). A measure of subjective happiness: Preliminary reliability and construct validation. *Social Indicators Research, 46,* 137–155.

Lyubomirsky, S., Sheldon, K. M., & Schkade, D. (2005). Pursuing happiness: The architecture of sustainable change. *Review of General Psychology, 9,* 111–131.

MacCorquodale, K., & Meehl, P. E. (1948). On a distinction between hypothetical constructs and intervening variables. *Psychological Review, 55,* 95–107.

MacIntyre, A. C. (1984). *After virtue: A study in moral theory* (2nd ed.). Notre Dame, IN: University of Notre Dame Press.

Mackintosh, N. J. (1975). A theory of attention: Variations in the associability of stimuli with reinforcement. *Psychological Review, 82,* 276–298.

Maddux, J. E. (2002). Stopping the "madness." In C. R. Snyder & S. J. Lopez (Eds.), *Handbook of positive psychology* (pp. 13–25). New York: Oxford University Press.

Maehr, M. L. (1991). The "psychological environment" of the school: A focus for school leadership. In M. L. Maehr & C. Ames (Eds.), *Advances in educational administration: Vol. 2. School leadership* (pp. 51–81). Greenwich, CT: JAI.

Maehr, M. L., Ames, R., & Braskamp, L. A. (1988). *Instructional Leadership Evaluation and Development program (I LEAD).* Champaign, IL: MetriTech.

Maehr, M. L., & Braskamp, L. A. (1986). *The motivation factor: A theory of personal investment.* Lexington, MA: Heath.

Maehr, M. L., & Midgley, C. (1996). *Transforming school cultures.* Boulder, CO: Westview.

Maehr, M. L., Midgley, C., & Urdan, T. (1992). School leader as motivator. *Educational Administration Quarterly, 18,* 412–431.

Mahoney, J. L. (2000). School extracurricular activity participation as a moderator in the development of antisocial patterns. *Child Development, 71,* 502–516.

Mahoney, J. L., & Cairns, R. B. (1997). Do extracurricular activities protect against early school dropout? *Developmental Psychology, 33,* 241–253.

Mahoney, J. L., & Stattin, H. (2000). Leisure activities and adolescent antisocial behavior: The role of structure and social context. *Journal of Adolescence, 23,* 113–127.

Mahoney, J. L., & Stattin, H. (2002). Structured after-school activities as a moderator of depressed mood for adolescents with detached relations to their parents. *Journal of Community Psychology, 30,* 69–86.

Mahoney, J. L., Stattin, H., & Magnusson, D. (2001). Youth recreation center participation and criminal offending: A 20-year longitudinal study of Swedish boys. *International Journal of Behavioral Development, 25,* 509–520.

Maier, S. F., & Seligman, M. E. P. (1976). Learned helplessness: Theory and evidence. *Journal of Experimental Psychology: General, 105,* 3–46.

Maier, S. F., Watkins, L. R., & Fleshner, M. (1994). Psychoneuroimmunology: The interface between behavior, brain, and immunity. *American Psychologist, 49,* 1004–1017.

Main, M., & Solomon, J. (1990). Procedures for identifying infants as disorganized/disoriented during the Ainsworth strange situation. In M. Greenberg, D. Cicchetti, & M. Cummings (Eds.), *Attachment in the preschool years: Theory, research, and intervention* (pp. 121–160). Chicago: University of Chicago Press.

Maio, G. R., Olson, J. M., Bernard, M. M., & Luke, M. A. (2003). Ideologies, values, attitudes, and behavior. In J. DeLamater (Ed.), *Handbook of social psychology* (pp. 283–308). New York: Plenum.

Marini, M. M. (2000). Social values and norms. In E. F. Borgotta & R. J. V. Montgomery (Eds.), *Encyclopedia of sociology* (pp. 2828–2840). New York: Macmillan.

Markus, H. R., & Kitayama, S. (1991). Culture and the self: Implications for cognition, emotion, and motivation. *Psychological Review, 98,* 224–253.

Marlatt, G. A., & Gordon, J. R. (1980). Determinants of relapse: Implications for the maintenance of behavior change. In P. O. Davidson & S. M. Davidson (Eds.), *Behavioral medicine: Changing healthy lifestyles* (pp. 410–452). New York: Brunner Mazel.

Marmor, M. G., Shipley, M. J., & Rose, G. (1984, May 5). Inequalities in death: Specific explanations of a general pattern? *Lancet,* pp. 1003–1006.

Masheter, C. (1990). Postdivorce relationships between ex-spouses: A literature review. *Journal of Divorce and Remarriage, 14,* 97–122.

Maslow, A. H. (1954). *Motivation and personality.* New York: Harper & Row.

Maslow, A. H. (1962). *Toward a psychology of being.* Princeton, NJ: Van Nostrand.

Maslow, A. H. (1966). *The psychology of science: A reconnaissance.* New York: Harper & Row.

Maslow, A. H. (1970). *Motivation and personality* (2nd ed.). New York: Harper & Row.

Massimini, F., & Delle Fave, A. (2000). Individual development in a bio-cultural perspective. *American Psychologist, 55,* 24–33.

Masten, A. (2001). Ordinary magic: Resilience processes in development. *American Psychologist, 56,* 227–238.

Matas, L., Arend, R. A., & Sroufe, L. A. (1978). Continuity of adaptation in the second year: The relationship between quality of attachment and later competence. *Child Development, 49,* 547–556.

Matlin, M., & Stang, D. (1978). *The Pollyanna Principle.* Cambridge, MA: Schenkman.

Maton, K., & Pargament, K. (1987). The roles of religion in prevention and promotion. *Prevention in Human Services, 5,* 161–205.

Maton, K., & Wells, E. (1995). Religion as a community resource for well-being: Prevention, healing, and empowerment pathways. *Journal of Social Issues, 51*(2), 177–193.

Matthews, S. H. (1986). *Friendships through the life course.* Beverly Hills, CA: Sage.

McAdam, D. (1989). The biographical consequences of activism. *American Sociological Review, 54,* 744–760.

McAdams, D. P. (1993). *The stories we live by: Personal myths and the making of the self.* New York: Guilford.

McAdams, D. P. (2005). *The redemptive self: Stories Americans live by.* New York: Oxford University Press.

McCann, I. L., & Holmes, D. S. (1984). Influence of aerobic exercise on depression. *Journal of Personality and Social Psychology, 46,* 1142–1147.

McClelland, D. C. (1961). *The achieving society.* Princeton, NJ: Van Nostrand.

McCombs, B. L. (1991). Motivation and lifelong learning. *Educational Psychologist, 26,* 117–127.

McCullough, M. E., Hoyt, W. T., Larson, D. B., Koenig, H. G., & Thoresen, C. (2000). Religious involvement and mortality: A meta-analytic review. *Health Psychology, 19,* 211–222.

McCullough, M. E., Kilpatrick, S. D., Emmons, R. A., & Larson, D. B. (1999). Gratitude as moral affect. *Psychological Bulletin, 127,* 249–266.

McCullough, M. E., Pargament, K., & Thoresen, C. T. (Eds.). (2000). *Forgiveness: Theory, research, and practice.* New York: Guilford.

McCullough, M. E., & Snyder, C. R. (2000). Classical sources of human strength: Revisiting an old home and building a new one. *Journal of Social and Clinical Psychology, 19,* 1–10.

McKenna, F. P. (1983). Accident-proneness: A conceptual analysis. *Accident Analysis and Prevention, 15,* 65–71.

McKillip, J., & Riedel, S. L. (1983). External validity of matching on physical attractiveness for same and opposite sex couples. *Journal of Applied Social Psychology, 13,* 328–337.

McWhirter, B. T. (1990). Loneliness: A review of current literature with implications for counseling and research. *Journal of Counseling and Development, 68,* 417–422.

Meehl, P. E. (1975). Hedonic capacity: Some conjectures. *Bulletin of the Menninger Clinic, 39,* 295–307.

Meier, A. (1993). Toward an integrated model of competency: Linking White and Bandura. *Journal of Cognitive Psychotherapy, 7,* 35–47.

Mellen, S. L. W. (1981). *The evolution of love.* San Francisco: Freeman.

Meyer, D. (1988). *The positive thinkers: Popular religious psychology from Mary Baker Eddy to Norman Vincent Peale and Ronald Reagan* (Rev. ed.). Middletown, CT: Wesleyan University Press.

Meyer, G. J., et al. (2001). Psychological testing and psychological assessment: A review of evidence and issues. *American Psychologist, 56,* 128–165.

Midgley, C., Anderman, E., & Hicks, L. (1995). Differences between elementary and middle school teachers and students: A goal theory approach. *Journal of Early Adolescence, 15,* 90–113.

Mikulincer, M., Florian, V., & Weller, A. (1993). Attachment styles, coping strategies, and posttraumatic psychological distress: The impact of the Gulf War in Israel. *Journal of Personality and Social Psychology, 64,* 817–826.

Milgram, S. (1963). Behavioral study of obedience. *Journal of Abnormal and Social Psychology, 67,* 371–378.

Miller, G. A. (1969). Psychology as a means of promoting human welfare. *American Psychologist, 24,* 1063–1075.

Miller, W. R., & Thoresen, C. (2003). Spirituality, religion, and health: An emerging research field. *American Psychologist, 58,* 24–35.

Mineka, S., & Henderson, R. W. (1985). Controllability and predictability in acquired motivation. *Annual Review of Psychology, 36,* 495–529.

Mischel, W. (1968). *Personality and assessment.* New York: Wiley.

Moneta, G. B., & Csikszentmihalyi, M. (1996). The effect of perceived challenges and skills on the quality of subjective experience. *Journal of Personality, 64,* 275–310.

Monk, R. (1990). *Ludwig Wittgenstein: The duty of genius.* New York: Free Press.

Mook, D. G. (1983). In defense of external invalidity. *American Psychologist, 38,* 379–387.

Morrow-Howell, N., Hinterloth, J., Rozario, P. A., & Tang, F. (2003). Effects of volunteering on the well-being of older adults. *Journals of Gerontology Series B: Psychological Sciences and Social Sciences, 58,* S137–S145.

Mortimer, J. T. (1976). Social class, work, and family: Some implications of the father's occupation for family relationships and son's career decisions. *Journal of Marriage and the Family, 38,* 241–256.

Mowbray, C. T., Oyserman, D., & Ross, S. (1995). Parenting and the significance of children for women with a serious mental illness. *Journal of Mental Health Administration, 22,* 189–200.

Mowrer-Popiel, E., Pollard, C., & Pollard, R. (1993). An examination of factors affecting the creative production of female professors. *College Student Journal, 27,* 428–436.

Mumford, D. B. (1993). Somatization: A transcultural perspective. *International Review of Psychiatry, 5,* 231–242.

Murray, C. (2003). *Human accomplishment: The pursuit of excellence in the arts and sciences, 800 BC to 1950.* New York: HarperCollins.

Murstein, B. I. (1974). *Love, sex, and marriage through the ages.* New York: Springer.

Murstein, B. I. (1976). *Who will marry whom.* New York: Springer.

Murstein, B. I., Merighi, J. R., & Vyse, S. A. (1991). Love styles in the United States and France: A cross-cultural comparison. *Journal of Social and Clinical Psychology, 10,* 37–46.

Myers, D. G. (1993). *The pursuit of happiness.* New York: Avon.

Myers, D. G. (2000). *The American paradox: Spiritual hunger in an age of plenty.* New Haven, CT: Yale University Press.

Myers, D. G., & Diener, E. (1995). Who is happy? *Psychological Science, 6,* 10–19.

Myers, J. E., Madathil, J., & Tingle, L. R. (2005). Marriage satisfaction and wellness in India and the United States: A preliminary comparison of arranged marriages and marriages of choice. *Journal of Counseling and Development, 83,* 183–190.

Myers, S. (1996). An interactive model of religiosity inheritance: The importance of family context. *American Sociological Review, 61,* 858–866.

Nakamura, J., & Csikszentmihalyi, M. (2002). The concept of flow. In C. R. Snyder &

S. J. Lopez (Eds.), *Handbook of positive psychology* (pp. 89–105). New York: Oxford University Press.

Nathan, P. E., & Gorman, J. M. (1998). *A guide to treatments that work.* New York: Oxford University Press.

Nathan, P. E., & Gorman, J. M. (2002). *A guide to treatments that work* (2nd ed.). New York: Oxford University Press.

Neill, A. S. (1960). *Summerhill: A radical approach to child rearing.* New York: Hart.

Neisser, U. (1967). *Cognitive psychology.* Englewood Cliffs, NJ: Prentice-Hall.

Nesse, R. M. (1990). Evolutionary explanations of emotions. *Human Nature, 1,* 261–289.

Nesse, R. M., & Williams, G. C. (1996). *Evolution and healing: The new science of Darwinian medicine.* London: Phoenix.

Neugarten, B. L. (1970). Adaptation and the life cycle. *Journal of Geriatric Psychiatry, 4,* 71–87.

Newberg, A., & d'Aquili, E. (2001). *Why God won't go away: Brain science and the biology of belief.* New York: Ballantine.

Newcomb, A. F., & Bagwell, C. (1995). Children's friendship relations: A meta-analytic review. *Psychological Bulletin, 117,* 306–347.

Nicholson, I. A. M. (1998). Gordon Allport, character, and the "culture of personality": 1897–1937. *History of Psychology, 1,* 52–68.

Nisbett, R. E., & Wilson, T. D. (1977). Telling more than we can know: Verbal reports on mental processes. *Psychological Review, 84,* 231–259.

Nock, S. L. (1995). A comparison of marriages and cohabiting relationships. *Journal of Family Issues, 16,* 53–76.

Noddings, N. (2003). *Happiness and education.* New York: Cambridge University Press.

Noller, P. (1996). What is this thing called love? Defining the love that supports marriage and family. *Personal Relationships, 3,* 97–115.

Norem, J. K. (2001). *The positive power of negative thinking.* New York: Basic.

Norem, J. K., & Cantor, N. (1986). Defensive pessimism: "Harnessing" anxiety as motivation. *Journal of Personality and Social Psychology, 51,* 1208–1217.

Norton, A. J. (1983). Family life cycle: 1980. *Journal of Marriage and the Family, 45,* 267–275.

Notarius, C. I., & Vanzetti, N. A. (1983). The marital agendas protocol. In E. E. Filsinger (Ed.), *Marriage and family assessment* (pp. 209–227). Beverly Hills, CA: Sage.

Novak, M. A., & Harlow, H. F. (1975). Social recovery of monkeys isolated for the first year of life: I. *Developmental Psychology, 11,* 453–465.

Nozick, R. (1974). *Anarchy, state, and utopia.* New York: Basic.

Nunnally, J. C. (1970). *Introduction to psychological measurement.* New York: McGraw-Hill.

Nussbaum, M. (1992). Human functioning and social justice: In defense of Aristotelian essentialism. *Political Theory, 20,* 202–246.

Oettingen, G. (1996). Positive fantasy and motivation. In P. M. Gollwitzer & J. A. Bargh (Eds.), *The psychology of action: Linking cognition and motivation to behavior* (pp. 236–259). New York: Guilford.

Ohira, H., & Kurono, K. (1993). Facial feedback effects on impression formation. *Perceptual and Motor Skills, 77,* 1251–1258.

O'Leary, K. D., & Smith, D. A. (1991). Marital interactions. *Annual Review of Psychology, 42,* 191–212.

Oliner, S. P., & Oliner, P. M. (1988). *The altruistic personality: Rescuers of Jews in Nazi Europe.* New York: Free Press.

O'Neill, M. (2001, September). Virtue and beauty: The Renaissance image of the ideal woman. *Smithsonian,* pp. 62–69.

Orne, M. T. (1962). On the social psychology of the psychological experiment: With particular reference to demand characteristics and their implications. *American Psychologist, 17,* 776–783.

Ornstein, R. E. (1988). *Psychology: The study of human experience* (2nd ed.). San Diego, CA: Harcourt Brace Jovanovich.

Owen, T. R. (1999). The reliability and validity of a wellness inventory. *American Journal of Health Promotion, 13,* 180–182.

Paffenbarger, R. S., Hyde, R. T., & Dow, A. (1991). Health benefits of physical activity. In B. L. Driver, P. J. Brown, & G. L. Peterson (Eds.), *Benefits of leisure* (pp. 49–57). State College, PA: Venture.

Pargament, K. (1997). *The psychology of coping.* New York: Guilford.

Pargament, K. (2002). The bitter and the sweet: An evaluation of the costs and benefits of religiousness. *Psychological Inquiry, 13,* 168–181.

Parish, T. S., & McCluskey, J. J. (1994). The relationship between parenting styles and young adults' self-concepts and evaluations of parents. *Family Therapy, 21,* 223–226.

Park, N. (2004a). Character strengths and positive youth development. *Annals of the American Academy of Political and Social Science, 591,* 40–54.

Park, N. (2004b). The role of subjective well-being in positive youth development. *Annals of the American Academy of Political and Social Science, 591,* 25–39.

Park, N. (2005, August 21). *Congressional Medal of Honor recipients: A positive psychology perspective.* Paper presented at the 113th Annual Meeting of the Conference of the American Psychological Association, Washington, DC.

Park, N., & Huebner, E. S. (2005). A cross-cultural study of the levels and correlates of life satisfaction among children and adolescents. *Journal of Cross-Cultural Psychology, 36,* 444–456.

Park, N., & Peterson, C. (2003). Virtues and organizations. In K. S. Cameron, J. E. Dutton, & R. E. Quinn (Eds.), *Positive organizational scholarship: Foundations of a new discipline* (pp. 33–47). San Francisco: Berrett-Koehler.

Park, N., & Peterson, C. (2004). Early intervention from the perspective of positive psychology. *Prevention and Treatment, 6*(35). Document available at http://journals.apa.org/prevention/volume6/pre0060035c.html. Accessed February 15, 2004.

Park, N., & Peterson, C. (2005). The Values in Action Inventory of Character Strengths for Youth. In K. A. Moore & L. H. Lippman (Eds.), *What do children need to flourish? Conceptualizing and measuring indicators of positive development* (pp. 13–23). New York: Springer.

Park, N., & Peterson, C. (in press a). Methodological issues in positive psychology and the assessment of character strengths. In A. D. Ong & M. van Dulmen (Eds.), *Handbook of methods in positive psychology.* New York: Oxford University Press.

Park, N., & Peterson, C. (in press b). Assessing strengths of character among adolescents: The Values in Action Inventory of Strengths for Youth. *Journal of Adolescence.*

Park, N., & Peterson, C. (in press c). Character strengths and happiness among young children: Content analysis of parental descriptions. *Journal of Happiness Studies.*

Park, N., & Peterson, C. (in press d). The cultivation of character strengths. In M. Ferrari & G. Poworowski (Eds.), *Teaching for wisdom.* Mahwah, NJ: Erlbaum.

Park, N., Peterson, C., & Seligman, M. E. P. (2004). Strengths of character and well-being. *Journal of Social and Clinical Psychology, 23,* 603–619.

Park, N., Peterson, C., & Seligman, M. E. P. (2005). *Strengths of character and well-being among youth.* Unpublished manuscript, University of Rhode Island.

Park, N., Peterson, C., & Seligman, M. E. P. (in press). Character strengths in 54 nations and all 50 U.S. states. *Journal of Positive Psychology.*

Parke, R. D., & Collmer, W. C. (1975). Child abuse: An interdisciplinary analysis. In E. M. Hetherington (Ed.), *Review of child development research* (Vol. 5, pp. 509–590). Chicago: University of Chicago Press.

Patrick, C. L., & Olson, K. (2000). Empirically supported therapies. *Journal of Psychological Practice, 6,* 19–34.

Patton, J. (1999). *Exploring the relative outcomes of interpersonal and intrapersonal factors of order and entropy in adolescence: A longitudinal study.* Unpublished doctoral dissertation, University of Chicago.

Pavot, W., & Diener, E. (1993). Review of the Satisfaction with Life Scale. *Personality Assessment, 5,* 164–172.

Peirce, C. S. (1878, January). How to make our ideas clear. *Popular Science Monthly, 12,* 286–302.

Pennebaker, J. W., Kiecolt-Glaser, J., & Glaser, R. (1988). Disclosure of traumas and immune function: Health implications for psychotherapy. *Journal of Consulting and Clinical Psychology, 56,* 239–245.

Pepler, D. J., & Slaby, R. (1994). Theoretical and developmental perspectives on youth and violence. In L. Eron, J. Gentry, & P. Schlegel (Eds.), *Reason to hope: A psychosocial perspective on violence & youth* (pp. 27–58). Washington, DC: American Psychological Association.

Perrett, D. I., May, K. A., & Yoshikawa, S. (1994). Facial shape and judgments of female attractiveness. *Nature, 368,* 239–242.

Peter, L. J., & Hull, R. (1969). *The Peter Principle: Why things always go wrong.* New York: Morrow.

Peters, T. J., & Waterman, R. H. (1982). *In search of excellence: Lessons from America's best-run companies.* New York: Warner.

Peterson, B. E., & Stewart, A. J. (1993). Generativity and social motives in young adults. *Journal of Personality and Social Psychology, 65,* 186–198.

Peterson, C. (1991). Meaning and measurement of explanatory style. *Psychological Inquiry, 2,* 1–10.

Peterson, C. (1992). *Personality* (2nd ed.). Fort Worth, TX: Harcourt Brace Jovanovich.

Peterson, C. (1996). *The psychology of abnormality.* Fort Worth, TX: Harcourt Brace.

Peterson, C. (1997). *Psychology: A biopsychosocial approach* (2nd ed.). New York: Longman.

Peterson, C. (1999). Helplessness. In D. Levinson, J. J. Ponzetti, & P. F. Jorgensen (Eds.),

Encyclopedia of human emotions (Vol. 1, pp. 343–347). New York: Macmillan Reference.

Peterson, C. (2000). The future of optimism. *American Psychologist, 55,* 44–55.

Peterson, C. (in press). The Values in Action (VIA) Classification of Strengths: The un-DSM and the real DSM. In M. Csikszentmihalyi & I. Csikszentmihalyi (Eds.), *A life worth living: Contributions to positive psychology.* New York: Oxford University Press.

Peterson, C., Bishop, M. P., Fletcher, C. W., Kaplan, M. R., Yesko, E. S., Moon, C. H., Smith, J. S., Michaels, C. E., & Michaels, A. J. (2001). Explanatory style as a risk factor for traumatic mishaps. *Cognitive Therapy and Research, 25,* 633–649.

Peterson, C., & Bossio, L. M. (1991). *Health and optimism.* New York: Free Press.

Peterson, C., & de Avila, M. E. (1995). Optimistic explanatory style and the perception of health problems. *Journal of Clinical Psychology, 51,* 128–132.

Peterson, C., & Lee, F. (2000, September–October). Reading between the lines: Speech analysis. *Psychology Today, 33*(5), 50–51.

Peterson, C., Maier, S. F., & Seligman, M. E. P. (1993). *Learned helplessness: A theory for the age of personal control.* New York: Oxford University Press.

Peterson, C., & Park, C. (1998). Learned helplessness and explanatory style. In D. F. Barone, V. B. Van Hasselt, & M. Hersen (Eds.), *Advanced personality* (pp. 287–310). New York: Plenum.

Peterson, C., & Park, N. (2003). Positive psychology as the evenhanded positive psychologist views it. *Psychological Inquiry, 14,* 141–146.

Peterson, C., & Park, N. (2004). Classification and measurement of character strengths: Implications for practice. In P. A. Linley & S. Joseph (Eds.), *Positive psychology in practice* (pp. 433–446). New York: Wiley.

Peterson, C., & Park, N. (in press). The psychology of religion. In A. Eisen & G. Laderman (Eds.), *Science, religion, and society: History, culture, and controversy.* Armonk, NY: Sharpe.

Peterson, C., Park, N., & Seligman, M. E. P. (2005a). Assessment of character strengths. In G. P. Koocher, J. C. Norcross, & S. S. Hill III (Eds.), *Psychologists' desk reference* (2nd ed., pp. 93–98). New York: Oxford University Press.

Peterson, C., Park, N., & Seligman, M. E. P. (2005b). Orientations to happiness and life satisfaction: The full life versus the empty life. *Journal of Happiness Studies, 6,* 25–41.

Peterson, C., Park, N., & Seligman, M. E. P. (2006). Strengths of character and recovery. *Journal of Positive Psychology 1,* 17–26.

Peterson, C., Schulman, P., Castellon, C., & Seligman, M. E. P. (1992). CAVE: Content analysis of verbatim explanations. In C. P. Smith (Ed.), *Motivation and personality: Handbook of thematic content analysis* (pp. 383–392). New York: Cambridge University Press.

Peterson, C., & Seligman, M. E. P. (1984). Causal explanations as a risk factor for depression: Theory and evidence. *Psychological Review, 91,* 347–374.

Peterson, C., & Seligman, M. E. P. (2003a). Character strengths before and after September 11. *Psychological Science, 14,* 381–384.

Peterson, C., & Seligman, M. E. P. (2003b). Positive organizational studies: Thirteen lessons from positive psychology. In K. S. Cameron, J. E. Dutton, & R. E. Quinn (Eds.), *Positive organizational scholarship: Foundations of a new discipline* (pp. 14–27). San Francisco: Berrett-Koehler.

Peterson, C., & Seligman, M. E. P. (2004). *Character strengths and virtues: A handbook and classification.* New York: Oxford University Press; Washington, DC: American Psychological Association.

Peterson, C., Seligman, M. E. P., & Vaillant, G. E. (1988). Pessimistic explanatory style is a risk factor for physical illness: A thirty-five-year longitudinal study. *Journal of Personality and Social Psychology, 55,* 23–27.

Peterson, C., Seligman, M. E. P., Yurko, K. H., Martin, L. R., & Friedman, H. S. (1998). Catastrophizing and untimely death. *Psychological Science, 9,* 49–52.

Peterson, C., Semmel, A., von Baeyer, C., Abramson, L. Y., Metalsky, G. I., & Seligman, M. E. P. (1982). The Attributional Style Questionnaire. *Cognitive Therapy and Research, 6,* 287–299.

Peterson, C., & Stunkard, A. J. (1989). Personal control and health promotion. *Social Science and Medicine, 28,* 819–828.

Peterson, C., & Vaidya, R. S. (2001). Explanatory style, expectations, and depressive symptoms. *Personality and Individual Differences, 31,* 1217–1223.

Peterson, C., & Vaidya, R. S. (2003). Optimism as virtue and vice. In E. C. Chang & L. J. Sanna (Eds.), *Virtue, vice, and personality: The complexity of behavior* (pp. 23–37). Washington, DC: American Psychological Association.

Philliber, W. W., & Hiller, D. V. (1983). Relative occupational attainments of spouses and later changes in marriage and wife's work experience. *Journal of Marriage and the Family, 46,* 161–170.

Piaget, J. (1950). *The psychology of intelligence.* New York: Harcourt, Brace.

Pierrehumbert, B., Iannotti, R. J., & Cummings, E. M. (1985). Mother-infant attachment, development of social competencies and beliefs of self-responsibility. *Archives de Psychologie, 53,* 365–374.

Pierrehumbert, B., Iannotti, R. J., Cummings, E. M., & Zahn-Waxler, C. (1989). Social functioning with mother and peers at 2 and 5 years: The influence of attachment. *International Journal of Behavioral Development, 12,* 85–100.

Pinker, S. (2002). *The blank slate: The denial of human nature and modern intellectual life.* New York: Viking.

Pinnacle Project. (2001–2002). *Winter Newsletter.* Document available at http://www.apa.org/ed/cpse/pinnew1.pdf. Accessed June 1, 2005.

Pinsker, H., Nepps, P., Redfield, J., & Winston, A. (1985). Applicants for short-term dynamic psychotherapy. In A. Winston (Ed.), *Clinical and research issues in short-term dynamic psychotherapy* (pp. 104–116). Washington, DC: American Psychiatric Association.

Pistole, M. C. (1989). Attachment in adult romantic relationships: Style of conflict resolution and relationship satisfaction. *Journal of Social and Personal Relationships, 6,* 505–510.

Pittman, T. S., & Heller, J. F. (1987). Social motivation. *Annual Review of Psychology, 38,* 461–489.

Pledge, D. S. (1992). Marital separation/divorce: A review of individual responses to a major life stressor. *Journal of Divorce and Remarriage, 17,* 151–181.

Plutchik, R. (1962). *The emotions: Facts, theories, and a new model.* New York: Random House.

Plutchik, R. (1980). *Emotion: A psychoevolutionary synthesis.* New York: Harper & Row.

Porges, S. W. (1998). Love: An emergent property of the mammalian autonomic nervous system. *Psychoneuroendocrinology, 23*, 837–861.

Porter, E. H. (1913). *Pollyanna.* London: Harrap.

Prenzel, M. (1992). The selective persistence of interest. In K. A. Renninger, S. Hidi, & A. Krapp (Eds.), *The role of interest in learning and development* (pp. 71–98). Hillsdale, NJ: Erlbaum.

Prochaska, J., DiClemente, C., & Norcross, J. C. (1992). In search of how people change. *American Psychologist, 47*, 1102–1114.

Prochaska, J., DiClemente, C., Velicer, W. F., & Rossi, J. S. (1993). Standardized, individualized, interactive, and personalized self-help programs for smoking cessation. *Health Psychology, 12*, 399–405.

Prochaska, J., Redding, C., & Evers, K. (1997). The transtheoretical model and stages of change. In K. Glanz, F. Lewis, & B. Rimer (Eds.), *Health behavior and health education* (2nd ed., pp. 60–84). San Francisco: Jossey-Bass.

Public Agenda. (1999). *Kids these days '99: What Americans really think about the next generation.* New York: Author.

Purtilo, D. T., & Purtilo, R. B. (1989). *A survey of human diseases* (2nd ed.). Boston: Little, Brown.

Putnam, R. D. (2000). *Bowling alone: The collapse and revival of American community.* New York: Simon & Schuster.

Quine, W. V., & Ullian, J. S. (1978). *The web of belief* (2nd ed.). New York: Random House.

Rachels, J. (1999). *The elements of moral philosophy* (3rd ed.). New York: McGraw-Hill.

Rachman, S. J. (1990). *Fear and courage* (2nd ed.). New York: Freeman.

Raimy, V. (1976). *Misunderstandings of the self: Cognitive psychotherapy and the misconception hypothesis.* San Francisco: Jossey-Bass.

Ralph, R. O., & Corrigan, P. W. (Eds.). (2005). *Recovery in mental illness: Broadening our understanding of wellness.* Washington, DC: American Psychological Association.

Rashid, T., & Anjum, A. (2005). *340 ways to use VIA character strengths.* Unpublished manuscript, University of Pennsylvania.

Rathunde, K. (1988). Optimal experience and the family context. In M. Csikszentmihalyi & I. Csikszentmihalyi (Eds.), *Optimal experience: Psychological studies of flow in consciousness* (pp. 343–363). New York: Cambridge University Press.

Rathunde, K. (1996). Family context and talented adolescents' optimal experience in school-related activities. *Journal of Research on Adolescence, 6*, 605–628.

Rathunde, K., & Csikszentmihalyi, M. (1993). Undivided interest and the growth of talent: A longitudinal study of adolescents. *Journal of Youth and Adolescence, 22*, 385–405.

Rawls, J. (1971). *A theory of justice.* Cambridge, MA: Harvard University Press.

Rean, A. A. (2000). Psychological problems of acmeology. *Psychological Journal, 21*, 88–95.

Redelmeier, D. A., & Kahneman D. (1996). Patients' memories of painful medical treatments: Real-time and retrospective evaluations in two minimally invasive procedures. *Pain, 116*, 3–8.

Redelmeier, D. A., & Singh, S. M. (2001). Survival in Academy Award–winning actors and actresses. *Annals of Internal Medicine, 134*, 955–962.

Reeves, D. J., & Booth, R. F. (1979). Expressed versus inventoried interests as predictors of paramedic effectiveness. *Journal of Vocational Behavior, 15*, 155–163.

Reis, H. T., & Gable, S. L. (2003). Toward a positive psychology of relationships. In

C. L. M. Keyes & J. Haidt (Eds.), *Flourishing: Positive psychology and the life well-lived* (pp. 129–159). Washington, DC: American Psychological Association.

Reivich, K. J., Gillham, J. E., & Shatté, A. (2004). *Penn Resiliency Program for Parents.* Unpublished manuscript, University of Pennsylvania.

Reivich, K. J., & Shatté, A. (2003). *The resilience factor: Seven essential skills for overcoming life's inevitable obstacles.* New York: Random House

Renninger, K. A. (1990). Children's play interests, representation, and activity. In R. Fivush and K. Hudson (Eds.), *Knowing and remembering in young children* (pp. 127–165). New York: Cambridge University Press.

Renninger, K. A. (2000). Individual interest and its implications for understanding intrinsic motivation. In C. Sansone & J. M. Harackiewicz (Eds.), *Intrinsic and extrinsic motivation: The search for optimal motivation and performance* (pp. 375–407). New York: Academic.

Renninger, K. A., & Hidi, S. (2002). Student interest and achievement: Developmental issues raised by a case study. In A. Wigfield & J. S. Eccles (Eds.), *Development of achievement motivation* (pp. 173–195). San Diego, CA: Academic.

Renninger, K. A., & Leckrone, T. G. (1991). Continuity in young children's actions: A consideration of interest and temperament. In L. Oppenheimer & J. Valsiner (Eds.), *The origins of action: Interdisciplinary and international perspectives* (pp. 205–238). New York: Springer-Verlag.

Renninger, K. A., & Shumar, W. (2002). Community building with and for teachers: The math forum as a resource for teacher professional development. In K. A. Renninger & W. Shumar (Eds.), *Building virtual communities: Learning and change in cyberspace* (pp. 60–95). New York: Cambridge University Press.

Rescorla, R. A. (1968). Probability of shock in the presence and absence of CS in fear conditioning. *Journal of Comparative and Physiological Psychology, 66,* 1–5.

Robbins, A. (1992). *Awaken the giant within: How to take immediate control of your mental, emotional, physical, and financial destiny.* New York: Simon & Schuster.

Robins, L. N., Helzer, J. E., Weissman, M. M., Orvaschel, H., Gruenberg, E., Burke, J. D., & Regier, D. A. (1984). Lifetime prevalence of specific psychiatric disorders in three sites. *Archives of General Psychiatry, 41,* 949–958.

Robinson, J. P. (1990). Television's effects on families' use of time. In J. Bryant (Ed.), *Television and the American family* (pp. 195–209). Hillsdale, NJ: Erlbaum.

Robinson-Whelen, S., Kim, C., MacCallum, R. C., & Kiecolt-Glaser, J. (1997). Distinguishing optimism from pessimism in older adults: Is it more important to be optimistic or not to be pessimistic? *Journal of Personality and Social Psychology, 73,* 1345–1353.

Roeser, R. W., & Eccles, J. S. (1998). Adolescents' perceptions of middle school: Relation to longitudinal changes in academic and psychological adjustment. *Journal of Research on Adolescence, 8,* 123–158.

Rogers, C. R. (1951). *Client-centered therapy: Its current practice, implications, and theory.* Boston: Houghton Mifflin.

Rogers, C. R., Gendlin, G. T., Kiesler, D. V., & Truax, C. B. (1967). *The therapeutic relationship and its impact: A study of psychotherapy with schizophrenics.* Madison: University of Wisconsin Press.

Rohan, M. J. (2000). A rose by any name? The values construct. *Personality and Social Psychology Review, 3,* 255–277.

Rokeach, M. (1971). Long-range experimental modification of values, attitudes, and behavior. *American Psychologist, 26,* 453–459.
Rokeach, M. (1973). *The nature of human values.* New York: Free Press.
Rokeach, M. (1979). *Understanding human values: Individual and social.* New York: Free Press.
Rokeach, M., & Grube, J. W. (1979). Can human values be manipulated arbitrarily? In M. Rokeach (Ed.), *Understanding human values: Individual and societal* (pp. 241–256). New York: Free Press.
Rosch, E., Mervis, C. B., Gray, W., Johnson, D., & Boyes-Braem, P. (1976). Basic objects in natural categories. *Cognitive Psychology, 8,* 382–439.
Rosenbaum, M., & Jaffe, Y. (1983). Learned helplessness: The role of individual differences in learned resourcefulness. *British Journal of Social Psychology, 22,* 215–225.
Rosenthal, R., & Rubin, D. B. (1982). A simple, general purpose display of magnitude of experimental effect. *Journal of Educational Psychology, 74,* 166–169.
Rosenwald, G. C. (1988). A theory of multiple-case research. *Journal of Personality, 56,* 239–264.
Ross, L., & Nisbett, R. E. (1991). *The person and the situation.* Philadelphia: Temple University Press.
Rotter, J. B. (1954). *Social learning and clinical psychology.* Englewood Cliffs, NJ: Prentice-Hall.
Rotter, J. B. (1966). Generalized expectancies for internal versus external control of reinforcement. *Psychological Monographs, 81*(1).
Rowe, D. C., & Osgood, D. W. (1984). Heredity and sociology theories of delinquency: A reconsideration. *American Sociological Review, 49,* 526–540.
Rozin, P. (1999). Preadaptation and the puzzles and properties of pleasure. In D. Kahneman, E. Diener, & N. Schwarz (Eds.), *Well-being: The foundations of hedonic psychology* (pp. 109–133). New York: Russell Sage.
Rubenstein, A. J., Kalakanis, L., & Langlois, J. H. (1999). Infant preferences for attractive faces. *Developmental Psychology, 35,* 848–855.
Rubin, Z. (1970). Measurement of romantic love. *Journal of Personality and Social Psychology, 16,* 265–273.
Rubin, Z. (1973). *Liking and loving: An invitation to social psychology.* New York: Holt, Rinehart, & Winston.
Ruff, G. F., & Korchin S. J. (1964). Personality characteristics of the Mercury astronauts. In G. H. Grosser, H. Wechsler, & M. Greenblatt (Eds.), *The threat of impending disaster* (pp. 197–207). Boston: MIT Press.
Runyan, W. M. (1981). Why did Van Gogh cut off his ear? The problem of alternative explanations in psychobiology. *Journal of Personality and Social Psychology, 40,* 1070–1077.
Rupp, D. E., & Spencer, S. (in press). When customers lash out: The effects of interactional justice on emotional labor and the mediating role of discrete emotions. *Journal of Applied Psychology.*
Rusbult, C. E. (1980). Commitment and satisfaction in romantic associations: A test of the investment model. *Journal of Experimental Social Psychology, 16,* 172–186.
Rusbult, C. E., Zembrodt, I. M., & Gunn, L. K. (1982). Exit, voice, loyalty, and neglect:

Responses to dissatisfaction in romantic relationships. *Journal of Personality and Social Psychology, 43,* 1230–1242.

Russell, B. (1930). *The conquest of happiness.* New York: Liveright.

Russell, B. (1945). *A history of Western philosophy, and its connection with political and social circumstances from the earliest times to the present day.* New York: Simon & Schuster.

Russell, R. J. H., & Wells, P. A. (1994). Predictors of happiness in married couples. *Personality and Individual Differences, 17,* 313–321.

Rutter, M. (1985). Resilience in the face of adversity: Protective factors and resistance to psychiatric disorder. *British Journal of Psychiatry, 147,* 598–611.

Rutter, M., & Garmezy, N. (1983). Developmental psychopathology. In P. H. Mussen & E. M. Hetherington (Eds.), *Handbook of child psychology: Vol. 4. Socialization, personality, and social development* (pp. 775–911). New York: Wiley.

Ryan, R. M., & Deci, E. L. (2000). On happiness and human potentials: A review of research on hedonic and eudaimonic well-being. *Annual Review of Psychology, 52,* 141–166.

Ryan, R. M., Sheldon, K. M., Kasser, T., & Deci, E. L. (1996). All goals are not created equal: An organismic perspective on the nature of goals and their regulation. In P. M. Gollwitzer & J. A. Bargh (Eds.), *The psychology of action: Linking cognition and motivation to behavior* (pp. 7–26). New York: Guilford.

Ryan, W. (1978). *Blaming the victim* (Rev. ed.). New York: Random House.

Ryff, C. D. (1989). Happiness is everything, or is it? Explorations of the meaning of psychological well-being. *Journal of Personality and Social Psychology, 57,* 1069–1081.

Ryff, C. D. (1995). Psychological well-being in adult life. *Current Directions in Psychological Science, 4,* 99–104.

Ryff, C. D., & Keyes, C. L. M. (1995). The structure of psychological well-being revisited. *Journal of Personality and Social Psychology, 69,* 719–727.

Ryff, C. D., & Singer, B. H. (1996). Psychological well-being: Meaning, measurement, and implications for psychotherapy research. *Psychotherapy and Psychosomatics, 65,* 14–23.

Ryff, C. D., & Singer, B. H. (1998). The contours of positive mental health. *Psychological Inquiry, 9,* 1–28.

Ryff, C. D., & Singer, B. H. (2001). *Emotion, social relationships, and health.* New York: Oxford University Press.

Ryff, C. D., Singer, B. H., & Love, G. D. (2004). Positive health: Connecting well-being with biology. *Philosophical Transactions of the Royal Society of London, 359,* 1383–1394.

Ryle, G. (1949). *The concept of mind.* Chicago: University of Chicago Press.

Sandage, S. J., Hill, P. C., & Vang, H. C. (2003). Toward a multicultural positive psychology: Indigenous forgiveness and Hmong culture. *Counseling Psychologist, 31,* 564–592.

Sandvak, E., Diener, E., & Seidlitz, L. (1993). Subjective well-being: The convergence and stability of self-report and non-self-report measures. *Journal of Personality, 61,* 317–342.

Sansone, C., Wiebe, D., & Morgan, C. (1999). Self-regulating interest: The moderating role of hardiness and conscientiousness. *Journal of Personality, 67,* 701–733.

Schachter, S. (1959). *The psychology of affiliation.* Stanford, CA: Stanford University Press.

Scheier, M. F., & Carver, C. S. (1985). Optimism, coping, and health: Assessment and implications of generalized outcome expectancies. *Health Psychology, 4,* 219–247.

Scheier, M. F., & Carver, C. S. (1987). Dispositional optimism and physical well-being: The influence of generalized outcome expectancies on health. *Journal of Personality, 55,* 169–210.

Scheier, M. F., & Carver, C. S. (1992). Effects of optimism on psychological and physical well-being: Theoretical overview and empirical update. *Cognitive Therapy and Research, 16,* 201–228.

Scheier, M. F., Carver, C. S., & Bridges, M. W. (2001). Optimism, pessimism, and psychological well-being. In E. C. Chang (Ed.), *Optimism and pessimism: Implications for theory, research, and practice* (pp. 189–216). Washington, DC: American Psychological Association.

Scheier, M. F., Matthews, K. A., Owens, J. F., Magovern, G. J., Lefebvre, R. C., Abbott, R. A., & Carver, C. S. (1989). Dispositional optimism and recovery from coronary artery bypass surgery: The beneficial effects on physical and psychological well-being. *Journal of Personality and Social Psychology, 57,* 1024–1040.

Scheier, M. F., Matthews, K. A., Owens, J. F., Schulz, R., Bridges, M. W., Magovern, G. J., Sr., & Carver, C. S. (1999). Optimism and rehospitalization following coronary artery bypass graft surgery. *Archives of Internal Medicine, 159,* 829–835.

Scheier, M. F., Weintraub, J. K., & Carver, C. S. (1986). Coping with stress: Divergent strategies of optimists and pessimists. *Journal of Personality and Social Psychology, 51,* 1257–1264.

Scherer, K. R., & Oshinsky, J. J. (1977). Cue utilization in emotion attribution from auditory stimuli. *Motivation and Emotion, 1,* 331–346.

Schimmack, U., Boeckenholt, U., & Reisenzein, R. (2002). Response styles in affect rating: Making a mountain out of a molehill. *Journal of Personality Assessment, 78,* 461–483.

Schimmack, U., Diener, E., & Oishi, S. (2002). Life-satisfaction is a momentary judgment and a stable personality characteristic: The use of chronically accessible and stable sources. *Journal of Personality, 70,* 345–384.

Schleifer, S. J., Keller, S. E., Siris, S. G., Davis, K. L., & Stein, M. (1985). Depression and immunity. *Archives of General Psychiatry, 42,* 129–133.

Schneider, C. D. (2000). What it means to be sorry: The power of apology in mediation. *Mediation Quarterly, 17,* 265–280.

Schneider, E. L. (1991). Attachment theory and research: Review of the literature. *Clinical Social Work Journal, 19,* 251–266.

Schneider, S. F. (2000). The importance of being Emory: Issues in training for the enhancement of psychological wellness. In D. Cicchetti, J. R. Rappaport, I. Sandler, & R. P. Weissberg (Eds.), *The promotion of wellness in children and adolescents* (pp. 439–476). Washington, DC: CWLA.

Schofield, W. (1964). *Psychotherapy: The purchase of friendship.* Englewood Cliffs, NJ: Prentice-Hall.

Schuessler, K. F., & Fisher, G. A. (1985). Quality of life research and sociology. *Annual Review of Sociology, 11,* 129–149.

Schull, W. J., & Rothhammer, F. (1981). The Multinational Andean Genetic and Health Program. In P. Baker & C. Jest (Eds.), *Environmental and human population problems at high altitude* (pp. 55–60). Paris: National Center for Scientific Research.

Schumaker, J. F. (Ed.). (1992). *Religion and mental health.* New York: Oxford University Press.

Schwartz, B. (2004). *The paradox of choice: Why less is more.* New York: HarperCollins.

Schwartz, B., & Sharpe, K. E. (in press). Practical wisdom: Aristotle meets positive psychology. *Journal of Happiness Studies.*

Schwartz, B., Ward, A., Monterosso, J., Lyubomirsky, S., White, K., & Lehman, D. R. (2002). Maximizing versus satisficing: Happiness is a matter of choice. *Journal of Personality and Social Psychology, 83,* 1178–1197.

Schwartz, C., Meisenhelder, J. B., Ma, Y., & Reed, G. (2003). Altruistic social interest behaviors are associated with better mental health. *Psychosomatic Medicine, 75,* 778–785.

Schwartz, S. H. (1992). Universals in the content and structure of values: Theoretical advances and empirical tests in 20 countries. *Advances in Experimental Social Psychology, 25,* 1–65.

Schwartz, S. H. (1994). Are there universal aspects in the structure and content of human values? *Journal of Social Issues, 50*(4), 19–45.

Schwartz, S. H. (1996). Value priorities and behavior: Applying a theory of integrated value systems. In C. Seligman, J. M. Olson, & M. P. Zanna (Eds.), *The psychology of values: The Ontario symposium* (Vol. 8, pp. 1–24). Mahwah, NJ: Erlbaum.

Schwartz, S. H., & Bilsky, W. (1987). Toward a universal structure of human values. *Journal of Personality and Social Psychology, 53,* 550–562.

Schwartz, S. H., & Bilsky, W. (1990). Toward a theory of the universal content and structure of values: Extensions and cross-cultural replications. *Journal of Personality and Social Psychology, 58,* 878–891.

Schwartz, S. H., Melech, G., Lehmann, A., Burgess, S., Harris, M., & Owens, V. (2001). Extending the cross-cultural validity of the theory of basic human values with a different method of measurement. *Journal of Cross-Cultural Psychology, 32,* 519–542.

Schwartz, S. H., & Sagiv, L. (1995). Identifying culture-specifics in the content and structure of values. *Journal of Cross-Cultural Psychology, 26,* 92–116.

Schwarz, N., & Strack, F. (1999). Reports of subjective well-being: Judgmental processes and their methodological implications. In D. Kahneman, E. Diener, & N. Schwarz (Eds.), *Well-being: The foundations of hedonic psychology* (pp. 61–84). New York: Russell Sage.

Scitovsky, T. (1993). The meaning, nature, and source of value in economics. In M. Hechter, L. Nadel, & R. E. Michod (Eds.), *The origin of values* (pp. 93–105). New York: de Gruyter.

Scott, D., & Willits, F. K. (1998). Adolescent and adult leisure patterns: A reassessment. *Journal of Leisure Research, 30,* 319–330.

Scott, W. A. (1958a). Research definitions of mental health and mental illness. *Psychological Bulletin, 55,* 29–45.

Scott, W. A. (1958b). Social psychological correlates of mental illness and mental health. *Psychological Bulletin, 55,* 65–87.

Scott, W. A. (1959). Empirical assessment of values and ideologies. *American Sociological Review, 24,* 72–75.

Scott, W. A. (1963). *Values and organizations: A study of fraternities and sororities.* Chicago: Rand McNally.

Sears, R. R. (1977). Sources of life satisfaction of the Terman gifted men. *American Psychologist, 32,* 119–128.

Seeman, J. (1989). Toward a model of positive health. *American Psychologist, 44,* 1099–1109.

Segerstrom, S. C., & Miller, G. E., (2004). Psychological stress and the human immune system: A meta-analytic study of 30 years of inquiry. *Psychological Bulletin, 130,* 601–630.

Segerstrom, S. C., Taylor, S. E., Kemeny, M. E., & Fahey, J. L. (1998). Optimism is associated with mood, coping and immune change in response to stress. *Journal of Personality and Social Psychology, 74,* 1646–1655.

Seligman, M. E. P. (1975). *Helplessness: On depression, development, and death.* San Francisco: Freeman.

Seligman, M. E. P. (1988). *Why is there so much depression today? The waxing of the individual and the waning of the commons.* Invited lecture at the 96th Annual Convention of the American Psychological Association, Atlanta, GA.

Seligman, M. E. P. (1991). *Learned optimism.* New York: Knopf.

Seligman, M. E. P. (1994). *What you can change and what you can't.* New York: Knopf.

Seligman, M. E. P. (1998). Positive social science. *APA Monitor Online, 29*(4). Document available at http://www.apa.org/monitor/apr98/pres.html. Accessed October 17, 2003.

Seligman, M. E. P. (1999). The president's address. *American Psychologist, 54,* 559–562.

Seligman, M. E. P. (2002). *Authentic happiness.* New York: Free Press.

Seligman, M. E. P. (2003, September). Love and positive events. *Authentic Happiness Newsletter.* Document available at http://www.authentichappiness.org/news7.html. Accessed June 20, 2005.

Seligman, M. E. P. (2004). Can happiness be taught? *Dædalus, 133*(2), 80–87.

Seligman, M. E. P., Castellon, C., Cacciola, J., Schulman, P., Luborsky, L., Ollove, M., & Downing, R. (1988). Explanatory style change during cognitive therapy for unipolar depression. *Journal of Abnormal Psychology, 97,* 13–18.

Seligman, M. E. P., & Csikszentmihalyi, M. (2000). Positive psychology: An introduction. *American Psychologist, 55,* 5–14.

Seligman. M. E. P., & Pawelski, J. O. (2003). Positive psychology: FAQs. *Psychological Inquiry, 14,* 159–163.

Seligman, M. E. P., Peterson, C., Kaslow, N. J., Tanenbaum, R. J., Alloy, L. B., & Abramson, L. Y. (1984). Attributional style and depressive symptoms among children. *Journal of Abnormal Psychology, 83,* 235–238.

Seligman, M. E. P., & Royzman, E. (2003, July). Happiness: The three traditional theories. *Authentic Happiness Newsletter.* Document available at http://www.authentichappiness.org/news6.html. Accessed January 2, 2005.

Seligman, M. E. P., Steen, T. A., Park, N., & Peterson, C. (2005). Positive psychology progress: Empirical validation of interventions. *American Psychologist, 60,* 410–421.

Sen, A. (1985). *Commodities and capabilities.* Amsterdam: North-Holland.

Sethi, S., & Seligman, M. E. P. (1993). Optimism and fundamentalism. *Psychological Science, 4,* 256–259.

Shaver, P. R., & Hazan, C. (1993). Adult romantic attachment: Theory and evidence. In D. Perlman & W. Jones (Eds.), *Advances in personal relationships* (Vol. 4, pp. 29–70). London: Kingsley.

Shaw, M. E. (1981). *Group dynamics: The psychology of small group behavior.* New York: McGraw-Hill.

Shaw, R. B. (1997). *Trust in the balance.* San Francisco: Jossey-Bass.

Sherif, M. (1936). *The psychology of social norms.* New York and London: Harper.

Shernoff, D. J., Csikszentmihalyi, M., Shneider, B., & Shernoff, E. S. (2003). Student engagement in high school classrooms from the perspective of flow theory. *School Psychology Quarterly, 18,* 158–176.

Sifton, E. (2003). *The serenity prayer: Faith and politics in times of war and peace.* New York: Norton.

Silverstein, A. M. (1989). *A history of immunology.* San Diego, CA: Academic.

Simon, H. (1956). Rational choice and the structure of the environment. *Psychological Review, 63,* 129–138.

Simon, S. B., Howe, L. W., & Kirschenbaum, H. (1995). *Values clarification.* New York: Warner.

Simonton, D. K. (1984). *Genius, creativity, and leadership: Historiometric methods.* Cambridge, MA: Harvard University Press.

Simonton, D. K. (1992). Gender and genius in Japan: Feminine eminence in masculine culture. *Sex Roles, 27,* 101–119.

Simonton, D. K. (1994). *Greatness: Who makes history and why.* New York: Guilford.

Simonton, D. K. (1997). Creative productivity: A predictive and explanatory model of career trajectories and landmarks. *Psychological Review, 104,* 66–89.

Simonton, D. K. (2000). Creativity: Cognitive, developmental, personal, and social aspects. *American Psychologist, 55,* 151–158.

Simpson, J. A., Rholes, W. S., & Nelligan, J. S. (1992). Support seeking and support giving within couples in an anxiety-provoking situation: The role of attachment styles. *Journal of Personality and Social Psychology, 62,* 434–446.

Simpson, W. F. (1989). Comparative longevity in a college cohort of Christian Scientists. *Journal of the American Medical Association, 262,* 1657–1658.

Singer, B. H., & Ryff, C. D. (2001). *New horizons in health: An integrative approach.* Washington, DC: National Academy Press.

Singer, I. (1984a). *The nature of love: Vol. 1. Plato to Luther.* Chicago: University of Chicago Press.

Singer, I. (1984b). *The nature of love: Vol. 2. Courtly and romantic.* Chicago: University of Chicago Press.

Singer, I. (1987). *The nature of love: Vol. 3. The modern world.* Chicago: University of Chicago Press.

Singer, P. (1981). *The expanding circle: Ethics and sociobiology.* Oxford: Clarendon.

Singer, P. (1993). *How ought we to live? Ethics in an age of self-interest.* New York: Oxford University Press.

Smart, J. C. (1982). Faculty teaching goals: A test of Holland's theory. *Journal of Educational Psychology, 74,* 180–188.

Smith, C. P. (Ed.). (1992). *Motivation and personality: Handbook of thematic content analysis.* New York: Cambridge University Press.

Smith, H. L., Reinow, F. D., & Reid, R. A. (1984). Japanese management: Implications for nursing administration. *Journal of Nursing Administration, 14*(9), 33–39.

Smith, M. L., & Glass, G. V. (1977). The meta-analysis of psychotherapy outcome studies. *American Psychologist, 32,* 752–760.

Snowdon, D. (2001). *Aging with grace: What the nun study teaches us about leading longer, healthier, and more meaningful lives.* New York: Bantam.

Snyder, C. R. (1988). Reality negotiation: From excuses to hope and beyond. *Journal of Social and Clinical Psychology, 8,* 130–157.

Snyder, C. R. (1994). *The psychology of hope: You can get there from here.* New York: Free Press.

Snyder, C. R. (1995). Conceptualizing, measuring, and nurturing hope. *Journal of Counseling and Development, 73,* 355–360.

Snyder, C. R. (Ed.). (2000). *Handbook of hope: Theory, measures, and applications.* San Diego, CA: Academic.

Snyder, C. R. (2002). Hope theory: Rainbows of the mind. *Psychological Inquiry, 13,* 249–275.

Snyder, C. R., Cheavens, J., & Sympson, S. C. (1997). Hope: An individual motive for social commerce. *Group Dynamics, 1,* 107–118.

Snyder, C. R., Harris, C., Anderson, J. R., Holleran, S. A., Irving, L. M., Sigmon, S. T., Yoshinobu, L., Gibb, J., Langelle, C., & Harney, P. (1991). The will and the ways: Development and validation of an individual differences measure of hope. *Journal of Personality and Social Psychology, 60,* 570–585.

Solomon, R. L., & Corbit, J. D. (1974). An opponent process theory of motivation: I. The temporal dynamics of affect. *Psychological Review, 81,* 119–145.

Southwick, C. H., Pal, B.C., & Siddiqui, M. F. (1972). Experimental studies of social intolerance in wild rhesus monkeys. *American Zoologist, 12,* 651–652.

Spearman, C. (1904). "General intelligence" objectively determined and measured. *American Journal of Psychology, 15,* 201–292.

Spiegel, D., Bloom, J. R., Kraemer, H. C., & Gottheil, E. (1989, October 14). Effect of psychosocial treatment on survival of patients with metastatic breast cancer. *Lancet,* pp. 888–891.

Spilka, B., Hood, R. W., & Gorsuch, R. L. (1985). *Psychology of religion: An empirical approach.* Englewood Cliffs, NJ: Prentice-Hall.

Spillman, M. A. (1988). Gender differences in worksite health promotion activities. *Social Science and Medicine, 26,* 525–535.

Spranger, E. (1928). *Types of men.* New York: Strehert-Hafner.

Sprecher, S., & Regan, P. C. (1998). Passionate and companionate love in courting and young married couples. *Sociological Inquiry, 68,* 163–185.

Sroufe, L. A. (1983). Infant-caregiver attachment and patterns of adaptation in preschool: The roots of maladaptation and competence. In M. Perlmutter (Ed.), *Minnesota symposium in child psychology* (Vol. 16, pp. 41–81). Hillsdale, NJ: Erlbaum.

Sroufe, L. A., Fox, N. E., & Pancake, V. R. (1983). Attachment and dependency in developmental perspective. *Child Development, 54,* 1615–1627.

Starker, S. (1989). *Oracle at the supermarket: The American preoccupation with self-help books.* New Brunswick, NJ: Transaction.

Starr, C. G. (1985). *The ancient Romans.* New York: Oxford University Press.

Staw, B., Bell, N. E., & Clausen, J. A. (1986). The dispositional approach to job attitudes: A life-time longitudinal test. *Administrative Science Quarterly, 31*, 56–77.

Steinberg, L. (1985). *Adolescence.* New York: Knopf.

Stern, W. (1914). *The psychological methods of testing intelligence.* Baltimore: Warwick & York.

Sternberg, R. J. (1985). *Beyond IQ: A triarchic theory of human intelligence.* Cambridge: Cambridge University Press.

Sternberg, R. J. (1998). A balance theory of wisdom. *Review of General Psychology, 2*, 347–365.

Sternberg, R. J., & Smith, E. E. (Eds.). (1988). *The psychology of human thought.* Cambridge: Cambridge University Press.

Stolzenberg, R., Blair-Loy, M., & Waite, L. (1995). Religious participation in early adulthood: Age and family life cycle effects on church membership. *American Sociological Review, 60*, 84–103.

Stone, A. A., Shiffman, S. S., & deVries, M. W. (1999). Ecological momentary assessment. In D. Kahneman, E. Diener, & N. Schwarz (Eds.), *Well-being: The foundations of hedonic psychology* (pp. 26–39). New York: Russell Sage.

Stotland, E. (1969). *The psychology of hope.* San Francisco: Jossey-Bass.

Strack, F., Martin, L. L., & Schwarz, N. (1988). Priming and communication: Social determinants of information use in judgments of life satisfaction. *European Journal of Social Psychology, 18*, 429–442.

Strack, S., Carver, C. S., & Blaney, P. H. (1987). Predicting successful completion of an aftercare program following treatment for alcoholism: The role of dispositional optimism. *Journal of Personality and Social Psychology, 53*, 579–584.

Strauch, B. (2003). *The primal teen: What the new discoveries about the teenage brain tell us about our kids.* Garden City, NY: Doubleday.

Strümpfer, D. J. W. (2005). Standing on the shoulders of giants: Notes on early positive psychology (psychofortology). *South African Journal of Psychology, 35*, 21–45.

Sun, S., & Meng, Z. (1993). An experimental study of examining [the] "facial feedback hypothesis." *Acta Psychologica Sinica, 25*, 277–283.

Sutton, W., & Linn, E. (1976). *Where the money was: The memoirs of a bank robber.* New York: Viking.

Swensen, C. H., Eskew, R. W., & Kohlhepp, K. A. (1981). Stage of family life cycle, ego development, and the marriage relationship. *Journal of Marriage and the Family, 43*, 841–853.

Symons, D. A. (1978). *Play and aggression: A study of rhesus monkeys.* New York: Columbia University Press.

Taylor, E. I. (2001). Positive psychology versus humanistic psychology: A reply to Prof. Seligman. *Journal of Humanistic Psychology, 41*, 13–29.

Taylor, H. (2001, August 8). *Harris Poll #38.* Document available at http://harrisinteractive.com/harris_poll. Accessed April 12, 2005.

Taylor, R., & Chatters, L. (1991). Religious life. In J. S. Jackson (Ed.), *Life in Black America* (pp. 105–123). Newbury Park, CA: Sage.

Taylor, R. B., Denham, J. R., & Ureda, J. W. (1982). *Health promotion: Principles and clinical applications.* Norwalk, CT: Appleton-Century-Crofts.

Taylor, S. E. (1985). Adjustments to threatening events: A theory of cognitive adaptation. *American Psychologist, 38,* 1161–1173.

Taylor, S. E. (1989). *Positive illusions.* New York: Basic.

Taylor, S. E., & Brown, J. D. (1988). Illusion and well-being: A social psychological perspective on mental health. *Psychological Bulletin, 103,* 193–210.

Taylor, S. E., Collins, R. L., Skokan, L. A., & Aspinwall, L. G. (1989). Maintaining positive illusions in the face of negative information: Getting the facts without letting them get to you. *Journal of Social and Clinical Psychology, 8,* 114–129.

Taylor, S. E., Klein, L. C., Lewis, B. P., Gruenewald, T. L., Gurung, R. A. R., & Updegraff, J. A. (2000). Biobehavioral responses to stress in females: Tend-and-befriend, not fight-or-flight. *Psychological Review, 107,* 422–429.

Taylor, S. E., & Lobel, M. (1989). Social comparison activity under threat: Downward evaluation and upward contacts. *Psychological Review, 96,* 569–575.

Teachman, J. D., Polonko, K. A., & Scanzoni, J. (1987). Demography of the family. In M. B. Sussman & S. K. Steinmetz (Eds.), *Handbook of marriage and the family* (pp. 3–36). New York: Plenum.

Tedeschi, R. G., & Calhoun, L. G. (1995). *Trauma and transformation: Growing in the aftermath of suffering.* Thousand Oaks, CA: Sage.

Tellegen, A., Lykken, D., Bouchard, T. J., Wilcox, K. J., Segal, N. L., & Rich, S. (1988). Personality similarity in twins reared apart and together. *Journal of Personality and Social Psychology, 54,* 1031–1039.

Tetlock, P. E. (1986). A value pluralism model of ideological reasoning. *Journal of Personality and Social Psychology, 50,* 819–827.

Thaler, R. (1980). Toward a positive theory of consumer choice. *Journal of Economic Behavior and Organization, 1,* 39–60.

Thayer, R. E. (1989). *The biopsychology of mood and arousal.* New York: Oxford University Press.

Thibaut, J. W., & Kelley, H. H. (1959). *The social psychology of groups.* New York: Wiley.

Thinley, J. Y. (1998, October 30). *Values and development: Gross national happiness.* Keynote speech delivered at the Millennium Meeting for Asia and the Pacific, Seoul, Republic of Korea.

Thomas, D. (1995, February 21). The world's firstborn: Guinness's record-holder turns 120 in France. *Washington Post,* p. D1.

Thurstone, L. L. (1938). Primary mental abilities. *Psychometric Monographs, 1.*

Tiger, L. (1979). *Optimism: The biology of hope.* New York: Simon & Schuster.

Tolman, E. C. (1932). *Purposive behavior in animals and men.* New York: Century.

Tomkins, C. (1976, January 5). New paradigms. *New Yorker,* pp. 30–36+.

Tomkins, S. S. (1962). *Affect, imagery, consciousness* (Vol. 1). New York: Springer.

Tomkins, S. S. (1963). *Affect, imagery, consciousness* (Vol. 2). New York: Springer.

Tomkins, S. S. (1982). *Affect, imagery, consciousness* (Vol. 3). New York: Springer.

Tooby, J., & Cosmides, L. (1989). Adaptation versus phylogeny: The role of animal psychology in the study of human behavior. *International Journal of Comparative Psychology, 2,* 175–188.

Tooby, J., & Cosmides, L. (1990). On the universality of human nature and the uniqueness of the individual: The role of genetics and adaptation. *Journal of Personality, 58,* 17–68.

Travers, R. M. W. (1978). *Children's interests.* Kalamazoo: Western Michigan University College of Education.

Triandis, H. C. (1995). *Individualism and collectivism.* Boulder, CO: Westview.

Troy, M., & Sroufe, L. A. (1987). Victimization among preschoolers: Role of attachment relationship history. *Journal of American Academy of Child and Adolescent Psychiatry, 26,* 166–172.

Tugade, M. M., & Fredrickson, B. L. (2004). Resilient individuals use positive emotions to bounce back from negative emotional experiences. *Journal of Personality and Social Psychology, 86,* 320–333.

Turner, A. N., & Miclette, A. L. (1962). Sources of satisfaction in repetitive work. *Occupational Psychology, 36,* 215–231.

Turner, R. H. (1976). The real self: From institution to impulse. *American Journal of Sociology, 84,* 1–23.

Twenge, J. M., & Im, C. (2005). *Changes in social desirability, 1958–2001.* Unpublished manuscript, San Diego State University.

Udelman, D. L. (1982). Stress and immunity. *Psychotherapy and Psychosomatics, 37,* 176–184.

Urban, H. B. (1983). Phenomenological-humanistic approaches. In M. Hersen, A. E. Kazdin, & A. S. Bellack (Eds.), *The clinical psychology handbook* (pp. 155–175). New York: Pergamon.

Urry, H. L., Nitschke, J. B., Dolski, I., Jackson, D. C., Dalton, K. M., Mueller, C. J., Rosenkranz, M. A., Ryff, C. D., Singer, B. H., & Davidson, R. J. (2004). Making a life worth living: Neural correlates of well-being. *Psychological Sciences, 6,* 367–372.

U.S. Department of Labor Statistics. (2004). *Occupational outlook handbook.* Document available at http://www.bls.gov/cps. Accessed April 24, 2005.

Vaihinger, H. (1911). *The psychology of "as if": A system of theoretical, practical, and religious fictions of mankind.* New York: Harcourt, Brace, & World.

Vaillant, G. E. (1977). *Adaptation to life.* Boston: Little, Brown.

Vaillant, G. E. (1983). *The natural history of alcoholism.* Cambridge, MA: Harvard University Press.

Vaillant, G. E. (1992). *Ego mechanisms of defense: A guide for clinicians and researchers.* Washington, DC: American Psychiatric Press.

Vaillant, G. E. (1995). *The wisdom of the ego.* Cambridge, MA: Harvard University Press.

Vaillant, G. E. (2000). Adaptive mental mechanisms: Their role in a positive psychology. *American Psychologist, 55,* 89–98.

Vaillant, G. E. (2002). *Aging well.* New York: Little, Brown.

Vaillant, G. E. (2003). Mental health. *American Journal of Psychiatry, 160,* 1373–1384.

Vaillant, G. E. (2004). Positive aging. In P. A. Linley & S. Joseph (Eds.), *Positive psychology in practice* (pp. 561–578). New York: Wiley.

Vaillant, G. E. (2005, May 26). *Religion and spirituality.* Lecture given at the Positive Psychology Center, University of Pennsylvania, Philadelphia.

Vandell, D. L., Owen, M. E., Wilson, K. S., & Henderson, V. K. (1988). Social development in infant twins: Peer and mother-child relationships. *Child Development, 59,* 168–177.

Van Ijzendoorn, M. H. (1992). Intergenerational transmission of parenting: A review of studies in nonclinical populations. *Developmental Review, 12,* 76–99.

Varey, C., & Kahneman, D. (1992). Experiences extended across time: Evaluation of moments and episodes. *Journal of Behavioral Decision Making, 5,* 169–186.
Velleman, J. D. (1991). Well-being and time. *Pacific Philosophical Quarterly, 72,* 48–77.
Verbrugge, L. M. (1989). Recent, present, and future health of American adults. *Annual Review of Public Health, 10,* 333–361.
Vernon, P., & Allport, G. W. (1931). A test for personal values. *Journal of Abnormal and ocial Psychology, 26,* 231–248.
Veroff, J., Douvan, E., & Kukla, R. A. (1981). *Mental health in America: Patterns of health-seeking from 1957 to 1976.* New York: Basic.
Viau, J. J. (1990). Theory Z: "Magic potion" for decentralized management? *Nursing Management, 21*(12), 34–36.
Volpicelli, J. R., Ulm, R. R., Altenor, A., & Seligman, M. E. P. (1983). Learned mastery in the rat. *Learning and Motivation, 14,* 204–222.
Voltaire, F. (1759). *Candide, ou l'optimisme.* Geneva, Switzerland: Cramer.
Wallach, M. A., & Wallach, L. (1983). *Psychology's sanction for selfishness: The error of egoism in theory and therapy.* San Francisco: Freeman.
Walsh, R. (2001). Positive psychology: East and West. *American Psychologist, 56,* 83–84.
Walster, E., Walster, G. W., & Berscheid, E. (1978). *Equity: Theory and research.* Boston: Allyn & Bacon.
Warr, P. B. (1987). *Work, unemployment, and mental health.* Oxford: Clarendon.
Wasserman, E. A., & Miller, R. R. (1997). What's elementary about associative learning? *Annual Review of Psychology, 48,* 573–607.
Waterman, A. S. (1993). Two conceptions of happiness: Contrasts of personal expressiveness (eudaimonia) and hedonic enjoyment. *Journal of Personality and Social Psychology, 64,* 678–691.
Waters, E., Wippman, J., & Sroufe, L. A. (1979). Attachment, positive affect, and competence in the peer group: Two studies in construct validation. *Child Development, 50,* 821–829.
Waters, M. C. (1990). *Ethnic options: Choosing identities in America.* Berkeley: University of California Press.
Watson, D. (2000). *Mood and temperament.* New York: Guilford.
Watson, D. (2002). Positive affectivity: The disposition to experience pleasurable emotional states. In C. R. Snyder & S. J. Lopez (Eds.), *Handbook of positive psychology* (pp. 106–119). New York: Oxford University Press.
Watson, D., Clark, L. A., & Tellegen, A. (1988). Development and validation of brief measures of positive and negative affect: The PANAS scales. *Journal of Personality and Social Psychology, 54,* 1063–1070.
Watson, D., Hubbard, B., & Wiese, D. (2000). General traits of personality and affectivity as predictors of satisfaction in intimate relationships: Evidence from self- and partner-ratings. *Journal of Personality, 68,* 413–449.
Watson, J. (1895). *Hedonistic theories from Aristippus to Spencer.* New York: Macmillan.
Watson, J. B. (1913). Psychology as the behaviorist views it. *Psychological Review, 20,* 158–177.
Watson, J. B. (1925). *Behaviorism.* New York: Norton.

Watson, R. E. L. (1983). Premarital cohabitation versus traditional courtship: Their effects on subsequent marital adjustment. *Family Relations, 32*, 139–147.

Watson, W. E., & Gauthier, J. (2003). The viability of organizational wellness programs: An examination of promotion and results. *Journal of Applied Social Psychology, 33*, 1297–1312.

Weil, A. (1988). *Health and healing* (Rev. ed.). Boston: Houghton Mifflin.

Weinstein, N. D. (1989). Optimistic biases about personal risks. *Science, 246*, 1232–1233.

Weiss, R. S. (1986). Continuities and transformations in social relationships from childhood to adulthood. In W. W. Hartup & Z. Rubin (Eds.), *Relationships and development* (pp. 95–110). Hillsdale, NJ: Erlbaum.

Weissberg, R. P., Barton, H., & Shriver, T. P. (1997). The social competence promotion program for young adolescents. In G. W. Albee & T. P. Gullotta (Eds.), *Primary prevention works* (pp. 268–290). Thousand Oaks, CA: Sage.

Weisse, C. S. (1992). Depression and immunocompetence: A review of the literature. *Psychological Bulletin, 111*, 475–489.

Werner, E. E. (1982). *Vulnerable but invincible: A longitudinal study of resilient children and youth.* New York: McGraw-Hill.

Wertheimer, M. (1912). Experimentelle Studien über das Sehen von Bewegung. *Zeitschrift fur Psychologie, 61*, 161–265.

Whalen, S. A. (1999). Challenging play and the cultivation of talent: Lessons from the Key School's flow activities room. In N. Colangelo & S. Assouline (Eds.), *Talent development III* (pp. 409–411). Scottsdale, AZ: Gifted Psychology Press.

White, B. L. (1967). An experimental approach to the effects of experience on early human behaviors. In J. P. Hill (Ed.), *Minnesota symposium on child psychology* (Vol. 1, pp. 201–225). Minneapolis: University of Minnesota Press.

White, J. K. (2003). *The values divide.* New York: Chatham House.

White, R. W. (1959). Motivation reconsidered: The concept of competence. *Psychological Review, 66*, 297–333.

Wigfield, A., Eccles, J. S., MacIver, D., Reuman, D., & Midgley, C. (1991). Transitions at early adolescence: Changes in children's domain-specific self-perceptions and general self-esteem across the transition to junior high school. *Developmental Psychology, 27*, 552–565.

Williams, R. M. (1951). *American society: A sociological interpretation.* New York: Knopf.

Wilson, T. D., Meyers, J., & Gilbert, D. T. (2001). Lessons from the past: Do people learn from experience that emotional reactions are short lived? *Personality and Social Psychology Bulletin, 27*, 1648–1661.

Wilson, T. D., Wheatley, T. P., Meyers, J. M., Gilbert, D. T., & Assom, D. (2000). Focalism: A source of durability bias in affective forecasting. *Journal of Personality and Social Psychology, 78*, 821–836.

Wilson, W. (1967). Correlates of avowed happiness. *Psychological Bulletin, 67*, 294–306.

Winch, R. F. (1958). *Mate selection: A study of complementary needs.* New York: Harper & Row.

Winett, R. A., King, A. C., & Altman, D. G. (1989). *Health psychology and public health: An integrative approach.* Elmsford, NY: Pergamon.

Wing, R. R. (1992). Behavioral treatments of severe obesity. *American Journal of Clinical Nutrition, 55*, 545–551.

Winn, K. I., Crawford, D. W., & Fischer, J. L. (1991). Equity and commitment in romance versus friendship. *Journal of Social Behavior and Personality, 6,* 301–314.

Winner, E. (2000). The origins and ends of giftedness. *American Psychologist, 55,* 159–169.

Winstead, B. A., Derlega, V. J., & Montgomery, M. J. (1995). The quality of friendships at work and job satisfaction. *Journal of Social and Personal Relationships, 12,* 199–215.

Wissing, M. P., & van Eeden, C. (2002). Empirical clarification of the nature of psychological well-being. *South African Journal of Psychology, 32,* 32–44.

Wong, P. T. (1989). Personal meaning and successful aging. *Canadian Psychology, 30,* 516–525.

Woodruff-Pak, D. (1988). *Psychology and aging.* Englewood Cliffs, NJ: Prentice-Hall.

World Health Organization. (1946). Preamble to the Constitution of the World Health Organization as adopted by the International Health Conference, New York, 19–22 June, 1946. In *Official Records of the World Health Organization.* Geneva, Switzerland: Author.

World Health Organization. (1990). *International classification of diseases and related health problems* (10th ed.). Geneva, Switzerland: Author.

Wright, R. (1994). *The moral animal: The new science of evolutionary psychology.* New York: Random House.

Wright, R. (1999). *Nonzero: The logic of human destiny.* New York: Pantheon.

Wright, T. A. (2003). Positive organizational behavior: An idea whose time has truly come. *Journal of Organizational Behavior, 24,* 437–442.

Wrzesniewski, A., McCauley, C., Rozin, P., & Schwartz, B. (1997). Jobs, careers, and callings: People's relations to their work. *Journal of Research in Personality, 31,* 21–33.

Wulff, D. W. (1991). *Psychology of religion: Classic and contemporary views.* New York: Wiley.

Yankelovich, D. (1981). *New rules.* New York: Random House.

Yearley, L. H. (1990). *Mencius and Aquinas: Theories of virtue and conceptions of courage.* Albany: State University of New York Press.

Young, L. J., Wang, Z., & Insel, T. R. (1998). Neuroendocrine bases of monogamy. *Trends in Neuroscience, 21,* 71–75.

Zajonc, R. B. (1965). Social facilitation. *Science, 149,* 269–274.

Zajonc, R. B. (1968). Attitudinal effects of mere exposure. *Journal of Personality and Social Psychology, 9,* 1–28.

Zeaman, D. (1959). Skinner's theory of teaching machines. In E. Galanter (Ed.), *Automatic teaching: The state of the art* (pp. 167–175). New York: Wiley.

Zimmerman, M. A. (1990). Toward a theory of learned hopefulness: A structural model analysis of participation and empowerment. *Journal of Research in Personality, 24,* 71–86.

Zullow, H., Oettingen, G., Peterson, C., & Seligman, M. E. P. (1988). Explanatory style and pessimism in the historical record: CAVing LBJ, presidential candidates, and East versus West Berlin. *American Psychologist, 43,* 673–682.

Zullow, H., & Seligman, M. E. P. (1990). Pessimistic rumination predicts defeat of presidential candidates, 1900 to 1984. *Psychological Inquiry, 1,* 52–61.

Zytowski, D. G. (Ed.). (1973). *Interest measurement.* Minneapolis: University of Minnesota Press.

Name Index

Subject Index